Introduction to Human Evolution

A Bio-Cultural Approach

First Edition

By Gillian Crane-Kramer
State University of New York - Plattsburgh

and Roman Gastrell Harrison
Mount Royal University, Calgary

Bassim Hamadeh, CEO and Publisher

Michael Simpson, Vice President of Acquisitions

Jamie Giganti, Managing Editor

Jess Busch, Senior Graphic Designer

John Remington, Acquisitions Editor

Monika Dziamka, Project Editor

Natalie Lakosil, Licensing Manager

Kaela Martin, Interior Designer

First published in the United States of America in 2015 by Cognella, Inc.

Cover image: Copyright © 2013 by Depositphotos Inc./mastaka

Printed in the United States of America

ISBN: 978-1-63189-866-2 (pbk)/ 978-1-63189-867-9 (br)

www.cognella.com   800-200-3908

Contents

The authors wish to dedicate this book to their PhD supervisor, Dr. M. Anne Katzenberg.

Dr. Harrison also dedicates the book to his parents, Tony and Virginia Harrison, and his significant other, Jane Cassidy. Dr. Crane-Kramer inscribes this book to her mother, Charmay L. Crane, for her endless support and love (and a good laugh when needed).

1

Introduction

By Gillian Crane-Kramer

This is a book about evolution. It does not promise an exhaustive discussion of the topic, or we would be providing you with a textbook that weighed more than you do. Instead, this book will introduce the reader to major issues surrounding the theory of evolution, and illuminate questions like what evolution is and is not, and how we know what we think we know about it. In addition, these discussions can serve as a backdrop from which other scholars can add their own specific scientific focus in the classroom. Whether you are an ecologist, geneticist, physicist, or anatomist, the rules of the scientific method that apply to you are identical. Good science always follows the strict rules of the scientific method, and this allows scholars from diverse geographic areas to compare their work in a meaningful and consistent way. There should never be "science-phobes" in the world. Science functions in very logical and predictable ways, and this notion that it is only understandable to the few members of a secret organization is unfortunate. Everyone can be a scientist, from the gardener who observes the structure of his plants to the runner who improves performance through different training techniques. Some of the greatest scientific discoveries have occurred either by laymen

Figure 1.1: Everyone can be scientists.

or by accident. This urges us to always maintain an amazed wonder at the complex natural world that surrounds us.

There is no question that the human-focused perspective that we adopt in this work directly results from the fact that we are both biological anthropologists. Biological anthropology is the area of anthropology that focuses upon the biological history of human beings. If we were chemists, we would definitely spend more time talking about protons. As fascinating as quarks, string theory, and cell receptors are, we are focused upon the 4.6-billion-year journey that led specifically to humans. Thus, while we will present several examples discussing the evolutionary history of other species, there is no question that we have a primate/human bias. It is best to be honest up front.

Before we begin our journey, it is important for us to fit biological anthropology into the wider anthropological perspective. Anthropology is the study of humans. Cultural anthropologists focus upon all aspects of learned behavior in contemporary or historic peoples. This includes areas such as belief, ritual, medical, political, and economic systems.

Figure 1.2: Scientists are not magicians.

Linguistic anthropologists are interested in examining human language and speech, both historically in terms of the evolution of languages, and in terms of modern languages.

Archaeologists focus on the examination of prehistoric and historic populations from the material remains that human activity leaves behind. This includes examining questions of settlement pattern, architecture, diet, human movement, and burial practices, to name a few. Biological anthropology traces the biological history of our primate relatives and ourselves, and encompasses many fields such as osteology (skeletal biology), primatology, paleoanthropology (the study of fossil ancestors), and population genetics. What all subdivisions of anthropology share in common is a universal interest in the human experience and a strong desire to illuminate the connection between human biology, culture, and the natural environment. This desire to understand the connection between biology, behavior, and the environment is shared by all scientists who study living things, whether they are plants or animals. The theory of evolution provides the foundation upon which studies of past and present organisms can be laid. In other words, it provides the bedrock upon which ideas about the emergence of life on planet Earth rest.

ARE SCIENTISTS MAGICIANS? REMOVING THE WAND!

When we are driving to work in the morning, we never stop to even consider why the sun is shining, or why the December temperature is cold outside in temperate climes. Earlier in our morning, when we dropped the soap in the shower and it fell down or we ate eggs for breakfast, these were experiences that were not worthy of reflection. Why is this? Because they are a given. They are a predictable and consistent element in our cyclical lives. These things had been explained to us in our salad days as schoolchildren as concepts such as gravity, embryology, and the rotation of the Earth around the sun. These phenomena were known to us as accepted scientific principles, and they ultimately govern the way we perceive the universe and our place within it as a living creature. The question that we do not reflect upon enough is how we know these givens. These theoretical tenets did not just fall out of the sky or magically appear by spontaneous generation (okay, maybe a few, like Newton's falling apple). This realm of knowledge has been developing for centuries, as humans attempted to organize and explain their natural and social environments through controlled experiment. Often, these experiments were not formal; if you place your finger in a fire, it will burn every time. One learns quickly not to put digits in the fire! This individual "trial-by-error" experiential learning is one very important way that we organize our

Figure 1.3: The scientific method begins with the formation of a question.

world. However, a wide range of human knowledge has been obtained in formalized experiments that established a question to be asked and a controlled manner in which to answer that question. A scientist sometimes has a Eureka moment, but much more commonly, a cohort of scholars working from separate angles ultimately piece together the answer to a complicated problem. Occasionally, this collaboration extends over several centuries, with each generation of scholars contributing a vital piece to the next generation, like a rung in a long, elaborate ladder. The result of these long ladders of knowledge is the organizational framework through which we experience our daily lives.

Most of us do not spend our time contemplating black holes, the genome of the 1918 flu virus, or acid rain. However, there are people who fill their days thinking about these things and investigating them via the use of the scientific method. Like any specialists, scientists like there to be some mystery to what they do. It is nice to have the mystery of the Wizard of Oz behind the curtain. However, no area of knowledge is more open to scrutiny than science. The scientific method functions according to very strict parameters, and these parameters are internationally and universally accepted by scientists as far apart as Japan, the Ivory Coast, and the United States.

One of the very important things about science is that it must play out in the public arena. Even though scientists are often highly trained individuals, their results must be presented to an audience of their peers for evaluation. This ultimately keeps science honest.

IS THIS MUMBO JUMBO? CAN SCIENCE ANSWER ALL QUESTIONS FOR US?

In the 21st century, the knowledge gained through centuries of scientific enquiry governs the assumptions that organize our lives. We do not even question that we can't breathe naturally underwater in our pool, or that a thrown football will not suddenly stop, suspended, in the air. These are inherently understood principles we have learned throughout our personal and academic experiences. As our understanding of the world rests upon these inherent assumptions, we often begin to think that science is capable of answering all of our questions and solving all of our problems. This is an incorrect assumption. The **scientific method** functions in a very specific way. It begins with an observation and the development of a question to be answered. This involves both inductive and deductive reasoning. Inductive reasoning is the process of creating general principles from particular facts (creating an idea to be tested). Deductive reasoning involves reasoning from the general to the specific in terms of conclusions (testing the idea). This question to be answered is called a hypothesis, and it is an educated guess that must be tested by way of experiment.

The creation of a testable hypothesis is the creative portion of the scientific process. A hypothesis must be able to be accepted or rejected via experimentation. The empirical part of science begins with the testing of a hypothesis by collecting relevant data. Developing and conducting experiments to test a hypothesis is very time consuming and costly. Ultimately, the results will lead to the acceptance or rejection of the hypothesis and the formation of a new set of questions to be addressed. The next part of the scientific process is the explanation. This is a process that correlates the collected data with the problem that has been tested. Science directs itself toward proximate causes (the how), rather than ultimate causes (the why). Scientific explanations strive to be parsimonious, in that they try not to be unnecessarily complicated—given all the evidence, the simplest explanation is likely the right one. This idea is known as **Occam's razor**, named after a medieval philosopher who believed in simplicity in explanation (Marks 2011).

When a hypothesis is repeatedly confirmed by numerous experiments, it may become what is called a theory. The formation of a hypothesis is the beginning of the scientific process, and the establishment of a theory is the end of the process after experimentation. The National Academy of Sciences (NAS) defines a scientific theory as "a well-substantiated explanation of some aspect of the natural world that can incorporate facts, laws, inferences, and testable hypotheses" (Rennie 2006). A theory does not become a law simply because of its consistent validation. There are several examples of laws in science (the law of gravity, laws of thermodynamics, Hardy-Weinberg law), but they are simply descriptive generalizations rather than explanations of natural phenomena. Theories essentially explain laws—that's a fact. When scientists refer to a theory rather than a law, they do not doubt its validity. Thus, science is essentially a cycle of asking questions, observing patterns, generating hypotheses, and testing those hypotheses. Even when a hypothesis is well supported enough to be accepted as a theory, it still must be subjected to scientific inquiry to support its validity and explain its elements. Science should always be skeptical and open to self-examination. Science is a never-ending process, where discoveries made by former generations lay the groundwork for future scientists. Science is a probabilistic endeavor, not a deterministic one. We can predict what outcomes can be expected, but we cannot predict the future like a soothsayer.

Figure 1.4: For centuries people believed that the Earth was flat.

Scientific questions change as technology improves. No one asked questions about germs or atoms in the 15th century! Sometimes, theories that have been accepted for decades, even centuries, are disproved in the light of new information. The scientific climate that was prevalent at the time of Copernicus in the 15th century was very different from when Ptolemy was alive in the second century AD. An improvement in technology and method allows scientists to test accepted notions and develop new theories. For over a millennium, people believed that the Earth was flat, and that sailors were in danger of not only terrifying sea monsters, but also the risk of sailing off the edge of the Earth into the abyss. The recognition in the 16th century that the Earth was round represented a Kuhnian, or scientific, revolution. This involves the replacement of an often long-held theory with a radically different one. This is typically associated with an explosion of new scientific inquiries and discoveries, because scientists are asking different questions in different ways. In a nutshell, the **scientific method** helps us to ask questions and set up experiments to answer those questions in a controlled manner.

HOW MANY ANGELS ON THE HEAD OF A PIN? THE DIFFERENCE BETWEEN SCIENCE AND PSEUDOSCIENCE

As scientific principles have provided us with the rules that govern our everyday lives, is it safe to assume that science can answer all of our queries, and help to solve the wide myriad of our problems? Like philosophy and faith, science is a realm of knowledge, and like all realms of knowledge, it has limits to what it can provide. Jonathan Marks points out that it is important to distinguish between ontology and epistemology in

Figure 1.5: Science cannot address all questions. How many ghosts are in the room right now?

Figure 1.6: The Abominable Snowman Yeti belongs to the realm of pseudoscience.

science. The term ontology is about being or the state of existence—what actually "is." This is not really the realm of science, as science is about epistemology—what CAN be known, and how we go about knowing it. Consider an interesting question: How many ghosts are there in the room right now?

Three or fewer ghosts
Four or more ghosts
None

Logic tells us that one of these answers must be correct. Even though there is a real answer to the question, science cannot discover it. As ghosts and angels are not tangible entities, they are not amenable to scientific detection and analysis. Thus, science is not actually about reality or what there "is"; rather, it is about what we are actually able to KNOW with some degree of certainty. One of the most important points to remember is that science can only investigate questions that can be tested via experiment, and these questions must be able to be either accepted or rejected. Science cannot answer questions like "Do God and angels exist?" "What is the meaning of life?" or "Do animals have souls?" because, given present method and theory, we cannot devise an experiment to test these questions. Such questions are investigated within other realms of knowledge.

Pseudoscientific claims are based on assertions that cannot be tested via experimentation, like the suggestion that aliens created the famous Nazca lines in South America, or that Bigfoot is alive and well and living undetected by nearby humans in the Pacific Northwest. As fascinating as these ideas may be, they are not science, and their advocates do not practice the scientific method. Unfortunately, pseudoscience often receives more public attention than legitimate science because it makes grandiose claims, or discusses fun topics like ghosts, sea monsters, and spaceships. The media attention that pseudoscience often receives misleads the general public, in terms of what real science is and what it isn't. Alien abductions do set the stage for a great story, and probably would capture the public's attention more than a story about global warming or a new strain of influenza virus emerging in Southeast Asia. However, these concerns of the scientific community will ultimately have a much greater impact upon your life than aliens will. The point of the story is, enjoy the pseudoscience as a hobby, but understand how it differs from legitimate science.

STAND YE AND BE JUDGED: WHO DETERMINES WHAT IS SCIENCE?

How do scientists determine what is science? As stated above, scientific examination must proceed via the use of the scientific method. Does this mean that if you do an experiment in the lab 50 times and always get the same result that this can now become an established scientific tenet? The answer to this question is NO.

Figure 1.7: Scientists add to the knowledge of their discipline with every generation.

Scientists are members of a wider international community, and the results of scientific inquiry must pass certain types of scrutiny before the results can be accepted. Firstly, scientific results must be replicable. This means that the experiment must be able to be reproduced by multiple scientists under similar conditions, and they must attain the same or similar results under controlled circumstances. This means that all scientists have to be extremely conscientious in terms of the methods and theories implemented in their work. Secondly, as honest and trustworthy as the majority of scientists are, their work cannot simply be generally accepted by the wider community just because they say so. Science is played out in the academic and subsequently the public arena—that is what ultimately makes it self-corrective! One must present the results of their work to their scientific peers for examination, comment, and scrutiny. This not only ensures that "bad" science comes to light, but it also stimulates discussion and future research within the community itself. Thus, scientists do have an obligation to present their work to the wider academic community, both for validation and for progress.

Lastly, scientists also have an obligation to the wider nonscientific community in which they live. While scientific examination is typically a purely academic enterprise, the discoveries of science often have tremendous impact on the wider society. Scientific discoveries have contributed in a myriad of

Figure 1.8: Scientists must present their results to their peers for review and discussion.

positive ways to the quality of human (and nonhuman) life (think of insulin, cell phones, mosquito nets, and airplanes, to name a few). However, scientists must recognize that the knowledge generated by them as an intellectual exercise may have a much wider social implication. In the last century, discoveries within the realm of genetics have demonstrated that humans are all members of the same polytypic species, and that there is no biological validity in dividing humans into distinctive "races." Thus, scientific results can contribute enormously to positive social change. However, once scientific results become public, the scientific community no longer has total control over how that knowledge will be used. There is a darker side here, where scientific knowledge can be politicized and used to justify negative applications that are not sanctioned by the majority of the scientific community (think of the eugenics movement, phrenology and criminal propensity, IQ and race, and the atom bomb, for instance). Therefore, science does not function in a vacuum or ivory tower, and it does have obligations, both to the academic community itself and the wider global community as well. Lastly, science is typically a multidisciplinary endeavor, where there are collaborations between scholars in diverse fields, each contributing a crucial piece of the puzzle. For example, archaeologists routinely consult not only with scholars from other anthropological specialties, but are often found working closely with geologists, environmental scientists, statisticians, chemists, and so on. In order to reconstruct a holistic picture of the human past, we need to collaborate with scholars who have a wide range of skills. This multidisciplinary approach has led to a large number of discoveries that could not have been achieved within a single discipline itself.

For example, in order to understand the elaborate picture of the peopling of the Americas, archaeologists must also consider complex geological and climatic processes such as glaciation or rising and falling ocean levels. You cannot move anywhere if an enormous glacier is in your way, or if the land bridge between Asia and North America is submerged in seawater! Without considering the complex geological past, one cannot truly understand the movement of humans into North and South America.

CAN YOU BELIEVE IN GOD AND EVOLUTION AT THE SAME TIME?

There is no homogeneous agreement between peoples today or in the past about how creation occurred. Diverse cultures have developed a wide range of philosophies to explain the creation of the universe, the planet Earth, the sun and moon, and living beings. According to the Chinese creation myth, the first living creature evolved inside a gigantic egg, and this cosmic egg contained all the elements of the universe totally intermixed.

Figure 1.9: The Judeo-Christian descriptions of creation are found in Genesis of the Old Testament.

The Samoan creation myth states that the supreme god Tangaroa created the world by simply thinking of it. In the Norse creation myth, the primordial giant Ymir is killed by Odin, Vili, and Ve. The Earth is formed from the dead body of Ymir. His flesh becomes the land, his blood becomes the sea, his bones become the mountains, and his hair becomes the trees. His skull becomes the vault of the heavens. A similar story occurs in the Babylonian creation myth recounted in the Babylonian epic *Enuma Elish*, which was written around 1100 BCE. The Babylonian god Marduk combats and slays Tiamat, the primordial goddess of the ocean. He cuts her body in two; one half becomes the Earth and the other half becomes the sky (Leeming and Leeming 1994, 1996).

The Cherokee creation belief describes the Earth as a great floating island surrounded by seawater. It hangs from the sky by cords attached at the four cardinal points. The story tells that the first Earth came to be when Dâyuni'sï (Beaver's Grandchild), the little water beetle, came from Gälûñ'lätï, the sky realm, to see what was below the water. He scurried over the surface of the water, but found no solid place to rest. He dived to the bottom of the water and brought up some soft mud. This mud flowed in every direction and became the Earth. To the Mandé peoples of southern Mali, the story begins when Mangala, the creator god, tries making a balaza seed, but fails. Then, he made two eleusine seeds of different kinds, which the people of Keita call "the egg of the world in two twin parts which were to procreate." After that, Mangala made three more pairs of seeds, and each pair became the four elements, the four directions, as corners in the framework of the world's creation. This he folded into a hibiscus seed. The twin pairs of seeds, which are seen as having opposite sex, are referred to as the egg or placenta of the world. This egg held an additional

Figure 1.10: In recent years, creationists have fought to remove evolution from the science classroom.

two pairs of twins, one male and one female, who were the archetype of people (Leeming and Leeming 1994, 1996).

What all these explanations have in common is an interest in explaining the complex world in which we live in ways that are culturally meaningful. While the investigation of human faith and belief is a fascinating area of study, it has no relationship to science. Science is not concerned with philosophical arguments or religious debate. These are questions that cannot be addressed within the scientific realm of knowledge. Likewise, the discoveries made by science are not then focused upon challenging people's religious beliefs. They are proven ideas that explain important processes in our world and beyond. While both science and belief are ways that humans make sense of their place in the world, they accomplish this by very different means. The theory of evolution explains the incredibly slow development of life on planet Earth; it does not address who got the ball rolling. Unfortunately, science cannot answer that question, and doesn't even try.

The vast majority of belief systems have reconciled evolutionary theory quite easily with religious doctrine. Most Christian denominations do not see a conflict between Christian doctrine and the tenets of evolutionary theory. This is essentially accomplished by holding that God created the universe, and the way in which God designed life to unfold was through evolution. Problem solved! The only circumstance in which one cannot reconcile Christian doctrine with evolutionary theory is if one believes in a literal translation of the Bible. In this case, the Bible is considered to relay the direct words of God, and the creation story contained within Genesis of the Old Testament is the only true version of creation. There can be no reconciliation between this view and evolutionary theory, or between this view and any other creation story. While this represents a true minority of

Christians, it has fueled a century-long legal challenge to the theory of evolution, commencing with the Scopes Trial (commonly called the **Scopes Monkey Trial**) of 1925 and continuing into the 21st century.

These legal challenges have principally focused upon the validity of teaching evolution in the public school classroom, with attempts being made to either remove the topic entirely from science curricula, or teaching "creationism" with equal time to the theory of evolution. While the Scopes Monkey Trial occurred in the 1920s, we are naive if we think that the theory of evolution is still not controversial. Attempts to insert "intelligent design" (the modern moniker for creationism) into the public school curriculum continues to this day. As recently as 2004–2005, a courtroom showdown occurred in Pennsylvania, where a newly elected Dover school board voted to require a statement promoting "intelligent design" be read out in ninth grade biology classes. They argued that it simply represented an alternative scientific view of the origins of life on Earth. The board was sued by several parents, and the trial ended with the U.S. District Court judge John E. Jones III stating that intelligent design was a principle based on religion, and that it "presents students with a religious alternative masquerading as a scientific theory" (*Kitzmiller v. Dover Area School District*, 2005). These legal challenges have repeatedly failed, principally because of the U.S. constitutional division between church and state.

In conclusion, science is not a secret, complex enterprise conducted by people in white coats in laboratories. Scientists crawl in caves, dive underwater, fly in the sky, and dig in jungles, as well as working in white lab coats. No theory—not even the theory of evolution—is sacred. We do not stop testing this idea simply because it is now a well-established and internationally recognized theory. The theory of evolution continues to be challenged by scientists all over the world; thus far, it has withstood these challenges.

CRITICAL REASONING QUESTIONS

- How is the discipline of anthropology divided? What are the different foci of the subdisciplines?
- You want to plant a garden in your backyard. You have a 12-foot-long plot that is half in direct sun and half in the shade. How do you select what plants to grow in each area?
- Your laptop won't turn on this morning. How do you form a hypothesis to find out why? How do you test this hypothesis by way of experiment?
- Your odd aunt Harriet tells you that aliens created the pyramids. How can you explain to her why this conclusion is not scientific?
- What is different about science and faith as realms of knowledge?
- Think of your own cultural beliefs about creation. Does it conflict with the idea of evolution? How might the two be reconciled?
- How might you feel if your child came home and told you that intelligent design will be taught in her ninth grade biology class? How might you make a case to the school that this is not recognized scientific material?

REFERENCES AND SUGGESTED READINGS

Leeming, D. A., and M. A. Leeming (1994). *Encyclopedia of creation myths*. Santa Barbara, CA: ABC-CLIO.

Leeming, D. A., and M. A. Leeming (1996). *A dictionary of creation myths* (Oxford Paperback Reference). Oxford, UK: Oxford University Press.

Kitzmiller v. Dover Area School District, Case No. 04CV2688, United States District Court for the Middle District of Pennsylvania. 2005 U.S. Dist. (court opinion found as PDF document at http://www.pamd.uscourts.gov./Kitzmiller/Kitzmiller-342.pdf).

Kuhn, T. (1962). *The structure of scientific revolutions.* Chicago: University of Chicago Press.

Marks, Jonathan (2011). *The alternative introduction to biological anthropology.* Oxford, UK: Oxford University Press.

Rennie, John (2006). "Answers to creationist nonsense." In Mary Courtis, ed., *Taking Sides: Clashing Views on Controversial Issues in Physical Anthropology,* pp. 72–81. Dubuque, IA: McGraw-Hill/Dushkin.

Sandford, M. K., and E. M. Jackson (2009). *Classic and contemporary readings in physical anthropology.* California: Wadsworth.

Taylor-Parker, S., and K. E. Jaffe (2008). *Darwin's legacy: Scenarios in human evolution.* New York: Altamira.

2

Leading Up To Evolution

Fathers of Evolutionary Thought

By Gillian Crane-Kramer

When one considers the concept of evolution, the name Charles Darwin immediately leaps to mind. Although Darwin is credited with conceiving of how the process of evolution actually functions (i.e., natural selection), he was not the first person to investigate the principles that guide the natural world. Charles Darwin published his influential tome *On the Origin of Species* in 1859, but natural scientists had been examining living organisms and geological processes on Earth long before Darwin's time. It is likely that our earliest hominid ancestors recognized processes such as the seasons, birth and death, and the passing of time. However, they did not set up controlled experiments to determine the reason for these events. In the ancient world, we begin to view a more sophisticated attempt to examine the natural world with classical scholars such as Aristotle and Plato. As early as the fourth century BC, Aristotle asserts that every living creature contains an essence that could not be changed (the immutability of species).

All creatures on Earth were organized in a hierarchical fashion, from the simplest to the most sophisticated (humans), and were forever linked to each other through this great chain of being. For many centuries, beginning in the Classical world and continuing well into the Middle Ages, well-established views concerning the creation and organization of the universe defined how humans viewed their place in the bigger scheme of things. Explanations were based upon theology, and any challenge to this worldview was punished swiftly and completely. These misconceptions severely hampered the development of modern science, and it was not until the 14th century that challenges to this pervasive way of thinking began to occur.

THE ELEPHANT IN THE ROOM: OUTDATED PERCEPTIONS OF THE UNIVERSE

In the modern age, we have essentially lost a true understanding of the influence of Christian doctrine on the everyday lives of individuals in the past. In medieval Europe, the Church influenced all aspects of social and professional life, establishing the calendar and religious festivals as well. People often attended services multiple times a day, and the Church was the most influential and important force in their daily lives. Biblical interpretation was essentially determined by Church doctrine. It told people how to live, how to die, and everything in between. As the clergy represented a considerable portion of the literate population, the everyday person relied on their presentation of biblical passages. It is important to remember that the Bible could only be read at this time in the classical languages (Latin, Greek, Hebrew, and Aramaic). The majority of the population was effectively illiterate, in that people could not often read or write in their native language, let alone the classical languages. This offered the medieval Church absolute control over biblical interpretation; not surprisingly, this view was considered to be the only true explanation of the universe. Challenging the authority of Church interpretation risked being labeled as a heretic. This was typically punished by imprisonment and/or death. Certainly, it was a career breaker. For centuries in Europe, biblical texts explained the history of humankind's creation and fall from grace. Biblical passages were considered the literal word of God. For devout Christians, there was only one way to explain the creation of the universe, and that explanation was contained in Genesis in the Old Testament.

Four ideas in particular presented significant impediments to the advance of a modern view of the universe: Fixity of species; a geocentric universe; a young Earth; and the notion that humans were separate from the animal kingdom. Until these ideas were challenged, it would be impossible to formulate any scientific view of the natural world. As discussed above, from classical times, it had been established that the natural world remained fixed and unchanging. Aristotle's **Great Chain of Being** was unanimously accepted as a true explanation of the

Figure 2.1: The Great Chain of Being explained the organization of the universe.

relationship between Earth's creatures. All were organized in this static hierarchical ladder with humans as the most sophisticated organism at the top (*Homo sapiens*, meaning wise man—if you believe that, I have some swamp land for sale). There is an inherent assumption that this ladder progresses from the simplest organism to the most complex and sophisticated (humans). If every organism was linked to every other in exactly the order that God had placed them during creation, where would you put the link of a new species? And if a species disappeared, then the chain would be broken. This plan was imperfect, and God was not imperfect! Thus, nothing new had appeared, and nothing had disappeared since creation. Period!

Figure 2.2: In Medieval European society, the Church was the most important institution in people's lives.

According to the Church, the universe was created in six days, as described in the biblical book of Genesis. No creatures have disappeared since creation, and no new species have appeared. The plan of the universe was seen as a "grand design." All organisms were perfectly designed by God to function in their individual environments. This can explain the large teeth in predators, the talons of eagles, the speed of cheetahs, and the dramatic coloration of birds and flowers. The idea of **fixity of species** is that all creatures have remained unchanged since creation, nothing new appearing and nothing disappearing. There is no need for change, as all life is considered to be perfectly adapted. This universally accepted notion of a stable and unchanging world served as a serious roadblock to the idea of evolution, where dynamic change is the focus.

As previously noted, the accepted description of how God created the universe was contained within the Book of Genesis in the Old Testament. As humans were a divinely favored species, it only made sense that Earth should also hold a central place in the organization of the wider universe. **Claudius Ptolemaeus** (Ptolemy) was a Greco-Egyptian scholar who lived in the second century AD. A well-respected mathematician, astronomer, and geographer, Ptolemy was very interested in how the universe was organized. His analysis of the heavens and its celestial bodies led him to support the earlier assertions of Aristotle, that the universe was **geocentric** (from the Greek *geo*, meaning Earth). He believed that the Earth was spherical and stationary at the center of the universe, and that all the other heavenly bodies moved around it in a circular motion and at constant speeds. This made sense in the intellectual climate in which Ptolemy was working; if humans were God's most important creation, then it was only logical that Earth was the center of the universe.

Figure 2.3: Ptolemy was a Greco-Egyptian scholar of the 2nd century A.D. who believed in a "geocentric" universe.

Prior to the 19th century, it was generally accepted by theologians, philosophers, and natural scientists that there was only a single creation event. It was natural to wonder when that monumental event occurred in relation to the modern calendar. The only means to investigate this question was to examine the Old and New testaments of the Bible itself for answers. For

Figure 2.4: Archbishop James Ussher.

example, the Gospel of St. Luke provides a genealogy for Jesus, extending back to the time of Adam and Eve. This question of the timing of the creation was reputedly first addressed by Bishop **John Lightfoot** in 1642. He stated that God created the universe beginning on September 12, 3928, and finally created humans in his image on Friday, September 17, 3928, at 9 A.M. This date was later revised by a well-respected Irish Anglican archbishop and scholar named **James Ussher** (1581–1656). On the basis of his analysis of the "begat" section of Genesis, a long genealogy listing the ages of important biblical figures, he concluded that creation commenced in 4004 BC on October 23rd. As James Ussher was a well-known and important scholar and clergyman, his calculations for the time of creation were not overtly questioned for over two centuries. Thus, it was generally held that God had risen on October 23, 4004 BC, and at 9 A.M. decided to create humans (presumably after having his coffee). If the Earth was created by God around 4004 BC, then this meant that the Earth

was geologically only roughly 6,000 years old. This young age of the Earth would dominate views of the Earth's antiquity for several generations; it continues to be accepted by fundamentalist Christians today.

Finally, as humans were God's most precious and important creation, and the only one to be created in his own image, medieval scholars were clear about our place in the wider organic world. It is

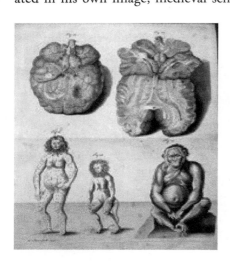

Figure 2.5: Edward Tyson's comparison of monkey, ape, and man.

clearly stated in the Book of Genesis that humans were a separate creation event. Thus, there was no biological relationship between humans and all other living organisms on earth. Humans were essentially the shepherds of the natural world, separate from it, but responsible for its care. This idea dominated science well into the 19th century and explains why Charles Darwin was so mercilessly mocked when he dared to suggest that humans descended from primates (although, again, he was not the first to make the connection between humans and primates). The prominent English anatomist **Edward Tyson** published a work in 1699 presenting an anatomical comparison of a modern human, ape, and monkey. On the basis of his analysis, he concluded that apes had many more anatomic similarities to humans (48, in fact) than they have to monkeys (only 34). This tremendous anatomic similarity between humans and apes seemed to directly challenge the generally accepted notion that humans were not part of the animal kingdom, as stated in Genesis. In fact, Tyson argues that it strongly implies a common thread among all living creatures, and the placement of humans within the natural world rather than outside of it. So, it appears that Charles Darwin took all the heat for an idea that had been circulating for over two centuries before he published *On the Origin of Species* in 1859.

Figure 2.6: Age of Exploration—Medieval ships.

A REVOLUTION OF IDEAS: THE BIRTH OF MODERN SCIENCE

In light of the strict control that Christian doctrine maintained upon perceptions of the natural world, it is not difficult to see why the pursuit of science—and the mere suggestion of evolution—was a tremendous risk. When do we begin to see the fires of revolution beginning to be set? It really begins during the Renaissance period between the 14th and 16th centuries, and this awakening results from a series of converging ideas and experiences. It is probably not a coincidence that this explosion of new knowledge occurs during the great Age of Exploration, when humans embarked on long sea voyages and circumnavigated the globe. At this time, Europeans were suddenly becoming aware of the vast diversity of plant and animal species that exist in the wider world. Europeans were now regularly coming into contact with new and vastly different ecosystems that were associated with hitherto unknown living species (and very different-looking people, as well). This stimulated scholars to reinvestigate accepted explanations, thereby stimulating the development of new types of questions and new methods and technology to answer those questions. This revolution in ideas also coincided with the first really significant and widespread criticism of Church doctrine, gaining momentum with Martin Luther's vocal criticism of Church excesses, laid out in detail and nailed to the Wittenberg Church in 1517. The invention of the printing press by Johannes Gutenberg allowed for a faster movement of new ideas. This removed the authority of the clergy to control the dissemination of ideas, and maintain their unchallenged authority over biblical interpretation. The famed Oxford theologian and philosopher John Wycliffe defied Church authority in the late 14th century and translated many biblical passages into Middle English, as he firmly believed that a vernacular Bible should be made available for all people to read. He felt that it was more important for people to read the Bible themselves than to just listen to the clergy in church. These translations had a significant influence on the Lollard movement, a pre-Reformation movement that strongly criticized many of the tenets of the Church. Not surprisingly, the Church moved quite rapidly to suppress it. It was banned by the Oxford Synod in 1408.

Figure 2.7: In the 17th Century John Ray developed the modern view of the term "species".

Particularly from the 14th century on, translations of biblical passages into the vernacular (the common language of the people) were beginning to occur throughout Europe. Even today, the best-known English translation of the Bible is the King James Version. In the year 1604, King James VI and I of Scotland and England (and a devout Protestant) authorized the translation of the Bible into English for the Church of England, and the project was completed in 1611. These biblical translations into the everyday language of the people severed the Catholic Church's control over biblical interpretation, and allowed the majority of the population access to the word of God for the first time.

By the 17th century, European scholars were beginning to truly investigate the enormous diversity of life forms on Earth. Prior to this time, there had been very little emphasis on the standard modern biological approach to investigating organisms. If anyone asked the question "How many types of butterflies are there?" the standard answer was "As many as God created." As comforting as this divinely organized universe may have been, there was no way to understand the incredible degree of variation in the world without actually going out and collecting, describing, and comparing all the variants.

With this new approach to examining the natural world came the necessity for some form of system to classify organisms. This, in turn, requires a method of grouping different types of organisms together and distinguishing between the different groups. The modern view of the term **species** did not develop until the 17th century with the work of the Cambridge-educated clergyman **John Ray**. Ray observed that groups of animals and plants could be distinguished from each other by their ability to mate and produce living, fertile offspring. These individual reproductively isolated groups he called species. Furthermore, Ray noted that often species share some biological/behavioral features in common with other species, and he created another category—the genus—to account for this observation. These terms are still in regular use in the biological sciences today, an impressive accomplishment for John Ray. In rare instances, there are different, but closely related, species that are able to produce living offspring (think of a horse and donkey producing a mule, or lions and tigers producing ligers). However, the offspring are always sterile; an evolutionary dead end, which defeats the whole purpose in the first place.

THE NAILS IN THE COFFIN: THE BUMPY ROAD TO EVOLUTION

A very interesting fact concerning some of the first modern scientists is that many of them were also clerics. This placed them in a unique and often very perilous position, given that their scientific results often directly contradicted the Church's position on a number of issues. Even the scientific laymen were expected to adhere to Church authority, under penalty of being labeled a heretic (and that was a decidedly BAD thing for you, your family, and sometimes your friends as well). When do we begin to see specific examples of natural scientists challenging these outdated views of the universe? It begins in the early 16th century with people like **Copernicus**, a Polish mathematician and astronomer who spent many years investigating the question of how the universe was organized. In Copernicus's day, the belief in a geocentric universe had dominated perceptions of the Earth's place in the wider plan of the universe for about a millennium and a

Figure 2.8: Ptolemy and Copernicus.

half (1500 years or more!). On the basis of complex mathematical calculations and observations of the heavens with the naked eye (as telescopes were yet to be invented), Copernicus determined that a **heliocentric**, or sun-centered, universe was a more likely possibility. Other heavenly bodies were still believed to rotate around the sun in a perfect series of concentric spheres, but the Earth was now relegated to a much less prominent position in the overall universe. Did that mean that humans were also less important to God? It is not surprising that Copernicus finally was convinced to allow the publication of his ideas as he was dying in 1543. He was well aware of the Church's reaction to this radical change in view, and he knew that it would likely result in excommunication or worse.

He was wise to foresee this theological opposition, because it came to fruition when the Italian mathematician/astronomer Galileo Galilei supported Copernicus's views in the early 1600s. Galileo's mathematical calculations and observations led him to support the notion of a heliocentric universe. This conclusion led to accusations of heresy by the Roman Inquisition, and the final nine years of his life were spent under house arrest. The Church was not fooling around, and punishment for these revolutionary ideas was a real possibility. Remarkable, really, that any of the early scientists were willing to risk the wrath of the Church. Thank heavens for us now that they did!

In the year 1543, another pivotal work was published that challenged many long-held beliefs in the very conservative discipline of medicine. This was the seven-volume *On the Fabric of the Human Body*, by the Flemish physician **Andreas Vesalius** (1514–1564). For centuries, physicians consulted earlier Greek, Roman, and Arab medical texts for diagnostic and treatment protocols. It was this reliance on earlier work that hindered new developments in the discipline. Prior to the 19th century, the discipline of anatomy was severely hampered by laws prohibiting the dissection of the human body. Since the 15th century, certain medical schools throughout Europe were allotted a small number of executed criminals for autopsy. However, this small number of legally obtained bodies was not nearly enough to sustain medical schools. Medical students could not be trained without a constant supply of cadavers. In order to obtain adequate numbers, they acquired their anatomical specimens by stealth (hence the famous English sack-'em-up men). Vesalius was a professor at the University of Padua, and is seen as the father of

Figure 2.9: Galileo Galilei.

PORTRAIT D'HOMME.

Figure 2.10: The Flemish physician Andreas Vesalius.

human anatomy. His great work presented extremely detailed and realistic drawings of the human body for the first time. Prior to this, medicine had relied upon stylized representations of the body inherited from the Classical world. Vesalius had broken a cardinal rule: he asserted that the only way to truly understand the structure and function of the human body was to dissect it and examine the individual elements. He challenged this long-held taboo against dissection that was not formally addressed in medical schools until the early 19th century. Prior to 1832, no provisions for the practical study of anatomy existed in Great Britain, Canada, or the United States.

In addition, by actually examining the human body in detail, Vesalius also began to question, and then directly challenge, the works of the fathers of medicine such as Galen and Hippocrates. This was a very important challenge, because Vesalius proved that there were actually mistakes with the wisdom of the ancient texts, and that medicine would never advance if it continued to adhere blindly to ancient descriptions. In 1541, while working in Bologna, Vesalius discovered that all of the famed Roman physician Galen's research had been based upon animal anatomy, rather than human.

The dissection of the human body was illegal in ancient Rome, and so Galen had dissected Barbary apes instead (which, he argued, would be anatomically similar to humans). Vesalius proved that an examination of human anatomy displayed considerable differences from animal anatomy, and that one could not make assumptions about human anatomy based upon that of animals. Vesalius's work was not only revolutionary in terms of the discipline of medicine, but it had wider influence, as it advocated empiricism—actually investigating issues directly—and this was an essential tenet for the development of modern science.

As an increasing number of new species were being discovered, it became necessary to place them in some form of logical and meaningful order. There was a good reason that early naturalists were often clergymen. They often had time during the day for observation and research; they had a natural interest in God's creations, and studying them was a wonderful way to glorify God. John Ray was a clergyman in addition to a naturalist, and Carolus Linnaeus, although not a cleric, was a devout Christian who saw

Figure 2.11: Carolus Linnaeus—the founder of binomial nomenclature.

natural science as a way to praise God. Linnaeus would have been an interesting man to have coffee with. He seems to have embodied such contradictory views, which makes him particularly intriguing. On the one hand, he was a very conservative man; devout Christian, and firm believer in the fixity of species for most of his life. In this way, his work supported the status quo by classifying all the miraculous creations of God to his glory. However, brewing inside and bubbling over was also a radical. We know that John Ray had provided a very useful means of beginning, with his designations of genus and species.

Enter the father of biological taxonomy, the Swedish naturalist **Carolus Linnaeus** (1707–1778). Linnaeus is famous for his influential study titled the *Systema Naturae*, published in 1735. In this work, he presents a system for classifying plants and animals called **binomial nomenclature** (*bi-* meaning two, and *-nomial* meaning names). It is a four-tired classification system, including John Ray's categories of genus and species, and adding two more of his own: class and order. This classification system of binomial nomenclature is still used internationally by scientists today, and if you discover a new species of plant or animal, it must be categorized in adherence to its rules. By examining living organisms in detail and placing them in distinct categories, it allows scholars to observe the pattern of relationships between organisms. Linnaeus rightly concluded that humans share a huge number of biological features in common with monkeys and apes, and thus placed us within the order Primates (although he placed humans and apes in separate families: Hominidae and Pongidae, respectively). It is fascinating to speculate how a man who believed in fixity of species could have made such a bold move as to assert that humans should be placed firmly within the animal kingdom. Not surprisingly, the Catholic Church placed his book upon the prohibited readings list, and the Lutheran Church authorities were enraged. Linnaeus had directly challenged the accepted notion that humans were a separate creation event as described in Genesis. However, the biological sciences would never be the same again because Linnaeus was establishing "a radical biological relativism to the natural world, tearing down the linear hierarchy of the Great Chain of Being and replacing it with a hierarchy of a very different kind—one wherein all species are equal, and can be more meaningfully arranged in relation to one another than in relation to an imaginary transcendent ideal: presumably us" (Marks 2011: 29).

Figure 2.12: Georges-Louis Leclerc, Comte de Buffon (1707–1788).

While Linnaeus and many scholars of his day were creationists and believers in the notion of a fixed, unchanging world, there were some scholars who were beginning to challenge these long-held ideas. One early proponent of change was **Georges-Louis Leclerc, Comte de Buffon** (1707–1788). Buffon was one of the first scholars to recognize that there is an active and dynamic relationship between the environment and the living organisms within it. As environments change, so must the organisms in order to survive. He noted that when a species moves to a new environment, it often changes in response to these new circumstances. However, he had no idea how this change took place, not surprising since the field of genetics did not exist at this time. In his great work *Natural History, General and Specific*, first published in 1749, he describes in great detail many species of plants and animals. He argues that sterile classification is not useful without an explanation for how these relationships developed. His outspoken views did get him into trouble; the theology faculty of the University of Paris would force him to retract some of his radical views (an ancient Earth, natural change) in 1751. However, although a creationist himself, Buffon continued to believe that biological similarities between living organisms suggested a notion of common descent (an idea never developed by Linnaeus).

Figure 2.13: Robert Hooke and Samuel Pepys.

During the 18th century, a large number of fossils were being uncovered with greater frequency around the world. This resurgence of interest in the natural world had led scientists to begin a thorough examination of these ancient remains. With the emergence of the

Figure 2.14: Georges Cuvier—The Father of Catastrophism.

Industrial Revolution, the increase in construction led to the discovery of large numbers of creatures that did not resemble modern species. In addition, scholars such as the English naturalist **Robert Hooke** (1635–1703) had proven that fossils were indeed evidence of ancient life through his microscopic analysis of fossil wood. If one still questioned the possibility of extinction, one had to look no further than the extinction of the famous dodo bird on the island of Mauritius in 1684 AD.

One of the first scholars to undertake a large systematic study of the fossil record was **Georges Cuvier** (1769–1832), a French zoologist and natural scientist. Cuvier, like the majority of scholars of his day, was a firm creationist. He is yet another potential coffee date, as he also embodies an interesting contradiction. He believes in the biblical description of creation; yet he rejects the idea of a Great Chain of Being, clearly stating that fossils are the remains of ancient creatures that are no longer alive today! This statement directly challenges the idea of fixity of species because it says that organisms have died out through time. In addition to asserting that extinction has occurred on Earth, he also recognizes that different geological layers (strata) seemed to be associated with a unique set of fossils. If these organisms have died out, than clearly they were not perfectly adapted to their environment.

Is God imperfect? Cuvier believed that God was perfect, and thus there must be a reasonable explanation for these extinctions in the fossil record. Cuvier did not believe in evolution; consequently, he was a staunch opponent of scholars like Jean-Baptiste Lamarck, Geoffroy Saint-Hilaire, and Erasmus Darwin (Charles's grandfather). As a result, Cuvier did not believe that an organism transforms over time into something else. Instead, he was crafty, and he devised an idea called **Catastrophism** to skirt around the whole evolution issue. The notion of catastrophism states that throughout the history of life on Earth, there has been a series of sudden and dramatic environmental catastrophes (think tsunamis, earthquakes, volcanic eruptions, and temperature change, to name a few). When one of these environmental disruptions occurs, it destroys the plant and animal life in

Figure 2.15: Volcanic eruption, Mt. St. Helens.

that region (hence the fossils), and afterward, new, more sophisticated creatures would appear in the area (he is a little fuzzy on where these new creatures come from; presumably it is surviving organisms from neighboring areas that have a more recent creation). Fossils are indeed ancient life forms that are gone from the modern world, but not because of evolution. Problem solved. While he was a very skilled anatomist, he was simply not willing to accept that the similarities he saw between fossil and modern species indicated an evolutionary relationship between the two. With catastrophism, he killed two birds with one stone; he dismissed the idea of evolution, and he accounted for the fact that fossils appear to become more complex over time.

Figure 2.16: Jean-Baptiste Lamarck.

A contemporary and major opponent of Georges Cuvier was a man named **Jean-Baptiste de Monet** (1744–1829), typically referred to by his title of chevalier de Lamarck. In many ways, he is Charles Darwin's only genuine precursor because he not only accepted that evolution occurs, but he attempted to explain how evolution actually functions. He believed that animals and plants change over the course of time to make themselves better adapted to their individual environments. As the environment changes over time and new biological traits are needed, organisms could become modified and then pass these improvements on to their offspring. This idea is called the **Inheritance of acquired characteristics**, and it was an idea that would have tremendous influence. The classic example is that of the giraffe

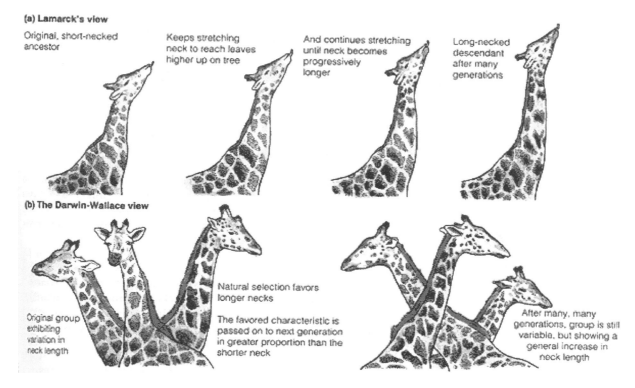

Figure 2.17: An example of Lamarck's "Inheritance of Acquired Characteristics."

Figure 2.18: Thomas Malthus.

that having depleted the leaves on the lower branches, has to stretch up to eat from the higher branches. Over time, their necks would become longer, and their children will be born with longer necks. Likewise, those organs that are no longer used will gradually reduce in size and ultimately disappear.

While Lamarck was very progressive in many ways—such as his rejection of the notion of the fixity of species and his staunch support of evolution—he was also conservative in some respects. He believed in the Great Chain of Being, in that offspring that had traits that were improved over their parents were one link higher in the Great Chain of Being. Add another person to the coffee klatch! Although Lamarck's notion of the inheritance of acquired characteristics was ultimately disproved with the development of the field of genetics, he is an important scientific figure: he was the first and only person to propose a theory of macroevolution prior to Charles Darwin and Alfred Russell Wallace. He also truly recognized the interrelationship between organisms and their environment, and the fact that it was this relationship that drove organic evolution.

This notion that organisms have evolved over time was also supported by scholars like **Erasmus Darwin** (1731–1802), who was a well-respected English physician, poet, and natural scientist, in addition to being Charles's grandfather. It is eerie how much his ideas are echoed in the work of his famed grandson—ideas like a common ancestry for all living creatures; the fact that evolution is a very slow process, taking enormous measures of time; that life emerged from water; that the environment dynamically interacts with living forms; and that there is competition among individuals for essential resources. While both Comte de Buffon and Erasmus Darwin recognized the crucial relationship between the environment and the flora and fauna within it, they did not take Lamarck's big leap and try and explain how organisms actually change.

Another Englishman who would go on to not only directly influence Charles Darwin, but have great influence on the scientists and politicians of his day, was the political economist and clergyman **Thomas Malthus** (1766–1834). In 1798, Malthus wrote a text titled *An Essay on the Principle of Population*, which had a tremendous impact on both the political and scientific communities. The Industrial Revolution is a name given to the era when human society was transitioning to new manufacturing techniques in the period from about 1760 to the mid-19th century. With it came the "Rise of Industry" and a rapid depopulation of the rural areas into the cities for work. The tremendous demographic shifts that were associated with this technological revolution presented new and difficult challenges for governing bodies. According to Robert Hughes in *The Fatal Shore*, the population of England and Wales, which had remained fairly stable at 6 million from 1700 to 1740, rose markedly after 1740. The population of England had more than doubled, from 8.3 million in 1801 to 16.8 million in 1850, and by 1901 had nearly doubled again to 30.5 million. Europe's population increased from about 100 million in 1700 to 400 million by 1900. This is a rapid increase in population in a very short period of time, and this brought with it all manner of problems concerning issues such as housing, health, employment, sanitation, poverty, and crime.

Malthus was very interested in the factors influencing human population growth. Interestingly, despite the enormous influence he had upon both Charles Darwin and Alfred Russell Wallace, he himself was not at all interested in the transformation of species. He notes that in nature, animal populations tend to increase over time, but the resources available in their environments remain reasonably constant. Animal populations are restricted in their numbers by the resource availability in their environment. He further observes that humans typically place population strains upon their environments, and even though we can artificially increase our food supply, it will never be able to increase at a rate rapid enough to maintain continuous growth. Therefore, Malthus concludes that there is a "**struggle for existence**," or competition among individuals for a limited number of resources. And the downside is that the majority of individuals do not win that competition. They are removed from the gene pool by positive checks like famine, war, disease, or accidents. These means are necessary to maintain the human (and presumably any) population below the carrying capacity of the environment. Where Darwin and Russell Wallace picked up the ball was extending this observation to the rest of the natural world, not just humans. Don't salmon and hummingbirds and reindeer reproduce faster than their food supply in nature? If so, then there must also be a struggle for existence between individuals in the animal and plant kingdoms. If only a small number of individuals actually survive to reproduce, then they are the successful ones in this game of life, and there must be something special about their features. Eureka!

Thus far, we have seen scholars challenge many of the traditional and incorrect theological views of how the universe is organized. Scientists like Copernicus, Kepler, and Galileo challenged the notion of a geocentric universe. Linnaeus disputed the notion of humans as separate from the animal kingdom, and scholars like Buffon, Hooke, Cuvier, and Lamarck questioned the idea of a fixed, unchanging natural world. The last holdout was this perception of a young Earth. Since the time of Ussher's calculation, it was generally accepted that the Earth was less than 10,000 years old. While this was far too short a time to explain the inherently slow process of organic evolution, it was an acceptable age, if one adhered to a creationist explanation. In order for any explanation of evolution to be presented, this notion of a young Earth had to be addressed.

Figure 2.19: James Hutton, the Scottish scientist (Scottish National Portrait Gallery).

SIR CHARLES LYELL.

Figure 2.20: Charles Lyell—the Father of Geology (from Sarah K. Bolton: "Famous Men of Science" (New York, 1889).

Figure 2.21: The Grand Canyon.

The first serious challenge to this idea came from the Scottish scientist **James Hutton** (1726–1797). He spent many years observing geological processes like water and wind erosion in action on the Scottish landscape. He concluded that the geological processes that we witness today are the same as those that acted on Earth throughout time. As geological processes are by their very nature slow-acting, he believed that the Earth must, in fact, be millions—rather than thousands—of years old. This notion of uniformitarianism did not really get much attention until the idea was rediscovered by the Scottish lawyer and geologist **Charles Lyell** (1797–1875). Lyell is generally considered the father of geology, and he wanted to make the field much more empirically rigorous. In his extremely influential three-volume tome written between 1830 and 1833, called the *Principle of Geology*, Lyell firmly establishes the notion of uniformitarianism, and argues that science can only examine geological processes that are witnessed today to explain the creation of landforms in the past (this means one could not refer to things like global floods that have never been witnessed in the modern age). In addition, Lyell argues that for the mostly slow-acting geological processes to have created the complex global landscape that we see today, the Earth must be a great deal older than 6000 years. This notion of **deep time** revolutionized the way that scientists perceived the geological history of Earth.

With this idea of an ancient Earth, Lyell had provided Charles Darwin with the time-depth he required to explain the inherently slow process of organic evolution. The stage was now set for the theory of natural selection to unfold. Like a long ladder, scholars from various times and places not only challenged and overturned many incorrect views of the natural world, but they also contributed pieces of the puzzle that would allow Darwin to publish a holistic theory of evolution in 1859.

CRITICAL REASONING QUESTIONS

- What is the idea of fixity of species? How did this belief impede the development of a notion of evolution?
- Think about how difficult it is to defy authority. What might these early scientists have endured at home and from the wider society?
- Prior to the work of Vesalius, how did physicians gain knowledge about the human body? Why might this hamper the development of modern medicine?
- Why did it matter how old the Earth was?
- How did theology dictate perceptions of the universe and the place of humans within it?
- You are sent to an unknown tropical island in the Indian Ocean and asked to record all plant and animal life. How do you make meaningful conclusions about the relationships between the native species?

REFERENCES AND SUGGESTED READINGS

Aczel, A. D. (2007). *The Jesuit and the skull: Teilhard de Chardin, evolution and the search for Peking Man.* New York: Riverhead Books (Penguin Books).

Berlanstein, Lenard R., ed. (1992). *The Industrial Revolution and work in nineteenth-century Europe.* London and New York: Routledge.

Boulanger, C. L. (2013). *Biocultural evolution: The anthropology of human prehistory.* IL: Waveland Press Inc.

Broberg, G. (1994). "*Homo sapiens:* Linnaeus' classification of Man," pp. 156–194. In T. Frangsmyr, ed., *Linnaeus: the Man and His Work*, rev. ed. Canton, MA: Science History.

Cahn, S. M., ed. (1977). *Classics of Western philosophy.* Indianapolis: Hackett Publishing Company.

Debus, Allen, ed. (1968). *Vesalius. Who's who in the world of science: From antiquity to present*, 1st ed. Hannibal, MO: Western Co.

Eddy, J. H. Jr. (1984). "Buffon, organic alterations, and man." *Studies in the History of Biology* 7:1–45.

Gillespie, C. C. (1951). *Genesis and geology: The impact of scientific discoveries upon religious beliefs in the decades before Darwin.* Cambridge, MA: Harvard University Press.

Gould, S. J. (1983). "Chimp on the chain." *Natural History* 98(12):18–27.

———— "Adam's navel." *Natural History* 93(6):6–14.

———— (2000). *The structure of evolutionary theory.* Cambridge, MA: Harvard University Press.

Green, J. C. (1954). "Some early speculations on the origin of human races." *American Anthropologist* 56:31–41.

Griffin, Emma (2010). *Short history of the British Industrial Revolution.* London: Palgrave.

Hodgson, M. H. (2004). Malthus, Thomas Robert (1766–1834). In D. Rutherford, ed., *Biographical Dictionary of British Economists.* Bristol, UK: Continuum.

Hughes, R. (1986). *The fatal shore: The epic of Australia's founding.* New York: Random House.

Jurmain, R., L. Kilgore, and W. Trevathan (2013). *Essentials of physical anthropology,* 9th ed. United States: Wadswoth Cengage Learning.

Koerner, L. (1999). *Linnaeus: Nature and nation.* Cambridge, MA: Harvard University Press.

Koestler, A. (1959). *The sleepwalkers: A history of man's changing vision of the universe.* London: Penguin Books.

Kuhn, T. (1970). *The structure of scientific revolutions,* 2nd ed. Chicago: University of Chicago Press.

Lightfoot, John (1602–1675) (1822–1825). *The whole works of the Rev. John Lightfoot: Master of Catharine Hall, Cambridge*. John Rogers Pitman, ed. London: J. F. Dove.

Lindberg, D. C., and R. L. Numbers, eds. (1986). *God and nature: Historical essays on the encounter between Christianity and science*. Berkeley: University of California Press.

Lovejoy, A. O. (1936). *The great chain of being*. Cambridge, MA: Harvard University Press.

Marks, J. (2011). *The alternative introduction to biological anthropology*. Oxford, UK: Oxford University Press.

Mayr, E. (1981). *The growth of biological thought*. Cambridge, MA: Harvard University Press.

Montagu, M. F. A. (1943). "Edward Tyson M.D., F.R.S., 1650–1708 and the rise of human and comparative anatomy in England." *Memoirs of the American Philosophical Society* 20.

O'Malley, C. D. (1964). *Andreas Vesalius of Brussels, 1514–1564*. Berkeley: University of California Press.

Porter, Roy, ed. (1994). *Vesalius. The biographical dictionary of scientists*, 2nd ed. New York: Oxford University Press.

Ray, J. (1977). *The wisdom of God manifested in the works of the creation* (1717). New York: Arno Press.

Robinson, H. W. (1970). *The Bible in its ancient and English versions*. Westport, CT: Greenwood Press.

Rosen, E. (1984). *Copernicus and the scientific revolution*. Malabar, FL: Robert E. Krieger.

Shea, W. R., and M. Artigas (2003). *Galileo in Rome: The rise and fall of troublesome genius*. Oxford, UK: Oxford University Press.

Stacey, J. (1964). *John Wyclif and reform*. London: Westminster Press.

Teresi, D. (2002). *Lost discoveries: The ancient roots of modern science—from the Babylonians to the Maya*. New York: Simon & Schuster.

"The UK population: Past, present and future" (PDF). Statistics.gov.uk

Young, D. (1992). *The discovery of evolution*. Natural History Museum Publications, Cambridge, UK: Cambridge University Press.

3

The Lights Turn On

Evolution at the Level of the Genes

By Gillian Crane-Kramer

The dramatic development of the biological sciences in the 20th century allowed humans for the first time to investigate the living world with a precision formerly unimaginable. Now, humans were able to examine minute structures like cells and genes that could not be seen with the naked eye. This allowed us to assess the relationship between living beings with a remarkable degree of accuracy, and permitted scholars to establish ancestral relationships with more clarity. These new developments stimulated the study of microevolution, or how evolution actually works at the level of the genes. We now know that evolution results from tiny fluctuations in the frequencies of genes in a population over long periods of time. Charles Darwin recognized that evolution results from a gradual accumulation of biological differences over countless generations, but as the field of genetics had yet to develop, he was unaware of the mechanisms of inheritance.

There are several wonderful textbooks that describe in detail the structure of the cell and DNA, mitosis and meiosis, the Hardy-Weinberg formula, and Punnett squares. While it will briefly describe these topics, this book is more concerned with how we apply this knowledge and what it can tell us about evolution. So, for biology majors who need a much more detailed account of these structures and processes, I propose you consult your professor's suggested standard textbook, as you are already set up to be disappointed here. However, if you would like to also know how this knowledge has changed our view of the natural world in which we live, please do read on.

CELLS: WHAT ARE THEY, AND WHY ARE THEY CONTROVERSIAL?

I always think of the cell as a fried egg. I will pause for a moment until the cell and micro biologists recuperate from this simplified blasphemy. Much to all of our great disappointment, the vast majority of students who read this book will not enter those illustrious fields. However, it is important that the rest of us unfortunate majority have a fundamental understanding of what a cell is and how it is structured. We estimate that the Earth and the moon are about 4.6 billion years old. Interestingly, we do not see evidence of life on Earth for almost a billion years, until sometime around 3.7 billion years ago. It may be that the environmental conditions on the planet were not conducive to support life, or it may be that we have never recovered evidence of these early life forms. Regardless, the earliest evidence of life are what we call prokaryotes. Every living organism is constructed of at least a single cell. In the case of prokaryotes, they comprise only a single cell. The earliest of life forms were prokaryotes like bacteria and blue-green algae. It was not until much later—at closer to a billion years ago—that we begin to see eukaryotes, multicellular organisms like plants and animals. While eukaryotes are far more complex than prokaryotes in terms of their structure, they also have much higher energy requirements to survive and reproduce themselves. The two major components of eukaryotic cells that are surrounded by membranes are the nucleus and the cytoplasm. Numerous exchanges occur between these two portions for normal functioning to occur. Eukaryotic cells are composed essentially of lipids (fats), carbohydrates, amino acids, and proteins. Every type of tissue in the human body, be it nerve, bone or brain, is composed of clusters of cells that perform specialized functions.

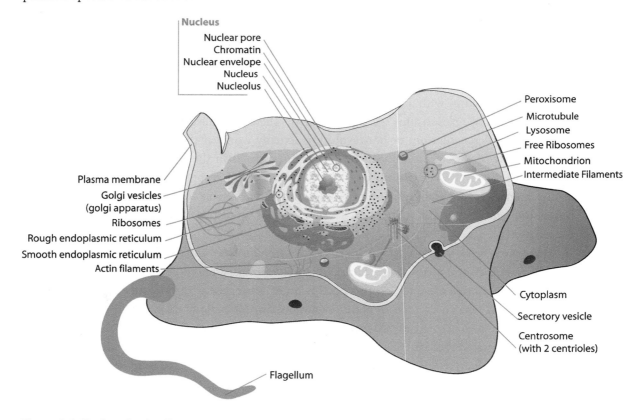

Figure 3.1: Basic animal cell structure.

The yolk of the egg is the nucleus. It is where we find the molecules that run the show. These molecules are **DNA** and **RNA** (**deoxyribonucleic acid** and **ribonucleic acid**); they contain the information that guides the functioning of the cell. The cytoplasm is the white of the egg, and there are many important structures (organelles) that are located within it such as mitochondria (energy producers) and ribosomes (seat of protein production). It does not matter what type of cell is involved (blood, muscle, lung): all of them are structured in the same way, and it is the DNA located in their nucleus that guides their proper functioning. In living organisms, there are two types of cell: somatic cells and gametes. **Somatic cells** (from

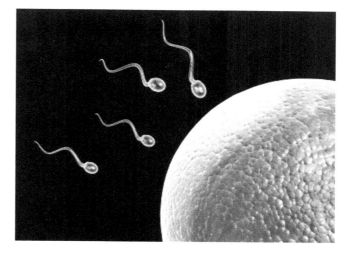

Figure 3.2: Sperm fertilizing human egg.

sōma, the Greek word for body) form body tissues like bone, muscle, skin, and blood. **Gametes** are sex cells that are formed within the reproductive organs. These gametes are ova (eggs) in females and spermatozoa in males. As gametes contain our genetic information, it is only when they unite with another gamete at fertilization that our genetic information is transferred to the next generation in the creation of a zygote. The source of gamete and somatic cell production lies in the chromosomes that are located in the nucleus of every cell. Different species have different numbers of chromosomes in their nucleus; humans have 46 chromosomes in their somatic cells and 23 chromosomes in their gametes (by comparison, salamanders have 24, algae have 148, and orangutans have 48). Gametes have only half the number of normal body cells, so that at conception, the first original cell has the correct human number—46—in its nucleus.

The most controversial issue relating to cells is centered upon stem cell research. **Stem cells** are marvelous things that have the potential to revolutionize many areas of medical treatment. They are undifferentiated cells that have not been given the instructions to form into a blood cell, or a nerve or kidney cell yet. They are able to make copies of themselves through mitosis, and come in two forms: embryonic and adult. During embryonic development, stem cells can differentiate into all the necessary specialized cells of the body. In adults, stem cells make up part of our tissue repair system. In particular, embryonic stem cells represent important possibilities for future therapies. Research into stem cells grew out of discoveries made by University of Toronto scholars Ernest A. McCulloch and James E. Till in the 1960s.

This technology has given rise to a myriad of ethical questions concerning the use of embryonic stem cells, with strong opposition being presented from the pro-life movement. Religious opposition centers upon the assertion that life begins at the moment of conception, and that destruction of human embryos

Figure 3.3: Stem cell.

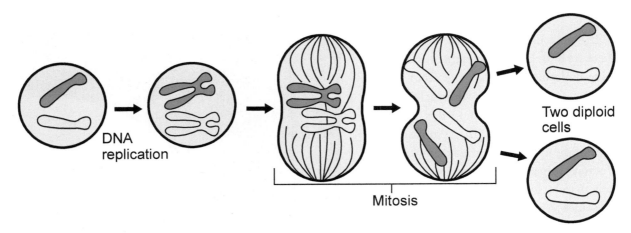

Figure 3.4: Mitosis.

is therefore technically murder. Most of the existing human embryonic stem cell lines internationally were derived from unused embryos created for couples seeking in vitro fertilization (IVF). The process of in vitro fertilization creates many embryos that will not, in fact, be used to create a baby and will therefore be destroyed. Scientists argue that it is much more ethical to use these embryos for research that may ultimately cure disease than to let them simply be destroyed intact. It is necessary to destroy human embryos in order to establish a stem cell line. However, research involving existing stem cell lines does not require the destruction of further embryos. Given the enormous positive potential of the avenue of research, it is logical to continue research upon stem cell lines already in existence.

Researchers working with these cells have found that they usually recover after freezing and thawing and can differentiate into assorted cell types in a culture dish. Embryonic stem cells have the potential to grow perpetually in a laboratory environment and can differentiate into almost all tissue types. This gives embryonic stem cells enormous potential for positive cellular therapies to treat conditions such as diabetes and Parkinson's, to name a few. Researchers widely suggest that stem cell research has the potential to revolutionize our understanding and treatment of many diseases, as well as greatly improve the quality of many people's lives. In the future, most medical researchers anticipate being able to use technologies derived from stem cell research to treat a variety of diseases and injuries such as Alzheimer's disease, spinal cord injuries, and Parkinson's disease.

HOW DO WE CONSTRUCT OUR BODY AND SEX CELLS, AND WHY DOES IT MATTER?

At the moment of conception, we all start out as one giant cell. Somehow, we have to get from this starting point to the final product with billions upon billions of cells. We do this through the process of **mitosis**, where somatic (body) cells are able to make perfect duplicates of themselves (in fact, creating two cells from one original cell). This process continues throughout our lives, as most cells die and are replenished continually.

The majority of cells (red blood cells and liver cells being the odd exceptions) are able to make copies of themselves when necessary (for healing, growth, or to replace aging cells). It is a complicated business because the cell has to make a perfect copy of itself, with the full complement of DNA as well. Mitosis involves a stage of chromosome replication and cell division. What results is the production of two daughter cells that are identical to the original, with 46 chromosomes in the nucleus if you are a human. That is why these cells are said to be diploid: they have the full complement of chromosomes in the nucleus.

While mitosis is the process through which we create new cells, as a process, it does not have the same evolutionary significance as **meiosis**, the production of our sex cells (gametes, which are ova in females and spermatozoa in males). Meiosis is a specialized form of cell division in the reproductive organs (ovaries and testes). It is these sex cells or gametes that have the potential to become actual human beings. The gametes are said to be haploid because they have only half the full complement of chromosomes (23 in humans). Unlike the body cells produced by mitosis, sex cells are not perfect duplicates of the parent cell or

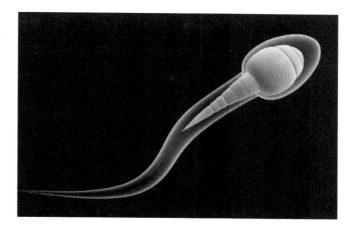

Figure 3.5: Spermatozoa gamete.

its DNA. This is because of a reshuffling of genes (sexual recombination, or crossing over) that takes place during this process. During meiosis, there is also a stage of chromosome replication, but this is followed by two cell divisions instead of just one. Thus, the process of meiosis produces four haploid daughter cells. When the two gametes meet at fertilization, the new offspring will have one chromosome of each pair from each parent, uniting to form the proper complement of 46 chromosomes in the nucleus of the original cell. Because genes get shuffled around during meiosis (they also can during mitosis, but this does not have evolutionary implications), it means that every organism can have a very large number of genetically different offspring. Genetic variation is extinction insurance. The more variation a species has, the more biological flexibility it has in the face of environmental change.

THAT MIRACLE JUICE: WHY IS DNA SO COOL?

Today in the media the term DNA is heard all the time. Every police or CSI show has this lovely molecule front and center, so it is important to have a sense of why DNA provides a wonderful way of examining evolutionary relationships and discovering ancient diseases and modern criminals. DNA stands for deoxyribonucleic acid, and it is a double-stranded molecule that contains the genetic code. Think of it as a blueprint that contains all the information to construct and properly run an organism.

It essentially directs all the activities in the cell, a very hefty responsibility. The physical and chemical properties of DNA were discovered in the 1950s by both the American and British scholars James Watson and Francis Crick, respectively, and their teams. This discovery was revolutionary—it completely changed forever the way scientists perceive the mechanisms that govern living organisms and their evolution. It also revolutionized the biological sciences and the field of genetics. The best way to think of DNA is like a ladder composed of two sides and several rungs.

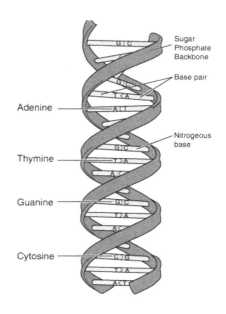

Figure 3.6: DNA structure.

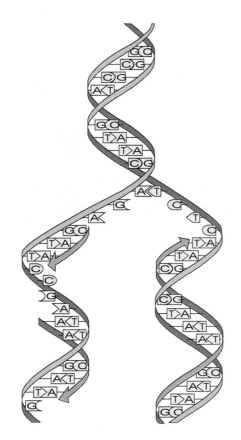

Figure 3.7: DNA replication.

The sides of the ladder are called nucleotides; in turn, they are composed of three elements: a sugar molecule, a phosphate, and one of four nitrogenous bases (adenine, cytosine, guanine, and thymine). The nucleotides are stacked on top of each other like a long chain that is bonded to another long chain at its base. When bonded together, the two individual strands twist to form a spiral shape we call a **double helix**. An important fact to remember is something called the base-pairing rule, which is that cytosine only bonds to guanine, and adenine only bonds to thymine. Thus, the rungs of the ladder are either AT (TA) or GC (CG).

First of all, there are two types of DNA. Nuclear DNA is found in the nucleus of every cell, and it is inherited by both parents. Mitochondria are structures that are located in the cytoplasm of the cell, and are a cell's energy producers. Mitochondria have their own unique type of DNA, and this is inherited only from one's mother. Thus, mitochondrial DNA has been an interesting tool to investigate maternal lineages through time. With the exception of identical twins, your DNA is individual to you, because you are a unique and against-all-odds creation of your parents. The fact that DNA is unique both within individuals and between species makes it a wonderful focus for research concerning evolutionary relationships. It allows us to investigate questions such as Where did modern humans first evolve? How closely are humans related to other primates? What disease organisms plagued people in the past? and Were you present at the crime scene?

Before we examine how scientists have applied DNA technology to a variety of questions, we need to discuss two very important functions that DNA has: DNA replication and protein synthesis. The chemical properties of the DNA molecule allow it to fulfill two very important functions: replication and protein synthesis. DNA has the ability to make a perfect copy of itself; it does this through a process called DNA replication.

The way it practically works is that in the nucleus of the cell, specialized enzymes are released that break apart the bonds between the two individual nucleotides. Everyone remembers from high school chemistry class that once bonds are pulled apart (open), they have a tremendous desire to re-bond to something. These exposed nitrogenous bases attract complementary nucleotides, and the ladder with both sides is then rebuilt. Hence, one ends up with two identical molecules of DNA. Why is this important? Firstly, it is vital because we all start out at the moment of fertilization as one large cell. That cell has to reproduce itself (a process called mitosis for body cells, meiosis for sex cells) billions of times to form all the cells of the human body in the womb. For every new cell that is reproduced, an exact copy of the original DNA must be placed in the nucleus to give and carry out genetic instructions. This means that replication has to occur perfectly, billions and billions of times. Impressive.

Another very important function of DNA is the production of proteins within the cell, or protein synthesis. We are essentially constructed of various proteins (the most common being collagen, a major constituent of connective tissue like bone and muscle). Proteins, in turn, are constructed of smaller units called amino acids that are linked together in various combinations to form different proteins. There are 20 different amino acids that compose living organisms that can be combined to create a great variety of different proteins. Thus, proteins differ from each other in terms of the number of and sequence of amino acids. The seat of protein production is in structures called ribosomes that are located in the cytoplasm of the cell. It is here that amino acids are produced. While nuclear DNA contains the instructions for production, it cannot communicate directly with the ribosomes in the cytoplasm. As a result, it enlists the help of Messenger and Transfer RNA, that codes the DNA message, transports and interprets it for the ribosomes.

A gene is a portion of DNA that determines the sequence of amino acids in a particular protein. Essentially, within the chromosome, DNA is packaged into genes. Genes are located on chromosomes, which are structures that are composed of DNA and proteins in the cell nucleus. The location of a gene on a chromosome is called its locus. Chromosomes come in pairs (and hence so do genes), and we inherit one chromosome of each pair from each of our parents. Chromosomes of the same pair are called homologous chromosomes, and while the locus for a particular gene is the same on each of the homologous chromosomes, the alleles at each locus may be different. At many genetic loci, there is more than one possible variant for a gene. These genetic variants at a particular locus are called alleles. For example, let's look at the ABO blood group. The locus for the ABO blood group system is on chromosome 9, and there are three possible alleles for this trait: A, B, or O. Genes come in pairs, which means

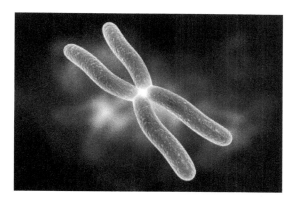

Figure 3.8: Chromosome.

that an individual can only have two of these genes in total (one from each parent). They can be combined in several different ways to form the four different ABO blood groups; A (AA or AO), B (BB or BO), OO, and AB.

Most of our DNA is what is often referred to as "junk" DNA, in that it does not appear to have any purpose in normal human functioning. The majority of this genetic material has been inherited from ancient ancestors and their parasites, many millions of years ago, and does not serve any necessary function today.

MITOCHONDRIAL EVE AND Y-CHROMOSOME ADAM: SOME IMPORTANT GENETIC RELATIVES

As stated above, mitochondria are organelles that are contained within the cytoplasm of the cell. Mitochondria produce energy for the cell by breaking down fats and sugars in the presence of oxygen to produce ATP (adenosine triphosphate), so that the cell can "breathe." Unlike nuclear DNA, mitochondrial DNA is only inherited from one's mother; it does not undergo recombination like nuclear DNA does. However, mitochondrial DNA does acquire mutations over time, random, but significant, events, and the mutation rate can be estimated over time during the course of human evolution. This allows mitochondrial DNA to act as a molecular clock that allows us to trace female lineages over many generations. There appears to be far less variation in human mitochondrial DNA than in other species of primate, such as our closest relative, the chimpanzee.

In the 1980s, Rebecca Cann, Allan Wilson, and Mark Stoneking designed a study to examine at what time and location the earliest modern human female originated. They took samples from living populations in diverse areas of the world. By tracing mutation rates in mitochondrial DNA

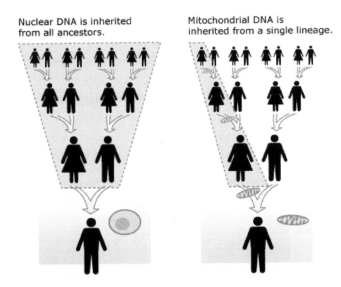

Figure 3.9: Inheritance of nuclear and mitochondrial DNA.

over time, they constructed family trees of mitochondrial lineages. Although some of the trees led to southwest Asia, the vast majority led to Africa. It appears that in terms of **mitochondrial DNA**, sub-Saharan African populations have more genetic diversity than any other groups on Earth. There are two ways of explaining this observation. Firstly, one could argue that populations that have been in existence the longest will have accumulated the largest numbers of mutations. This would indicate that Africa appears to be the origin of modern humans. Alternatively, the geneticist and anthropologist John Relethford argues that the greater genetic diversity in sub-Saharan African groups may result from the population structure of Africa compared to other continents. He points out that population size has a tremendous influence upon genetic diversity. This puts into question whether or not Africa is the sole source of modern humans, or whether Africa simply had a larger breeding population size than other continents. This would lead Africa to have greater genetic diversity. Thus, the female dubbed Mitochondrial Eve seems to represent human ancestry upon the African continent. In addition, the team calculated the time of this emergence at between 140,000 and 200,000 years ago. There has been considerable controversy over the implications of this work, particularly in terms of calculating mitochondrial mutation rates and ancient population size (Corruccini 1994, Conroy 1997, Relethford and Harpending 1994). A recent estimate in 2013 from scholars at the Max Planck Institute for Evolutionary Anthropology suggests that Mitochondrial Eve lived about 160,000 years ago, and also that the non-African humans were separated from Africans about 95,000 years ago. In recent years, this position has been bolstered by complementary work looking at variations in the **Y-chromosome** of males, again finding much less variation in humans than in other primates. Research looking at patrilineal lineages (tracing back along the male side of the family tree) have focused on the Y chromosome, leading to Y-Chromosome Adam (Y-MRCA, the most recent common ancestor).

Further work looking at DNA sequences on chromosome 12 found that modern African populations have more variation than all other world populations combined (Dorit et al. 1995, Tishkoff et al. 1996). In August 2013, a study led by geneticists from the Stanford University School of Medicine estimates the age of Mitochondrial Eve to be about 99,000 and 148,000 years, and the Y-MRCA to have lived between 120,000 and 156,000 years ago, based on the sequencing of genes from 69 people from 9 different populations. It is possible that the genetic ancestral Adam and Eve may have existed at the same time, but further work is necessary to clarify the molecular methodology.

Figure 3.10: Ape-human evolution.

A MOLECULAR CLOCK: TRACING THE APE-HUMAN SPLIT

One of the earliest studies to experiment with a "molecular clock" was that conducted by Allan Wilson and Vincent Sarich in the1960s. They were interested in seeing if we could estimate the time when the human lineage split off from a common ancestor we share with the great apes. Many diverse sources of evidence—from morphology to genetics to immunology—have demonstrated a very close biological relationship between humans and the great apes. We are most closely related to the chimpanzee, differing in only roughly 1.2 percent of our genes.

Figure 3.11: Donald Johansen and a potential human ancestor.

This would suggest a fairly recent common ancestry in geological time. Wilson and Sarich look at this question by examining how the rabbit immune system responds to both the human and nonhuman primate protein, albumin. When an animal's immune system recognizes a foreign protein or antigen has entered its body (whether that is mold, bacteria, or peanuts), one of the things that it does to protect the body is to create antibodies against that specific antigen. The more distant the biological relationship between the organisms, the more extreme the immune reaction should be. The protein albumin is very important for regulating fluid movement in the body, and it is specific to each species. The experiment injected albumin from several different primate species into rabbits. Naturally, as rabbits and primates are not closely related, the rabbits had a strong immunological reaction to the foreign albumin, but it differed, depending on the primate species. By measuring these different reaction rates, scientists estimate that human and chimpanzee lineages split from each other (ape-human split) around five million years ago. At first, this date rocked the scientific world, as paleoanthropologists were forced to accept a very recent date for human-ape common ancestry. However, today, this date has generally been accepted as representing the approximate period of hominid differentiation sometime in the late Miocene period.

ARE NEANDERTHALS ANCESTORS OR COUSINS?

Since the first *H. neanderthalensis* was discovered in the Neander Valley in Germany in 1856, humans have been trying to sort out what position the species represents on the modern human family tree. Are they direct ancestors to modern humans, or are they simply more distant cousins? The reaction to Neanderthals has been very interesting in the last century and a half. On the one hand, we can see the similarities between them and us; Neanderthals are clearly a highly adapted and intelligent species, who created sophisticated tools, manufactured clothing and jewelry, and buried their dead. However, they also maintained some biological and behavioral differences from modern humans. Several interesting

Figure 3.12: *Australopithecus africanus* adult female head model (Smithsonian Museum of Natural History).

molecular studies have been conducted to assess the Neanderthal genetic relationship to modern humans.

Supporters of the Out-of-Africa theory like Chris Stringer argue that the appearance of modern humans in Africa was a speciation event, and there could be no genetic admixture (interbreeding) between modern humans and archaic *Homo sapiens* groups like Neanderthals because technically they were different species. Remember what John Ray said about a species: it is defined by a population of interbreeding individuals who can produce fertile offspring. Different species = no children (or, in rare cases, sterile children). If this is true, Neanderthal genes should show little similarity to modern humans. However, what if modern humans were not a different species and they could interbreed with archaic groups? Firstly, one should find evidence of these hybrids in the skeletal record. Provocative examples like the child recovered from Lagar Velho in Portugal suggest this might just be a possibility (Duarte et al. 1999). Some scholars argue that the juvenile specimen from this site does not represent a modern human/Neanderthal hybrid, but simply a hefty modern child (Tattersall and Schwartz 1999).

Early on, it appears that the molecular scholars agreed with the paleoanthropologists, as it was generally held that the genetic evidence did not support interbreeding (Serre and Pääbo 2008, Krings et al. 1997, 2000, Schmitz et al. 2002). The mitochondrial DNA retrieved from Neanderthal specimens is all similar to each other, and appear to cluster together as a group to the exclusion of early or modern *Homo sapiens*. Like modern humans, there is little apparent diversity in Neanderthal mitochondrial DNA, considerably less than in modern African great apes. However, recent investigations directly question this assertion based on the sequencing of nuclear DNA samples (Green et al. 2006, Noonan et al. 2006). This work suggests that the

Figure 3.13: Skeleton and restoration model of Neanderthal La Ferrassie 1 (National Museum of Nature and Science, Tokyo, Japan).

split between Neanderthals and *Homo sapiens* occurred at some time between 440,000 and 270,000 years ago. It further suggests that Neanderthals contributed at least one percent, and possibly as much as four percent, of the genome of modern non-African populations (Green et al. 2010). Other scholars estimate that the last common African ancestor from the Y-chromosome evidence dates to roughly 60,000 years ago (Underhill, Shen et al. 2000, Wells 2002). In terms of Neanderthal mitochondrial DNA, it appears that Neanderthals shared the last common ancestor with modern humans roughly 500,000 years ago (Krings, Stone, et al. 1997). Interestingly, the earliest fossil evidence of modern humans comes only from the African continent; it is dated to roughly 160,000 years ago (White, Asfaw, et al. 2003).

The jury is still out on this debate, but there is no question that the ride will be very exciting! Interesting recent research using nuclear DNA also indicates that some Neanderthal individuals at the El Sidrón site in Spain had red hair and pale skin (Lalueza-Fox 2007). This indicates that like modern humans, Neanderthals had adapted genetically to temperate areas with low UV radiation, as seen by traits like skin depigmentation. However, interestingly, the mutation for this is different for

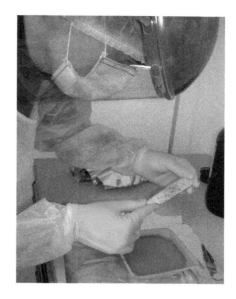

Figure 3.14: Neanderthal DNA extraction (Max Planck Institute for Evolutionary Anthropology, Leipzig, Germany).

modern humans and Neanderthals, suggesting that they developed these features independently of each other.

RECAPTURING THE NASTY CRITTERS OF THE PAST: ANCIENT DNA AND HUMAN DISEASE EVENTS

One of the specialties within the field of osteology (skeletal biology) is called paleopathology, and it focuses on an examination of ancient health and illness. On rare occasions, researchers have access to soft tissue associated with intentional or natural mummification (think of Egyptian mummies or the Iceman, for example). However, in the vast majority of cases, we have only the skeletal remains of the individual left for examination. The majority of human aDNA (ancient DNA) studies have focused on extracting DNA from bone and teeth samples, which tend to preserve most often in archaeological contexts. Recently, several other types of biological evidence have yielded DNA, including paleofeces (Poinar et al. 2001) and hair (Gilbert et al. 2004). A major impediment to aDNA research has been the issue of contamination, which continues to present a major problem today. In addition, retrieving usable DNA from pathogens in ancient skeletal and mummified tissue is very difficult, as the amount of bacterial or viral DNA recovered is typically small, even in an individual who is severely affected.

Prior to the development of techniques to retrieve ancient DNA from bone tissue, scholars could really only examine diseases and conditions that left an imprint on bone. This can be a very difficult task in and of itself, as bone has a limited number of ways in which it can respond to stress: either bone growth or bone loss. While we have many documentary descriptions and artistic representations of conditions like cholera, the Black Death, or malaria that affected ancient groups, it was impossible for us to obtain a signature of

Figure 3.15: Medieval Plague, Josse Lieferinxe (1497–1499).

these pathogens until the rise of the specialty of ancient DNA analysis. This new area has not only allowed scholars to retrieve the history of many pathogens that do not leave their mark on bone, but they also assist us in confirming diagnoses made on the basis of macroscopic bone changes as well. This technology has presented a very important new method of examining the complex interaction between organisms and their environment in terms of overall health.

In addition to work in immunology, DNA studies have allowed us to identify specific diseases in prehistoric skeletons such as cholera, tuberculosis, leprosy, treponemal disease, bubonic plague, malaria, Chagas disease, influenza, ascariasis, and schistosomiasis. The list is continuously expanding (Greenblatt and Spigelman 2003). This research can contribute enormously to our knowledge of the history and distribution of specific prehistoric and historic diseases. It assists us in identifying specific pathogens in areas where skeletons display no bone pathology; it strengthens paleopathological diagnoses based upon gross pathology; and it helps us to correlate the rate of visible pathology with the actual prevalence of disease in a cemetery population (Cohen and Crane-Kramer 2007). Through the use of ancient DNA, we have a much better understanding of the origins and transmission history of diseases like leprosy, tuberculosis, malaria, and bubonic plague (Donoghue et al. 1998, Kappelman et al. 2008, Wiechmann 2005, Harbeck et al. 2013, Schuenemann et al. 2013).

Fascinating results are presented in this field continuously. Salo et al. (1994) were able to retrieve tuberculosis DNA from the lung tissue of a thousand-year-old Peruvian mummy. This proves that tuberculosis plagued New World populations for a long time prior to European contact. This result was confirmed by other studies like the one that identified tuberculosis in the 900-year-old remains of a

Figure 3.16: Influenza (flu) virus.

12-year-old child from Chile (Arriaza et al. 1995). The causative agent of the bubonic plague, *Yersinia pestis*, was recovered from dental DNA retrieved from several individuals who died in the plague epidemics of France between 1590 and 1722 (Drancourt et al. 1998). Leprosy was identified in several individuals found at the Romano-Christian cemetery of Kellis II at Dahkleh Oasis in Egypt. The cemetery was in use from roughly 50 to 450 AD. (Molto 1997, 2001, 2002). Thus, this disease was clearly well entrenched in North Africa long before it became endemic during the medieval period in Europe.

In addition, we can also begin to examine ancient genetic diseases. In 1995, Filon et al. examined ancient DNA samples from the 3800-year-old remains of a Phoenician child in Israel. The eight-year-old child was associated with skeletal pathology that implied the presence of severe anemia. They concluded that the child suffered from a serious form of thalassemia (genetic anemia), which is found in between two and ten percent of modern populations living in the eastern Mediterranean area. Furthermore, DNA has been used to map the sequences of the deadly 1918 influenza virus. The sample was provided by a U.S. soldier who died during the epidemic (Taubenberger et al. 1997).

Interesting work has also applied the use of ancient DNA to determining the sex of children. As the skeletal changes that differentiate males from females do not develop until sexual maturity, it has been extremely difficult to assess the sex of juvenile remains. Faerman et al. (1997) investigated the sex of 43 newborns found in the sewer below a Roman bathhouse at Ashkelon, an Israeli coastal site. Only 19 (44 percent) of the samples yielded results, and it was determined that these were 14 males and 5 females. The authors suggest that these may be the undesired children of the female bathhouse workers.

Figure 3.17: Ancient mummies from Cuzco, Peru (Museo di Storia Naturale, Florence).

Ancient DNA has revolutionized the way scientists examine living organisms in the past, from plants and animals to bacteria and viruses. It allows us to retrieve a signature of pathogens that leave no visible trace on the skeleton, both in terms of genetic and infectious diseases. It has also been used to investigate the plants that were discovered with the Iceman (Rollo et al. 1994), or to illuminate the history of corn, wheat, and cattle domestication (Brown and Brown 1992, Bailey et al. 1996, Goloubinoff et al. 1993). It is also applied to investigating the source of certain paints and parchment used in the past (Reese et al. 1996). As DNA theory and methodology have only been developed over the last 30 years, it is a relatively new area of investigation. There is no question that this area of research will prove very fruitful in terms of examining the biological history of living creatures.

THE SCENE OF THE CRIME: NUCLEAR DNA AND WHODUNITS!

The application of DNA technology to the field of criminal justice has provided a new and powerful tool for solving crime. Not only does it help us make a case against a guilty party in court, it also helps to exonerate innocent people in jail, convicted on the basis of circumstantial evidence. The technique that is applied to forensic evidence is called **DNA fingerprinting**, and it was presented in 1984 by the British geneticist Alec Jeffreys. He coined this term because, just like actual fingerprinting, this technology was clearly able to identify individuals. Although 99.9 percent of human DNA sequences are the same in all

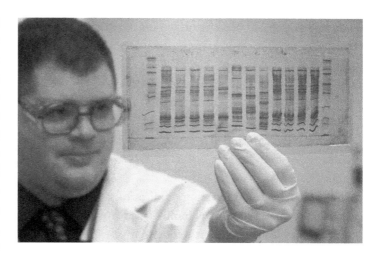

Figure 3.18: Chemist reads a DNA profile.

people, a small percentage differs between people, and this allows us to distinguish one individual from another, unless they are identical twins. DNA profiling uses repetitive (repeat) sequences that are highly

Figure 3.19: Tsar Nicholas Romanov and his family.

variable. These are called variable number tandem repeats (VNTRs), particularly short tandem repeats (STRs). VNTR genetic loci are very similar between closely related humans, but are variable enough that individuals who are not relatives are extremely unlikely to have the same VNTRs (Jeffreys 1984, Wambaugh 1989, Watson 2003). The process of DNA amplification implemented is called polymerase chain reaction (PCR), which is able to provide a DNA fingerprint from the tiniest of original samples. This means that DNA fingerprinting can be conducted on a single drop of blood, a tiny smear of semen, or from saliva cells left on a discarded cigarette butt. It makes it very difficult for one to deny their presence at the crime scene when their DNA has been identified on the evidence! The judiciary system was wisely cautious in using this technology, until it could be repeatedly scientifically validated as a reliable investigative tool. Only in 1993, in the case of *Daubert vs. Merrell Dow Pharmaceuticals*, did the Supreme Court rule that judges had the right to determine whether or not offered evidence is reliable (in other words, whether or not the evidence is scientifically accepted)(Watson 2003).

In addition to techniques applied to identify individuals from nuclear DNA, Peter Gill devised a DNA fingerprinting technique that uses mitochondrial DNA. Mitochondrial DNA is particularly useful because it is far more abundant than nuclear DNA, and can be used in cases where nuclear DNA is degraded or contaminated.

One of the most interesting applications of this technology to a famed forensic case is the supposed execution of the Russian royal family (the Romanovs) in Ekaterinburg on July 17, 1918. In July 1991, nine skeletons were uncovered that were tentatively identified by Russian forensic scientists as the remains of the Russian tsar Nicholas Romanov, his wife, Tsarina Alexandra, three of their five children, three servants, and the royal doctor. Nuclear and mitochondrial DNA samples were retrieved from the skeletal remains and compared to each other and to samples from both living and deceased relatives. Investigators concluded that the DNA evidence indicated a family unit present in the grave. The tests indicated that five of the skeletons were members of one family, and four were unrelated. Three of the five skeletons were determined to be the children of two parents. The mother was linked to the British royal family (Alexandra was the granddaughter of the British queen Victoria). The plot thickens when, in the summer of 2007, a Russian amateur archaeologist discovered a second grave nearby. In the grave were the remains of two subadult individuals who were thought to represent the two missing Romanov children. Subsequent DNA analysis has confirmed that these are the remains of the crown prince Alexei and one of his sisters (Coble et al. 2009). Researchers now feel confident that they have recovered the remains of the entire family, the first grave containing the tsar and tsarina and three of their daughters: Olga, Tatiana, and Anastasia or Maria. A further high-profile case came from the DNA identification of the remains of the notorious Nazi, Josef Mengele, the so-called Angel of Death, from exhumed skeletal remains in Brazil (Jeffreys et al. 1992).

New investigative tools developed in the 20th century have opened up a brave new world to us. We are now able to begin the long, slow process of understanding the microscopic world, in terms of minute genetic structures and disease-causing microorganisms. With every new development, we are learning in ever greater detail the wonderful journey that life on Earth has taken and the unimaginable links between the complex web of life.

CRITICAL REASONING QUESTIONS

- How is DNA used to investigate human ancestry? Does this evidence support the fossil record?
- How do we produce our body cells? Why is this process important?
- You are born in southern Kenya in a malarial region. What genetic mutation might save your life?
- Would Jack the Ripper get away with his crimes today?
- What are stem cells, and how might they revolutionize your health?
- Are apes and humans related at the genetic level? When was the last time we shared a common ancestor?

REFERENCES AND SUGGESTED READINGS

Abrahams, P., ed. (2009). *How the body works*. London: Amber Books.

Arriaza, B. T., W. Salo, A. C. Aufderheide, and T. A. Holcomb (1995). "Pre-Columbian tuberculosis in northern Chile: Molecular and skeletal evidence." *American Journal of Physical Anthropology* 98:37–45.

Bailey, J. F., M. B. Richards, V. A. Macauley, et al. (1996). "Ancient DNA suggests a recent expansion of European cattle from a diverse wild progenitor species." *Proc. Roy. Soc. Lond. B. Biolo. Scien.* 263:1467–1473.

Balloux, F., L. J. Handley, T. Jombart, et al. (2009). "Climate shaped the worldwide distribution of human mitochondrial DNA sequence variation." *Proceedings of the Biological Sciences* 276 (1672):3447–3455. Becker, A. J., E. A. McCulloch, and J. E. Till (1963). "Cytological demonstration of the clonal nature of spleen colonies derived from transplanted mouse marrow cells," Nature 197 (4866):452–454.

Behar, D. M., R. Villems, H. Soodyall, et al. (May 2008). "The dawn of human matrilineal diversity." *American Journal of Human Genetics 82* (5):1130–1140.

Brown, W. M. (June 1980). "Polymorphism in mitochondrial DNA of humans as revealed by restriction endonuclease analysis." *Proc. Natl. Acad. Sci. U.S.A. 77* (6):3605–3609.

Brown, T. A., and K. A. Brown (1992). "Ancient DNA and the archaeologist." *Antiquity* 66:10–23.

Cann, R. L. (2013). "Genetics. Y weigh in again on modern humans." *Science 341* (6145):465–467.

Cann, R. L., A. C. Wilson, and M. Stoneking (1987). "Mitochondrial DNA and human evolution." *Nature* 325:31–36.

Cavalli-Sforza, Luigi Luca (2007). "Human evolution and its relevance for genetic epidemiology." *Annual Review of Genomics and Human Genetics* 8:1–15.

Coble M. D., O. M. Loreille, M. J. Wadhams, et al. (2009). Mystery solved: The identification of the two missing Romanov children using DNA analysis. *PLoS ONE, 4* (3)

Cohen, M. N., and G. M. M. Crane-Kramer (2007). *Ancient health: Skeletal Indicators of agricultural and economic intensification.* University of Florida Press.

Conroy, G. C. (1997). *Reconstructing human origins: A modern synthesis.* New York: Norton.

Corruccini, R. S. (1994). "Reaganomics and the fate of the progressive Neandertals." In R. Corruccini and R. Ciochon, eds., *Integrative Paths to the Past: Paleoanthropological Advances in Honor of F. Clark Howell.* Englewood Cliffs, NJ: Prentice Hall.

Cummins, J. M. (2000). Fertilization and elimination of the paternal mitochondrial genome. *Human Reproduction* 15 (Suppl. 2):92–101.

Current Regulation of Human Embryonic Stem Cell Research (2005). Guidelines for Human Embryonic Stem Cell Research, pp. 63–80. Washington, DC: National Academies Press.

Donnelly, P., S. Tavaré, D. J. Balding, and R. C. Griffiths (May 1996). "Estimating the age of the common ancestor of men from the ZFY intron." *Science 272* (5266):1357–1359; author reply 1361–1362.

Donoghue, H., A. Marcsik, C. Matheson, et al. (2005). "Co-infection of myobacterial tuberculosis and *Myobacterium leprae* in human archaeological samples: A possible explanation for the historical decline of leprosy." *Proc. Royal Soc. B.* 582.1–582.6.

Donoghue, H. D., M. Spigelman, J. Zias, et al. (1998). *Mycobacterium tuberculosis* complex DNA in calcified pleura from remains 1400 years old. *Lett. Appl. Microbiol.* 27:265–269.

Dorit, R. L, H. Akashi, and W. Gilbert (1995). "Absence of polymorphism at the Zfy locus on the human Y chromosome." *Science* 268:1183–1185.

Drancourt, M., G. Aboudharam, M. Signoli, et al. (1998). "Detection of 400-year-old *Yersinia pestis* DNA in human dental pulp: An approach to the diagnosis of ancient septicemia." *Proceedings of the National Academy of Sciences USA* 95:12637–12640.

Duarte, C., J. Mauricio, P. B. Pettitt, et al. (1999). "The early Upper Paleolithic human skeleton from the Abrigo do Lagar Velho (Portugal) and modern human emergence in the Iberian Peninsula." *Proceedings of the National Academy of Sciences of the USA* 96, 13:7604–7609.

Endicott, P., S. Y. Ho, M. Metspalu, and C. Stringer (September 2009). "Evaluating the mitochondrial timescale of human evolution." *Trends Ecol. Evol. (Amst.) 24* (9):515–521.

Faerman, M., D. Filon, G. Kahila, et al. (1995). "Sex identification of archaeological human remains based on amplification of the X and Y amelogenin alleles." *Gene* 167:327–332.

Francalacci P., L. Morelli, A. Angius, et al. (2013). "Low-pass DNA sequencing of 1200 Sardinians reconstructs European Y-chromosome phylogeny." *Science 341* (6145):565–569.

Fu, Q., A. Mittnik, P. L. F. Johnson, et al. (2013). "A revised timescale for human evolution based on ancient mitochondrial genomes." *Current Biology 23* (7):553–559.

Gilbert, M. T. P., A. S. Wilson, M. Bunce, et al. (2004). Ancient mitochondrial DNA from hair. *Current Biology* 14:463–464.

Gill, P., P. L. Ivanov, et al. (1994). "Identification of the remains of the Romanov family by DNA analysis." *Nature Genetics* 2:135–138.

Goloubinoff, P., S. Pääbo, and A. C. Wilson (1993). "Evolution of maize inferred from sequence diversity of an Adh2 gene segment from archaeological specimens." *Proceedings of the National Academy of Sciences USA* 90:1997–2001.

Gonder, M. K; H. M. Mortensen, F. A. Reed, et al. (December 2007). "Whole-mtDNA genome sequence analysis of ancient African lineages." *Molecular. Biol. Evol 24* (3):757–768.

Green, R. E., J. Krause, S. E. Ptak, et al. (2006). "Analysis of one million base pairs of Neanderthal DNA." *Nature* 444:330–336.

Green, R. E., et al. 2010). "A draft sequence of the Neandertal genome." *Science* 328:710–722.

Greenblatt, C., and M. Spigelman (2003). *Emerging pathogens.* New York: Oxford University Press.

Hammer, M. F. (1995). "A recent common ancestry for human Y chromosomes." *Nature 378* (6555):376–378.

Harbeck M., L. Seifert, S. Hänsch, et al. (2013). *Yersinia pestis* DNA from skeletal remains from the 6th century AD reveals insights into Justinianic plague. *PLoS Pathog.* 9(5):e1003349. doi:10.1371/journal.ppat.1003349

Harrub, B., and B. Thompson (2003). *The demise of Mitochondrial Eve.* Apologetics Press, Inc.

Healey, J., ed. (2003). *Stem cell research, vol. 178, Issues in society.* New South Wales, Australia: Spinneypress.

Ivanov, P. L., M. J. Wadhams, R. K. Roby, et al. (1996). Mitochondrial DNA sequence heteroplasmy in the Grand Duke of Russia Georgij Romanov establishes the authenticity of the remains of Tsar Nicholas II. *Nature Genetics* 12:417–420.

Jeffreys, A. J., V. Wilson, and S. W. Thein (1984). "Hypervariable 'minisatellite' regions in human DNA." *Nature* 314:67–73.

Jeffreys, A. J., M. J. Allen, E. Hagelberg, and A. Sonnberg (1992). "Identification of the skeletal remains of Josef Mengele by DNA analysis." *Forensic Science Int. 56*:65–76.

Kappelman, J., M. C. Alçiçek, N. Kazanci, et al. (2008). "First *Homo erectus* from Turkey and implications for migrations into temperate Eurasia." *American Journal of Physical Anthropology* 135(1):110–116.

Karafet, T. M., F. L. Mendez, M. B. Meilerman, et al. (2008). "New binary polymorphisms reshape and increase resolution of the human Y chromosomal haplogroup tree." *Genome Research 18* (5):830–838.

Katzenberg, M. A., and S. R. Saunders, eds. (2000). *Biological anthropology of the human skeleton.* New York: Wiley-Liss.

Krings, M., C. Capelli, F. Tschentscher, et al. (2000). "A view of Neandertal genetic diversity." *Nature Genetics* 26:144–146.

Krings, M., A. Stone, R. W. Schmitz, et al. (1997). "Neandertal DNA sequences and the origin of modern humans." *Cell* 90:19–30.

Lalueza-Fox, C., D. Caramelli, G. Catalano, et al. (2007). "A melanocortin 1 receptor allele suggests varying pigmentation among Neanderthals." *Science,* vol. 318, no. 5855:1453–1455.

Molto, J. E. (2001). The Comparative Skeletal Biology and Paleoepidemiology of Population Samples From the Ein Tirghi and Kellis Cemeteries, Dakhleh Oasis, Egypt. In *The Oasis Papers I, Proceedings of the First Conference of the Dakhleh Oasis Project,* ed. C. A. Marlow and A. J. Mills, pp. 81–100. Monograph 6. England: Oxbow Press.

——— (2002). Leprosy in Roman Period Skeletons from Kellis 2, Dakhleh, Egypt. In *Proceedings of the 3rd International Congress on the Evolution and Paleoepidemiology of the Infectious Diseases. The Past and Present of Leprosy,* ed. Charlotte A. Roberts, Mary E. Lewis, and K. Manchester, pp. 183–196. British Archaeological Reports International Series 1054. Oxford, UK: Archaeopress.

Molto, Joseph Eldon (1997). "Leprosy: A perspective from the Dakhleh Oasis, Egypt" [Abstract]. In Eve Cockburn, ed. *Papers on Paleopathology Presented at the Twenty-Fourth Annual Meeting of the Paleopathology Association,* St. Louis, Missouri, 1 and 2 April 1997, p. 10.

——— (2001). "Leprosy in Egypt: New Cases from Kellis 2, Dakhleh" [Abstract]. In Mary Lucas Powell, ed. *Paleopathology Association, Scientific Program, Twenty-Eighth Annual Meeting of the Paleopathology Association,* Kansas City, Missouri, 27 and 28 March *2001,* p. 9.

Noonan, J. P., G. Coop, S. Kudaravalli, et al. (2006). "Sequencing and analysis of Neanderthal genomic DNA." *Science* 314:1113–1118.

Pääbo, S. (1985a). "Preservation of DNA in ancient Egyptian mummies." *Journal of Archaeological Science 12* (6):411–417.

——— (1985b). "Molecular cloning of ancient Egyptian mummy DNA." *Nature 314* (6012):644–645.

Poinar, H. N., M. Hofreiter, W. G. Spaulding, et al. (July 1998). "Molecular coproscopy: Dung and diet of the extinct ground sloth *Nothrotheriops shastensis*." *Science 281* (5375):402–406.

Poznik, G. D., B. M. Henn, M. C. Yee, et al. (2013). "Sequencing Y chromosomes resolves discrepancy in time to common ancestor of males versus females." *Science 341* (6145):562–565.

Reese, R. L., M. Hyman, M. W. Rowe, et al. (1996). "Ancient DNA from Texas pictographs." *Journal of Archaeological Sciences* 23:269–277.

Relethford, J. H. (1995). "Genetics and Modern Human Origins." *Evolutionary Anthropology* 4:53–63.

——— (1998). "Genetics of modern human origins and diversity." *Annual Review of Anthropology* 27:1–23.

——— (2001). *Genetics and the search for modern human origins.* New York: Wiley-Liss.

Relethford, J. H., and H. C. Harpending (1994). "Craniometric variation, genetic theory, and modern human origins." *American Journal of Physical Anthropology* 95:249–270.

Rollo, F., W. Asci, S. Antonini, I. Marota, and M. Ubaldi (1994). "Molecular ecology of a Neolithic meadow: The DNA of the grass remains from the archaeological site of the Tyrolean Iceman." *Experientia* 50:576–584.

Salo, W. L., A. C. Aufderheide, J. Buikstra, and T. A. Holcomb (1994). "Identification of *Mycobacterium tuberculosis* DNA in a pre-Columbian Peruvian mummy." *Proceedings of the National Academy of Sciences* USA 91:2091–2094.

Sarich, V. M., and A.C. Wilson (1967). "Immunological time scale for hominid evolution." *Science* 158:1200–1203.

Schmitz, R. W., D. Serre, G. Bonani, et al. (2002). "The Neandertal type site revisited: Interdisciplinary investigations of skeletal remains from the Neander Valley, Germany." *Proceedings of the National Academy of Sciences* 99:13342–13347.

Schuenemann, V. J., P. Singh, T. A. Mendum, et al. (2013). "Genome-wide comparison of medieval and modern *Mycobacterium leprae*." *Science* 341(6142):179–183.

Serre, D., and S. Pääbo (2008). "The fate of European Neanderthals: Results and perspectives from ancient DNA analysis." In K. Harvati and T. Harrison, eds. *Neanderthals Revisited: New Approaches and Perspectives,* pp. 211–219. Dordrecht, Netherlands: Springer.

Siminovitch L., E. A. McCulloch, and J. E. Till (1963). "The distribution of colony-forming cells among spleen colonies." *Journal of Cellular and Comparative Physiology 62* (3):327–336.

Soares, P., L. Ermini, N. Thomson, *et al.* (June 2009). "Correcting for purifying selection: An improved human mitochondrial molecular clock." *Am. J. Hum. Genet. 84* (6):740–59

Stone, A. C. (2000). "Ancient DNA from skeletal remains." In M. A. Katzenberg and S. R. Saunders, eds. *Biological Anthropology of the Human Skeleton*, pp. 351–371. New York: Wiley-Liss.

Tattersall, I., and J. H. Schwartz (1999). "Hominids and hybrids: The place of Neanderthals in human evolution." *Proceedings of the National Academy of Sciences of the USA 96*, 13:7117–7119.

Tishkoff, S. A., E. Dietzsch, W. Speed, et al. (1996). "Global patterns of linkage disequilibrium at the CD4 locus and modern human origins." *Science* 271:1380–1387.

Thompson, B., and B. Harrub (2003). *How many times does "Mitochondrial Eve" have to die?* Apologetics Press, Inc.

Underhill, P. A., P. Shen, et al. (2000). "Y chromosome sequence variation and the history of human populations." *Nature Genetics* 26:358–361.

Vigilant, L., R. Pennington, H. Harpending, et al. (December 1989). "Mitochondrial DNA sequences in single hairs from a southern African population." *Proc. Natl. Acad. Sci. U.S.A. 86* (23):9350–9354.

Vigilant, L., M. Stoneking, H. Harpending, et al. (September 1991). "African populations and the evolution of human mitochondrial DNA." *Science 253* (5027):1503–1507.

Wambaugh, J. (1989). *The blooding.* New York: Perigord Press.

Watson, E., P. Forster, M. Richards, and H. J. Bandelt (September 1997). "Mitochondrial footprints of human expansions in Africa." *Am. J. Hum. Genet. 61* (3):691–704.

Watson, J. D., with A. Berry (2003). *DNA: The secret of life.* New York: Alfred A. Knopf.

Wells, S. (2002). *The journey of man.* New York: Random House.

White, T., B. Asfaw, et al. (2003). "Pleistocene *Homo sapiens* from Middle Awash, Ethiopia." *Nature* 423:742–747.

Wiechmann, I., and G. Grupe (2005). Detection of Yersinia *pestis* DNA in two early medieval skeletal finds from Aschheim (Upper Bavaria, 6th century AD). *Am J Phys Anthropol.* Jan. 126(1):48–55.

4

Population Genetics

How I Acquired the Family Nose

By Gillian Crane-Kramer

At the time Charles Darwin and Alfred Russell were formulating their ideas about evolution, there was much confusion surrounding the mechanisms of inheritance. Darwin knew that natural selection (and hence evolution) acts upon variation in a population, but he had no idea what the source of that variation was. Likewise, he knew that traits were passed from one generation to the next, but the manner in which this occurred was poorly understood. People have been tinkering with the genetics of other species for millennia—it is called domestication. We realized fairly early on that we could accentuate what features we wanted and eliminate the features that were not desirable by controlling what individuals were allowed to breed. If you are a dairy farmer and you want to maximize your milk production, you only breed those females that are high milk producers. People recognized that parents passed their traits on to their offspring, but no one knew how it was actually accomplished.

There were two general ideas around at the time that attempted to explain heredity: the inheritance of acquired characteristics and blending. We discussed in Chapter 2 about the work of Lamarck and his explanation for how traits are passed on to the next generation. The inheritance of acquired characteristics essentially states that an organism can change itself during its lifetime (increased muscle mass, faster running speed, stretching to eat leaves on higher branches), and those acquired traits could be passed on to its offspring. Today, this idea has been disproven, so everyone with a tattoo on their bottom or a tongue piercing can breathe a collective sigh of relief. You will not be handed babies in the delivery room with those distinctive features. However, it is important to remember that this

49

idea was generally accepted in the mid-19th century. While Darwin and Wallace knew that there were problems with this idea, in the absence of any other viable alternative, it had to be considered.

Blending, the other explanation, states that the biological traits of children should always be intermediate between the features of the parents like a blending of paints. If Dad is 6 feet tall and Mom is 5 feet tall, you will be 5 feet 6 inches tall! It should have been apparent very quickly that there is a problem with this concept. All people have physical traits that are not intermediate between their parents. My parents both have brown hair. My mother has brown eyes and my father hazel eyes. However, I have blond hair and blue eyes. So … unless my mother is hiding the fact that the milkman was delivering more than dairy products, I am clearly not a blending of my parents, in terms of several biological traits. To further muddy the waters, people also believed in a concept called spontaneous generation: the idea that life can arise from nonliving matter by some fantastic and mystical transformation.

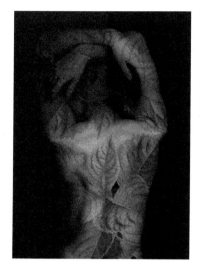

Figure 4.1: Tattooed woman with leaves representing Mother Nature.

Well into the 19th century, people generally held that microorganisms emerged spontaneously from broths or other rotting foods. It was generally accepted that maggots developed automatically from rotting meat, or that snakes and frogs arose spontaneously from mud at the bottom of a lake; or that dirty old rags transformed into rodents; or that sperm injected into cucumbers turned into people (wouldn't you love to know where that idea came from).

Today, the French scholar **Louis Pasteur** and the German scholar **Robert Koch** are recognized as the fathers of the field of bacteriology and germ theory. Their work proved that a specific microorganism causes a specific disease—the one germ, one disease theory. By the latter half of the 19th century, both Pasteur and Koch had gained great prestige for establishing a causal link between microbes and infectious disease. Louis Pasteur's work showed that the process of fermentation results from the growth of microorganisms. Furthermore, he noted that the subsequent growth of bacteria in nutrient broths was not a result of spontaneous generation, but instead resulted from colonization from outside. The way that Pasteur discovered this fact was very clever. He placed boiled (and thus sterile) broth in specially designed flasks that contained a filter. This filter prevented any particles from reaching the broth, but still allowed it to be exposed to the air. Pasteur noted that as long as the filter remained intact, nothing grew in the broth. However, when the filter was broken, things began to grow in the broth. Pasteur realized that the microorganisms that grew in the broth came from outside, in particles from the air, and that they were not spontaneously generated. Pasteur's experiments were crucial because they finally disproved the idea of spontaneous generation and also proved the idea

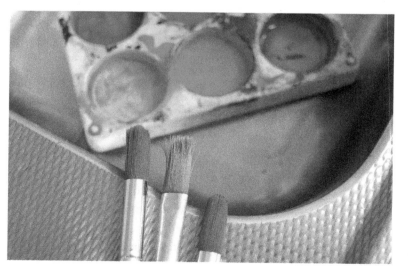

Figure 4.2: Blending was like a mixing of paints.

of **germ theory**. As a result, this theory rapidly spread throughout the medical and scientific communities; and it revolutionized the way we perceive disease causation. Unfortunately, this knowledge was yet to be discovered at the time Darwin was writing *On the Origin of Species*.

THE FATHER OF GENETICS: PLEASE, NO MORE PEAS FOR SUPPER

Today, we have a very good understanding of the complex chemical and molecular processes involved in the transference of genetic material from one generation to the next. The modern view of genetics began with a monk named **Johann (Gregor) Mendel**. He was born in 1822 in what was part of the Austrian Empire and what is now the Czech Republic. Mendel became an Augustinian monk in 1843 and spent the remainder of his life in Brno, Moravia. Mendel had

Figure 4.3: The Father of Bacteriology, Luis Pasteur, in his lab (Albert Edelfelt, 1885, Musee d'Orsay).

always had an interest in botany and the process of hybridization. In order to understand more about how traits (presumably desirable) were passed on from parents to offspring, he began a series of experiments that would revolutionize the way we understand the mechanisms of inheritance. This was the foundation upon which many fascinating genetic discoveries in the 20th century would be laid.

Mendel conducted his experiments on the common pea plant (*Pisum sativum*) in the monastery garden.

Figure 4.4: Gregor Mendel, the Father of Genetics.

These humble plants would assist him in revealing the secrets of heredity (plants are too often underappreciated for their contributions to great breakthroughs—think of Newton's apple). He conducted his experiments between 1856 and 1863 with purebred plants. He focused upon seven different features of the common pea plant, all of which could be expressed in only one of two ways: it could be only short or tall, have wrinkled seeds or smooth, etc. Mendel discovered that the traits in the offspring did not demonstrate a blending of the parents' traits. Quite the contrary; inheritance is the result of discrete units that he called factors, and these are segregated. These factors (what we now refer to as genes) could be followed through generations, and inheritance could be determined by mathematical laws (in this case, a 3:1 ratio). The results of these experiments allowed Mendel to contribute three important ideas to our understanding of heredity. Firstly, these genes come in two forms—**dominant** or **recessive**. Dominant genes mask recessive genes when they are paired together. Thus, recessive traits (like blue eyes, for example) can only be expressed when there are two copies (one from each parent). The **Law of Segregation** says that sex cells (ova and sperm) contain one of each

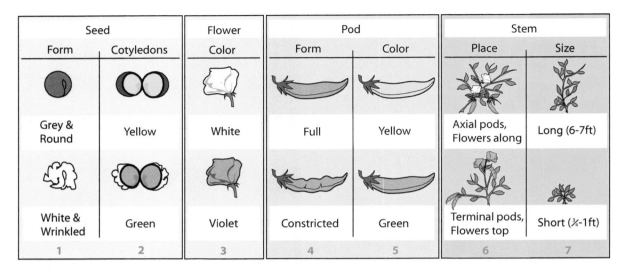

| Seed | | Flower | Pod | | Stem | |
Form	Cotyledons	Color	Form	Color	Place	Size
Grey & Round	Yellow	White	Full	Yellow	Axial pods, Flowers along	Long (6-7ft)
White & Wrinkled	Green	Violet	Constricted	Green	Terminal pods, Flowers top	Short (¾-1ft)
1	2	3	4	5	6	7

Figure 4.5: Seven traits of the common pea plant.

pair of genes. They are inherited as entire units, and they always come in pairs. Lastly, what is now called the **Law of Independent Assortment** states that biological traits and the factors that determine them are independent. In other words, genes on separate chromosomes are inherited independently of each other. Genes on the same chromosome are said to be linked because they are always inherited together as a unit. Mendel published his work during his lifetime, but it had not attracted much attention. It was not until his work was rediscovered and replicated over 30 years later by scholars such as the Dutch botanist Hugo de Vries (1848–1935) that Mendel's contribution to the field of heredity was truly appreciated. It is estimated that Mendel used over 28,000 pea plants for his experiments over that eight-year period. The monks of his monastery must have been so sick of eating peas!

WHAT IS A POPULATION?

Evolution works at the level of the population. It involves minute changes in the frequency of genes from generation to generation over very long periods of time. How do we then define a population? Think of it this way: For most of human history, there were no cars, cruise ships, or airplanes. The only way to get anywhere was by walking or by animal transport. This meant that most people did not travel very far from home in their entire lives. A population is essentially a group of individuals who live in the same general geographic region and are likely to find mates within that region. We can divide larger populations into smaller groupings representing breeding populations. These groups are generally characterized by a degree of genetic relatedness (which makes sense if for generations you have mostly mated with people from the same area). A gene pool represents the overall genetic variation in the population, and this is where evolution takes place. Lock this idea in your brain:

Figure 4.6: What is a population-family of zebra?

Genetic variation is extinction insurance! With that in mind, you don't want to have such an overwhelming amount of variation that negative traits are present in significant numbers. Everything is a trade-off, and the forces of evolution act upon genes by increasing or decreasing them through time, ultimately leading an organism to evolve.

FORCES OF EVOLUTION: THE MOVERS AND SHAKERS

If microevolution results from changes in gene frequencies over time, there must be some forces that lead to change. The magical entity that is the source of all new genetic variation is mutation. It provides the new possibilities (a new gene). What happens to that new gene, in terms of whether or not it will increase or decrease over time, depends upon other forces of evolution. Some forces of evolution like gene flow, genetic drift, or sexual recombination (mutation as well) increase variation over time. Other forces of evolution, namely natural selection, genetic drift (especially founder's effect), and sexual selection decrease variation over time. One would expect that over time, organisms should become better adapted to their respective environments rather than less adapted. Thus, genes that are adaptive in that particular environment should increase in that population over time, and deleterious genes should be eliminated or maintained at low levels over time. As environments change, so do the features that are adaptive and hence selected for. It is important to remember that evolution is not a goal-directed enterprise. Nature tinkers with different plans and systems; some simply work out better than others. It is to the advantage of any plant or animal species to have as much genetic variation as possible in their gene pool. The more genetic variation a population has, the more biological flexibility it has in a changing environment. This also reduces the likelihood of extinction. How do we know whether a gene is being acted upon by any of the forces of evolution? Well, this is where the dreaded Hardy-Weinberg formula comes in. The **Hardy-Weinberg equilibrium** is an algebraic equation that represents a state of evolutionary equilibrium, or stasis. The Hardy-Weinberg equation ($p2+2pq=q2$) is used in order to investigate whether or not evolution is occurring at a specific locus where we have only two allele forms (p and q). If evolution is not affecting these genes, the proportions should remain the same from generation to generation. If we do observe changes from a state of equilibrium, this indicates that one or more of the forces of evolution is acting upon those genes. The forces of evolution that increase variation are mutation, gene flow, genetic recombination (crossing over), and genetic drift. The forces that decrease variation are natural selection, sexual selection, and genetic drift. **Mutations** are the only source of new genetic variation—they can be positive, neutral, or negative. Mutation presents new genetic possibilities in the form of new genes. However, mutations are rare and random events; we never know where and when they will occur, and they do not commonly occur in the best of circumstances. The most basic form of change is called a point mutation. This occurs when somewhere along the strand of DNA there is a substitution of one base for another. You may think, a tiny glitch, a minor concern, a single nitrogenous base substitution—big deal. Sometimes, it does have no observable effect.

However, sometimes this little glitch leads to serious conditions like the genetic disease sickle cell anemia. In sickle cell anemia, on chromosome 11, a point mutation occurs in the sixth codon of the beta-globin gene. This error leads to a substitution of the amino acid valine for glutamic acid in the resulting protein. The disease is caused by the production of abnormal red blood cells that are sickle shaped. People with sickle cell disease (two copies of the recessive gene for this condition) have shortened life expectancy, and they suffer both acute and chronic pain, swelling, leg ulcers, and a myriad of other symptoms. The majority of people who carry the gene for sickle cell descend from ancestors who lived in tropical/subtropical areas

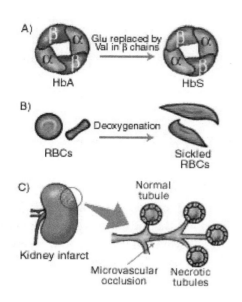

Figure 4.7: Diagram of sickle cell anemia.

where malaria is present. People with only one copy of the gene have a condition called sickle-cell trait, and they appear to be considerably more resistant to developing malaria. This is a major advantage in malarial areas, where mortality from the disease can be very high, especially for those under the age of five years of age. However, the homozygous condition (the genes at that locus on the chromosome are the same) leads to a substantial disease experience. For most of human history, these individuals likely did not survive to reproduce.

There are also more serious alterations in the DNA like reading frame shifts that are genetic mutations, which occur when there are deletions or insertions of a number of nucleotides in a sequence of DNA. This results in incorrect translation of the original message and essentially the production of the incorrect protein. Negative mutant alleles can be either dominant or recessive. If they are recessive, then the organism must inherit copies from both parents. An example of an autosomal recessive condition is the metabolic genetic disease PKU (phenylketonuria). Untreated PKU can lead to severe mental retardation, seizures, and other serious symptoms. This condition is well controlled if identified and treated early upon birth, and affects roughly 1 in every 12,000 births in the United States. Many more people will carry one copy of the mutated recessive allele, but it is not observed phenotypically. Most negative mutations or chromosomal abnormalities lead to death of the organism in the womb. However, there are instances when those individuals with a negative mutation do survive. Down syndrome, or Trisomy 21, results from an extra copy (hence the term *tri-*, meaning three) of the 21st chromosome. It is associated with a spectrum of mental, social, and physical disabilities that typically in the past led the affected individual to be less likely to survive to adulthood and contribute to the future gene pool. Remember that mutations are rare events, and thus they cannot in themselves lead to major changes in gene frequencies over time. What will determine what happens to these new mutated genes depends upon whether they are increased or decreased by the other forces of evolution.

Gene flow is exactly that, a flow of genes between at least two populations. Through this process of mating (and hence genetic exchange), the variation between the groups is decreased, and the variation within the groups is increased. Very few human populations are truly breeding isolates, where there is no exchange between that population and nearby human groups (as if you were on an island in the middle of the Pacific Ocean, for example). Thus, there is typically an exchange of mating partners between neighboring groups, and this allows for a constant movement of genes across cultural and social boundaries. Think of an extreme example if a population of

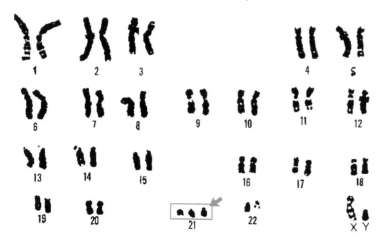

Figure 4.8: Trisomy 21 Down Syndrome genotype.

red people and a population of white people interbreed. Both the red and white groups have increased variation because all of these new genes are being transferred from the other population. However, the pink children share traits from both groups, and thus the offspring represent decreased variation between the groups.

Revealing research has investigated the contribution of non-African genes to the African American population over the last three centuries in the United States. By examining a number of genes at different loci, geneticists were able to examine the amount of non-African genes that have entered the mostly West African American gene pool. Interesting results were observed that differed, depending upon geography. Data from western and northern U.S. cities (like New York and Oakland) showed that the admixture rate (inclusion of non-African genes) was between 20 percent and 25 percent.

Figure 4.9: 8-Year-Old boy with Down Syndrome.

However, in the South (rural Georgia, Charleston, etc.), the admixture was far less at roughly between 4 percent to 11 percent (Cummings 1994).

An interesting example of gene flow involves the ABO blood group. A cline (a trait that changes along a line of geographic transition) is seen in the reduction in blood group B as one moves from Eurasia to western Europe. Some argue that this reduction as one moves west results from considerable gene flow that occurred between indigenous Europeans and migrating Mongol populations in the period between 500–1500 AD. In the past, Mongol populations had much higher frequencies of type B blood, and this allele was introduced at higher frequency due to this genetic admixture (Candela 1942). Gene flow is occurring today at an unheard-of rate in history, as populations that would never have traditionally come into contact are regularly interacting as a result of rapid global travel. This variation can only strengthen us as a species—food for thought!

Figure 4.10: Gene flow.

Genetic or sexual recombination involves a crossing over or exchange of genes between two homologous chromosomes (ones of the same pair) during mitosis or meiosis. It only has evolutionary significance if it occurs during meiosis, or during the creation of our gametes (sex cells), as these are what get transferred to the next generation. Essentially, sometimes when we are creating our body or sex cells, there is a swapping of genes at the same locus between chromosomes of the same pair. This random reshuffling of the genes greatly increases variation. It increases the chance that favorable new combinations of genes may occur, and it also allows beneficial genes to sometimes become separated from dangerous new mutations that may occur on the same chromosome. If crossing over did not occur, that favorable gene would be stuck being inherited with the dangerous mutation forever. This recombining

Figure 4.11: African American family.

Figure 4.12: Native American Gathering of Nations Pow Wow.

of the genes means that each individual has the potential to produce veritably thousands of genetically different children. Wow! This also explains why sometimes siblings do not look that much alike. My brother and I demonstrate a decided lack of physical similarity (except that we both have our father's eyes). It also would let the milkman off the hook.

Genetic Drift is the random change in allele frequencies from one generation to the next. Sometimes a gene increases randomly from one generation to the next, and sometimes it decreases. This drift is much more significant in small populations and less significant in large breeding populations. For example, if the rate of people with blue eyes is 20 out of 1000 in the parent generation and 25 out of 1000 in the children's, this does not make a huge genetic difference. However, if it changes from 20 to 25 in a group of 50 individuals, that is much more significant. Random, unpredictable events sometimes occur to change the allele frequencies in a population, like an accident that removes some individuals from the group before they reproduce. As genetic drift is a random process where allele frequencies can change in either direction, it is the only force of evolution that is said to either increase or decrease genetic variation. There is an additional very special form of genetic drift called the **Founder Effect**. It occurs when a smaller group breaks off from a larger parental population to found a new population. What occurs is essentially a genetic bottleneck, as the new, much smaller group is reproductively isolated. The founder effect is said to decrease variation because this new smaller population does not represent all of the genetic variation contained within the larger group from which they have come. We see evidence of genetic drift in terms of the distribution of ABO blood types and higher frequencies of some genetic anomalies. For example, prior to 12,000 years ago, ancestors of modern Native Americans crossed the Bering Land Bridge from Southeast Asia. We can observe genetic ancestral relationships in interesting ways, in that today, Native Americans have very high frequencies of blood type O. In many populations, this allele is fixed and is found in 100 percent of individuals. When we compare them to modern Southeast Asians, the latter have substantially lower

Figure 4.13: Amish Children on their way to school.

rates of blood type O, suggesting that the early ancestors of modern Native peoples had substantially higher frequencies of the allele in the past. This suggests again that the initial Amerindians evolved from an isolated population with a small number of total individuals. In terms of trends in genetic disease, a classic example of founder effect is the prevalence of Ellis-van Creveld syndrome among the Pennsylvania Amish. This condition is characterized by dwarfism, often malformations of the heart, and extra fingers on the hand. The syndrome is quite rare, with fewer than 50 cases being known outside the Amish. Yet among the small Amish population alone, over 80 definite cases are known. The majority of these individuals can trace their descent back to three common ancestors, one of whom was probably a carrier. The Amish community is an orthodox Anabaptist sect in the United States, focusing particularly in Pennsylvania. As they do not practice marriage outside of their small religious community, they are genetically more closely related to each other than to the wider American population. In the case of a negative recessive gene, it is most likely to thrive in this form of small, breeding community.

Natural selection is another force of evolution that decreases variation. It acts like a filter or sieve, weeding out the genes that are less adaptive in any environment because those individuals with those genes are less likely to survive and reproduce. Think of it as nature selecting out those alleles that are not well adapted. Natural selection is essentially a force that favors the survival and reproduction of some organisms over others because of their biological traits. Therefore, some individuals pass their genes on disproportionately to the next generation (only those who survive). What traits are considered adaptive are completely environment specific. Those features favored in an arid desert will be very different from those in a tropical rain forest. The classic example of natural selection at work is the global distribution of sickle-cell trait and the wonderful peppered moth. We discussed earlier in this chapter the fact that the recessive sickle-cell gene causes the disease state only when it is homozygous (inherited from both parents). The highest frequencies of sickle-cell trait are in central and West Africans, where values can be as high as 20 percent. Abnormal sickled red blood cells result from the presence of hemoglobin with one incorrect amino acid. Such cells fail to transport oxygen properly to the body's tissues. Malaria is an infectious disease caused by members of the genus *Plasmodium* (*Plasmodium vivax, ovale,* and *falciparum*) and is transmitted by mosquitoes. Malaria is one of the leading causes of illness and death in warm regions

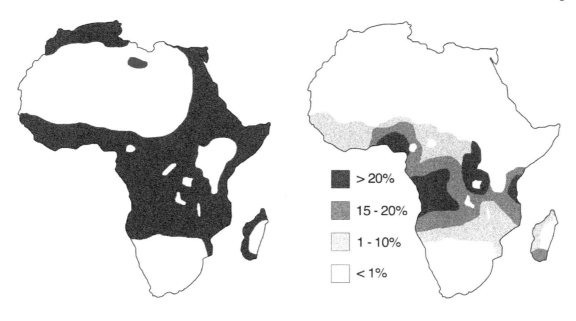

Figure 4.14: Malaria versus sickle cell trait distributions (original work by Anthony Allison).

of the world today. Every year, over 400 million people are infected, and one to three million people die, mostly African children under the age of five years. Those individuals who live in malarial areas often have a reduced reproductive success due to high infant mortality and adult morbidity.

Much of the early pivotal work was conducted by the English Kenyan biologist Anthony Allison during the 1950s. Allison noted that in areas affected by malaria, especially along Kenya's coast (southeast) and near Lake Victoria (southwest), a remarkably high number of people (20–30 percent) carried the gene for sickle cell anemia. In the highlands (west) of Kenya, where there was no malaria, Allison noted that less than one percent of the population carried the sickle cell gene. Allison concluded that individuals with one copy of the sickle cell gene (sickle cell trait) were resistant to malaria, and that in malarial areas, natural selection is acting upon this gene. Thus, carriers of the gene are much more likely to survive and reproduce than are noncarriers; hence, natural selection favors the carriers. In malarial areas, those individuals with normal hemoglobin are highly susceptible to dying from malaria. Individuals who carry one copy of the sickle cell gene (sickle cell trait) either do not contract malaria, or suffer a less severe malarial infection. This sickle cell genotype represents what we call a balanced polymorphism. A polymorphism is essentially a genetic trait where there is more than one allele found in a frequency above one percent. The ABO blood group is a great example of this, as most human populations have all three alleles in appreciable frequency. A balanced polymorphism is when two or more alleles are found in significant frequencies because the heterozygous (the alleles at a particular locus, thus of the same pair, are different) condition is beneficial. Sickle-cell trait in malarial areas is a wonderful example of this process. In this case, both the allele for normal hemoglobin and the sickle cell allele are maintained in appreciable numbers because the AS (one normal and one sickle) condition is advantageous for survival in malarial regions of the world.

Figure 4.15: Peppered moth *Biston betularia* on a birch tree.

As for the peppered moths, prior to the Industrial Revolution (the mid-1800s), the peppered moth had exactly that—a peppered appearance of gray flecked with black (non-melanic form). This peppered appearance was highly adaptive for this species, because it allowed them to camouflage themselves on the lichen of trees, thus evading their principal predators, birds. At some time prior to the mid-19th century, a new species of peppered moth (with a new mutated dominant gene) was observed that was a solid black color (melanic form). Prior to the late 19th century, the melanic (dark) form was fairly low in number. However, starting in the late 19th century, the melanic form began to increase quite substantially, and the non-melanic forms slowly began to decrease. What would cause such a dramatic turn of events? With the introduction of the Industrial Revolution commencing in earnest in the mid-19th century, the environmental pollution resulting from the use of coal in industry was enormous. Over time, the coal dust in the atmosphere contributed to killing off the lichen on the trees; now it was a selective advantage to be a melanic moth and blend into the darker bark of the trees. By the 1950s roughly 85–90 percent of peppered moths were dark in coloration. We see natural selection in action again with these species from the 1960s on. At this time, there was increasing concern about atmospheric pollutants, which led to stricter pollution laws. In addition to these policy changes, considerable reductions in the industry sector also contributed to a decline in environmental contaminants. As a result, over time, a substantial decrease was observed in the melanic population (in Manchester, England, the frequency of melanic moths went from 90 percent in 1983 to roughly 10 percent in the following decade) (Larsen 2010). Natural selection leads to biological change over countless populations, as a population responds to the specific stresses of their environment. Those individuals who have important biological traits that make them better adapted to their specific environment are the ones likely to survive and pass on those beneficial genes to their children. Is it fair? No. But it is only not fair in the short run. Environments are not static; when they change, the features that are best adapted to those new circumstances change as well. In the long run, no one really gets an unfair advantage in nature. The key is really to keep your neck above water (at least for us air-breathing creatures)!

Last but not least, another of the forces of evolution that decreases variation is sexual selection. This was an ingenious idea that Darwin developed to explain the many extravagances witnessed in nature.

Peacocks were not Charles Darwin's favorite birds. In fact, he disliked them immensely because they seemed to directly challenge Darwin's theory of natural selection. This theory beautifully explains why polar bears have thick fur, or why birds have hollow bones: because these are features that make these organisms better adapted to their environments. The peacock's tail should make him less likely to survive rather than more likely: it is very visible, it is very heavy and cumbersome, and it requires a lot of calories to grow. According to natural selection, the male peacock's tail should never have developed in the first

place. Darwin also made another interesting observation: it is usually the males in nature that are ornamented—think of the lion's mane or the moose's antlers. If the whole goal of evolution is to reproduce oneself, then perhaps males have developed these traits to attract females. Darwin concluded that when the notion of competition or choice enters into mating, we have what he labeled **Sexual Selection**. Males compete with other males for access to females, and the females choose which males they wish to mate with. Eureka!—the male peacock

Figure 4.16: Peacock male and beautiful tail.

has a beautiful, large tail because female peahens like that, and the males with the most glorious tails are the ones who pass their genes on to the next generation. Females look for males who seem to be healthy and fertile, and for peacocks, the larger and more beautiful the tail, the better the genes. Sexual

Figure 4.17: Zebras fighting.

selection reduces variation because those individuals with less-than-desirable traits do not mate and pass on those traits to the next generation.

COMPLEX PHYSICAL TRAITS, SELECTION, AND PLEIOTROPY: WHAT A MOUTHFUL!

There are many genetic traits that are determined by a single locus (pair) of genes such as eye color and ABO blood type. However, there are also many biological traits that are polygenic, meaning that many genes are involved in the expression of the trait. This brings us to complex physical traits. These are features like height, weight, and skin color, for example. Many genes at different locations contribute to these traits. **Complex Physical Traits** are interesting in that unlike most genetic traits, they are affected by the environment. For example, you are born with a genetic blueprint for a specific height, but if you do not get proper nutrition during the period of growth and development, you may not actually reach your genetic height. In addition, complex physical traits are found in a continuous distribution (moving from the shortest person on the one end all the way continuously to the tallest at the other). Complex physical traits tend to produce values that are distributed mostly around the average rather than the extremes. In other words, in any population there will be a small number of people who are unusually short and unusually tall. However, the vast majority of the population falls within the average range for height. Even when a population appears to be relatively stable, natural selection is still at work. When we look at how selection acts upon these traits, we focus upon what is called **stabilizing selection** and **directional selection**. Stabilizing selection involves selection against the extremes of a trait's range in values. It means those individuals with extreme high and low values are less likely to survive to reproduce. A good example of this is birth weight. Prior to remarkable 20th-century develop-ments in neonatal medicine, most babies born below a certain weight did not survive. Likewise, very large babies often died with their mothers in childbirth. One was most likely to survive if one had an average birth weight (in North America, roughly seven pounds today).

Directional selection involves selection in favor of one direction to the discrimination of the other, like the increase in hominid brain size in the last five million years. Brain size seems to consistently increase over time, suggesting that those with larger brains were the ones surviving and contributing more genes to the next generation than other smaller-brained individuals. Not surprising, given that surviving on the open savanna can't have been a picnic. We see this movement in one direction when we have a trait that is selectively adaptive, and thus it increases over time in a population—as long as that trait continues to be beneficial in that specific ecological scenario.

Figure 4.18: Complex physical traits like height have a continuous distribution and are influenced by the environment.

Pleiotropy is sort of like the opposite of polygenic traits. In polygenic traits, many genes act to influence the expression of a single trait. In the case of pleiotropy, a single gene affects multiple phenotypic traits in an organism. Tricky, isn't it! A great example of pleiotropy in humans is phenylketonuria (PKU). This genetic condition is caused by a deficiency of the enzyme phenylalanine hydroxylase, which is necessary to convert the essential amino acid phenylalanine to tyrosine. A defect in the single gene that codes for this enzyme results in the multiple phenotypes associated with PKU, including mental retardation, eczema, and pigment defects that make

Figure 4.19: White cat with blue eyes—pleiotropy.

affected individuals lighter skinned (Paul 2000). Another interesting example of pleiotropy involves the beloved house cat. Approximately 40 percent of cats with white fur and blue eyes are deaf (Hartl and Jones 2005). This link between pigmentation and deafness was suggested by the fact that white cats with one blue eye and one yellow eye were deaf only on the blue-eyed side.

Today, we know that evolution functions as a result of changes in gene frequencies over time. Mutation is the source of new genetic variation, while the other forces of evolution act to increase or decrease preexisting genes. We have certainly come a long way from blending theory and the inheritance of acquired characteristics. A biological trait's adaptive value is totally environmentally specific. As environmental conditions change, so do the traits that will be selected.

CRITICAL REASONING QUESTIONS

- Record the genetic traits you can observe in your own family (grandparents, parents, and siblings). Can you observe any pattern in heritable traits?
- You are transported to a new desert world where you will have to adapt to survive. What features might be an advantage in this environment?
- Before the work of Gregor Mendel, how did scientists explain heredity? Where did they go wrong?
- Why can you make potentially millions of genetically distinct children?
- What is sexual selection? What traits might have emerged in humans as a result of sexual selection?

REFERENCES AND SUGGESTED READINGS

Allison, A. C. (2002). "Mini-series: Contributions to biological chemistry over the last 125 years. The discovery of resistance to malaria of sickle-cell heterozygotes." *Biochemistry and Molecular Biology Education* 30(5):279–287.

Bickel, H., C. Bachmann, R. Beckers, et al. (1981). "Neonatal mass screening for metabolic disorders: Summary of recent sessions of the committee of experts to study inborn metabolic diseases." Public Health Committee, *European Journal of Pediatrics* (137):133–139.

Bowler, Peter J. (2003). *Evolution: The history of an idea*. Berkeley: University of California Press.

Candela, P. B. (1942). "The introduction of blood-group B into Europe." *Human Biology* 14:413–443.

Chown, B., and M. Lewis (2005). "The blood group genes of the Cree Indians and the Eskimos of the Ungava District of Canada." *American Journal of Physical Anthropology* 14 (2):215–224.

Condit, C. (1999). *The meanings of the gene: Public debates about human heredity.* Madison: University of Wisconsin Press.

Cummings, M. (1994). *Human heredity. Principles and issues,* 3rd ed. St. Paul, MN: Wadsworth West Publishing Co.

Estrada-Mena, B., F. J. Estrada, R. Ulloa-Arvizu, et al. (May 2010). "Blood group O alleles in Native Americans: Implications in the peopling of the Americas." *American Journal of Physical Anthropology* 142 (1):85–94.

Falk, R. (1986). "What is a gene?" *Studies in History and Philosophy of Science* 17:133–173.

Filiano, J. J. (May 2006). "Neurometabolic diseases in the newborn." *Clinics in Perinatology* 33 (2):411–479.

Gribbin, J., and M. White (1995). *Darwin: A life in science.* London: Simon & Schuster.

Hartl, D. L., & E. W. Jones (2005). *Genetics: Analysis of genes and genomes,* 6th ed. Boston: Jones and Bartlett.

Henig, Robin Marantz (2000). *The monk in the garden: The lost and found genius of Gregor Mendel, the father of genetics.* Boston: Houghton Mifflin.

Hubbard, R., and E. Wald (1993). *Exploding the gene myth.* Boston: Beacon Press.

Keigwin, L. D., J. P. Donnelly, M. S. Cook, et al. (October 2006). "Rapid sea-level rise and Holocene climate in the Chukchi Sea." *Geology* 34(10):861–864.

Larsen, C. S. (2010). *Essentials of physical anthropology: Discovering our origins.* New York: W. W. Norton and Company.

Losick, R., J. D. Watson, T. A. Baker, et al. (2008). *Molecular biology of the gene.* San Francisco: Pearson/Benjamin Cummings.

Malowany, J. I., and J. Butany (February 2012). "Pathology of sickle cell disease." *Seminars in Diagnostic Pathology* 29 (1):49–55.

Marks, J. (1992). "Beads and string: The genome in evolutionary theory." In E. J. Devor, ed., *Molecular Applications in Biological Anthropology,* pp. 234–255. New York: Cambridge University Press.

Marks, J. (2009). "The construction of Mendel's Laws." *Evolutionary Anthropology* 17:250–253.

McKusick, V. A. (2000). "Ellis-van Creveld syndrome and the Amish." *Nature Genetics* 24:203–204.

McKusick V. A., J. A. Egeland, R. Eldridge, and D. E. Krusen (October 1964). "Dwarfism in the Amish I. The Ellis-van Creveld syndrome." *Bulletin of Johns Hopkins Hospital* 115:306–336.

Mendel, W. B., and W. Bateson (2009). *Mendel's principles of heredity: A defence, with a translation of Mendel's original papers on hybridisation* (Cambridge Library Collection—Life Sciences). Cambridge, UK: Cambridge University Press.

Orel, Vitezslav (1984). *Mendel.* Trans. Stephen Finn. Oxford, UK: Oxford University Press.

Paul, D. (2000). "A double-edged sword." *Nature* 405, 515.

Platt, O. S., D. J. Brambilla, W. F. Rosse, et al. (June 1994). "Mortality in sickle cell disease. Life expectancy and risk factors for early death." *New England Journal of Medicine* 330 (23):1639–1644.

Sherman, I. W. (2006). *The power of plagues.* Washington, DC: ASM Press.

Stearns, F. W. (2010). "One hundred years of pleiotropy: A retrospective." *Genetics* 186(3):767–773.

Wade, M. S., J. Wolf, and E. D. Brodie (2000). *Epistasis and the evolutionary process.* Oxford, UK: Oxford University Press.

Waller, J. (2003). "Parents and children: Ideas of heredity in the 19th century." *Endeavour* 27:51–56.

5

An Epic Journey And An Epic Idea

The Path to Natural Selection

By Gillian Crane-Kramer

Charles Darwin (1809–1882) was fortunate that he was born into an educated and affluent family. This not only exposed him to the important knowledge of his day, but also fostered a curiosity about the natural world. He was one of six children, and as his mother died when he was eight years old, he was essentially raised by his older sisters. In the 1820s, Darwin spent two years studying medicine at the University of Edinburgh in Scotland. He did not enjoy medicine in the slightest, but this short period was a very important point in Darwin's intellectual development. At this time, he was exposed to many of the important scientific debates of the day, one of which was evolution. He would have been exposed to the work of people like Lamarck (as several of his professors were staunch supporters of the notion of evolution). He also was able to attend important lectures on diverse topics in the natural sciences and had access to impressive museum collections for analysis. Eventually, Darwin would complete a degree in theology from Christ's College, Cambridge, during which4 time he seriously pursued interests in diverse areas of natural science like geology, botany, beetles, and—strangely—barnacles!

When he graduated in 1831, Darwin signed on to be the naturalist on the ship *HMS* Beagle, whose journey would take almost five years and would circumnavigate the globe. This is a stunning achievement that is lost on today's jet-setters, who can have lunch in Toronto and supper in London. For most of human history, people did not travel far from home. Firstly, you either had to walk everywhere, or you had to be financially comfortable enough to have a horse (which most people were not). Only the

Figure 5.1: Charles Darwin (Photo by J. Cameron, 1869).

wealthy traveled, even after train and boat travel became widespread. To have the opportunity to participate in an excursion of this magnitude gave Darwin the opportunity of a lifetime. If, as Louis Pasteur said, it is that "chance favors the prepared mind," then Charles Darwin's life up until his journey upon the *Beagle* had prepared his mind to investigate, examine, and draw conclusions about the exciting range of life forms he would encounter in his travels. Throughout this five-year period, Darwin collected plant and animal specimens from a dizzying array of organisms in very different ecosystems. The largest portion of his trip was spent in South America and the Galapagos Islands. Darwin marveled at the continuity that he could see between fossil and modern species there. It is fascinating to contemplate the fact that Darwin believed in fixity of species at the beginning of his journey. However, it is not surprising that he became increasingly uncomfortable with the idea as his travels progressed. He was particularly intrigued during the five-week period that he examined the life forms found on the Galapagos Islands. He immediately noted that the unique creatures found there resembled ones on the South American mainland, and that they all differed slightly from each other, depending upon the specific island they inhabited. The most famous of these creatures are the little birds known as finches. He realized at the time that the finches must have descended from South American ancestors, but he recognized that they had changed since that time. In addition, they differed from each other, depending upon the specific microclimate of the individual islands. It was only later upon his return to England that he realized how important characteristics like beak shape were, and how these different biological features were modified through time.

When Charles Darwin returned home in 1856, he set about spending decades conducting research in a wide variety of different scientific areas and cultivating relationships with many of the leading biological scientists of the day. In addition, he began to interact with animal breeders, who helped him to see first-hand that one could accentuate artificially whatever features one wished, and eliminate the traits that were not desired through controlling which animals were allowed to reproduce. Depending upon the environment and which specific

Figure 5.2: Satellite view of the Galapagos Islands.

features were desirable (hence, selected for), one could artificially select specific traits. This idea of artificial selection could be translated into Darwin's idea of natural selection. Instead of humans selecting features to create a greyhound, an Australian shepherd, or a border terrier, perhaps God had determined that nature should unfold in the same way. Thus, it was the unique qualities of each environment that established what features are beneficial for survival and reproduction. Plus, if we consider this observation in light of Malthus's struggle for existence, we are edging even closer to the modern view of evolutionary change. Charles Darwin and Alfred Russell

Figure 5.3: Galapagos Cactus Finch.

Wallace were independently asking an important question that really did not interest Malthus much: What is different about the few who survive and pass their traits on to the next generation?

Darwin had not been in a hurry to publish his findings. He had presented an amazing amount of work at scholarly proceedings, but was very hesitant to take the next step. This was in part due to his concern that his views would deeply upset his devoutly Christian wife. While he had been raised in a Christian household his whole life and had been a strong believer well into his adult years, Darwin's faith in a loving, kind God was seriously shaken at the death of his beloved ten-year-old daughter, Annie, in 1851 (Keynes 2001). He also knew that his ideas were likely to be viewed as radical or blasphemous, as they implied that nature—rather than God—shaped the living world. He also stated that he believed humans descended from apes, that they emerged on the African continent, and that female choice drove evolution. All of these ideas directly challenged many deeply held beliefs in European society, so now he was not only in trouble with the Church, but the wider populace as well. After he became aware of Alfred Russell Wallace's work, they both presented papers to the Linnaean Society in London in 1858. Interestingly, neither of the papers garnered much interest. However, it was the publication of his famous work *On the Origin of Species by Means of Natural Selection* in 1859 that forever changed the course of the biological sciences.

WHAT IS NATURAL SELECTION, ANYWAY?

Charles Darwin did not invent the idea of evolution. His genius lay in his ability to explain how evolution actually functions, and this explanation is called natural selection. **Natural selection** is a force of evolutionary change that favors the survival and reproduction of some individuals over others because of their biological traits. In any environment, there will be certain biological traits that make you more likely to survive in that environment. Those organisms that have that trait (or suite of traits) are more likely to survive and reproduce; thus, they pass their genes on disproportionately to the next generation. One would expect those beneficial traits to increase over time, and every successive generation is slightly different from their parents'. This was a natural process that occurred without divine intervention, and placed humans squarely within the animal kingdom. We had been formed by the same processes as every other living creature. Not surprisingly, these ideas caused quite an explosion.

Darwin had two major limitations to his theory of natural selection that were never resolved during his lifetime. He knew that most populations have a tremendous amount of observable variation, and no two individuals (except identical twins) are exactly the same. When we look at people in different parts of the world, we can easily see this incredible variation within our own species. This variation allows us some flexibility in the face of a changing environment. However, Darwin was endlessly frustrated by the fact that he could not establish where that variation came from. We now know that there is only one source of new variation, mutation, but this fact was yet to be discovered. The other major limitation that Charles Darwin had was that he did not understand the mechanisms of inheritance. He knew that parents pass their traits on to their children, but as we have already discussed in Chapter 3, no one knew how that actually occurred. Ironically, this very problem was being addressed by his contemporary, Gregor Mendel; alas, the two paths never converged.

AM I "FIT" IN EVOLUTIONARY TERMS BECAUSE I GO TO THE GYM?

One of the best-known concepts that has extended from Darwin's work is the notion of survival of the fittest (even if he didn't exactly call it that). How do we establish who is "fit" in evolutionary terms? Actually, it is remarkably easy to establish the level of fitness for an individual. Your fitness depends upon success in only one area: reproduction. How fit you are depends on how many genes you contribute to the next generation, compared to other members of your population. It is essentially only a measure of individual reproductive success. You must have children who survive to reproduce, and not all individuals will pass on their genes to the next generation. Therefore, we say that some organisms pass on their genetic material disproportionately to the next generation. It is important to remember that this is a relative measure, as the features that are considered better adapted change with the environment. When we look at people, in evolutionary terms, no one is interested in how wealthy, famous, or successful you are. Leonardo di Caprio is a big zero on the fitness scale, as he has no children, despite his unquestioned success in other areas. If you have no children, then your genes die with you—you are an evolutionary dead-end. That is a little dramatic; if you have siblings, it is possible that some of your genes may survive to be passed down to the next generation via your nieces and nephews. Many of us share more than 50 percent of our genes with our siblings. Ironic, isn't it, that the very people that you spend years in childhood trying to remove from the gene pool (I have apologized to my younger brother on multiple occasions) are precisely the people you should be most invested in surviving.

Figure 5.4: Twin babies.

Figure 5.5: Mother and child.

WHAT IS A SPECIES? AND THE DOMESTICATION OF THE BELOVED DOG

Scientists like to speak in absolutes, but this luxury is rarely possible. When we define what a species is, it is generally considered to be a grouping of organisms that breed successfully to produce fertile offspring. These groups are reproductively isolated from each other, as they cannot successfully interbreed (on rare occasions they can, but all offspring are sterile; think of the ligers in Chapter 2). These species are further divided into populations that are spread out on the geographical landscape, and contain individuals that tend to mate within that grouping. As self-explanatory as these definitions are, they are actually trickier than they seem. There are over 400 recognized breeds of domestic dog, but they are all the same species—*Canis lupus familiaris*. Thus, we would assume that all individuals should be able to produce offspring successfully. While technically it should be possible, one does wonder about the mechanical problems of

Figure 5.6: My greyhound "Blitzen".

mating a Great Dane and a miniature poodle, not to mention the difficulty in a poodle mother carrying and delivering the puppies successfully. So, this idea is not necessarily as straightforward as we would like.

We can trace the origin of the domestic dog (*Canis lupus familiaris*) to its ancestor, the gray wolf (*Canis lupus*), several tens of thousands of years ago. It appears from both the archaeological and the genetic evidence that dog domestication did not occur in only one location, but happened on more than one occasion. The modern domestic dog appears unequivocally no later than 15,000 years ago, as supported by the Bonn-Oberkassel site. Mitochondrial DNA evidence retrieved from a Paleolithic dog from the Razboinichya Cave in the Altai Mountains of southern Siberia suggests that this process may have occurred as early as 33,000 years ago (Germonpré et al. 2009, 2012, 2013). Researchers have not agreed whether or not humans intentionally domesticated wolves, or whether it was a form of wolf self-domestication.

As domestic dogs share roughly 99 percent of their genes with gray wolves, it is interesting to question whether dogs are simply wolves that have been raised and socialized by humans. Yet again, we go back to the famous question of nature versus nurture. A fascinating investigation of this question was provided by breeding research conducted in Siberian Russia on silver foxes. From the 1950s on, researchers working with wild silver foxes selectively bred over 35 generations for the

Figure 5.7: Afghan hound.

Figure 5.8: Child playing with dog.

sole trait of tameness; they created foxes that interacted with humans like dogs. After less than ten generations, the domesticated foxes seek out human interactions and are warm and friendly. As Lyudmilla Trut says in her 1999 *American Scientist* article:

The least domesticated foxes, those that flee from experimenters or bite when stroked or handled, are assigned to Class III. Foxes in Class II let themselves be petted and handled but show no emotionally friendly response to experimenters. Foxes in Class I are friendly toward experimenters, wagging their tails and whining. In the sixth generation bred for tameness we had to add an even higher-scoring category. Members of Class IE, the "domesticated elite," are eager to establish human contact, whimpering to attract attention and sniffing and licking experimenters like dogs. They start displaying this kind of behavior before they are one month old. By the tenth generation, 18 percent of fox pups were elite; by the 20th, the figure had reached 35 percent. Today elite foxes make up 70 to 80 percent of our experimentally selected population. (Trut 1999:160)

A further intriguing result of this study was the demonstration that when you select for tameness, the changes in behavior are paralleled by physical changes as well. The experimental design did not originally include selection for physical traits, as the focus was upon behavioral characteristics. However, with tameness came several new biological traits like spotted or black-and-white coats, tails that curl

Figure 5.9: Grey wolf howling.

over the foxes' backs, barking, floppy ears, and earlier sexual maturity. There is a noticeable retention of juvenile characteristics, like what we see in the modern dog versus the gray wolf. It appears that selection for tameness involves both morphological (genetic) and behavioral adjustments over time. These features move as a suite together, rather than having each feature selected independently.

Recent research by Kathryn Lord suggests that dogs are not simply socialized wolves. The study focuses on examining the development of the sensory systems in dogs and wolves. They recorded weekly the responses of seven wolf pups and 43 dog pups (two to seven weeks of age) to familiar and novel auditory, olfactory, and visual stimuli. Lord concludes that there is a difference between wolves and dogs during the critical early period of socialization, when they are experiencing their environment. These differences lead to significant differences in their ability to form interspecies social relationships with humans.

A great deal of interesting research is being conducted on the evolution of the domestic dog. Some fascinating work is being conducted at the Family Dog Project established in 1994 in the Department of Ethology at the Eötvös Loránd University in Budapest, Hungary. One study investigated whether human listeners could categorize played-back dog (*Canis familiaris*) barks in various situations and associate them with emotions. In a remarkable number of cases, humans could properly interpret the emotion behind the bark. The researchers concluded that this ability to recognize meaning suggests that barks could serve as an effective means of communication between humans and dogs (Pongrácz et al. 2005). This is a truly remarkable suggestion—that dogs have developed a vocal repertoire to communicate specifically with humans. It further confirms what humans have asserted all along: that their dogs had an uncanny ability to sense their emotion and communicate. These diverse investigations into the process of evolution not only offer us a far greater understanding of the phylogeny (evolutionary history) of man's best friend, but they have given us provocative new insights into the process of domestication.

WAS THE WOOL PULLED OVER OUR EYES? EVIDENCE FOR EVOLUTION

There are countless ways we can find evidence for evolution, both from modern living organisms and from the fossil record. With every new scientific breakthrough comes ever ingenious ways for us to investigate the history of life on this planet. The benefit of investigating modern living plants and animals is that we can examine them with a precision that is impossible for ancient life forms. We can search an organism's genes, and look at their blood and tissues in microscopic detail. This has not only revealed the amazing complexity of various creatures, but has also allowed us to describe, compare, and classify living beings with an amazing degree of accuracy. The negative to focusing upon an examination of living organisms is the fact that you have no time depth. You can describe the end product—say, the zebra—in great detail, but you cannot say anything about the road that led to the zebra. Why are zebras different from their close equine relatives? That is a question that can only be answered through an investigation of the fossil record. Therefore, for any holistic understanding of the process of evolution to be achieved, one must consider both the modern and the fossil evidence in concert.

It is important to remember that much of the technology and theory required to discover this knowledge did not develop until the 20th century. From the late 19th century, we see an explosion of development in a wide range of scientific disciplines. In the 1730s, when Linnaeus was collecting and classifying living organisms into his system known as binomial nomenclature, he did not have at his disposal the vast range of investigative tools that we have today. There were no genes, no viruses, and no DNA. How were scientists of the past able to compare organisms and draw conclusions about biological relationships? Taxonomists essentially had

Figure 5.10: Pair of zebras.

anatomy to rely on; specifically, the field of morphology (the study of form and structure). The basis for comparing living plants and animals was biological similarities and differences. It made sense that those organisms that are more closely related should share more biological similarities; the more distant the relatedness, the more biological differences.

Classification systems were established by analyzing things like primitive and derived traits, homologous and analogous traits, and vestigial organs. **Primitive traits** are ones that have been inherited from an ancestral form. A great example of this is pentadactyly (*penta-* = five, *-dactyl* = digit) in primates. We share this trait of five fingers and toes on each appendage because we inherited this from an earlier ancestral form. This trait continues to be adaptive, despite changes in the descendants' environment, and this is why we see little to no change in this feature over time.

Figure 5.11: Human baby hand pentadactyly.

Derived traits are ones that have changed from an ancestral state, and this change results from adaptation to a changing environment over very long periods of time. An example of this is bipedalism (*bi-* = two, *-ped* = feet) in humans. Our normal form of locomotion is the striding gait on two legs. However, we know that we descend from quadrupedal (four-legged) primate ancestors. All other primates are still quadrupeds. Therefore, this is a trait where we have changed from our ancestral state (there is considerable debate as to why this happened; I will leave that to my illustrious colleague in Chapter 9).

Homologous traits (*homo-* = same) are those that share the same structure, but may not share the same function. The classic example of this is the fin of a whale, the arm of a human, and the wing of a bat. We all share the same structure—one upper limb bone and two lower limb bones, even though the size and shape may differ significantly. However, the arm of a human, the fin of a whale, and the wing of a bat all function in very different ways. Homologous traits indicate common ancestry. In this case, we are all mammals, but we are also all descendants of terrestrial vertebrates (land-living animals with a backbone), so we share this feature in common.

Figure 5.12: Whale.

Analogous traits are the opposite of homologous traits. Analogous traits have the same function, but may not have the same structure. This is because they are features that have been developed independently in different species. This independent evolution of the same trait can occur in two ways: parallel evolution and convergent evolution. **Parallel evolution** occurs when two related species split from each other, adapt in different environmental circumstances, and end up developing many of the same traits. Thus, parallel evolution is when you have the independent development of the same phenotypic trait in distinct species that are closely related. Parallel evolution probably occurs because similar environmental pressures actually lead to different species evolving similar traits. An example is the wildebeest, which is native to the dry, flat grasslands of the African savanna and North American cattle, which are native to the dry, flat grasslands of the North American plains. Although they are related, these species evolved geographically isolated from each other. However, they have developed striking morphological similarities because they are both adapting to similar arid, open environments.

Convergent evolution (hooplas) is the independent development of the same phenotypic trait in species that are not closely related. We can see this in plants, in that the photosynthetic pathways such as CAM (crassulacean acid metabolism) and C-4 photosynthesis have evolved independently in distantly related plant families. In addition, succulent plants like the North American cactuses (family Cactaceae) and the South African euphorbias (family *Euphorbiaceae*) are not closely related, and are only distant relatives in the phylogeny of flowering plants. As both groups have been adapting for countless generations to arid climates with little natural rainfall, they both

Figure 5.13: African cactus garden.

have succulent, thick stems that store water, and they both have developed spines for protection. If we look under the sea at dolphins (mammals), sharks (cartilaginous fish), swordfish (bony fish), and ichthyosaurs (long-extinct reptiles), we see that they share the same streamlined and torpedolike body shape, and have tall dorsal fins and wide tails. None of these creatures is closely related, but they have tried to adapt to the same environment—life under the sea as marine predators. Thus, they have developed an entire suite of biological and behavioral features in common. This reminds us that organisms can develop similar traits without the link of a recent common ancestor. Make sure that you do not get led down the garden path by thinking

Figure 5.14: Shark.

that organisms that share some observable similarities must be closely related. Although dolphins and sharks do indeed share many observable traits in common, it is not because of recent common ancestry, but because they both are adapting to a life underwater. Dolphins are more closely related to elephants (and other mammals) than they are to sharks.

Vestigial organs are another way that we can establish ancestral relationships. These are biological structures that were well developed and important in ancestral forms, but are reduced in size and importance in derived species (descendants). There are many species that show evidence of vestigial organs, both plant and animal. Both whales and some species of primitive snakes (boas and pythons) maintain vestigial hind limb bones. Clearly, neither of these organisms has legs, but the presence of hind limb bones tells us a lot about their ancestors (who did have legs), as well as their evolutionary journey since that time. The fact that some primitive snakes contain vestiges of lower

Figure 5.15: Dolphin.

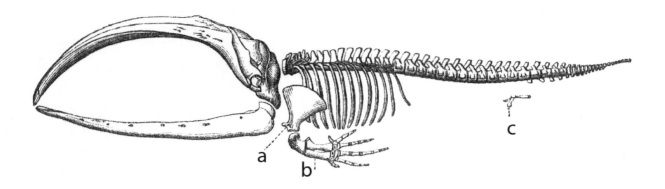

Figure 5.16: Whale vestigial organs—hind limb bones.

limb bones confirms the 95-million-year-old fossil evidence of early snakes that had limbs (Tchernov et al. 2000). The fact that modern whales demonstrate vestiges of hind limbs can also be linked to fossils of early whales with reduced hind limbs (Gingerich et al. 1990). Whales diverged from other mammals roughly 50 million years ago, and it appears that some mammals after this date returned to a life in the sea. The fossil record strongly suggests that whales descended from wolflike terrestrial mammals and that snakes derived from lizards. These vestigial organs not only tell us a great deal about ancestral forms, but they also help us to understand the changing environmental circumstances that led to the feature becoming less important for survival.

Figure 5.17: Pakicetus—whale quadrupedal ancestor.

Humans also have a number of vestigial organs that offer clues about our ancestors. We get goose bumps and we have a tailbone, ear-wiggling muscles, a vermiform appendix, and wisdom teeth. Goose bumps are considered to be vestigial in humans, even though they are technically a reflex rather than a permanent anatomical feature. The pilomotor reflex (the official term) occurs when the tiny muscle at the base of a hair follicle contracts and pulls the hair upright. In birds or mammals with fur, spines, or feathers, this action creates a layer of insulating warm air when it is cold, or a significant deterrent to potential predators (think of when your cat is startled and the hair on their back stands up). Throughout the course of human history, we have seen a dramatic reduction in the amount of overall body hair when compared to our modern primate cousins. Human hair is so thin and reduced that it is not capable of either of the original functions. Another good example of a vestige in humans is the human coccyx (tailbone). This is generally three to five small vertebrae at the terminal end of the spinal column. This is a vestige of the mammalian tail (used as an organ of balance in the trees or as a grasping appendage), which has taken on a modified function, notably as an anchor point for the muscles that hold the anus in place. Humans descend from arboreal primates, whose tails were an extremely beneficial adaptive feature. As humans have been adjusting entirely or in part to a terrestrial environment for roughly five million years, the tail has become ever reduced in size until it is a vestige—the coccygeal vertebrae. Throughout the past several million years, as our ancestors adapted to this new terrestrial environment, their diet shifted away from leaves and fruit and more toward an omnivorous diet of meat and a variety of plant species. Modern apes like gorillas, whose diet is principally folivorous (leaves), have developed intestinal specializations to break down cellulose efficiently. The human appendix is a vestige of this far more complicated digestive system in our primate ancestors, where vegetable cellulose is stored in order to be digested with the assistance of bacteria. We no longer consume high-cellulose plants as the major component of our diet; this system has become reduced over time, until we see it as a vestige in the appendix. When we look at our early hominid ancestors (or cousins, depending on who you are examining), they are associated with much larger dental complexes than modern humans. As our teeth, faces, and jaws were larger in the past, we had enough room in our mouth for the permanent third molars (wisdom teeth). However, modern humans are associated with small teeth, faces, and jaws, and most people simply no longer have enough room in their mouths to accommodate those third molar teeth. They are removed to prevent infection and misalignment of the other permanent dentition. One can clearly see the benefits of examining vestigial organs when investigating ancestral relationships. They not only provide critical

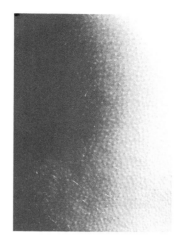

Figure 5.18: Human vestige—goose bumps.

evidence of the link between earlier forms and modern descendants, but vestigial organs also assist us in reconstructing the changing environmental conditions through time.

Dramatic scientific breakthroughs from the climax of the 19th century on have revolutionized the manner in which we investigate organic forms. The development of new fields such as genetics, immunology, embryology, and biochemistry have allowed us to describe and classify organisms at the microscopic and developmental level. One forceful piece of evidence

First coccygeal vertebra

Second coccygeal vertebra

Third, fourth and fifth coccygeal vertebrae

Figure 5.19: Human tailbone—coccygeal vertebrae.

to suggest common roots among all plants and animals is that essentially all organisms encode their genetic information in the DNA molecule. It is difficult to interpret this evidence in any other way than to suggest common ancestry. **Biochemical evidence** is also indicative of common ancestry. All proteins on Earth are constructed of the same 20 amino acids (although there are 64 total amino acid possibilities). Likewise, an examination of the alpha chain of the blood's hemoglobin shows identical amino acid sequences between humans and chimpanzees, and only one difference (out of 141 possible differences) between humans and gorillas (Berra 1990).

Comparative immunological studies have also established a close relationship between humans and the great apes. Interesting research involved the injection of human blood serum (the liquid clear part of the blood) into a rabbit. When the system of any living organism recognizes a foreign protein (called an antigen), it is stimulated to create antibodies against that specific antigen. The blood serum of different animals is composed of different serum proteins. When a rabbit was injected with human blood serum, it created antibodies against it. Those antibodies were then tested against

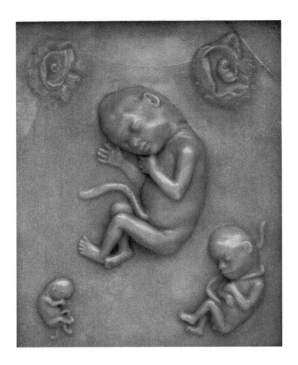

Figure 5.20: Embryo at five states (Wellcome Trust Images).

the blood serum of other animal species. The closer the relationship of an animal to humans, the more serum proteins that we should share in common, and the more substantial the rabbit's immunological reaction. The more distantly related to humans, the fewer serum proteins shared, the less the immune reaction of the rabbit. Results of these studies indicate that the closest relatives to humans are the great apes, followed by Old World and then New World monkeys. Thus, the immunological evidence supports evidence from diverse fields (like morphology) that indicate a close ancestral relationship between humans and the great apes in particular. This is further confirmed by the genetic evidence showing 1.2 percent difference between humans and chimpanzees, 1.4 percent genetic difference between humans and gorillas, and 2.4 percent difference between humans and orangutans (Lewin 2004). You simply cannot get much more closely related than this: it indicates that our evolutionary split from the great apes must have occurred very recently in geological time.

Another way we can find evidence for evolution is by comparing the development of organisms in the womb via **comparative embryology**. The field of embryology is concerned with an investigation of the developmental process, from fertilized egg to birth (or hatching). Related organisms tend to show remarkable similarities in embryonic development. If we look at the vertebrate classes—animals with a backbone: mammals, birds, fish, reptiles, and amphibians—there are remarkable similarities in embryonic development in the early stages of life in the womb. A fascinating tidbit is the fact that nonaquatic vertebrates (mammals, birds, and reptiles) still move through a gill-slit stage in early embryonic development. The fact that all vertebrates (including us) move through a gill-slit stage in early life in the womb is because ultimately, we descend from fish that had these features (Ayala 2007). It also informs us that the vertebrates clearly carry a number of ancestral genes that are either turned on or turned off during a process we call ontogeny. Ontogeny is the period of growth and development from fertilization of the egg to sexual maturity and adulthood. For mammals, birds, and reptiles, at some stage in early embryonic development, the genes that lead to gill development are turned off, and the genes that lead to lung development are turned on. All this action is controlled by regulatory genes that govern the activity of other genes.

Another example of how comparative embryology can be used to examine ancestral relationships can be seen in whales. Baleen whales (like blue whales or humpbacks) lack teeth and instead strain plankton through fine baleen plates. However, the embryos of baleen whales have rudimentary teeth, indicating that baleen whales must have evolved from toothed whales (Deméré et al. 2005, 2008, Wallace 2007). The recent discovery that reptilelike teeth could be grown in chicken embryos further strengthens the fossil evidence that suggests birds evolved from reptiles (Harris et al. 2006). Clearly, some modern bird species like chickens have retained these ancestral genes that remain off under normal developmental circumstances. The study of comparative embryology is obviously another extremely useful tool for examining ancestral relationships, and gives us a wonderful glimpse into the process of evolution from the earliest stages of life in utero.

A final example (and there are thousands of possibilities) that I will discuss for the process of evolution in living species is the discipline of **biogeography**. This is the study of the geographical distribution of plants and animals around the world. Between 1831–1836, when Darwin was traveling on the *Beagle*, he made some observations that later would be critical for the generation of the theory of natural selection. He noticed that individuals of the same species varied from geographic region to region. Think of the variety in humans around the world. He reasoned that there must be a great deal of variation in most living species. He also noted that these differences make sense in light of individual environments.

Figure 5.21: Arctic fox.

This explains why the arctic fox has thick white fur and predators have big pointy canines for puncturing and tearing.

Lastly, there is a dynamic relationship between the environment and the organisms that live within it. The environment shapes organisms over long periods of time. Darwin observed this directly himself during his closer examination of the variation between the finches on Galapagos and those from different islands. The finches had clearly all descended from one original ancestral species from the South American mainland. Yet no—although they were all clearly still finches—they

Figure 5.22: Tyrannosaurus Rex skull.

were different species. How did one original group of immigrants lead to several different closely related species? Darwin reasoned that as small populations radiated to the different islands, they then had to adapt to the individual climatic and environmental (microenvironment) conditions of the different islands. Likewise, he recognized that the different species found on the Cape Verde islands off the coast of Africa resembled very closely forms on the African mainland. This evidence convinced Darwin that the notion of fixity of species was incorrect, and that organisms in nature not only demonstrate tremendous variation (and hence plasticity), but they also have a remarkable ability for change. Furthermore, it is the environment that governs and directs that change.

WHAT ABOUT THE FOSSIL RECORD? IS THERE EVIDENCE FOR EVOLUTION THERE?

There are benefits and limitations to any approach, and examining the fossil record can help us tremendously in tracing the course of how life unfolded on Earth. We must accept that in the vast majority of cases, the fossil record preserves only the hard tissues of organisms—things like shells, bones, and teeth. We lose a large amount of biological information through the process of fossilization, and this means that we cannot investigate ancient creatures with anywhere near the precision that we can examine modern species. We cannot take blood samples, and only rarely is usable DNA present. This means that right at the beginning, we have a limited knowledge about the overall organism—no question, a problem.

Figure 5.23: Spider trapped in amber.

However, what the fossil record does provide us is a wonderful (yet undoubtedly incomplete) snapshot of a family's journey through time. It allows us to answer, at least in part, how a zebra became a zebra. The fossil record allows us to trace the phylogeny, or evolutionary history, of a lineage over long periods of time. We can actually view the accumulation of different biological traits over millions of years, and correlate this with a diverse range of environmental information (ancient climate, botany, geology, etc.) to reconstruct not only the organism's information, but also the ecological niche in which it lived. The problem is that fossils are rare events. This is not surprising, in that organic remains had to survive millions of years of climatic and geological processes to be uncovered by humans. Paleontologists are unsung heroes. They are out there with their tools in pelting rain, intense heat, and brutal winds to uncover often minute traces of ancient life (kind of like archaeologists). But each tiny piece that is recovered adds another crucial piece of the puzzle, which will lead to the reconstruction of ancient organisms and conditions on Earth.

On rare occasions, ancient life is preserved in amber. Amber is ancient tree resin that has changed from a liquid to a solid state. The oldest amber retrieved dates to the Upper Carboniferous period, roughly 320 million years ago (Bray and Anderson 2009, Grimaldi 2009). Amber sometimes contains animals or plant material that became caught in the resin in its liquid form. A variety of insects, worms, frogs, spiders and evidence of their webs, crustaceans, as well as tiny beings like amoeba and bacteria (not surprisingly, bacteria were some of Earth's first living inhabitants) are preserved in amber. In addition, ancient amber as old as 130 million years has preserved evidence of marine microfossils, wood cells, feathers, hair, plant material like flowers and fruit, and a myriad of other ancient creatures (Poinar and Cannatella 1987, Waggoner 1996, Girard et al. 2008, Grimaldi 2009). It was reported in August 2012 that contained within 230-million-year-old amber from northern Italy were two tiny mites, representing the oldest organisms

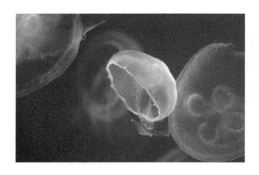

Figure 5.24: Jellyfish.

ever preserved in the material (Kaufman 2012). On rare occasions as well, the remains of soft-bodied organisms or features like jellyfish, feathers, or sharks are preserved.

Another great source of evidence for life in the distant past is coprolites, lovely pieces of preserved poop. At first thought, many would wonder why anyone would ever dream of studying ancient poop (people actually do PhD work on this topic). However, it can provide amazing insight into creatures and environments in the past. Contained within feces are tiny pieces of other animal and plant species, which not only can help to reconstruct past living beings and identify parasitic organisms, but also help us to understand the diversity of organisms through time and space.

Figure 5.25: *Kelaeno Scutellaris Muensterella*—squid fossil.

One of the arguments that opponents of evolution use is the fact that there are gaps in the fossil record. They argue that if evolution is true, then there should be a seamless and continuous stream of one form into another without any interruptions. When one looks at all the factors that contribute to fossils being created—from the death of the organism to its discovery potentially millions of years later by an observer—what is truly amazing is the amount of material that we do have. It is a surprisingly destructive process where biological processes like bacteria, carnivores, and insects are the first line of attack, and geological processes like tectonic activity, wind and water action, and exposure to sunlight become the great destructors later on. Only a very small percentage of all organisms will have their remains fossilized, and of those that do, only a fraction will be discovered by humans. Despite this small window we are peering through, we have actually been able to discover a startling amount about the 4.6-billion-year history of our planet.

HOW DO WE KNOW HOW OLD ANYTHING IS? DATING THE UNKNOWN

Prior to the middle of the 20th century, scientists who investigated the distant past had a huge problem: they could not accurately date anything. From the time of Cuvier in the 18th century, scholars recognized the progressive nature of the fossil record. It was obvious that different organisms were found in different layers. These layers were on top of each other, and organisms appeared to become more complex and sophisticated over time, rather than less. However, there were no techniques available to provide accurate dates for either rock layers or the fossils contained within them. How then did scientists begin to form conclusions about the Earth's history in any meaningful way? Sedimentary rock is formed by small particles that are carried by forces like wind, water, and ice and deposited in layers. Each layer is called a stratum; thus, the study of rock layers is called stratigraphy.

Before the 1950s, scholars used methods of relative dating to try and reconstruct the complex geological record. Relative dating was principally based upon the **Law of Superposition**. This law states that in undisturbed sedimentary rock, the oldest layers are at the bottom, and the layers become younger as one moves up toward the surface. It does not allow you to say that Layer B is ten million years old. It only lets you say

Figure 5.26: Law of Superposition—stratigraphic sequence.

that Layer B is older than Layer A and younger than Layer C. This allows you to organize the layers into a general sequence, and then compare those sequences in different geographic areas. The information gathered from the law of superposition was added to information from other developing areas like an examination of indicator fossils or faunal/floral succession. **Indicator fossils** are the fossils of a particular species that lived for a short span of time. They are found in a specific layer, often in geographic areas that are thousands of miles apart. For example, the species *Anadara devincta*, the most common marine fossil in Oregon and resembling the modern cockle, is a worldwide indicator fossil for the Miocene epoch. Indicator fossils assist geologists in establishing which strata are of similar age in different geological areas, and they allow geologists to establish a general geological timetable for a variety of regions around the world. This timetable was established by the early 1840s, roughly 20 years before Darwin published *On the Origin of Species*.

A further advance in geology resulted from the work of William Smith, who was an English surveyor and amateur geologist. Throughout his career as a surveyor, he had had the opportunity to examine stratigraphic sequences in a wide range of different English locations. This understanding of the geology of England allowed Smith to make a few really important observations. First, he noticed that different fossils were associated with different rock layers. Next, he saw that the sequence was the same throughout England. These observations led him to the idea of **faunal** (animal) and **floral** (plant) succession. Smith pointed out that fossils, as well as strata, proceed in a pattern that is consistent and observable. He argued that one could use fossils to establish the order of rock layers in a stratigraphic sequence, and this allowed him to create a complete geologic map of England. This idea of faunal/floral succession assisted geologists internationally in organizing fossils and rock layers into their relative temporal order. Faunal correlation is also a very useful tool. It allows you to get an age for undated species because of their association with fossils of known age. For example, if you know that a particular species of horse lived between 2 and 2.5 million years ago, then if you find other fossils in the same layer as those of the horse species, you can establish that they are likely of the same date.

The way that we humans understood the antiquity of the Earth was revolutionized in the 1950s with the development of radiometric dating (also called absolute or chronometric dating) techniques. **Radiometric dating** works like this: All rocks contain minerals, and many minerals contain a radiometric isotope of an element (such as carbon, uranium, potassium, etc.). This radiometric isotope acts like a kind of natural clock because it is unstable and deteriorates over time at a predictable rate that is not affected by environmental forces. This last point is very important, because if the rate of decay sped up or slowed down over time, this would be a useless endeavor. The radioisotope breaks down into a stable isotope called the disintegration product. There are several different radiometric techniques, depending upon what material you wish to date and the general antiquity of the material. In order to use radiometric dating as a natural clock, you must be able to provide three things. First, you have to be able to accurately measure how much radiometric material remains in the sample. Secondly, you must be able to accurately measure the amount of disintegration product that is present in the sample. Lastly, you must know the half-life of the isotope that you are using. The half-life is the amount of time that it takes for half of the radioactive isotopes to disintegrate. It varies widely, depending on the radioisotope used—carbon 14 has a half-life of 5,730 years, whereas potassium 40 has a half-life of 1.25 billion years, and uranium 238 a half-life of 4.5 billion years. If you know these three things, you can calculate back in time to the period when the organism was alive or the rock was formed. Archaeologists most often use radiocarbon 14 dating because it is used to date only organic remains

Figure 5.27: English Geologist William Smith (1769–1839), portrait by French painter Hugues Fourau (1803–1873).

(organisms that were once alive). Thus, we cannot use radiocarbon to date ceramics, stone tools, or rock layers. The limitation to radiocarbon dating is that it only allows you to date material that is younger than roughly 50,000 years. After that, there is simply too little of the radioactive isotope left to measure with precision. This means that ancient life must be dated indirectly, often by other means. Just like the law of superposition presents limitations in that it can only be applied to undisturbed sedimentary rock and does not provide an accurate age for samples, so radiometric techniques have limitations. Among them, the techniques are extremely expensive to generate and require very well-trained scholars with very expensive dating equipment. Additionally, radiometric dating can really only be applied to igneous rocks (ones that

have cooled from a molten state, i.e., volcanic rock). Although we typically do not recover fossils from volcanic lenses, they are often found sandwiched between volcanic layers, which allows the fossil to be dated.

Thus, we can finally answer a question that has plagued humans for countless generations: How old is the Earth, really? In order to achieve our modern understanding of the antiquity of the planet, thousands of radiometric dates have been provided by labs all over the globe. As a result, we now know that the Earth and the moon are roughly 4.5 billion years old. This is a major leap from Reverend Ussher's calculation of 4004 BC, and even would have shocked Charles Lyell. When do we see the first life forms appear? As discussed in an

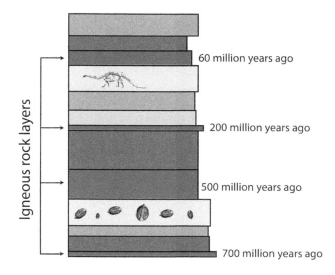

Figure 5.28: Law of Superposition.

EON	ERA	PERIOD		EPOCH		Ma
Phanerozoic	Cenozoic	Quaternary		Holocene		0.011 –
				Pleistocene	Late	0.8 –
					Early	2.4 –
		Tertiary	Neogene	Pliocene	Late	3.6 –
					Early	5.3 –
				Miocene	Late	11.2 –
					Middle	16.4 –
					Early	23.0 –
			Paleogene	Oligocene	Late	28.5 –
					Early	34.0 –
				Eocene	Late	41.3 –
					Middle	49.0 –
					Early	55.8 –
				Paleocene	Late	61.0 –
					Early	65.5 –
	Mesozoic	Cretaceous		Late		99.6 –
				Early		145 –
		Jurassic		Late		161 –
				Middle		176 –
				Early		200 –
		Triassic		Late		228 –
				Middle		245 –
				Early		251 –
	Paleozoic	Permian		Late		260 –
				Middle		271 –
				Early		299 –
		Pennsylvanian		Late		306 –
				Middle		311 –
				Early		318 –
		Mississippian		Late		326 –
				Middle		345 –
				Early		359 –
		Devonian		Late		385 –
				Middle		397 –
				Early		416 –
		Silurian		Late		419 –
				Early		423 –
		Ordovician		Late		428 –
				Middle		444 –
				Early		488 –
		Cambrian		Late		501 –
				Middle		513 –
				Early		542 –
Precambrian	Proterozoic	Late		Neoproterozoic (Z)		1000 –
		Middle		Mesoproterozoic (Y)		1600 –
		Early		Paleoproterozoic (X)		2500 –
	Archean	Late				3200 –
		Early				4000 –
	Hadean					

Figure 5.29: Geological time scale.

earlier chapter, the first evidence of life on this planet appears about 3.5 billion years ago in the form of bacteria and blue/green algae. There are rare fossils from the Precambrian period (4.5 billion to 543 million years ago), and we are lucky to have any at all, given that many organisms were soft-bodied; plus, the geological record has been through considerable upheaval. However, with the commencement of the Cambrian period around 570 million years ago, we see a significant increase in the numbers of fossils recovered.

We also are fortunate to have a substantial number of invertebrate fossils like jellyfish and sponges. The first vertebrates to appear were primitive fish called ostracoderms, and they appear in the Late Cambrian period around 500 million years ago. The first corals appear soon after during the Ordovician period. The first placoderms (fish with jaws) appear in the Silurian period (roughly 438 million years ago), and this is also the time we see the appearance of the first land plants and insects. Amphibians and the first vascular plants like ferns and mosses appear around 408 million years ago in the Devonian. Reptiles make their first appearance in the Carboniferous period roughly 320 million years ago. The Mesozoic period spans from roughly 248 to 65 million years ago, and is associated with three periods: the Triassic (248–208 million years ago, or mya), the Jurassic (208–144 mya), and the Cretaceous (144–65 mya). The Mesozoic (middle animal age) is associated with the rise of the mammals (Triassic) and the appearance of birds (Jurassic), but it is usually seen as the age of reptiles, as the dinosaurs dominated the Earth at this time. Interestingly, the earliest flowering plants also occur during the Cretaceous. The Cretaceous-Tertiary (K-T) Boundary roughly 65 million years ago marks an era of mass extinction where we see the disappearance of the dinosaurs and the rise of the mammals. This boundary marks a period of very dramatic change in the distribution of life forms on this planet.

The recent age of animals, the Cenozoic, covers the period between 65 million years ago and the present. It is divided into main periods, the Tertiary and Quaternary. The Tertiary period spans from 65 to 2.5 million years ago and is further divided into five epochs: the Paleocene (65–54.8 mya), the Eocene (54.8–33.7 mya), the Oligocene (33.7–23.8 mya), the Miocene (23.8–5.3 mya), and the first portion of the Pliocene (5.3–2.5 mya). The Tertiary-Quaternary boundary marks the beginning of glacial activity in the Northern Hemisphere, a situation that had a profound impact upon living species of the time. Large mam-

mals, including the first primates, appear around 65 million years ago during the Paleocene epoch. The earliest grasses (which would much later become the staple of the modern human diet) emerge in the Eocene epoch. The Quaternary period spans from 2.5 million years ago to the present and is divided into three epochs: the Pliocene (2.5–1.8 mya), the Pleistocene (1.8 mya to 10,000 years ago), and the Holocene (10,000 years ago to the present). Primates first appear in the Paleocene, and are widespread by the time of the Oligocene epoch roughly 38 million years ago (Berra 1990, Stanford et al. 2013, Merriam-Webster 1998).

Figure 5.30: Earth from satellite.

When we consider how amazingly old the planet is, it places in perspective what a young species we are, emerging only in the last 200,000 years.

TRANSITIONAL FOSSILS: DESCENT WITH MODIFICATION

Remember that Charles Darwin's perception of evolution is a gradual accumulation of biological differences over very long periods of time. Thus, transitional fossils should be abundant in the fossil record, and these would beautifully illustrate what Darwin called descent with modification. There are many examples of transitional fossils around the world. Perhaps the most famous of these is *Archaeopteryx*, a transitional fossil between reptiles and birds and dating to the Jurassic period about 150 million years

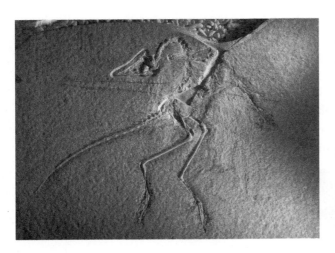

Figure 5.31: *Archaeolpteryx.*

ago. Multiple examples of this species have been discovered in Bavarian limestone deposits. *Archaeopteryx* is characterized by biological features that are reptilian and avian (bird). It has three claws on the front of its wings, reptilian teeth in the jaw, a long bony tail, and abdominal ribs that are reptilian in structure. However, *Archaeopteryx* also had feathers, an avian pelvis, and a furcula (wishbone)—all decidedly birdlike traits. It is impossible for us to say whether this form was actually ancestral to modern birds, but it certainly represents a stop on the evolution of birds from reptilian ancestors. This also beautifully illustrates the process of evolution in action, and forcefully argues for Darwin's idea of descent with modification.

Another good example of transitional fossils can be viewed through the evolution of the horse, the *Equidae.* The horse family represents the most complete series of fossils for any animal lineage and is therefore a wonderful representation of evolution in action. Although horses went extinct in the Americas in more recent geological time, they actually first emerged in North America roughly 54 million years ago. However, the earliest member of the horse family would not be recognizable as such to humans. This early form, called *Hyracotherium,* was a very small, forest-dwelling creature, with multiple toes and simple cusp patterns on the teeth designed to eat soft vegetation. The Miocene period sees an explosion of different horse species emerging. However, we begin to see a change in a number of features, as the family adapts to a much drier and cooler climate. Forests are being replaced by large, open grasslands, and it is during this middle period of the horse family's evolution (with species like *Mesohippus*) that we see a substantial increase in body size and the development of teeth with complex enamel ridges and high crowns, indicating a diet of tough grasses. Of the three toes present, the lateral toes are beginning to fuse to the body of the foot, as we see the beginning of the hoof developing. With the modern horse, Equus, we see a creature that is large with long limbs, a single toe (the hoof), and teeth well designed for masticating hard-to-chew grasses. Naturally, the million-dollar-question is, Why did the horse family transform from a small, forest-dwelling, leaf-eating creature to a very large, grass-eating creature? As the environment of North America became cooler and drier, there was a replacement of more tropical forests with large, open grasslands (think of the American Plains today). Horses are herbivores, and because they are not predators at the top of the food chain, they had to adapt to living in an environment where they are a great deal more visible. Thus, speed and size became ever important features in this new environment. Longer limbs, the adaptation of the hoof, and a dramatic increase in size allowed the horse not only to make smaller predators think twice about eating them, but also greatly increased their speed, and hence ability to evade a predator. The success of this family is demonstrated by the fact that during the Pleistocene, they dispersed through North and South America and into Africa (where we finally get our zebra developing) and Eurasia. For reasons unknown, they become extinct in the Americas at the end of the Pleistocene, and this may have resulted from significant climate change and perhaps human predation as well. Fortunately, horses had moved across the land bridge into the Old World prior to this time, and there would not be any further hooves on North American soil until Columbus brought horses with him on his second voyage to the New World. We now have thousands of fossils for the horse family from five continents spanning the last 54 million years. This transformation illustrates beautifully the adaptation to an altering

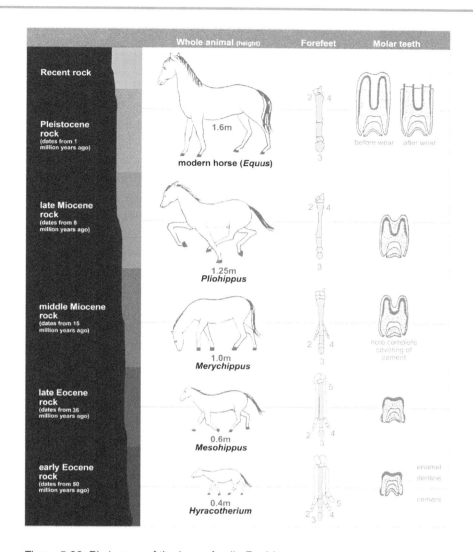

Figure 5.32: Phylogeny of the horse family *Equidae*.

environment over long periods of time, and clearly demonstrates that the process of evolution is ongoing (Berra 1990).

SLOW AND STEADY OR SPEEDING UP AND SLOWING DOWN: MAKE UP YOUR MIND

One of the important questions to ask when one looks at the development of life on Earth is, What is the tempo of evolution? Does it always occur at the same pace, or does it speed up and slow down sometimes, or both? Charles Darwin's perception of the tempo of evolution was one of gradualism. The notion of gradualism states that there will be a gradual accumulation of biological differences over very long periods of time. Evolution unfolds at a gradual, consistent rate. Clearly, there are many instances in the fossil record that demonstrate a gradual transition from one form to another; this idea of **gradualism** has dominated the

Figure 5.33: Early mammal, *Gobiconodon* sp. from the early to mid Cretaceous (Museum of Texas Tech University).

general perception of the pace of evolutionary change since Darwin proposed it. But in recent years, some scholars have noted that the pace of evolution can accelerate sometimes, particularly in small populations. This typically occurs when a population inhabits a new environment (think of the finches), or when there is environmental change (think of the onset of an Ice Age). In these instances, populations must face new environmental stresses and challenges, but if they succeed, we often see the emergence of new species (what is called a speciation event). This idea is called **punctuated equilibrium**, and it is defined by long periods (millions of years) of stasis associated with very little change, punctuated (interrupted) by brief periods (maybe tens of thousands of years) of rapid change typically associated with the emergence of a new species (Eldredge and Gould 1972). Thus, if we look at the horse family again, every species existed for long periods of time (millions of years) with very little change, and then there was a brief time (perhaps tens of thousands of years) of rapid evolutionary change, followed by the appearance of a new species of horse. Once the new species appears, there is a return to a long period of stasis. Thus, proponents of punctuated equilibrium argue that when an old species disappears in the fossil record and a new species emerges, it is an indication of a speciation event. However, Richard Dawkins (1986) points out that one must be cautious with this interpretation; as it may also be explained by migration of an already existing species into a new environment, where the new species is able to out-compete the old.

MASS EXTINCTION: BRACE YOURSELF

In the 1600s, humans became well aware that extinction was a reality when they witnessed the extinction of the dodo on the island of Mauritius. What became clear was that many organisms are not able to adapt to changing environments, and as a result are driven to extinction. How do we explain these extinctions in the fossil record? A large amount of the evidence for mass extinction has been retrieved from cores from polar ice caps and the bottom of the oceans.

A tremendous amount of multidisciplinary work is being conducted on the topic of mass extinction. There is no question that the majority of the work has concentrated on the Cretaceous-Tertiary boundary extinction event approximately 65 million years ago. It is at this time that we see the decline and eventual extinction of the dinosaurs, and subsequently the rise of the mammals. Much research focuses upon the extinction of the dinosaurs, and there is certainly not a simple explanation for this event. Apparently, multiple interrelating factors came into play to lead to small declines in number in every generation. We know that at the end of the Mesozoic Era (and the beginning of the Cenozoic), drastic environmental changes led to a much cooler and drier global climate. There has been great debate concerning the factors that led to the extinction of the dinosaurs. Some suggest that dramatic climatic events led to substantial changes in temperature, either making it too hot or too cold for dinosaurs to adapt. Reptiles are ectothermic (a poikilotherm), in that they regulate their body temperature largely by exchanging heat with their surroundings. That is why they bask in the sun to warm up. Mammals are homeothermic, meaning we are capable of maintaining a constant body temperature, despite large fluctuations in outside environmental temperatures. This means that mammals have considerably more flexibility in terms of temperature parameters than reptiles do. Some scholars suggest that large meteors struck the Earth, leading to devastating environmental changes (Alvarez et al. 1980). This focuses on the impact of a large meteor that struck the Earth, causing a large amount of particulates to be released into the atmosphere, blocking out the sun, and leading to the eventual extinction of plant and animal forms. Evidence of this extraterrestrial impact is found at a giant crater in Mexico called Chicxulub in the Yucatán Peninsula. It is likely that in addition to the release of this enormous dust cloud, there would also have been a fairly significant reduction in overall global temperature. During the last 15 million years of the Cretaceous, there was a substantial decrease in global temperature and a dropping of sea level, in addition to dramatic volcanic events. This would have led to an increase in seasonality, with a considerable negative impact upon plant species (Hallam 1987). The dramatic shift in local ecosystems and available food favored newly evolved mammalian herbivores—at the expense of the large, terrestrial dinosaurs.

Recent research indicates that there may be a cyclical pattern to some mass extinctions, with events occurring roughly every 26 million years, the result of episodic showers of comets. This assertion is based on an analysis of deep-sea cores containing hundreds of fossils of different marine families (Berra 1990). It is important to point out that not all mass extinctions adhere to this 26-million-year cycle. Other factors that may have contributed to the elimination of the dinosaurs is the evolution of poisonous plants, mammals feeding upon dinosaur eggs, or epidemic disease events.

Figure 5.34: Extinction of the dinosaurs.

Figure 5.35: Meteor.

It is also important to note that mass extinctions do not occur rapidly. For example, data from western North America suggests that the extinction of the dinosaurs here took at least seven million years to occur, and the final extinction occurred roughly 40,000 years after the supposed asteroid impact (Sloan and Keith Rigby Jr. 1986). This implies that there must have been multiple contributing factors that led to the decline and disappearance of the dinosaurs, not just an extraterrestrial impact. Mass extinctions are very important to evolution. They vacate environments, thus allowing surviving species to take advantage of new opportunities. For instance, the extinction of the dinosaurs allowed the rise of the mammals. When the dinosaurs were present, mammals were really regulated to marginal environments, as they simply could not compete with the larger reptiles. Mass extinctions are often associated with an explosion of new species, and so they really promote evolution. The extinction of the dinosaurs and the rise of the mammals was a crucial boost for us. Otherwise, the present picture might have looked very different!

CRITICAL REASONING QUESTIONS

- What is natural selection? What features might be selected for in a carnivore that lives in an open savanna environment versus a marine predator? How does environment shape the organisms that exist within it?
- Who is more fit in evolutionary terms, Mel Gibson or Leonardo di Caprio? Why?
- Are dogs simply socialized wolves? What biological and behavioral features define the domestic dog? What features benefit their interactions with humans?
- What types of morphological features indicate common ancestry? What is the difference between parallel and convergent evolution? Give examples.
- Why are vestigial organs wonderful indicators of ancestral history?
- Define three ways that we can find evidence of evolution from modern living organisms. Now define three types of information retrieved from the fossil record.
- How old is the Earth, and when does life first emerge on it?
- What is the pace of evolution? Discuss the differences between gradualism and punctuated equilibrium.
- Mass extinctions are very important events in terms of evolution. Why?

REFERENCES AND SUGGESTED READINGS

Alvarez, L. W., W. Alvarez, F. Asaro, and H. V. Michel (1980). "Extraterrestrial cause for the Cretaceous-Tertiary extinction." *Science* 208:1095–1108.

Ayala, F. J. (2007). *Darwin's gift to science and religion.* Washington, DC: Joseph Henry Press.

Berra, T. (1990). *Evolution and the myth of creationism. A basic guide to the facts in the evolution debate.* Stanford, CA: Stanford University Press.

Bray, P. S., and K. B. Anderson (2009). "Identification of carboniferous (320 million years old) class ice amber." *Science* 326 (5949):132–134.

Browne, J. (1995). *Charles Darwin: Voyaging* (Volume 1 of a biography in two volumes). New York: Alfred A. Knopf.

———— (1995). *Charles Darwin: The power of place* (Volume 2 of a biography in two volumes). New York: Alfred A. Knopf.

Charig, A. J., F. Greenaway, A. C. Milner, et al. (1986). "Archaeopteryx is not a forgery." *Science* 232:622–626.

Coyne, J. A. (2009). *Why evolution is true.* Oxford, UK: Oxford University Press.

Crockford, S. J., and Y. V. Kuzmin (2012). Comments on Germonpré et al., *Journal of Archaeological Science* 36, 2009: "Fossil dogs and wolves from Palaeolithic sites in Belgium, the Ukraine and Russia: Osteometry, ancient DNA and stable isotopes." Germonpré, Laznickova-Galetova, and Sablin (2012). "Palaeolithic dog skulls at the Gravettian Predmosti site, the Czech Republic." *Journal of Archaeological Science* 39: 2797–2801.

Crowley, T. J., and G. R. North (May 1988). "Abrupt climate change and extinction events in Earth history." *Science* 240(4855):996–1002.

Dawkins, R. (1986). *The blind watchmaker.* New York: Norton & Company.

Demére, T., M. McGowen, A. Berta, and J. Gatesy (2008). "Morphological and molecular evidence for a stepwise evolutionary transition from teeth to baleen in mysticete whales." *Systematic Biology* 57 (1):15–37.

Demére, T. A., A. Berta, and M. R. McGowen (2005). "The taxonomic and evolutionary history of fossil and modern balaenopteroid mysticetes." *Journal of Mammalian Evolution* 12 (1/2):99–143.

Desmond, A., and J. Moore (1991). *Darwin.* New York: Warner Books.

Eldredge, N., and S. J. Gould (1972). "Punctuated equilibria: An alternative to phyletic gradualism. In T. J. M. Schopf, ed. *Models in paleobiology,* pp. 82–115. San Francisco: Freeman Cooper and Company.

Eldredge, N., and I. Tattersall (1982). *The myths of human evolution.* New York: Columbia University Press.

Estes, G., T. Grant, and P. Grant (2000). "Darwin in the Galapagos. His footsteps through the archipelago." *Notes and Records of the Royal Society* 54:343–368.

Germonpré, M., M. V. Sablin, R. E. Stevens, et al. (2009). "Fossil dogs and wolves from Palaeolithic sites in Belgium, the Ukraine and Russia: Osteometry, ancient DNA and stable isotopes." *Journal of Archaeological Science* 36:473–490.

Germonpré, M., M. Laznickova-Galetova, and M. V. Sablin (2012). Palaeolithic dog skulls at the Gravettian Predmosti site, the Czech Republic. *Journal of Archaeological Science* 39:184–202.

Germonpré, M., M. V. Sablin, V. Despres, et al. (2013). Palaeolithic dogs and the early domestication of the wolf: A reply to the comments of Crockford and Kuzmin (2012). *Journal of Archaeological Science* 40:786–792.

Gingerich, P. D., B. H. Smith, and E. L. Simons (1990). "Hind limbs of Eocene *Basilosaurus*: Evidence of feet in whales." *Science* 249:154–157.

Girard, V., A. Schmidt, S. Saint Martin, et al. (2008). "Evidence for marine microfossils from amber." *Proceedings of the National Academy of Sciences of the United States of America* 105 (45):17426–17429.

Gould, S. J. (1985). "Darwin at sea—and the virtues of port." In S. J. Gould, *The Flamingo's Smile. Reflections in Natural History,* pp. 347–359. New York: W. W. Norton.

———— (1993). *Eight little piggies: Reflections in natural history.* New York: W. W. Norton & Company.

Grimaldi, D. (2009). "Pushing back amber production." *Science* 326 (5949):51–2.

Hallam, A. (November 1987). "End-Cretaceous mass extinction event: Argument for terrestrial causation." *Science* 238(4831):1237–1242.

Harris, M. P., S. M. Hasso, M. W. J. Ferguson, and J. F. Fallon (2006). "The development of archosaurian first-generation teeth in a chicken mutant." *Current Biology* 16(4):371–377.

Kaufman, Rachel (28 August 2012). "Goldbugs." *National Geographic.*

Keynes, R. (2001). *Annie's box: Charles Darwin, his daughter and human evolution.* London: Fourth Estate (HarperCollins).

Koler-Matznick, J. (2002). "The origin of the dog revisited." *Anthrozoös* 15 (2):98–118.

Kukekova, Anna V., L. N. Trut, K. Chase, et al. (2007). "Measurement of segregating behaviors in experimental silver fox pedigrees." *Behavior Genetics* 38 (2):185–194.

Larson, G., E. K. Karlsson, A. Perri, et al. (2012). Rethinking dog domestication by integrating genetics, archeology, and biogeography. *Proceedings of the National Academy of Sciences USA* 109:8878–8883.

Lewin, R. (2004). *Human evolution: An illustrated introduction,* 5th ed. New York: Wiley-Blackwell.

Lindberg, Julia, Susanne Björnerfeldt, Peter Saetre, et al. (2005). "Selection for tameness has changed brain gene expression in silver foxes." *Current Biology* 15 (22):R915–R916.

Lord, K. (2013). "A comparison of the sensory development of wolves (*Canis lupus lupus*) and dogs (*Canis lupus familiaris*)." *Ethology* vol. 119(2):110–120.

Mayr, E. (1942). *Systematics and the origin of species.* New York: Columbia University Press.

——— (1997). *What is biology?* Cambridge, MA: Harvard University Press.

Mish, F. C., ed. in chief (1998). *Merriam Webster's Collegiate Dictionary,* 10th ed. Springfield, MA: Merriam-Webster, Inc.

Péter, A., Á. Miklósi, and P. Pongrácz (2013). "Domestic dogs' (*Canis familiaris*) understanding of projected video images of a human demonstrator in an object-choice task." *Ethology* 119:1–9.

Poinar Jr., G. O., and D. C. Cannatella (Sept. 1987). "An Upper Eocene frog from the Dominican Republic and its implication for Caribbean biogeography." *Science* 237(4819):1215–1216.

Pongrácz, P., Á. Miklósi, Cs. Molnár, and V. Csányi (2005). Human listeners are able to classify dog barks recorded in different situations. *Journal of Comparative Psychology* 119:136–144.

Ratliff, Evan (March 2011). "Animal domestication: Taming the wild." *National Geographic.*

Savolainen, P., Y. Zhang, L. Jing, et al. (November 2002). "Genetic evidence for an East Asian origin of domestic dogs." *Science* 298 (5598):1610–1613.

Schluter, D., E. A. Clifford, M. Nemethy, and J. S. McKinnon (2004). "Parallel evolution and inheritance of quantitative traits." *American Naturalist* 163:809–822.

Scott, J. P., and J. L. Fuller (1974). *Dog behavior: The genetic basis,* 2nd ed., illustrated. Chicago: University of Chicago Press.

Serpell, J. (1995). *The domestic dog: Its evolution, behaviour, and interactions with people.* Cambridge, UK: Cambridge University Press.

Sloan, R. E., and J. Keith Rigby Jr. (December 1986). "Response: Cretaceous-Tertiary dinosaur extinction." *Science* 234(4781):1173–1175.

Stanford, C., J. S. Allen, and S. C. Antón (2013). *Exploring biological anthropology,* 3rd ed. New York: Pearson.

Tchernov, E., O. Rieppel, H. Zaher, et al. (2000). "A fossil snake with limbs." *Science* 287:2010–2012.

Topál, J., M. Gácsi, Á. Miklósi, et al. (2005). Attachment to humans: A comparative study on hand-reared wolves and differently socialized dog puppies. *Animal Behaviour* 70:1367–1375.

Trut, Lyudmila (1999). "Early canid domestication: The farm-fox experiment." *American Scientist* 87(2):160.

Vas, J., J. Topál, M. Gácsi, et al. (2005). A friend or an enemy? Dogs' reaction to an unfamiliar person showing behavioural cues of threat and friendliness at different times. *Applied Animal Behaviour Science* 94:99–115.

Vila, C., P. Savolainen, J. E. Maldonado, et al. (1997). "Multiple and ancient origins of the domestic dog." *Science* 276:1687–1689.

von Holdt, B., et al. (2010). "Genome-wide SNP and haplotype analyses reveal a rich history underlying dog domestication." *Nature* 464 (7290):898–902.

Waggoner, B. M. (July 1996). "Bacteria and protists from Middle Cretaceous amber of Ellsworth County, Kansas." *PaleoBios* 17 (1):20–26.

Wallace, D. R. (2007). *Neptune's ark: From ichthyosaurs to orcas.* Berkeley: University of California Press.

6

The Primates

By Roman Gastrell Harrison

The primates include humans, the various species of apes (for example, chimpanzees and gorillas), monkeys (baboons and macaques, for instance), and prosimians
(for example, lemurs and lorises). Primatology is the study of the nonhuman primates.
This chapter will discuss the primary environment to which primates have adapted,
features used to define whether a particular animal species is a primate or not, the
classification of the primates, and characteristics associated with the various different
types of primates.

In the present day, nonhuman primates are found in most tropical regions of both
the Old and New worlds. Some species have a wider distribution and are found not
only in tropical regions of the world, but also some temperate zones. These regions
include sub-Saharan Africa, Gibraltar in Europe, the Indian subcontinent, Southeast
Asia, southern China, Japan, the northern part of South America, and Central America
(Figure 6.1). In the past, nonhuman primates had a wider distribution, including
both tropical and temperate regions of the world, encompassing all of Africa, southern
Europe, the Middle East, the Indian subcontinent, Southeast Asia, southern China,
Japan, all of South America, Central America, and the western portion of the United
States in North America.

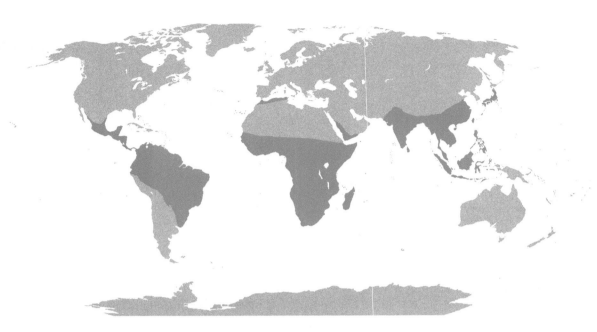

Figure 6.1: Present-day worldwide range of non-human primates.

WHAT IS A PRIMATE?

The earliest true primate species first evolved toward the end of the Paleocene epoch, approximately 55 to 60 million years ago. Just prior to this period of time, the dinosaurs became extinct, and the first fruit-bearing plants evolved. Many fruit-bearing plants are trees. This created a new ecological niche: forested areas containing trees that bore fruit. Early primates evolved to take advantage of this new type of food found in forested areas. Accessing fruit requires primates to spend a considerable amount of time moving between branches and trees above the ground. The environment in a forest up in the trees is called an arboreal environment. Many primate traits are adaptations to life up in trees, so as to be able to move effectively in the environment where fruit is found. Fruit is a major food source for most primate species.

The majority of modern primate species are found in forested areas. However, some primate species (including humans) have adapted to life on the ground, and can be found in woodland environments (regions with both treed areas and grassland areas) such as east Africa.

Primates are distinguished from other animal species by several features. Some of the features are exclusive to the primates (in other words, found in all primate species, and not found in any non-primate species), while other features are not exclusive to the primates, and may be found in some non-primate species. One feature is a tendency toward an erect posture. The trunk of the body is more frequently in a vertical position. For example, when a primate jumps from one branch to another between trees, as they fly through the air, the trunk of the body is more vertical than horizontal.

Another feature exclusive to primates is increased flexibility of the limbs, particularly the upper limb, which can be rotated 360°. This is an evolutionary adaptation to the arboreal environment. Effective movement between branches up in the trees requires enhanced flexibility of the upper limb in particular, in order to facilitate the grasping of branches above, below, behind, and in front of the individual, to prevent the individual from falling to the ground.

All primate species have evolved prehensility, or the ability to grasp objects. This is the ability to oppose the thumb to the other fingers and oppose the big toe to the other toes. All primate species have prehensile thumbs, and all primate species—with the exception of humans—have some degree of prehensility of the big toe. Grasping ability is important when moving in trees high above the ground. Primates have retained the primitive mammal trait of five digits on hands and feet and have enhanced tactile pads at the ends of their digits, in order to more effectively ensure a solid grip on branches. Primates also use these tactile pads as one way to tell whether fruit is ripe and hence edible. All primate species have nails instead of claws. While most species have nails at the ends of all of their digits, some species have one claw on each of their index fingers.

Another characteristic of the primates is a generalized, omnivorous diet, with fruit the most commonly consumed type of food. However, there is considerable variation in diet between different primate species. Some species eat almost exclusively fruit. In other species, fruit comprises the largest portion of the diet, but also includes other plant foods such as leaves, nuts, seeds, and roots. A few primate species, for example, chimpanzees, incorporate meat into their diet. Other species include insects or tree gum in their diet. While most primate species incorporate significant amounts of fruit into their diet, there are some exceptions. A few of the monkey species eat almost exclusively leaves. In order to be able to consume and process a wide variety of foods, primates have retained all four types of teeth (incisors, canines, premolars, and molars), and have no emphasis on one type of tooth over another.

Most primate species have color vision, which enhances their ability to distinguish between branches and other objects in the complex arboreal environment. Color vision is another way that primates distinguish whether a particular piece of fruit is ripe. A certain color is associated with ripe, and hence edible, fruit. All primate species have stereoscopic vision, which permits increased depth perception. Stereoscopic vision is achieved by having eyes that face frontward on the face, which increases the overlap between each eye's field of view. Enhanced depth perception is important when navigating the arboreal environment high above the ground.

In general, primates have a relatively poor sense of smell. Smell is less important in the arboreal environment as compared to life on the ground. However, primates do use smell as another method for telling whether fruit is ripe. A ripe piece of fruit has a particular odor associated with it.

All of the primates have a larger brain size in proportion to overall body size than all other animal species. Brain/body size is not constant for all primate species, but increases from the earliest to the latest evolving species. The prosimians have the smallest brain/body size among the primates, monkeys somewhat larger, apes larger still, and humans have the largest brain/body size. Intelligence is poorly correlated to brain size alone. Instead, there is a good correlation between intelligence and the proportion of brain/body size. For example, although elephants have larger brains when compared with humans, humans have a larger brain/body size. A primate's larger brain/body size and increased intelligence permit a greater range of behavior and increased flexibility of behavior (discussed in greater detail in Chapter 7). All primate species have a greater component of flexible, learned behavior in relation to instinctual, or hard-wired, behavior.

Most primate species have a tendency to single births, with an increased period of time of infant dependency. As a result, there is enhanced learning by offspring from their parents, more so from their mother. Most primate species live in social groups, where all individuals within the group have conscious knowledge of the relationship between themselves and all other group members. Primates are able to distinguish the degree of kin relationship between themselves and others in the group; for example, between cousins and siblings and between aunts and uncles and grandparents. Primates are also consciously aware of their own rank in the group's dominance hierarchy relative to other group members' rank (also discussed in greater detail in Chapter 7). A final feature of the primates is that most species are diurnal (active during the day, sleeping at night), whereas only a few species are nocturnal (sleeping during the day, active at night).

COPYRIGHTED MATERIAL — DO NOT DUPLICATE, DISTRIBUTE, OR POST

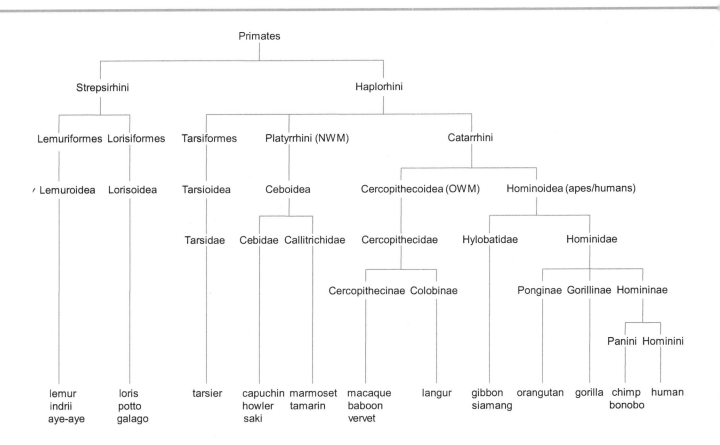

Figure 6.2: Cladistic classification of the primates.

PRIMATE CLASSIFICATION

Until the application of DNA technology to the question of the degree of relatedness between species, only similarity of morphological characteristics between species was used in the classification of living things. DNA analyzes how similar or dissimilar the base sequences are between species in order to determine the evolutionary genetic distance between those species. Analysis of DNA has shown that some classifications using only morphological characteristics are incorrect. As a result, over the past couple of decades, there has been some debate over whether and how the traditional taxonomic classification should be altered. Some researchers maintain that greater emphasis should be placed on morphological characteristics because it is physical traits upon which natural selection operates. Others maintain that only DNA genetic distance should be used because it is DNA that is passed from one generation to the next; therefore, it is a better indicator of evolutionary relationships between species through time.

One area of this debate centers on the classification of the primates. For instance, traditionally, the classification of the humans and the great apes (common chimpanzees, bonobos, gorillas, and orangutans) has separated the humans in one family (Hominidae) and included all of the great apes in a second family (Pongidae). This is because morphologically, humans are the least similar. However, humans genetically are not the least similar. Of the five great ape and human species, common chimpanzees and bonobos are the most genetically similar. Humans are more genetically similar to common chimpanzees and bonobos than they are to gorillas and orangutans. Of the five species, orangutans are the least genetically similar. As a result, based on DNA data, humans should not be distinguished from the other four species by placing them in a separate taxonomic category.

This book uses a classification of the primates based on genetic distance data (Figure 6.2). In this cladistic classification, the order Primates is split into two subor-

Figure 6.3: Vertical clinging and leaping.

ders, Strepsirhini and Haplorhini. The Strepsirhini contains two infraorders: Lemuriformes (for example, lemur, indri, and aye-aye), and Lorisiformes (loris, potto, and galago, for instance). The Haplorhini contains three infraorders: Tarsiformes (tarsier), Platyrrhini (New World monkeys), and Catarrhini (Old World monkeys, apes, and humans). The Platyrrhini includes one superfamily, Ceboidea, which is divided into two families, Cebidae (for example, capuchin, howler monkey, and saki) and Callitrichidae (marmoset and tamarin). The Catarrhini are divided into two superfamilies, Cercopithecoidea and Hominoidea. The Cercopithecoidea (Old World monkeys) includes one family, Cercopithecidae, which is divided into two subfamilies, Cercopithecinae (macaque, baboon, and vervet) and Colobinae (for example, langur). The Hominoidea (apes and humans) is divided into two families: Hylobatidae (lesser apes such as the gibbon and siamang) and Hominidae (great apes and humans). The Hominidae include three subfamilies, Ponginae (orangutan), Gorillinae (gorilla), and Homininae (both species of chimpanzees and humans). The Homininae include two tribes, Panini (common chimpanzee and bonobo) and Hominini (humans).

CHARACTERISTICS OF THE PRIMATES

Primate species within the suborder Strepsirhini most closely resemble the earliest evolved primates (discussed in Chapter 8). Most of these species are nocturnal, and most spend the majority of their time up in the trees. Their mode of locomotion while up in the trees is called vertical clinging and leaping, which involves using their lower limbs to push off from one branch, flying through the air with the trunk of their bodies in a more vertical position, and using all four limbs to grab onto another branch (Figure 6.3). The possession of a dental comb is characteristic of the Strepsirhini, where the four mandibular incisors project outward rather than being vertical. In some species, the dental comb is used for grooming, and in others it is used for feeding; for example, to extract tree sap by galagos. While all Strepsirhini species possess nails, they have retained one claw on each index finger, which is used for grooming. When compared with other primates, the Strepsirhini have a relatively well-developed sense of smell and possess a rhinarium (a moist nose), which enhances the sense of smell. In the present day, the various lemur species

Figure 6.4: Ring-tailed lemur.

Figure 6.5: Galago.

(Figure 6.4) are restricted to the island of Madagascar, where they did not face competition from the later evolving monkey species. Lorises (Figure 6.5) are found in the tropical forests of Africa and Southeast Asia.

Figure 6.6: Tarsier.

They are nocturnal, thus reducing competition with other local primate species.

The suborder Haplorhini includes the tarsiers, New World monkeys, Old World monkeys, apes, and humans. Commonly, the tarsiers, lemurs, and lorises are referred to as prosimians, and all of the monkeys, apes, and humans are referred to as anthropoids. Tarsiers (Figure 6.6) are found in the tropical forests of Southeast Asia and possess many traits similar to those of the lemurs and lorises, but in contrast do not have a rhinarium (they have a dry nose), and do not have a dental comb. The New World monkeys (Platyrrhini) are found in the tropical forests of Central America and the northern portion of South America; they are arboreal, spending the majority of their time up in the trees. They are herbivorous, with fruit and leaves comprising the greatest proportion of most species' diet.

Movement in the trees involves running and walking on the tops of branches and jumping from branch to branch. Some species brachiate (swing arm over arm beneath branches) from time to time, but do not do this habitually; spider monkeys, for instance (Figure 6.7). Many New World monkey species such as howler monkeys (Figure 6.8) have evolved a prehensile tail, which functions as a fifth limb and is used to grasp onto branches and can support the entire animal's weight. The end of a prehensile tail has

Figure 6.7: Spider monkey.

Figure 6.8: Red Howler monkey.

Figure 6.9: Macaque.

Figure 6.10: Baboon.

strong muscles and a hairless gripping pad to increase the grasp on branches. The Callitrichidae species have retained one grooming claw in each index finger, while Cebidae species have all nails.

All Catarrhini species have all nails, no claws. The Old World monkeys (Cercopithecoidea) are widely distributed throughout Africa and Asia, occupying both tropical forest and mixed woodland environments. One species of macaque, likely first introduced by the Romans, has colonized Gibraltar at the southern tip of the Iberian Peninsula in Europe. Some macaques (Figure 6.9) can also be found in temperate regions like Japan. Other Old World monkey species include baboons and vervets (Figures 6.10 and 6.11). When moving up in the trees, Old World monkey species typically run and walk on the tops of branches, and when on the ground usually move quadrupedally, but occasionally stand up and walk bipedally. Old World monkeys possess ischial callosities (hairless patches on the buttocks), used as sitting pads. The Cercopithecinae monkeys are omnivorous. Most eat a wide variety of plant foods (fruit, leaves, nuts, seeds, roots), with a concentration on fruit. Some include meat in their diet, obtained by catching small animals. The Colobinae monkeys such as langurs (Figure 6.12) are distinguished from the Cercopithecinae by their diet, which is folivorous, eating mostly leaves. In comparison to other primate foods, leaves are less nutritious, so the Colobinae monkeys must eat a large volume. Most leaves are mature leaves which contain cellulose, which is difficult to digest. A sacculated stomach aids in the digestion of this folivorous diet.

In contrast to the Cercopithecoidea, the Hominoidea do not have tails. The Hylobatidae include the lesser ape species (so called because they are the smaller of the ape species), and are found in the tropical forests of Southeast Asia. Their typical mode of locomotion is brachiation; consequently, movement is concentrated in the upper limbs. The lesser apes have particularly long arms in relation to leg length. Of all the ape species, only the lesser apes have ischial callosities. Gibbons

Figure 6.11: Vervet.

Figure 6.12: Langur.

Figure 6.13: Gibbon.

Figure 6.14: Orangutan.

and siamangs (Figure 6.13) are distinguished by their diet, with the former being frugivorous (eating mostly fruit) and the latter eating both fruit and leaves.

The Hominidae include the great apes (the larger of the ape species) and the humans, and is divided into three subfamilies. The Ponginae include the orangutans (Figure 6.14), who are found in the tropical forests of Southeast Asia. The mode of locomotion for orangutans is quadrumanual climbing, using all four limbs to move through the trees. Their diet is frugivorous. The Gorillinae include the gorillas (Figure 6.15), and are found in the tropical forests of central Africa. Gorillas are herbivorous, eating a variety of plant foods, and spend much of their time on the ground due to their size. Gorillas occasionally walk bipedally, but their usual mode of locomotion is knuckle walking, a type of quadrupedal locomotion, which involves placing the weight of the forelimbs on the knuckles rather than the palms.

Both species of chimpanzees and humans are contained within the Homininae, which include two tribes. Humans are contained within the tribe Hominini. The tribe Panini includes common chimpanzees and bonobos (sometimes referred to as pygmy chimpanzees). Bonobos are more lightly built than common chimpanzees. Common chimpanzees (Figure 6.16) are found in the tropical forests of west and central Africa, and also in mixed woodland areas of east Africa, whereas bonobos (Figure 6.17) occupy a more restricted range in the tropical forests of central Africa. Both species are omnivorous, concentrating on fruit and other plant foods such as leaves and nuts, and also may include meat, obtained through cooperative hunting. Both species combine knuckle walking with bipedal locomotion. However, bonobos walk bipedally more frequently than common chimpanzees. Common chimpanzee social groups are led by the alpha male; by contrast, bonobo social groups are led by the alpha female. In situations of conflict, common

Figure 6.15: Gorilla.

chimpanzees exhibit aggressive behavior, while bonobos have sex (with both the opposite and the same sex) to resolve the situation (Figure 6.18). Bonobos are the only species in addition to humans who have sex for reasons other than reproduction.

CRITICAL REASONING QUESTIONS

- Briefly describe two characteristics that are possessed by all primate species, but not possessed by non-primate species.
- How many million years ago did the first primate species appear? To which category of modern primates are these earliest primate species most similar?
- To what type of environment did the early primates evolve? What type of food found in this environment did primates take advantage of?
- What are the two suborders of primates named? What types of primates are classified in each of these suborders?
- Over the past decade, the word we use to refer to species within the human lineage has changed from hominid to hominin. Why has this change in terminology occurred?
- How does the study of chimpanzees help us understand human evolution?

Figure 6.16: Common Chimpanzee.

Figure 6.17: Bonobo.

Figure 6.18: Bonobo sexual behavior.

SUGGESTED READING

Rowe, N. (1996). *The pictorial guide to the living primates.* East Hampton, New York: Pogonius.

7

Primate Behavior

By Roman Gastrell Harrison

In the previous chapter, we explored features that are characteristic of the primates and how the primates are classified. Although the primates share many features, there is also considerable variability among the primates: for example, in appearance, modes of locomotion, diet, and aspects of behavior. Many of these features are evolutionary adaptations to the environments in which primates live. In this chapter, we focus on the diversity of primate behavior, including ranging behavior, social organization, dominance and rank, and primate intelligence.

PRIMATE RANGING BEHAVIOR

All primate social groups occupy a certain area over time. The size of this area is variable. In species like chimpanzees, for example, groups range over several kilometers, whereas other species such as tarsiers range over a few hundred meters. During the course of a day, most primate groups follow a similar pattern of activities. Depending on whether the species is diurnal or nocturnal, the group will wake up at their sleeping area at dawn or dusk. For diurnal species, when they wake up at dawn, they do not immediately move from their sleeping area. Instead, they will spend a period of time, perhaps an hour or two, undergoing social activities such as grooming, play, and sexual activity. Grooming behavior occurs when one individual cleans the fur of another individual (Figure 7.1).

Figure 7.1: Grooming—Japanese macaques.

Its purpose is for hygiene, but more importantly, it functions as a mechanism for creating and reinforcing social bonds between individuals. Grooming occurs more frequently between kin (related individuals), but also occurs between non-kin in order to form friendships.

After the morning period of social activity, the group will move from their sleeping area at the instigation of the alpha individual (group leader), and begin to travel within the area which the group occupies. As they move through this area, they will frequently stop at various locations to feed. At midday, when the sun is highest in the sky, the group will stop for a rest period, when individuals may have a nap or engage in social activities. The location of the midday rest is often the furthest point reached during the course of the day from the sleeping area. During the afternoon, the group will gradually travel back to their sleeping area, again stopping at various feeding locations. When they reach their sleeping area, typically at dusk, there will be another period of social activity prior to the group going to sleep.

As primates, humans also indirectly follow this pattern. For example, when each of the authors of this book wakes up in the morning, they do not immediately leave their house. Instead, there is a period of social activity, which may include having coffee and breakfast with the family. Afterward, we travel within the city in which we live to go to work. During the morning, we teach classes at each of our universities. Although we are not directly feeding during the morning, one reason we are teaching classes is to earn money to buy food in order to feed. At midday, we will have a break from work when we eat lunch and socialize. After our break, we will again teach classes in order to earn money to buy food. After our workday is finished, we will travel home and partake in social activities before going to sleep.

All of these activities occur in a particular area. The home range of a primate social group is the total area used by that group for all daily and seasonal activities, and is not defended against individuals from other conspecific (of the same species) social groups. Therefore, the home ranges of conspecific groups may overlap, and from time to time different groups meet. When groups meet, there may be social activity between individuals from each of the groups and individuals from one group may transfer to the other group, providing a mechanism for maintaining genetic diversity.

Some parts of the home range may be used more frequently than other parts. The part of the home range that has the heaviest usage is called the core area, which contains locations such as the sleeping area, a water source, and favored feeding sites; for example, preferred clumps of fruit trees. The location of the core area within the home range changes from season to season because the location of resources, particularly edible food (ripe fruit), changes over time. Fruit is a seasonal food. Particular types of fruit are ripe, and therefore edible, at certain times of the year. Fruit is a major dietary component of most primate species. Primates are able to track the changing conditions within their home range in order to efficiently utilize different locations of clumps of fruit trees at different times of the year.

Many, but not all, primate social groups maintain a territory, an area exclusively used by the group and actively defended against conspecific groups. In order to actively defend a territory, individuals within the group must know the location of the boundaries of the territory. Therefore, the territory is a conscious construct within the individual's mind, whereas the home range is not necessarily a conscious construct. Whether a territory is maintained is dependent on the particular characteristics of the environment that a particular group occupies. Since different groups of the same species occupy areas that are not exactly the same, in some primate species, some groups may be territorial, while others may not be.

A group may maintain a territory for two potential reasons. Resource defense territoriality may occur when preferred food resources (typically fruit trees) are clumped in space. Because these food resources are not available everywhere, a group may maintain a territory in order to stop non-group individuals from being able to access those locations. Mate defense territoriality may occur when that primate species' mating behavior involves a relatively large component of males competing among themselves for female sexual partners (intrasexual selection). If this is the case, then males must compete with other males within their group. In order to increase their chances of mating success, males may exclude non-group males from their territory in order to reduce the amount of competition for females. In primate species, where mating behavior is influenced less so by male competition and more so by female choice of mate (intersexual selection), there is less of a reason for males to maintain a territory.

Question: How is territoriality expressed? If a group maintains exclusive access to a particular area, individuals must do something to guard the boundary of that territory. Some species, indris and howler monkeys, for instance, express their territoriality through vocalization, where individuals make specific loud calls indicating to non-group individuals the boundaries of their territory. Other species use scent to mark the boundaries of their territory. For example, male ring-tailed lemurs use scent from glands located on the wrists to mark branches, whereas marmosets use scented urine. Still other species will patrol the boundaries of their territory and employ physical confrontation if required; chimpanzees do this. Confrontation usually do not involve physical fighting, and more often is expressed in the form of threats or displays (where one chimpanzee may pick up a branch and wave it around in order to intimidate another individual) against incurring individuals.

Even if preferred fruit trees are clumped in space or there is a high component of male competition for females in mating behavior, the maintenance of a territory is not guaranteed because there are costs of maintaining a territory. Time must be spent patrolling or marking the boundary of the territory, and there is the risk of confrontation with non-group individuals, which may result in injury or death. Each group must consciously weigh the benefits versus the costs of maintaining a territory. For example, sometimes, even if fruit trees are clumped in space, the costs of maintaining a territory to protect those fruit trees may not be worth it.

Question: How do primates perceive their range? Primates have a conscious awareness of their surroundings and know the locations of the various resources in their home range. Foraging travel studies of primate social groups in the wild indicate that groups travel in an efficient route between different locations. Among

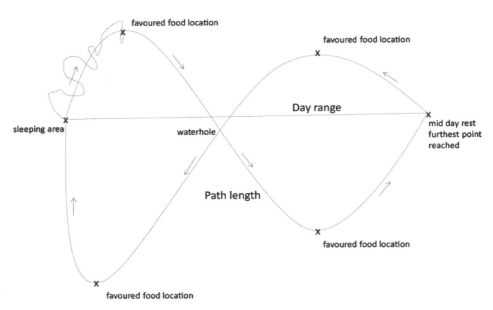

Figure 7.2: Path length and day range.

other things, foraging travel studies make observations of a social group's daily travel route and distance, including curves (path length) and the straight-line distance from the sleeping area to the furthest point reached in a day (day range) (Figure 7.2). These studies provide evidence that primates possess a conscious mental map of their surroundings (a cognitive map), which permits efficient movement between various locations within their range. For example, primates do not randomly wander until they happen to come across a preferred clump of fruit trees, but rather follow the most efficient route.

PRIMATE SOCIAL ORGANIZATION

Most primate species live in social groups. This entails group members having conscious knowledge of the relationship between themselves and other group members (both relative degree of kinship and rank). The composition of social groups of primates varies between different species, and is based primarily on mating behavior. Of the five types of primate social organization, only solitary primate species do not form social groups. Adult individuals lead solitary lives, with the exception of adult females with immature young or when an adult male and female come together for mating. Most solitary species like lorises are nocturnal, although orangutans are diurnal.

Other types of primate social organization involve some type of group living. The social group of monogamous primates is comprised of one adult male, one adult female, and immature young. Gibbons and owl monkeys are examples. Males and females will typically form a pair bond shortly after puberty, and this bond will continue for life. For the most part, mating between these two individuals is exclusive, although one or the other of the pair may occasionally mate with another individual; as a result, paternity of offspring is likely the male member of the pair. Monogamous males participate in the caring and raising of offspring. Monogamous primates are usually territorial for resource defense purposes in order to maintain exclusive access to food resources (favored clumps of fruit trees) for the pair's offspring.

The largest social groups among primates are those with multi-male/multi-female social organization, where the group is comprised of several adult males, several adult females, and immature young. Groups may number in the hundreds. Examples include Japanese macaques and both species of chimpanzees. Adult males and females form short-term bonds for the purpose of mating. The composition of these pairings changes from one episode to the next, and can be best described as promiscuous. Paternity is not known, but is likely a male from the female's social group. Multi-male/multi-female species have a relatively high degree of male competition for females, although females will have the final choice of whom to mate with. Since males must compete with other males within their group, multi-male/multi-female species are typically territorial for mate defense reasons, so that males do not have to compete with non-group members.

The composition of multi-male/multi-female groups in many species is fluid. Subgroups will form and disperse over time, with the composition of individuals in these subgroups changing from one event to the next (fission-fusion). For instance, types of fission groups among chimpanzees include foraging parties composed of several females, territorial boundary patrols composed of several males, or hunting parties composed of several males.

Chimpanzees hunt a variety of small animals. For example, at Gombe Stream National Park in Tanzania, chimpanzees hunt red colobus monkeys, with over half of the hunts killing at least one monkey or more (Stanford 1998). Different hunting strategies are used in different chimpanzee groups. In the woodlands of Gombe, when hunting monkeys, each male in the hunting party acts individually to try to catch one. Success of the hunting group as a whole is increased because several hunters are acting in the same place at the same time. In contrast, in the Tai Forest in Ivory Coast, there is greater cooperation between hunters, with different hunters carrying out different roles. Some hunters will carefully direct the group of monkeys in a specific direction within the forest, while others will circle ahead of the monkeys; still others will climb high in the treetops in order to block potential escape routes. This coordinated effort increases the likelihood of success. The rules for sharing the monkey meat vary between different chimpanzee groups. For example, in the Tai Forest, typically the hunter who made the kill will share the meat with his friends and relatives, which may exclude the alpha male from getting any meat (Boesch and Boesch-Achermann 1991). At Gombe, by contrast, the kill is often confiscated from the successful hunter by the alpha male and shared with his friends and relatives.

Uni-male/multi-female (polygynous) social groups are comprised of one adult male (the breeding male), several adult females, and immature young. Other adult males are nonbreeding and do not live in this group, but instead form all-male groups, or live solitarily before joining an all-male group. Gorillas are an example of uni-male/multi-female organization. Nonbreeding males will challenge the breeding male, and if successful will transfer to the breeding group as the breeding male, replacing the former breeding male. Male reproductive success depends on the ability to challenge the breeding male; therefore, larger and stronger males are more likely to mate and reproduce. As a result, uni-male/multi-female species have a large degree of sexual dimorphism, with males being up to twice the size of females. Breeding males have a high level of intolerance for nonbreeding males. Uni-female/multi-male (polyandrous) species are rare among the primates. The social group is comprised of one adult breeding female, two (and sometimes more) adult males, and immature young. From a biological point of view, reproduction in uni-female/multi-male organization is relatively inefficient, since the minimum time requirement for the reproduction of females is the period of gestation, whereas for males, it is the time required for copulation. Males participate in the care and raising of offspring in uni-female/multi-male groups. Marmosets are an example.

At puberty, individuals of one or both sexes will leave the group of their birth (natal emigration). This serves to maintain genetic diversity within groups. Individuals who remain in their natal group are referred to as philopatric individuals, while those who leave their natal group and reside in another group are referred to as immigrants or transferred individuals. Male dispersal is the most common pattern among primates. This occurs among ring-tailed lemurs and macaques, for example. Female dispersal is less common, and is seen in hamadryas baboons and both species of chimpanzees. In monogamous species (gibbons), both sexes disperse. If females are the sex to leave their natal group, they typically join another group (for instance, vervets). However, when males leave their natal group, in some species they may immediately join another group (such as macaques), but in other species, they may live solitarily before joining an all-male group (as gorillas do). Secondary emigration occurs when subsequent movement between groups occurs after natal emigration. For example, a gorilla male will leave his natal group at puberty and may join an all-male group (natal emigration) and later challenge a breeding male, subsequently taking his place in another breeding group (secondary emigration).

DOMINANCE AND RANK

One feature of life in social groups is the variable degrees of power that individuals possess. Dominance is the power to influence another individual's behavior. Some individuals within the group may have a greater ability to influence others, while some have less influence. Each individual within the group has a particular level of dominance (or rank) in relation to all other members of the group. An individual's rank influences their behavior. Rank is expressed through interactions between individuals, and can involve both situations of conflict and friendly interactions.

Agonistic behavior is associated with situations of conflict, and involves both aggressive and submissive behavior. Aggressive behavior may include physical fighting, but more frequently is exhibited in the form of threats, which can include one individual chasing or lightly cuffing another individual (for example, baboons), or through the use of displays (chimpanzees). Symbols may be employed as aggressive signals; the eyebrow flash used by baboons, for instance, where the eyebrow is raised and the eyelid is simultaneously closed. Examples of submissive behavior include cringing and may also be symbolic, such as a wide toothy grin in chimpanzees.

Interactions between individuals are often of a friendly, affiliative nature. Grooming behavior functions as a social bonding experience and serves to establish and reinforce friendships between individuals. Once friendships are established, those individuals are more likely to provide assistance to each other in the future; for example, in agonistic situations. In olive baboons, males may establish friendships with unrelated females to increase the likelihood of future mating, and may babysit that female's infant so they are less likely to be the object of other individuals' aggression (they use the proximity of the infant as protection) (Strum 1983).

Question: What determines an individual's rank? At birth, an individual inherits the rank of his or her mother. Individuals retain this rank while they reside in their natal group. To illustrate, in olive baboons, females do not leave their natal group at puberty and will retain their inherited rank throughout their lives. In all primate species, individuals of at least one sex will leave their natal group at puberty and transfer to another group. When these individuals join their new group, they will lose their inherited rank and establish a new rank through interactions with members of the new group. We see this in chimpanzees, as females leave their natal group at puberty and will join a new group and establish a new rank. An individual may be able to raise their rank to some degree through interactions with other members of their group. For example, in chimpanzees, where males remain in their natal group all of their lives, upon reaching adulthood, an individual may be able to increase their rank through having consistently positive outcomes in interactions with other males. These interactions include agonistic interactions, and forming alliances and friendships with others, both kin and non-kin. Social skill also may play a role in establishing or altering rank: in one of the chimpanzee groups at Gombe, a small, low-ranked male included empty kerosene cans in his displays, intimidating the other chimpanzees, eventually deposing the alpha male and replacing him (Riss and Goodall 1977).

Question: How do primatologists determine dominance and rank? Primatologists determine the relative dominance level of each individual in a social group by observing interactions between pairs of individuals (dyads), taking note of the direction of agonistic signals, approach and avoidance behavior, and access to food resources. Over time, all possible dyads in the group are observed. Several interactions within a dyad are recorded, in order to determine which individual has the higher rank and which has the lower rank. The higher-ranked individual will more frequently approach the lower-ranked individual, use aggressive signals, and have preferential access to food.

Question: Does an individual's rank have an effect on their reproductive success? An individual's rank within its social group may have an influence on reproductive success. Higher-ranking females on average will have greater access to resources—particularly food—and will have better health. This correlates with higher-ranking females bearing more infants than lower-ranking ones due to enhanced fetal nutrition. Infants of higher-ranking females have greater survivorship than those of lower-ranking females. For example, Pusey and colleagues have shown that higher-ranking females at Gombe Stream National Park in Tanzania are more likely to have infants who survive to the age of weaning than infants of lower-ranking females (Pusey et al. 1997). Mating behavior may influence the reproductive success of males. When males compete among each other for females, higher-ranking males are more likely to win the competition, thus mating more frequently with greater reproductive success. Higher-ranking males are more likely to be chosen by females, also enhancing their reproductive success.

PRIMATE INTELLIGENCE

Collectively, the primates have an increased level of intelligence relative to non-primates. Primates have large brains as a proportion to body mass. Brain size itself has a relatively low correlation with level of intelligence. For example, elephants have larger brains than humans, but are not as intelligent. However, humans have a larger brain size in relation to body mass.

On average, primate brains comprise approximately two percent of overall body mass. Brain-to-body proportion increases from the earliest to the latest evolving primates, from the prosimians through the monkeys, apes, and humans. Although primate brains comprise a relatively small proportion of body mass, they are expensive organs to maintain, on average consuming approximately 20 percent of metabolic energy taken in through diet. Most primate species have a particularly nutritious diet, including fruit, nuts, meat, and insects, in order to feed their larger brains. Leaves are less nutritious compared to these other foods. Species such as Colobine monkeys, whose diet is made up primarily of leaves, counter this by consuming a large volume of leaves.

Increased intelligence among the primates allows an increased proportion of flexible problem-solving behavior in their overall behavioral repertoire, as opposed to instinctual, hard-wired behavior. Primates have a greater ability to develop new behavior and incorporate novel solutions into preexisting behavior. An example comes from a social group of Japanese macaques who live on Koshima Island off the coast of mainland Japan (Kawai 1965). During the 1950s, in order to better observe the macaques, primatologists

Figure 7.3: Japanese macaques bathing in natural hot springs.

provisioned the group with food. Initially, sweet potatoes were left on the beach for the group to access. One female named Imo began to wash her sweet potatoes before eating them, presumably to remove adhering sand. The problem was that it is unpleasant to eat sand, and the solution was to wash the potatoes prior to consuming them. After a period of time, most other individuals in the group also washed their potatoes. In time, this same female began taking her potatoes to the ocean to wash them, most probably to add salt to the potatoes so as to enhance their taste. Later, the primatologists changed the provisioned diet to rice, thinking that it would take a long time for the macaques to pick the rice from the sand. However, Imo realized that all she had to do was pick up a handful of rice and sand and drop it into a pool of water. The sand sank and the rice floated, allowing her to skim off just the rice. Again, soon after, most other individuals in the group began doing the same. In a second example, a social group of macaques living in the Japanese Alps incorporated a new behavior as a response to the cold temperatures of winter. This social group had moved to a new area with natural hot springs. They soon discovered that they could get some respite from the cold by bathing in the hot springs (Figure 7.3).

A greater proportion of primate behavior is conscious. which allows choice of action to play a greater role. For example, if someone were to suddenly approach you with their fist raised, you have a choice of how to react. You may choose to duck to avoid the punch, or you may choose to hit them back. This choice may be made very quickly, but the choice must be made according to factors such as the relative size and level of social power (rank) of the individuals.

Question: *Why did primates evolve increased intelligence?* Increased intelligence among the primates likely evolved as an adaptation to life in a complex environment. Theories that have been proposed as an explanation for the evolution of increased primate intelligence focus on the ecological and social aspects of primates' lives. Many foods consumed by primates like various types of fruit are short-lived and patchy (Milton 1988). Primates must be able to track the changing conditions in their home range from season to season and be able to anticipate the availability, quantity, and location of different types of fruits over time. Primates' possession of a cognitive map assists in keeping track of food availability. Some foods consumed by primates are hidden from view and require enhanced intelligence to locate and process these foods (Gibson 1986). Nuts are hidden within a shell. In order to effectively access nuts, primates must associate a particular shape of shell with a particular type of nut. Some nut shells require tools to open; for instance, the use of a hammer and anvil by some chimpanzee social groups. Root foods are hidden from view, and require the association of particular types of leaves above ground with particular types of roots below ground. Life in a social group requires increased intelligence. An individual must consciously analyze other individuals' likely behavior, based on the relative degree of kinship and rank. The potential costs and benefits of a particular action must be considered prior to carrying out that action. If the costs outweigh the benefits, an individual is less likely to proceed with that action. For example, a higher-ranked individual is more likely to challenge a lower-ranked individual who is holding a piece of fruit because they have an increased chance of getting the piece of fruit. The lower-ranked individual will likely realize that the higher-ranked individual has a larger social backup, and therefore will surrender the piece of fruit.

Grooming behavior is an important aspect of social group living. It facilitates the formation of friendships between individuals. These friendships may be exploited in the future in agonistic situations. Altruistic behavior (where one individual does something for another individual, with a potential risk to the giving individual) occurs among the primates. Altruistic behavior among related individuals may be explained with the theory of kin selection. Helping a related individual who shares some genetic material (variable, according to how close the relationship is) will help some of one's genes to be passed to the next generation. Altruistic behavior has also been observed among unrelated individuals and may be explained with the theory of reciprocal altruism, where an individual may act helpfully toward an unrelated individual, with the expectation of some sort of return in the future. An example of evidence for reciprocal altruism comes from a study of savanna baboons, where males formed alliances in order to overpower higher-ranking males for mates (Smuts 1985). The alliances were formed with the expectation of future cooperation. Deceptive behavior has been observed in primates. For example, a vervet individual may give an alarm call warning of a predator when no predator is in the vicinity, causing other group members to vacate a favored fruit tree, providing unhindered access to the fruit for the call-giver (Byrne and Whiten 1988).

Deception requires a theory of mind: the ability to place oneself in the mind of another. This involves the ability to distinguish between what you and others know, and also the capacity to understand another's state of mind—the ability to feel empathy, as an example. Among nonhuman primates, the best examples of the presence of a theory of mind come from apes. Among Tai Forest chimpanzees, for instance, mother chimpanzees have been observed teaching their offspring how to crack open nutshells using a hammer and anvil (Boesch 1991).

There is some debate over whether nonhuman primates are capable of language. One aspect of this debate concerns the definition of language. How language is defined has a bearing on the question of nonhuman primate language capabilities. This book defines language as a type of communication that uses abstract symbols that have specific meanings. Among humans, language includes verbal, gestural, and written abstract symbols. Studies of nonhuman primate language capabilities have concentrated on the great ape species, with particular emphasis on chimpanzees, the focus of the following discussion. Earlier language capability studies concentrated more so on captive chimpanzees, but more recently have focused on wild chimpanzees.

Question: Are chimpanzees capable of human spoken language? In the 1950s, Keith and Catherine Hayes attempted to teach spoken human language to Vicki, a common chimpanzee. Vicki was able to imperfectly vocalize four human words, but was unable to expand her spoken vocabulary because chimpanzees are unable to articulate the wide range of sounds required for human language. The human larynx (voice box) is placed lower in the throat than in chimpanzees, facilitating the wide range of human sounds.

The morphological inability by chimpanzees to vocalize human language does not necessarily mean they are incapable of understanding human language. With this in mind, studies in the 1960s began to focus on gestural and visual symbolic language. One of these studies used an exclusively gestural human language, American Sign Language. Over the first four years of training, Washoe, a female common chimpanzee, mastered the correct use of over 132 signs. She was able to combine signs into simple sentences, carrying out simple conversations with her handlers (Gardner and Gardner 1969). Washoe was also observed teaching signs to other chimpanzees. Another example of a captive language study used lexigram symbols, where the symbols were pointed to in sequence to form sentences. Kanzi, a male bonobo, learned the lexigram language on his own by observing his mother while she was taught by her handlers (Savage-Rumbaugh and Rumbaugh 1993). Kanzi was also able to understand spoken English without being specifically taught. Critics of these and other studies suggest that the subjects were simply mimicking their handlers without full comprehension.

Wild chimpanzees use both vocalizations called pant-hoots and gestures in communication. Pant-hoots vary in the number of pants and hoots and the length of time of the vocalization, and are used in different specific contexts. For example, different pant-hoots correspond to different types of food (Slocombe and Zuberbuhler 2006). Examples of gestural symbols include leaf grooming, leaf clipping, and the grooming hand clasp. Leaf grooming involves taking a leaf, rubbing it, and bringing it to the mouth, perhaps lightly touching it to the mouth, and occurs before taking a nap. Leaf clipping involves taking a leaf and ripping parts of the leaf with the mouth, and in some social groups occurs prior to displaying; it occurs in other social groups prior to mating (Whiten et al. 2001; Matsumoto-Oda and Tomonaga 2005). The grooming hand clasp involves two individuals raising their arms and clasping hands prior to grooming behavior (Nakamura and Nishida 2013). Comparison of different chimpanzee social groups has provided evidence that the repertoire of vocalizations and gestures varies between different groups (Mitani et al. 1992).

Many animal species make use of tools in the wild: birds use twigs and other materials to build nests. However, they do not modify objects in a specific way for a specific purpose to manufacture tools. Other than humans, only chimpanzees and orangutans manufacture tools. While tool manufacture has been observed in all known wild chimpanzee populations, it appears that only some orangutan populations do

Figure 7.4: Bonobo using termite wand.

(van Schaik et al. 2003). Examples of tools manufactured by chimpanzees include probes fashioned from twigs ("wands") used to extract insects from ant or termite mounds (Figure 7.4); hammers (rock or branch) and anvils (large rock or protruding root) employed to crack open nutshells; sponges made from balled up leaves used to soak up water; and branches used as weapons (Panger 2007).

Question: *Have chimpanzees grasped the concept of medicine?* One chimpanzee social group in Uganda occasionally will eat a particular type of bitter-tasting leaf. Shortly after eating the leaf, an intestinal parasite is expelled from their body (McLennan and Huffman 2012). The only time a chimpanzee eats the leaf is prior to parasite expulsion. It appears that if the chimpanzees recognizes that it has an intestinal parasite, it has learned that eating this type of leaf will expel it. If we define medicine as recognizing that something is wrong with your body and then doing something to fix it, this chimpanzee group may have grasped the concept of medicine.

Not all chimpanzee groups use the same set of tools. For instance, while Tai Forest chimpanzees use rocks as tools, Gombe chimpanzees do not (McGrew 1992). The use and manufacture of tools is learned behavior passed from one generation to the next, a tradition handed down through time within the group. In other words, different chimpanzee groups have different cultural traditions. Studying these different traditions provides insight into early human cultural development. Stone tool use among chimpanzees may have considerable time depth. Stones recovered from the Tai Forest in Ivory Coast dating to 4300 years ago show evidence of having been used as tools, in the same way as present-day chimpanzees from the same region (Mercader et al. 2002). These stones had traces of starch residue, suggesting they had been used to open nutshells.

CRITICAL REASONING QUESTIONS

- Briefly define the terms home range and territory.
- Under what conditions might resource defense territoriality and mate defense territoriality occur?
- What do studies of path length and day range tell us about primates' knowledge of their surroundings? What is a cognitive map?
- What is grooming behavior? What are the two primary purposes of this behavior?
- Briefly define the terms dominance and rank.
- What determines an individual's rank?
- What learned behavior observed in macaques living on Koshima Island demonstrates increased flexible intelligence?
- What is the theory of mind? What type of learning is facilitated by this theory?

REFERENCES AND SUGGESTED READINGS

Boesch, C. (1991). Teaching in wild chimpanzees. *Animal Behaviour* 41:530–532.

Boesch, Christophe, and Hedwige Boesch-Achermann (September 1991). Dim forest, bright chimps. *Natural History* 1991:50, 52–56.

Byrne, R. W., and A. Whiten (1988). Towards the next generation in data quality: A new survey of primate social deception. *Behavioral and Brain Sciences* 11:267–273.

Gardner, R. Allen, and Beatrice T. Gardner (1969). Teaching sign language to a chimpanzee. *Science, New Series* 165:664–672.

Gibson, K. R. (1986). Cognition, brain size and the extraction of embedded food. In J. G. Else and P. C. Lee, eds., *Primate Ontogeny: Cognitive and Social Behavior*, pp. 93–104. Cambridge, MA: Cambridge University Press.

Kawai, M. (1965). Newly acquired precultural behaviour of the natural troop of Japanese monkeys on Koshima Island. *Primates* 6:1–30.

Matsumoto-Oda, Akiko, and Masaki Tomonaga (2005). "Intentional" control of sound production found in leaf-clipping display of Mahale chimpanzees. *Journal of Ethology* 23(2):109–112.

McGrew, W. C. (1992). Chimpanzee material culture. Cambridge, UK: Cambridge University Press.

McLennan, Matthew R., and Michael A. Huffman (2012). High frequency of leaf swallowing and its relationship to intestinal parasite expulsion in village chimpanzees at Bulindi, Uganda. *American Journal of Primatology* 74(7):642–650.

Mercader, J., M. Panger, and C. Boesch (2002). Excavation of a chimpanzee stone tool site in the African rainforest. *Science* 296:1452–1455.

Milton, K. (1988). Foraging behaviour and the evolution of primate intelligence. In R. Byrne and A. Whiten, eds., *Machiavellian Intelligence: Social Expertise and the Evolution of Intellect in Monkeys, Apes and Humans*, pp. 285–306. Oxford, UK: Clarendon Press.

Mitani, John C., Toshikazu Hasegawa, Julie Gros-Louis, et al. (1992). Dialects in wild chimpanzees. *American Journal of Primatology* 27(4):233–243.

Nakamura, Michio, and Toshisada Nishida (2013). Ontogeny of a social custom in wild chimpanzees: Age changes in grooming hand-clasp at Mahale. *American Journal of Primatology* 75(2):186–196.

Panger, Melissa (2007). Tool use and cognition in primates. In Christina J. Campbell, Agustin Fuentes, Katherine C. MacKinnon, et al., eds., *Primates in Perspective*, pp. 665–676. New York: Oxford University Press.

Pusey, A., J. Williams, and J. Goodall (1997). The influence of dominance rank on the reproductive success of female chimpanzees *Science* 277:828–831.

Riss, D., and J. Goodall (1977). The recent rise to the alpha-rank in a population of free-living chimpanzees. *Folia Primatologica* 27(2):134–151.

Savage-Rumbaugh, S., and D. Rumbaugh (1993). The emergence of language. In K. R. Gibson and T. Ingold, eds., *Tools, Language, and Cognition in Human Evolution*, pp. 86–108. Cambridge, UK Cambridge University Press.

Slocombe, K. E., and K. Zuberbuhler (2006). Food-associated calls in chimpanzees: Responses to food types or food preferences. *Animal Behaviour* 72:989–999.

Smuts, B. B. (1985). Sex and friendship in baboons. New York: Aldine Press.

Stanford, C. B. (1998). Chimpanzee and red colobus: The ecology of predator and prey. Cambridge, MA: Harvard University Press.

Strum, S. C. (1983). Use of females by male olive baboons (*Papio anubis*). *American Journal of Primatology* 5:93–109.

van Schaik, Carel P., Marc Ancrenaz, Gwendolyn Borgen, et al. (2003). Orangutan cultures and the evolution of material culture. *Science* 299(5603):102–105.

Whiten, A., J. Goodall, W. C. McGrew, et al. (2001). Charting cultural variation in chimpanzees. *Behaviour* 138(11/12):1481–1516.

8

Primate Evolution

by Roman Gastrell Harrison

P rimates are mammals, a group of species that share characteristics such as being warm-blooded, having mammary glands, and bearing fur or hair. Mammals first appear in the fossil record between 250 and 300 million years ago (mya). Of the various major taxa of mammals extant in the present day, the order Primates first appeared approximately 55 mya. In this chapter, we will discuss the geological time scale, the dating of fossils, and aspects of primate evolution, including the earliest fossil evidence for the primates and the evolution of the major categories of primates, with a focus on the lineage leading to the evolution of the earliest human species.

TIME FRAME FOR PRIMATE AND HUMAN EVOLUTION

In order to understand the evolution of the primates, it is necessary to organize fossil species in a time frame. Paleoanthropologists use the geological time scale, which divides the history of the Earth into eras, periods, and epochs (Figure 8.1). In terms of the age of the Earth, primates appeared relatively late, at the beginning of the Cenozoic era. The Tertiary period is the earlier of the two periods of the Cenozoic era and is divided into five epochs. The final extinction of the dinosaurs occurred at the beginning of the Paleocene epoch (65–54 mya). The earliest primate species likely evolved from a small Paleocene

113

PERIOD	EPOCH	TIME RANGE
Tertiary	Paleocene	65-54mya
	Eocene	54-34mya
	Oligocene	34-23mya
	Miocene	23-5mya
	Pliocene	5-1.7mya
Quaternary	Pleistocene	1.7mya-10kya
	Holocene	10kya-present

Figure 8.1: Geologic time scale—Cenozoic Era.

mammal that was similar to the modern tree shrew. The first true primates appear in the fossil record at the beginning of the Eocene epoch (54–34 mya), and resemble the modern prosimians. Anthropoids first appear toward the end of the Eocene, with the evolution of the first monkeys. The anthropoids include all monkey, ape, and human species. Several anthropoid monkey species have been identified from the Oligocene epoch (34–23 mya). The earliest hominoids appear toward the end of the Oligocene epoch, with the evolution of the first apes. The hominoids include all ape and human species. Hominin (human) fossil species first appear toward the end of the Miocene epoch (23–5 mya), and continue to evolve through the Pliocene epoch (5–1.7 mya). The Quaternary period is the more recent in the Cenozoic era. The earliest fossil evidence for anatomically modern *Homo sapiens* dates to approximately 200,000 years ago, toward the end of the Pleistocene epoch (1.7 mya–10,000 years ago). We are currently in the Holocene epoch (10,000 years ago to the present day), which begins with the end of the last ice age and, in terms of human development, the first appearance of settled agricultural communities. Prior to about 10,000 years ago, all human groups were hunter/gatherers.

DATING FOSSILS

Several different techniques have been developed for the dating of fossils. In this section, we will discuss three of the more commonly used techniques. Relative dating places fossils in a sequence from earlier to more recent dates using the principle of superposition, which states that lower stratigraphic layers (and the fossils within them) are older than upper stratigraphic layers, since the lower layers would have been deposited before the upper layers, and therefore date earlier in time. The age of fossils in a stratigraphic layer can be bracketed if the age of the two adjacent layers is known. The age of a fossil may be determined if it is found in association with other fossils of known age found in the same layer.

Radiometric dating provides absolute dates. The two most commonly used are radiocarbon and potassium-argon dating. Both of these techniques measure the spontaneous decay of an unstable radioactive isotope into a stable isotope. Decay occurs at a constant rate through time, and thus age can be computed from the proportion of the remaining radioactive isotope to the stable isotope in a sample. Radiocarbon dating measures the decay of radioactive C14 to stable C12. The rate of decay is expressed as the half-life of the radioactive isotope. For carbon, the half-life is 5730 years, which means that after 5730 years, half of the original C14 in a sample has decayed to C12. Radiocarbon dating determines the age of organic materials up to 50,000 years ago during the later phases of human evolution. Prior to this date, organic fossil remains are too degraded to analyze. Potassium-argon (K-Ar) dating may be used on materials dating earlier than 100,000 years ago, and is used to date volcanic rock layers that either contain fossils or bracket fossil-bearing layers. Radioactive K40 decays to stable Ar40 and has a half-life of 1.3 billion years. K-Ar dating has been used to date human fossils from in and around the Rift Valley in east Africa, where volcanic activity has occurred throughout the period of human evolution.

THE FIRST PRIMATES

The earliest fossil primate species appear at the beginning of the Eocene epoch, approximately 55 mya. A great many primate species have been identified in the fossil record. The focus of this book is

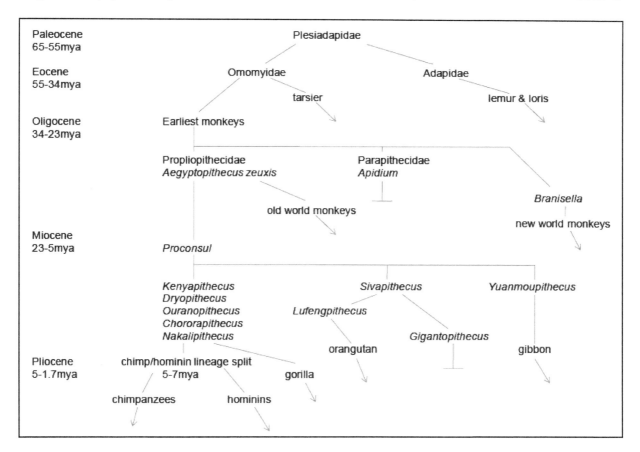

Figure 8.2: Primate evolution (one possible branching phylogeny).

Figure 8.3: *Plesiadapis cookei.*

paleoanthropology, the study of human evolution, and an exhaustive treatment of all fossil primate species is beyond this book's scope. Therefore, the following discussion and accompanying primate evolution phylogeny (Figure 8.2) is selective, concentrating on fossil species in the line leading to humans.

The primates likely evolved from small, insect-eating mammals similar to modern tree shrews that lived during the Paleocene epoch and are classified in the family Plesiadapidae (Figure 8.3). These fossils have been found throughout Europe and North America. The Plesiadapidae were nocturnal and quadrupedal, and had a diet that included seeds and insects. Fossils can tell us more than simply what a species looked like, and can provide evidence for behavioral characteristics. For example, larger eye orbits indicate a nocturnal lifeway (active at night, sleeping during the day), since possessing larger eyes provides better vision at night. Whether a species is quadrupedal (using all four limbs for locomotion) or bipedal (using only the hind limbs for locomotion) can be determined through examination of skeletal features; the type of diet can be determined through features of the dentition (these and other features will be further discussed in Chapter 9). While the Plesiadapidae are similar to the earliest true primates, they lack some key primate features; for example they do not have an opposable big toe and have all claws. There is some debate over whether the Plesiadapidae should be included within the order Primates (Silcox 2007).

During the Paleocene, trees bearing fruit first evolved, providing a new source of food. Early primates took advantage of this new food source, and evolved features that enhanced their ability to access fruit. Fruit typically is found in trees. The majority of primate species, both modern and fossil, incorporate a significant amount of fruit into their diet. In order to access fruit, the primates evolved features that allow them to efficiently move in an arboreal environment (an environment up in trees).

At the beginning of the Eocene epoch, the Earth's climate became warmer, tropical forests increased in size, and several new mammal species evolved, including the first true primates (the euprimates). Eocene fossil primate species are classified into two families. The Omomyidae are most similar to modern tarsiers; they had a small body size and large eye orbits, suggesting a nocturnal

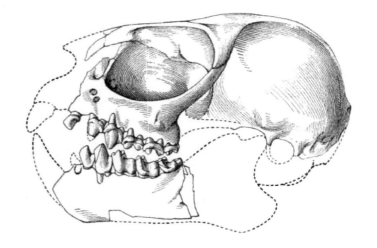

Figure 8.4: *Omomyidae: Tetonius homunculus.*

lifeway (Figure 8.4). Some species were insectivores (a diet containing a high proportion of insects), while other species were frugivores (a diet comprised of a high proportion of fruit). The Adapidae are similar to modern lemurs (Figure 8.5). Compared to the Omomyidae, their body size was somewhat larger, they had smaller eye orbits reflecting a diurnal lifeway, and their diet was comprised of leaves and fruit.

THE FIRST MONKEYS

Toward the end of the Eocene epoch, the Earth's temperature began to cool. Fossil evidence of

Figure 8.5: *Adapidae—Notharctus osborni.*

early anthropoids during this period is sparse and, as a result, the identity of the ancestor of the earliest anthropoids remains unresolved. There is debate over whether an omomyid, adapid, or some other species was the root ancestor of the anthropoids (Williams et al. 2010).

During the Oligocene epoch, many fossil anthropoid species have been identified. Much of our evidence for this anthropoid radiation comes from the Fayum in Egypt. Today, this region is a desert, but during the Oligocene, it was moister, with treed and swampy areas. Many of the Fayum fossil anthropoids fall into two families: the Propliopithecidae and the Parapithecidae. The Propliopithecidae were frugivorous, had a diurnal lifeway, and had a dental formula of 2.1.2.3. A dental formula is a numerical way of describing the type and number of teeth in one half of the mandible (lower jaw) or maxilla (upper jaw), from the front midline of the jaw to the back. A dental formula of 2.1.2.3 indicates that there are two incisors, one canine, two premolars, and three molars. All Old World species of monkeys, apes, and humans, both fossil and modern, have a dental formula of 2.1.2.3. Consequently, the consensus is that the Propliopithecidae are the ancestors of the Old World monkeys, apes, and humans. *Aegyptopithecus zeuxis* is one example of an Oligocene species in the family Propliopithecidae (Figure 8.6). The family Parapithecidae (which includes the genus *Apidium*) is similar to those of the Propliopithecidae, but had a diet consisting of both fruit and seeds, resulting in a different dental formula: 2.1.3.3. The majority of New World monkey species have a 2.1.3.3 dental formula, suggesting that *Apidium* or its close relatives may be the ancestor of the modern New World monkeys. The earliest New World monkey fossils date to 27 mya, and are placed in the genus *Branisella*. These fossils were discovered in Bolivia; the monkeys' diet was frugivorous. At this time, Africa and South America had separated. There is debate as to how the earliest New World monkey species got to South America, since there would have been a considerable expanse of ocean to cross. Hoffstetter (1974) hypothesizes that early New World

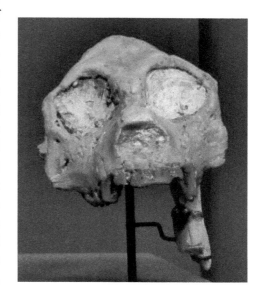

Figure 8.6: *Aegyptopithecus zeuxis.*

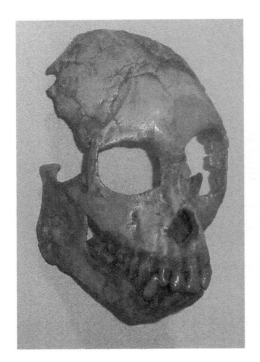

Figure 8.7: *Proconsul africanus.*

monkeys reached South America by crossing the Atlantic on floating masses of vegetation. During the Oligocene, sea levels were lower, exposing numerous islands in the South Atlantic, allowing for the possibility of island hopping.

THE FIRST APES

The early Miocene climate was warmer and wetter than that of the Oligocene, causing the enlargement of the African tropical forests in which early apes evolved. The earliest primates with features characteristic of the apes date to 27 mya and include the genus *Proconsul* (Figure 8.7). Although the postcranial skeleton of the proconsuloids is more similar to that of the monkeys, they likely had the hominoid characteristic of lacking a tail, and possessed the hominoid Y5 molar cusp pattern in contrast to the typical X4 bilophodont cusp pattern of the monkeys. These apelike primates occupied forest and woodland environments, eating mostly fruit. There is a general consensus that the proconsuloids were the ancestors of all later hominoids (Harrison 2010). Because the proconsuloids possess features that are characteristic of both apes and monkeys, there is debate over whether they should be classified in the superfamily Hominoidea along with other ape species, or be classified in a separate superfamily, the Proconsuloidea.

During the middle Miocene, beginning approximately 16 mya, the first true hominoids appeared, radiating out of Africa into Eurasia and diversifying into many forms. Consequently, the middle Miocene is often referred to as the Age of the Apes. Several middle Miocene ape species have been identified in the fossil record, including *Kenyapithecus*, *Chororapithecus* and *Nakalipithecus* from Africa; *Dryopithecus* and *Ouranopithecus* from Europe; *Sivapithecus* and *Lufengpithecus* from east Asia; and *Yuanmoupithecus* from China (Figure 8.8). *Gigantopithecus*, from east and south Asia is named for its large size; it appeared during the late Miocene and became extinct during the Pleistocene (Figure 8.9).

There is considerable debate surrounding which of the middle Miocene apes was ancestral to the various modern ape species and humans. *Yuanmoupithecus* has been proposed as the ancestor of the lesser apes (gibbons and siamangs) (Harrison et al. 2008). The cranial—and in particular, facial—features of *Sivapithecus* resemble that of modern orangutans (Pilbeam 1982). It has been proposed that *Sivapithecus* gave rise to *Lufengpithecus* and *Gigantopithecus* (Harrison et al. 2008). Features of the teeth, face, and phalanges suggest that *Lufengpithecus* is the likely ancestor of orangutans (Harrison 2010). Until recently, because of a similarity of facial features, it was thought that *Ouranopithecus* was the likely

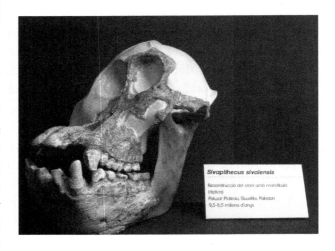

Figure 8.8: *Sivapithecus sivalensis.*

ancestor of the living African apes and humans. However, the recent discovery in Africa of *Chororapithecus* and *Nakalipithecus*, which have features in common with the African apes, has caused many researchers to propose that one of these may be the ancestor of later African apes and humans (Bernor 2007).

CRITICAL REASONING QUESTIONS

- Briefly describe how potassium-argon dating works. What does it date?
- Briefly define anthropoid, hominoid, and hominin. Which of these includes humans?
- What are the taxonomic names of the two families of Eocene primates? To what modern primates are they most similar?
- As far as primate evolution, what is the significance of the Fayum region in Egypt?
- What are two characteristics that distinguish Miocene ape species from monkeys?
- What is meant by the Age of the Apes? When did it occur?

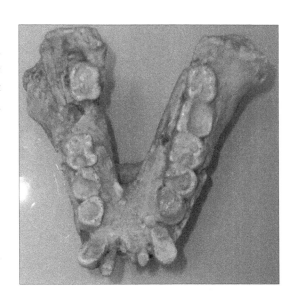

Figure 8.9: *Gigantopithecus blacki.*

REFERENCES AND SUGGESTED READINGS

Bernor, R. L. (2007). New apes fill the gap. *Proceedings of the National Academy of Sciences* 104:19661–19662.

Harrison, T. (2010). Apes among the tangled branches of human origins. *Science* 327:532–534.

Harrison, T., X. Ji, and L. Zheng (2008). Renewed investigations at the late Miocene hominoid locality of Leilao, Yunnan, China. *American Journal of Physical Anthropology* 135(S46):113.

Hoffstetter, R. (1974). Phylogeny and geographical deployment of the primates. *Journal of Human Evolution* 3:327–350.

Pilbeam, D. (1982). New hominoid skull material from the Miocene of Pakistan. *Nature* 295:232–234.

Silcox, M. T. (2007). Primate taxonomy, plesiadapiforms, and the approaches to primate origins. In M. J. Ravosa and M. Dagosto, eds., *Primate Origins: Adaptations and Evolution*, pp. 143–178. New York: Plenum Press.

Williams, B. A., R. F. Kay, and E. C. Kirk (2010). New perspectives on anthropoid origins. *Proceedings of the National Academy of Sciences* 107:4797–4804.

9

Early Hominin Evolution

By Roman Gastrell Harrison

Toward the end of the Miocene epoch and into the Pliocene, the Earth's climate was changing. In Africa, the climate was becoming cooler, drier, and more seasonal. This led to a reduction in size and the fragmentation of tropical forests, an expansion of savanna grasslands, and an increase in mixed woodland/grassland transitional zones. As a result, some of the Miocene African ape species began to increasingly utilize these transitional zones where fruit was less abundant. Evidence for the early hominins is associated with these zones in east Africa. Migration from tropical forest to mixed woodland/grassland presented certain problems to which the early hominins had to adapt. This chapter will explore what it means to be a hominin and the fossil evidence for the evolution of the early hominins.

DEFINITION OF A HOMININ

The distinguishing feature of hominins from the other primates is their mode of locomotion. Whereas the nonhuman primates habitually move around quadrupedally (using all four limbs), the hominins move around bipedally (using only the back limbs). Mode of locomotion can be determined from fossil evidence through the examination of features of the skeleton, including the position of the foramen magnum, curvature of the spine, and two characteristics of the foot. The foramen magnum is the large hole at the bottom of modern human skulls and articulates with the cervical (upper) vertebrae. In bipedal

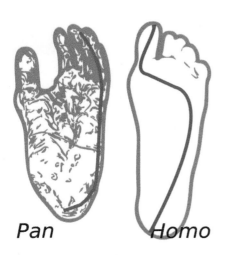

Figure 9.1: *Pan* divergent big toe, primary pressure on outer edge of foot. *Homo* in line big toe, primary pressure more central.

hominins, the foramen magnum is at the base of the skull, which allows for a front-facing orientation of the eyes. In quadrupedal species, the foramen magnum is placed more posterior than it is in bipeds. The spine in bipedal hominins is vertical and forms a gentle S-shape, whereas in the quadrupedal primates, the spine is horizontal and is not S-shaped. Nonhuman primate species have a divergent big toe, while it is in line with the other toes in the bipedal humans. The bipedal humans have a more distinct arch to the foot relative to the nonhuman primates (Figure 9.1).

WHEN DID THE HOMININS FIRST APPEAR?

Prior to the 1970s, estimates of the timing of the divergence of the chimpanzee and human lineages were based on fossil evidence and ranged between 10 mya and 15 mya. However, with more recent fossil discoveries and the application of DNA technology to the question of hominin origins over the past two decades, a more recent picture of the time of divergence has emerged. Over the past decade, a general consensus has emerged, based on both the fossil and genetic evidence: the chimpanzee/human divergence occurred 5–7 mya (Patterson et al. 2006). However, recent comparative studies of DNA suggest that the panin-hominin divergence occurred 4–5 mya (Hobolth et al. 2007). Genetic analysis compares differences in the base sequence between modern chimpanzees and humans. These differences are the result of mutations occurring in each of the lineages over time. Based on the assumption that mutation rates are approximately constant through time, dating of divergence can be calculated.

WHY DID BIPEDALITY EVOLVE?

Over time, as the African environment was changing during the late Miocene and Pliocene, early hominins began to colonize transitional areas between the contracting tropical forests and expanding savanna grasslands, eventually moving on to the grasslands in east Africa. This migration presented problems for the early hominins, particularly in relation to diet. The African apes inhabiting tropical forests incorporate fruit as a major portion of their diet. In the transitional woodland/grassland zones and on the savanna grasslands, fruit is scarce. On the east African savanna, fruit is found in small, isolated clumps of trees. The hominins adapted their diet in varying ways, as will be discussed in the next chapter.

Bipedality arose in the hominins during the same time period they left the tropical forests and colonized the savanna grasslands. Several hypotheses have been proposed as explanations for the evolution of bipedality in the hominins, some of which focus on adaptation to the savanna. The following discussion focuses on five of these hypotheses.

In transitional woodland/grassland areas and on the savanna, food resources would have been patchy compared to the tropical forests, requiring increased travel time and distance when moving from one food location to another. Human bipedal locomotion is more efficient when compared to chimpanzee locomotion in more open environments (Rodman and McHenry 1980). This would have been advantageous for accessing widely spaced food sources on the savanna grasslands. Humans are capable of walking or jogging continuously over large distances (for example, 42-kilometer marathons), but cannot run particularly fast. Animals such as gazelles and leopards that are capable of running fast tire quickly, and can maintain those high speeds only over short distances. This model suggests that the evolution of bipedal locomotion among the hominins was an adaptation to accessing widely spaced food resources on the open savanna.

The evolution of bipedalism may have evolved in response to life on the savanna as a way to stay cool where there is little shade (Wheeler 1991). East Africa straddles the equator, where the sun is close to or directly overhead for a considerable portion of the day. This model proposes that bipedality evolved as a cooling mechanism. In quadrupeds, the sun directly strikes the back and the head. In bipeds, the sun directly hits the shoulders and head, thus reducing the skin surface area that is directly exposed to the sun. Air is hottest close to the ground. A bipedal posture raises a greater proportion of the body higher off the ground, away from the warmer air at ground level. When there is a breeze, wind speeds are greater one or two meters above the ground than at ground level. A bipedal posture takes advantage of these higher wind speeds, allowing greater cooling of the body and evaporation of sweat.

Not all individuals within a group are capable of traveling large distances; toddlers, pregnant females, and older individuals may have difficulty. In this scenario, other individuals would travel to collect food and bring it back to those remaining behind. Bipedal locomotion would leave hands free to carry food and other objects. Lovejoy (1981) suggests that early hominins were K-selected (producing fewer offspring, but with increased infant dependency and parental care), and that males and females were monogamously pair bonded, resulting in increased paternal investment and care of offspring. In this scenario, adult males would travel widely to provision females and offspring.

When nonhuman primates access fruit, they usually climb trees. Occasional bipedalism to pick fruit has been observed in some species; chimpanzees, for instance (Stanford 2002). Standing in order to reach fruit expends less energy than climbing a tree. A bipedal posture may have evolved as an effective way to feed from trees (Hunt 1996).

Traveling in the open savanna grasslands presents a greater risk of being attacked by predators. Isbell and Young (1996) propose that this risk for early hominins may have been reduced by increasing group size (safety in numbers) and by increasing apparent body size by standing up bipedally. A bipedal stance raises an individual's field of view higher off the ground, above the height of small bushes and grass, increasing the chance of spotting predators. This model indicates that a bipedal posture evolved as a defense mechanism.

PROTOHOMININS

The recent DNA evidence suggesting that the divergence of the human and chimpanzee lineages may have occurred as recently as 4–5 mya (Hobolth et al. 2007) has led to debate over whether fossil species that date earlier than approximately 4 mya are hominins (Wood and Lonergan 2008). These species exhibit morphological features that suggest a functional ability for—but not necessarily habitual—bipedal locomotion, combined with features adaptive for arboreal movement. This book will refer to these pre–4 mya species as protohominins, as do other researchers (Keenleyside and Lazenby 2011). These species include *Sahelanthropus tchadensis*, *Orrorin tugenensis*, *Ardipithecus ramidus*, and *Ardipithecus kadabba*.

The earliest of these species is *Sahelanthropus tchadensis*, whose fossil remains were discovered in 2001 and 2002 at sites in northern Chad in central Africa; the remains have been dated to between 7.4 mya and 6.5 mya (Brunet et al. 2002) (Figure 9.2). The remains include a mostly complete cranium, teeth, and mandibular fragments. *Sahelanthropus* is unique in that it is the only protohominin or early hominin species to be found outside of the east African Rift Valley region. Associated floral and faunal fossil remains suggest that *Sahelanthropus* occupied a woodland lakeside environment. Currently, there is debate over whether *Sahelanthropus* was bipedal or quadrupedal. Brunet and colleagues (2002) argue that the position of the foramen magnum is closer to that of hominins at the base of the cranium, and therefore *Sahelanthropus* moved bipedally, but Wolpoff and colleagues (2002) suggest that the foramen magnum has a more posterior position closer to that of ape species, indicating quadrupedal locomotion. To date, no postcranial remains of *Sahelanthropus* have been recovered, hence other morphological features indicative of bipedality such as those of the foot are unavailable. Debate surrounding the mode of locomotion for *Sahelanthropus* continues. At present, it is probably best to view *Sahelanthropus* as a possible early hominin species.

Another recent discovery occurred in 2001, when fossils of teeth and a lower limb were recovered from a deposit in the Tugen Hills in Kenya in east Africa. These remains have been ascribed to a new species, *Orrorin tugenensis*, and have been dated to between 6.0 mya and 5.7 mya (Senut et al. 2001)(Figure 9.3). Floral remains found in association indicate that *Orrorin tugenensis* occupied a woodland environment with open areas. There is considerable, though not complete, agreement that *Orrorin* moved bipedally, as indicated

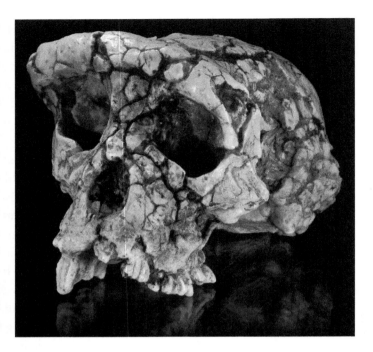

Figure 9.2: *Sahelanthropus tchadensis,* Chad.

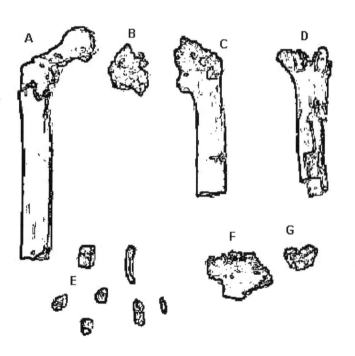

Figure 9.3: *Orrorin tugenensis,* Tugen Hills, Kenya.

by morphological features, including those of the head and neck of the femur. *Orrorin tugenensis* is best viewed as being a probable—but not definite—early hominin.

Beginning in the 1990s, fossils ascribed to a new genus, *Ardipithecus*, have been recovered from the site of Aramis in the Afar region of Ethiopia, also in east Africa. These remains are fragmentary and include cranial, dental, and postcranial fragments. They have been placed into two species: *Ardipithecus kadabba,* dating to between 5.8 mya and 5.2 mya; and *Ardipithecus ramidus*, dating to 4.4 mya (White et al. 1994)(Figure 9.4). *Ardipithecus* lived in woodland environments, as indicated by the associated floral and faunal remains. The earlier *Ardipithecus kadabba* displays some features that are somewhat more primitive (for example, a more pointed canine) than seen in *Ardipithecus ramidus*. Features of the pelvis and upper and lower limbs indicate that *Ardipithecus* was bipedal.

There is debate over whether morphological features associated with *Sahelanthropus, Orrorin*, and *Ardipithecus* are distinct enough to warrant placement in separate genera. White and colleagues (2009) advocate placement of all three in the genus *Ardipithecus*. (Note: taxonomic naming practice requires the retention of the earliest designated taxonomic name when taxonomic categories are to be combined; in this case, *Ardipithecus*, first discovered and named in 1994). Regardless of taxonomic naming issues, many researchers agree that *Ardipithecus ramidus* was the precursor to the later australopithecine and *Homo* species (White et al. 2006).

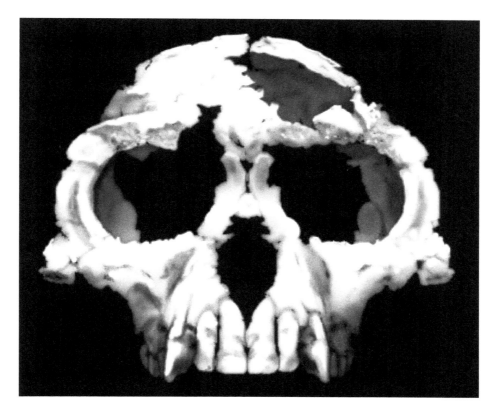

Figure 9.4: *Ardipithecus ramidus,* Aramis, Ethiopia.

CRITICAL REASONING QUESTIONS

- What characteristic distinguishes the hominins from other primate species?
- Briefly describe three features of the skeleton that can determine whether a primate fossil species is habitually bipedal or quadrupedal.
- How is DNA used to determine the date of the divergence of the human and chimpanzee lineages? When did this divergence occur?
- How was the African environment changing at the end of the Miocene and the beginning of the Pliocene?
- What type of environment did the early hominins colonize? To what problem in this environment did they have to adapt?
- Briefly explain how we know in what type of environment a particular fossil hominin species lived.
- What is the name of an early dating fossil species that was found in Chad? Why can't we currently definitely classify this species as a hominin?

REFERENCES AND SUGGESTED READINGS

Brunet, Michel, Franck Guy, David Pilbeam, et al. (2002). A new hominid from the Upper Miocene of Chad, central Africa. *Nature* 418:145–151.

Hobolth, Asger, Ole F. Christensen, Thomas Mailund, and Mikkel H. Schierup (2007). Genomic relationships and speciation times of human, chimpanzee, and gorilla inferred from a coalescent hidden Markov model. *PLoS Genetics* 4(2):294–304.

Hunt, K. D. (1996). The postural feeding hypothesis: An ecological model for the evolution of bipedalism. *South African Journal of Science* 92:77–90.

Isbell, L., and T. Young (1996). The evolution of bipedalism in hominids and reduced group size in chimpanzees: Alternative responses to decreasing resource availability. *Journal of Human Evolution* 30:389–397.

Keenleyside, Anne, and Richard Lazenby (2011). *A human voyage: Exploring biological anthropology*. Toronto: Nelson Education Ltd.

Lovejoy, C. O. (1981). The origin of man. *Science* 211:341–350.

Patterson, N., D. J. Richter, S. Gnerre, et al. (2006). Genetic evidence for complex speciation of humans and chimpanzees. *Nature* 441:1103–1108.

Rodman, P. S., and H. M. McHenry (1980). Bioenergetics and the origin of hominid bipedalism. *American Journal of Physical Anthropology* 52:103–106.

Senut, Brigitte, Martin Pickford, Dominique Gommery, et al. (2001). First hominid from the Miocene (Lukeino formation, Kenya). *Comptes Rendus de l'Académie des Sciences-Series IIA-Earth and Planetary Science* 332(2):137–144.

Stanford, C. B. (2002). Arboreal adaptation in Bwindi chimpanzees. *American Journal of Physical Anthropology* 119:87–91.

Wheeler, P. E. (1991). The thermoregulatory advantages of hominid bipedalism in open equatorial environments: The contribution of increased convective heat loss and cutaneous evaporative cooling. *Journal of Human Evolution* 21:107–115.

White, T. D., G. Suwa, and B. Asfaw (1994). *Australopithecus ramidus*, a new species of early hominid from Aramis, Ethiopia. *Nature* 371:306–312.

White, Tim D., Giday WoldeGabriel, Berhane Asfaw, et al. (2006). Asa Issie, Aramis, and the origin of *Australopithecus*. *Nature* 440(7086):883–889.

White, Tim D., Berhane Asfaw, Yonas Beyene, et al. (2009). *Australopithecus ramidus* and the paleobiology of early hominids. *Science* 326(5949):75–86.

Wolpoff, M. H., B. Senut, M. Pickford, and J. Hawks (2002). *Sahelanthropus* or "Sahelpithecus"? *Nature* 419:581–582.

Wood, B. A., and N. Lonergan (2008). The hominin fossil record: Taxa, grades, and clades. *Journal of Anatomy* 212:354–376.

The Australopithecines

By Roman Gastrell Harrison

After approximately 4.2 million years ago (mya), fossil evidence for the evolution of the hominins becomes somewhat more diverse. This marks the first appearance of a group of species called the australopithecines. By the time of this appearance, migration from the tropical forests onto the expanding savanna grasslands of east Africa was essentially complete.

Some of these species are more heavily built in features of the cranium, and are called the robust australopithecines. Other species have somewhat more lightly built cranial features; these are called the gracile australopithecines. The earliest of the australopithecines are the gracile australopithecines. There is some discussion relating to the taxonomic classification of these two groups of australopithecines. In this chapter, we will discuss the fossil evidence for the australopithecine species, the relationship between australopithecine cranial features and their dietary adaptation to the savanna, and provide a brief overview of the debate relating to taxonomic classification.

GRACILE AUSTRALOPITHECINES

The earliest of the australopithecine species, *Australopithecus anamensis*, was first identified in the fossil record in the 1990s, and dates to between 4.2 mya and 3.8 mya. Remains include over four dozen fragments of the cranium, dentition, and postcranium, first recovered from the sites of Kanapoi and Allia Bay on the eastern side of Lake Turkana in Kenya (Leakey et al. 1998), with subsequent discoveries at the sites of Asa Issie and Aramis in Ethiopia (White et al. 2006). Skeletal evidence indicates that *Australopithecus anamensis* moved bipedally and occupied both the grassland and woodland environments of east Africa. There is general consensus that *Australopithecus anamensis* evolved from the earlier *Ardipithecus ramidus*, and was the precursor of the later *Australopithecus afarensis*, forming a phyletic sequence through time (White et al. 2006).

In 1974, a skeleton that was 40 percent complete and dated to 3.2 mya was discovered at the site of Hadar in the Afar region of Ethiopia by a team led by Donald Johanson. At the time of discovery, the Beatles' song "Lucy in the Sky with Diamonds" was playing on the radio, and so this individual was given the nickname Lucy. Prior to this discovery, it had been thought that expansion of the brain was an ancestral hominin trait, and that the evolution of bipedalism came somewhat later. However, Lucy had a relatively small cranial capacity of approximately 380 cc (not much larger than modern chimpanzees) in combination with bipedal locomotion, indicating that the advent of bipedal locomotion preceded enlargement of the brain in hominin evolution. Soon after the discovery of Lucy, the fossil remains of several other individuals also possessing these same features were recovered from Hadar. As a result, a new hominin species was defined: *Australopithecus afarensis* (Figures 10.1, 10.2). Since these initial discoveries at Hadar, *Australopithecus afarensis* remains have been recovered from several sites in east Africa. Collectively, the *Australopithecus afarensis* fossil remains date to between 3.9 mya and 3.0 mya. Faunal and floral evidence indicates that *Australopithecus afarensis* lived predominantly in grassland environments.

Features of the pelvis such as the subpubic angle and the shape of the obturator foramen indicate that Lucy was female. When compared with a modern human female skeleton, Lucy's skeleton has many similarities, but also shows some differences. These differences demonstrate some of the evolutionary changes that have occurred in humans over the last three million years. For example, Lucy (who was of average height for an *Australopithecus afarensis* female) is shorter than the modern human female, indicating a trend to increased stature through time. Other trends in hominin evolution evidenced by the differences between Lucy and the modern female include an increase in cranial capacity, a reduction in the size of the brow ridges, reduced subnasal prognathism, and a reduction in the length of the arms in proportion to the length of the legs.

Another significant discovery was made at the site of Laetoli in Tanzania in 1978 by Mary Leakey (Leakey and Hay 1979), where thousands of footprints of various animal species, including hominins, were preserved in a layer of volcanic ash dating to 3.5 mya (Figure 10.3). The hominin footprints cover a distance of 24 meters and represent at least two individuals, and possibly a third with smaller feet than the other two. This presents the intriguing possibility that these hominin footprints may have been made by a family unit consisting of an adult male and female and their child. These footprints show conclusive evidence of bipedalism, including the fact that they come in pairs not fours; that the big toe is in line with the other toes; and that there is the presence of a distinct arch. Fossil remains attributed to *Australopithecus afarensis* have also been recovered at Laetoli. The general consensus is that the Laetoli footprints were made by *Australopithecus afarensis*.

Of the species that have been previously discussed in this book, there is a general consensus that the fossil evidence indicates the presence of bipedality—and therefore hominin status—in *Ardipithecus ramidus*, *Australopithecus anamensis*, and *Australopithecus afarensis*. Remains of these species all come from sites located in east Africa, the cradle of humanity. It is not until after approximately 3.5 mya that definite hominin sites are found outside of east Africa.

The earliest hominin fossil discovery in southern Africa occurred in 1924, when Raymond Dart found a child's skull at the site of Taung in South Africa. Dart classified the Taung skull as *Australopithecus africanus* (southern ape of Africa)(Figure 10.4). Subsequent finds of *Australopithecus africanus* remains have occurred at other southern African sites, including Makapansgat and Sterkfontein caves. Dating of these southern African cave sites has been somewhat problematic. Generally, radiometric techniques are not applicable to the dolomitic limestone found in the caves. Stratigraphic faunal association has typically been used to date hominin fossils found in these caves, providing a generally accepted time range of 3.3 mya to 2.3 mya for *Australopithecus africanus*. However, recent reanalysis of the dating of the southern African cave sites suggests a somewhat later time range of 3.0 mya to 2.0 mya for *Australopithecus africanus* (Walker et al. 2006). Recent fossil discoveries at the site of Malapa, South Africa, dated to almost 2 mya, may be those of a new distinct gracile australopithecine species. Named *Australopithecus sediba*, the discoverers suggest that these fossils represent the transitional species between earlier *Australopithecus africanus* and later early *Homo* (Berger et al. 2010). However, a majority of researchers do not recognize these fossils as a distinct species, and consider them to be later *Australopithecus africanus*, the position taken by the authors of this book.

The discovery in 1997 at the site of Bouri in the Awash region of Ethiopia of hominin fossils dating to 2.5 mya has provided a potential candidate for the australopithecine species which gave rise to the genus *Homo*. These remains include fragments of cranial, dental, and postcranial bones representing more than one individual, and have been classified in a new species named *Australopithecus garhi* (Asfaw et al. 1999). Morphological features on these remains show similarity to those of both the earlier dating *Australopithecus afarensis* and the later dating *Homo* species. Bones of animals found in association with *Australopithecus garhi* remains at Bouri show evidence of intentional breaking of the bones and cut marks on the bones made using

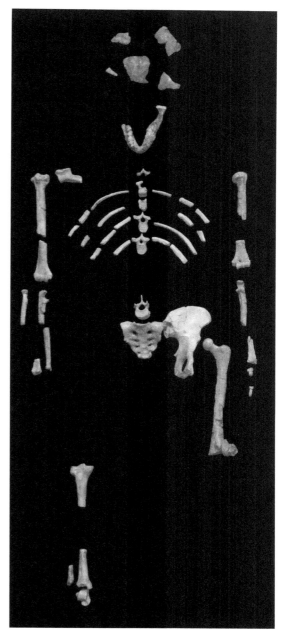

Figure 10.1: 'Lucy' fossil, *Australopithecus afarensis,* Hadar, Ethiopia.

stone tools. In addition, simple stone tools were found nearby, and appear to have come from the strata containing the *Australopithecus garhi* remains. This suggests that *Australopithecus garhi* made and used stone tools. In combination, both the morphological skeletal evidence and the stone tool cultural evidence make a strong case for *Australopithecus garhi* being the immediate ancestor of *Homo*.

Question: Are there other distinct gracile australopithecine species? Two recent fossil discoveries have led some researchers to question whether other australopithecine species existed contemporaneous with *Australopithecus afarensis*. In 1995, the remains of a partial hominin jaw and teeth were found in Chad, north central Africa, dating to between

Figure 10.2: 'Lucy' reconstruction, *Australopithecus afarensis*.

3.5 mya and 3.0 mya. The team that unearthed the remains announced that they represented a separate species distinct from *Australopithecus afarensis*, and named it *Australopithecus bahrelghazali* (Brunet et al. 1995). However, the majority of researchers maintain that these remains are those of *Australopithecus afarensis*, or that they are too fragmentary for a taxonomic designation to be made.

In 2001, hominin remains dating to 3.5 mya were discovered at Lomekwi on the western side of Lake Turkana in Kenya. It was announced that these represented a new species, and were given the name *Kenyanthropus platyops*, since the face appeared to be flatter than that of *Australopithecus afarensis* (Leakey et al. 2001)(Figure 10.5). However, many researchers consider these facial differences to be intraspecies variation, and thus classify the Lomekwi fossils as *Australopithecus afarensis*.

Question: When should a set of fossils be classified as one single species, and when should they be separated into separate species? There is no easy answer to this question; consequently, it has precipitated debate among paleoanthropologists. The recognition and classification of ancient species is based on the analysis of the physical morphology as observed in the fossil evidence. The central question in this debate is: How much morphological difference is required in order to separate a set of fossils into two species? This is what is commonly referred to as the splitters versus lumpers debate. Splitters have a greater tendency to explain morphological difference in fossil sets in terms of species differentiation, whereas lumpers tend to view these differences as variation within a single species. For example, splitters would view *Australopithecus afarensis*, *Australopithecus bahrelghazali*, and *Kenyanthropus platyops* as three distinct species. Lumpers would view these three fossil sets as one single species named *Australopithecus afarensis*. In this book's discussion of human evolution, where there is debate concerning splitting versus lumping, in each instance, we take the viewpoint of the majority of researchers. For example, the hominin phylogeny used in this book (discussed in Chapter 11) subsumes *Australopithecus bahrelghazali* and *Kenyanthropus platyops* into *Australopithecus afarensis*, the majority view.

As a generalization, the hominins became more gracile over time, particularly in features of the cranium. Our own species, *Homo sapiens*, is the most gracile of all of the hominins. The gracile australopithecines, while somewhat less heavily built as compared with the robust australopithecines, are considerably more robust than more recent *Homo* species.

Average cranial capacity of the gracile australopithecines is approximately 440 cc, about one third that of modern humans. Compared to modern humans, they have pronounced brow ridges, considerable subnasal prognathism, a relatively large lower jaw, large molars, and thick enamel. The canine teeth project somewhat beyond the other teeth. In order to fully close the jaws, there is a gap called the diastema, between the second incisor and canine in the maxilla, and between the canine and first premolar in the mandible. Diastemas provide slots for the projecting canines to fit in when the jaws are closed. Over the course of human evolution, the canines and the diastema become smaller, to the point that modern human canines do not project beyond the other teeth and have no diastema.

The shape of the tooth row, or dental arcade, of the maxilla and mandible has changed over the course of human evolution. Apes have a dental arcade that is more rectangular in shape. The common ancestor of chimpanzees and humans 5–7 mya was an ape, and therefore had a rectangular dental arcade. By approximately 3 mya, the dental arcade in *Australopithecus afarensis* became U-shaped; the shape is parabolic in modern humans.

The canines and first premolar teeth have also changed over the course of human evolution. The canines have become less pointed, smaller, and less sexually dimorphic. Collectively, these three changes are called incisorization because over time, hominin canines have come to look more like incisors. The first premolar has become less pointed and has developed a second cusp in a process called molarization.

Figure 10.3: *Australopithecus afarensis,* footprints, Laetoli, Tanzania.

ROBUST AUSTRALOPITHECINES

Dating later in time are three species with more robust features of the cranium, as compared with the gracile australopithecines. Originally, both the gracile and robust australopithecine species were classified in a single genus: *Australopithecus*. However, more recently, there has been debate over whether the robust australopithecines should be placed in their own genus: *Paranthropus*. Here, the central question is whether there is enough morphological difference between the two groups to warrant classification in two genera. This book will take the two-genera viewpoint, here using *Paranthropus* for the robust australopithecines.

Among the earlier fossil finds coming from Africa are those of *Paranthropus robustus*, first discovered by Robert Broom in 1938 at Kromdraai, South Africa (Broom 1938). Sites containing *Paranthropus robustus* remains are restricted to southern Africa, and are dated to between 2.0 mya and 1.2 mya (Figure 10.6). In 1959, the first east African discovery of robust australopithecine remains occurred at Olduvai Gorge, Tanzania, by Louis and Mary Leakey (Leakey 1959). Olduvai Gorge has been one of the most prolific locations for the discovery of hominin fossils (Figure 10.7). Originally named *Zinjanthropus boisei* by the Leakeys, this fossil and others of the same species from other east African sites (for example, Koobi Fora), dating to between 2.2 mya and 1.2 mya, are now classified in the same genus as *Paranthropus robustus*, and are named *Paranthropus boisei* (Figure 10.8).

A more recent discovery in 1986 from west Lake Turkana, Kenya, is that of the earliest dating (2.7 mya to 2.3 mya) of the robust australopithecines. Originally considered to be early *Paranthropus boisei*, this

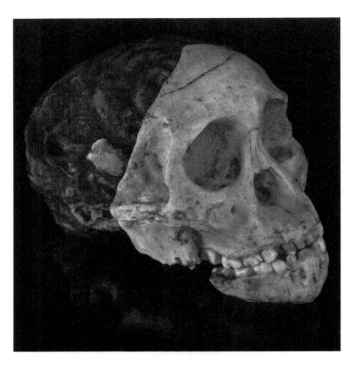

Figure 10.4: *Australopithecus africanus,* child, Taung, South Africa.

and subsequent discoveries (from the Omo region of Ethiopia, for instance) are now classified as a distinct species named *Paranthropus aethiopicus* (Walker et al. 1986)(Figure 10.9).

As a group, the robust australopithecine species have an average cranial capacity of 530 cc, somewhat larger than the earlier dating gracile australopithecines. The cranial features that distinguish the robust australopithecines from the gracile australopithecines include larger molars, thicker enamel, a very large mandible, a sagittal crest (ridge of bone down the center of the top of the cranium), and projecting zygomatic arches (cheekbones). These features are related to diet, as discussed below. The latter three features serve as anchors for the large temporalis (chewing) muscles associated with the robust australopithecines. In modern humans, smaller temporalis muscles attach to a more lightly built mandible, non-projecting zygomatic arches, and continue approximately halfway up the side of the cranium. In the robust australopithecines, the large temporalis muscles require larger muscle attachment sites, including the large mandible, projecting zygomatic arches, and sagittal crest, which serve as an anchor for the upper portion of the temporalis muscles.

Figure 10.5: *Kenyanthropus platyops,* Lomekwi, Kenya.

TEETH AND DIET

As a generalization, the morphology of the dentition of a species is largely related to the type of diet consumed by that species. For example, carnivorous species tend to have larger canines in order to hunt prey; by contrast, herbivorous grazers are inclined to have larger molars in order to process grasses. Species whose diet consists of tough crunchy foods usually have thicker enamel, so that with life-long wear, the enamel will last an animal's lifetime. In contrast, species whose diet is softer tend to have thinner enamel, since there is less life-long wear on the teeth. Modern humans have small molars and thin enamel, since the modern human diet is highly processed and soft. Humans

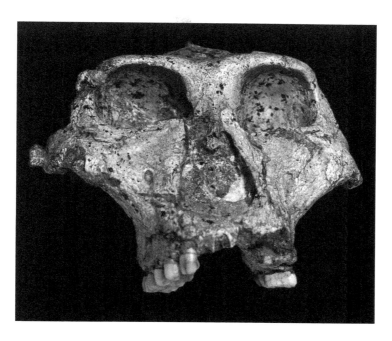

Figure 10.6: *Paranthropus robustus,* Swartkrans, South Africa.

Figure 10.7: Olduvai Gorge, Tanzania.

acquire meat through the use of tools, and thus have small canines. Chimpanzees have small molars and thin enamel, reflecting a soft diet concentrating on fruit and leaves. The moderately projecting canines of chimpanzees are used in agonistic encounters.

Teeth are particularly durable and tend to preserve well, and are the most frequently discovered fossil type. A picture of the diet of a fossil species can be deduced through the examination of features of the teeth, and with knowledge of the food resources available in the environment in which that fossil species lived. The early hominins migrated from the African tropical forests on to the expanding savanna grasslands where fruit was scarce, but other plant foods were abundant, including seeds and nuts.

As time progressed, the australopithecines increased their exploitation of harder foods. The robust australopithecines' large molars and thick enamel, in combination with a large mandible, flared zygomatic arches, and sagittal crest (which served as anchors for large chewing muscles) (Figure 10.10) indicate their adaptation to the savanna grasslands by concentrating on tougher, crunchier, and more readily available foods. As will be further discussed

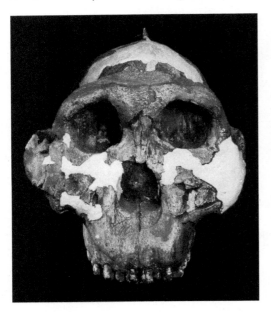

Figure 10.8: *Paranthropus boisei,* Olduvai Gorge, Tanzania.

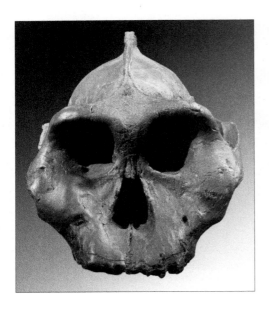

Figure 10.9: *Paranthropus aethiopicus,* West Turkana, Kenya.

Figure 10.10: Robust Australopithecines: Cranial features.

in the next chapter, the early *Homo* dietary adaptation contrasts with that of the australopithecines and is reflected in their dentition.

CRITICAL REASONING QUESTIONS

- In what year was the first hominin fossil discovered in Africa? Who discovered this fossil? What taxonomic name was this fossil given?
- Who is Lucy? How does she differ from a modern human female?
- What is the significance of the Laetoli footprints?
- Briefly describe how the dental arcade, diastema, and canine and first premolar teeth changed during hominin evolution.
- What morphological features distinguish the robust australopithecines from the gracile australopithecines?
- Briefly describe why the robust australopithecines evolved these features.

REFERENCES AND SUGGESTED READINGS

Asfaw, B., T. White, O. Lovejoy, et al. (1999). *Australopithecus garhi*: A new species of early hominid from Ethiopia. *Science* 284:629–635.

Berger, Lee R., Darryl J. de Ruiter, Steven E. Churchill, et al. (2010). *Australopithecus sediba*: A new species of *Homo*-like australopith from South Africa. *Science* 328(5975):195–204.

Broom, R. (1938). The Pleistocene anthropoid apes of South Africa. *Nature* 142:377–379.

Brunet, Michel, Alain Beauvilain, Yves Coppens, et al. (1995). The first australopithecine 2,500 kilometres west of the Rift Valley (Chad). *Nature* 378:273–275.

Leakey, L. (1959). A new fossil skull from Olduvai. *Nature* 184:491–493.

Leakey, M. D., and R. L. Hay (1979). Pliocene footprints in the Laetoli beds at Laetoli, northern Tanzania. *Nature* 278:317–323.

Leakey, M. G., C. S. Feibel, I. McDougall, et al. (1998). New specimens and confirmation of an early age for *Australopithecus anamensis*. *Nature* 393:62–66.

Leakey, Meave G., Fred Spoor, Frank H. Brown, et al. (2001). New hominin genus from eastern Africa shows diverse Middle Pliocene lineages. *Nature* 410:433–440.

Walker, A., R. E. Leakey, J. M. Harris, and F. H. Brown (1986). 2.5 myr *Australopithecus boisei* from west of Lake Turkana, Kenya. *Nature* 322:517–522.

Walker, J., R. A. Cliff, and A. G. Latham (2006). U-Pb isotopic age of the Stw 573 hominid from Sterkfontein, South Africa. *Science* 314:1592–1594.

White, Tim D., Giday WoldeGabriel, Berhane Asfaw, et al. (2006). Asa Issie, Aramis, and the origin of *Australopithecus*. *Nature* 440(7086):883–889.

11

The Genus *Homo*

By Roman Gastrell Harrison

Between two and a half and two million years ago, new, larger-brained hominins appear in the fossil record. These fossils are commonly referred to as early *Homo*, and represent the earliest appearance of our own genus. This period also marks the earliest physical evidence for human culture in the form of stone tools. As time progressed, even larger-brained hominins appear in the fossil record, and evidence for various aspects of culture increases. In this chapter, we will discuss the fossil evidence for premodern *Homo* species, selected aspects of the lifeway of these species, and evidence for early culture, including the manufacture of stone tools, how meat was obtained, the controlled use of fire, and the construction of shelters.

EARLY *HOMO*

Early *Homo* remains were first discovered in 1960 at Olduvai Gorge in east Africa by Louis and Mary Leakey, who suggested that early *Homo* had been responsible for the production of associated simple stone tools, and gave them the name *Homo habilis* (handy man) (Leakey et al. 1964). Since this initial discovery, early *Homo* remains have been found at a variety of sites in east Africa (for example, Koobi Fora in Kenya, the Omo River basin in Ethiopia) and southern Africa (Sterkfontein in South Africa, Uruha in Malawi). Early *Homo* fossils may date as early as 2.5 million years ago (mya) and as late as 1.4 mya.

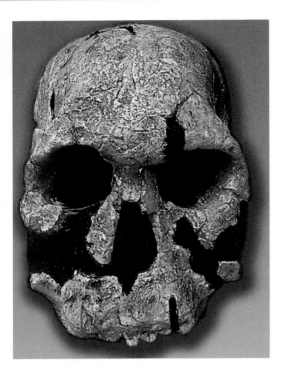 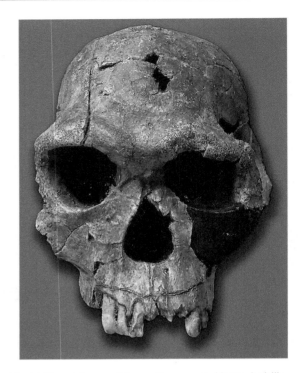

Figure 11.1: Early *Homo* (a) larger group, *Homo rudolfensis*, Koobi Fora, Kenya, (b) smaller group, *Homo habilis*, Koobi Fora, Kenya.

Early *Homo* cranial capacity is significantly larger than that of any of the australopithecine species, ranging between 600 cc and 750 cc. This enlarged brain size is the hallmark distinguishing feature of the genus *Homo*. Compared with the australopithecines, early *Homo* has smaller molars and thinner enamel, reflecting a softer diet. Cranial muscle attachment sites are smaller, indicating smaller temporalis chewing muscles. There is less subnasal prognathism and the cranium is more rounded, reflecting the larger brain size. Manufactured stone tools are found in association with early *Homo* fossils.

The early *Homo* fossil set contains considerable variability in terms of the size of the cranium, falling into two overlapping groups: a larger and a smaller group (Figure 11.1). This has led to debate over whether the early *Homo* fossil set represents one single species (named *Homo habilis*), or two distinct species (the larger named *Homo rudolfensis* and the smaller called *Homo habilis*). Those researchers who favor the single-species hypothesis explain the variation as representing a high degree of sexual dimorphism within one species, the larger group males and smaller group females. Other researchers suggest that the amount of difference between the two groups is too large to be explained as sexual dimorphism. The average cranial capacity of the large group is approximately 735 cc, and the smaller group 650 cc. These researchers maintain that this difference of 85 cc in cranial capacity is too great a disparity to be explained as males and females of the same species. In modern humans, average male brain size is approximately 20–30 cc larger than female brain size. This is to be expected, since males on average have larger overall body size. Currently, the consensus is moving toward considering the early *Homo* fossil set as representing two distinct species.

EARLY *HOMO* LIFEWAYS

Hominin colonization of the savanna grasslands of east Africa required adaptation to different dietary resources compared to those found in the tropical forests. Whereas the australopithecines adapted by concentrating on tough, crunchy plant foods, early *Homo* began to incorporate regular meat eating into their diet, combined with some tough, crunchy plants, as well as what fruit they could find in isolated clumps of trees. Morphological features of the cranium provide evidence for this different adaptation. In contrast to the australopithecines, early *Homo* displays more gracile cranial features, including a less robust mandible, receding zygomatic arches, and no sagittal crest, indicating a softer diet (meat is a soft food). Additional evidence is provided by the analysis of microwear on the enamel surface of teeth. The australopithecines have a more pitted enamel surface, compared with the smoother surface associated with early *Homo* (Unger et al. 2006). Stone tool cut marks on prey bones are associated with early *Homo* sites (Shipman 1986). With the exception of *Australopithecus garhi*, prey bones with stone tool cut marks are not associated with the australopithecines.

Question: Was meat eating by early Homo *advantageous?* The simple answer to this question is that early *Homo* continued to evolve into later hominin species and finally modern humans, whereas the robust australopithecines became extinct, suggesting that the early *Homo* dietary adaptation was more advantageous. Nevertheless, obtaining meat is more difficult than obtaining plants. Animals tend to run away from humans, but plants do not. If an animal is caught, it will likely struggle to get away. It would not have been easy to kill an animal of significant size with simple stone tools. Let's say you are an early *Homo* individual armed with a simple stone tool who wants gazelle for dinner. The gazelle can run faster than you, and even if you managed to catch the gazelle, you would not likely inflict much damage. In other words, the chances of you having gazelle for dinner would be extremely small. But if we change this scenario such that several individuals work together instead of a single individual acting alone, then the chances of catching a gazelle increase. Increased brain size and intelligence of early *Homo* may have facilitated the ability for increased group cooperation and planning.

In the above scenario, the assumption was that meat was obtained through hunting. However, meat may also be obtained through scavenging. At first glance, it might seem that it would be easier to access meat by scavenging. All that is required is that a freshly dead carcass is located and butchered using stone tools. However, there are problems associated with scavenging. The majority of savanna prey animals do not die a natural death, but rather are killed by carnivores such as lions for food. With their simple stone tools, if a group of early *Homo* were to try to scare away the lions before they had finished feeding on their kill, the early *Homo* would likely be attacked and become dessert for the lions. If they waited for the lions to finish feeding and move away, early *Homo* could then access the leftover scraps of meat on the carcass. However, there are other scavengers such as hyenas to contend with.

Question: Did early Homo *obtain their meat primarily through hunting or scavenging?* Evidence associated with cut marks indicates that early *Homo* obtained meat primarily through scavenging. Studies that have analyzed prey bones associated with early *Homo* indicate the presence of marks made by both stone tools and the teeth of large carnivores. Stone tools leave more jagged cut marks, while those made by large carnivore teeth are more rounded (Figure 11.2). The stone tool cut marks overlay the large carnivore tooth marks, indicating that early *Homo* was accessing the leftover meat scraps of carnivore kills (Shipman 1986). In addition, breakage patterns on these bones indicate that early *Homo* took advantage of marrow as a dietary resource.

Question: Did early Homo *have home bases?* A home base is a specific location a group of hominins come back to repeatedly, where activities such as sleeping, socializing, and food sharing occur.

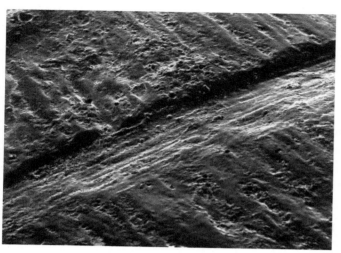

Figure 11.2: Scanning Electron Microscope image of stone tool cut marks.

Typical hunter/gatherer home bases are used for a period of weeks and are then abandoned. At Olduvai, Bed 1, dating to 1.9 mya, a circular concentration of stones, prey bones, and stone tools is present. Many of the prey bones show cut marks made by stone tools and the teeth of large carnivores. It has been suggested that these sites are the remains of home bases (Isaac 1978). On the other hand, these sites appear to have accumulated over longer periods of time—in the range of five to ten years—and were visited by carnivores. This suggests that they likely do not represent home bases (Lewin 2005). More recently, it has been suggested that sites such as Olduvai, Bed 1, are either butcher sites, where carcasses were disarticulated and carried elsewhere, or that they are tool caches, where stone tools were stored (Potts 1988).

HOMO ERGASTER AND HOMO ERECTUS

After 2.0 mya, hominins with increasing brain size (averaging approximately 1000 cc) initially appear at various sites in Africa, including Olduvai Gorge in Tanzania, along the shores of Lake Turkana in Kenya, and at Swartkrans in South Africa, and after about 1.5 mya outside of Africa in Asia and Europe. This represents the first migration of hominins to areas outside of Africa, including temperate zones, where cultural adaptations were made in order to live in regions where portions of the year were characterized by cooler temperatures (further discussed below).

Collectively, this fossil set dates to between 1.8 mya and 500,000 years ago. These fossils have less subnasal prognathism and smaller teeth compared with earlier hominins, but have large supraorbital torii (brow ridges). Features characteristic of this fossil set include a sagittal keel (a slight angularity of the cranium when viewed from the front) and an angled occiput (where the rear portion of the cranium forms an angle when viewed from the side) (see Figure 11.5). An almost complete skeleton discovered in 1984 at the site of Nariokotome on the western side of Lake Turkana, dated to 1.6 mya, is of a boy who died at eight years of age and stood about 5 feet 3 inches tall (Walker and Leakey 1993) (Figure 11.3). This and other individuals indicate that by about 1.5 mya, the stature of hominins had increased to that of the range of modern humans.

Question: Does the hominin fossil set dating to between 1.8 mya and 500 kya represent one species or two? Over the time period for this fossil, set there is considerable variation in brain size, with earlier fossils in the range of 800–900 cc and the later fossils increasing to 1000–1100 cc. As with other debates of this nature, the question is whether this difference represents intraspecies variation, or whether the degree of variation indicates two distinct species. Those researchers who hold the first viewpoint classify this entire fossil set as one single species named *Homo erectus*, while those of the second standpoint name the earlier

 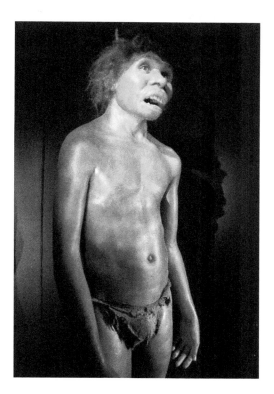

Figure 11.3: *Homo ergaster,* Nariokotome, Kenya, (left) fossil skeleton, (right) reconstruction.

smaller-brained African fossils *Homo ergaster* (Figure 11.4), and the later larger-brained fossils from Africa, Asia, and Europe *Homo erectus* (Figure 11.5). This book takes the view that two species are represented by this fossil set.

Figure 11.5: *Homo erectus* (Sangiran, Java, Indonesia).

Figure 11.4: *Homo ergaster* (Koobi Fora, Kenya).

ARCHAIC HUMANS

Hominin fossil remains with even larger brain sizes averaging 1200 cc appear by approximately 600,000 years ago. This fossil set is found in both temperate and tropical areas of Africa, Asia, and Europe. The craniums of these fossils more closely resemble those of modern humans. The occipital area of the cranium is more rounded, and the maximum breadth of the skull is located higher than in earlier species, reflecting the larger brain size compared with *Homo erectus*. In many ways, the morphology of this fossil set is transitional between the earlier *Homo erectus* and later *Homo sapiens*. There is debate as to whether this fossil set represents a distinct species named *Homo heidelbergensis*, or whether they are simply transitional forms—in which case, they are not given a distinct taxonomic name and are referred to as archaic *Homo sapiens*.

By 200,000 years ago in Europe, the Middle East, and central Asia, a distinct hominin appears: the Neanderthals. The traditional view is that Neanderthals disappeared by approximately 30,000 years ago. A recently dated Neanderthal site in Gibraltar suggests that they may have persisted in this area until 28,000 years ago (Finlayson et al. 2006). However, it has been recently suggested that there is no solid evidence for Neanderthals later that 35,000 years ago (Joris and Street 2008).

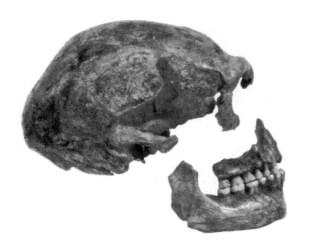

Figure 11.6: *Homo neanderthalensis* (Spy, Belgium).

The remains of a Neanderthal individual was the first fossil find, which at the time of discovery (in 1856 in the Neander Valley in Germany) was recognized to be those of an earlier human species predating modern humans. Neanderthals had large brains averaging 1520 cc, a characteristic occipital bun (a large protrusion on the rear part of the cranium) (Figure 11.6), and relative to modern humans a shorter, stockier body shape, which was an evolutionary adaptation to the colder environment of Europe, the Middle East, and central Asia during the last ice age (Figure 11.7). A stockier, shorter body shape minimizes skin surface area in proportion to overall body mass, reducing heat loss through the skin, and therefore is adaptive in colder environments. Conversely, a taller, slimmer body shape maximizes heat loss and is an adaptation to hotter environments.

After 200,000 years ago, Neanderthals were the occupants of Europe, the Middle East, and central Asia, until they were supplanted by modern humans. During this period in eastern Asia, hominins of the archaic *Homo sapiens* type continue until approximately 50,000 years ago, at which time anatomically modern *Homo sapiens* appear. It is in Africa after 200,000 years ago where the

Figure 11.7: Neanderthal sculpture, reconstruction (Neanderthal Museum, Dusseldorf, Germany).

earliest dating sites containing the fossil remains of anatomically modern humans are found. These earliest modern humans will be further discussed in Chapter 12.

Question: What happened to the Neanderthals? Debate concerning what happened to the Neanderthals has been ongoing since their initial discovery in the 19th century. One side of the debate suggests that they became extinct, unable to compete with modern humans, or unable to cope with the deteriorating ice age conditions (and thus are classified as a species distinct from modern humans; they are named *Homo neanderthalensis*). The opposing view suggests that Neanderthals were ancestral to modern European and Middle Eastern humans (and hence should be classified as a subspecies of modern humans; these are named *Homo sapiens neanderthalensis*). This question is directly related to the origin of modern humans, and will be further discussed in the next chapter.

Until the advent of technology capable of analyzing the similarity of DNA (and hence the degree of relatedness) between species in the 1990s, the formulation of phylogenies was based on the degree of similarity of physical traits. Currently, some researchers maintain that only genetic data should be used in the construction of phylogenies, since it is DNA that is passed from one generation to the next during evolution. Researchers of the opposing viewpoint maintain that morphological traits cannot be ignored, since natural selection operates on an individual's physical traits, not their DNA. In the past, prior to our ability to study DNA, various interpretations of the degree of similarity or difference between Neanderthal and modern human morphology and associated cultural evidence led to vigorous debate over whether the Neanderthals were ancestral to modern humans. With the more recent addition of genetic distance information, there is now an increasing consensus among researchers that the Neanderthals were not ancestral to modern humans, and became extinct. This is the view taken by the authors of this book. Since Neanderthal DNA was first iso-

lated and analyzed in 1997, several studies have compared the DNA of modern humans with that of Neanderthals (see, for example, Krings et al. 1997, Serre et al. 2004). These studies show that the analyzed Neanderthal DNA sequences fall outside of the range of variation found among modern humans, indicating that Neanderthals did not significantly contribute to the modern human gene pool—if at all.

Question: Who were the "hobbits of Flores Island?" Recently, beginning in 2003, the remains of particularly small individuals were discovered on Flores Island in Indonesia: the "hobbits of Flores Island." These fossils date to between 95,000 years ago and 18,000 years ago, stood 3 to 4 feet tall, had small brains ranging between 380 and 410 cc, and have been given the taxonomic name *Homo floresiensis* (Figure 11.8). While the size of the brain is in the range of the australopithecines, the shape of the

Figure 11.8: *Homo floresiensis* (Flores Island, Indonesia).

brain is similar to *Homo erectus*. One suggestion that has been proposed to explain the evolution of *Homo floresiensis* involves a phenomenon named insular dwarfism (Brown et al. 2004), which may occur when a population is reproductively isolated from other populations and occupies a small geographic range (such as a small island). If, in this environment, food resources are relatively scarce and there are few predators (no disadvantage for smaller individuals), the evolution of smaller size over time would be adaptive. If this explanation is correct, *Homo floresiensis* represents the descendants of a small population of either *Homo erectus* or archaic *Homo sapiens* that became isolated on Flores Island; over time, evolutionary forces in this particular environment resulted in smaller size being adaptive.

HOMININ PHYLOGENY

Over the past two decades, our knowledge of human evolution has greatly increased with new fossil finds and the definition of new hominin species. Currently, there is much debate among researchers over how many hominin species are represented in the fossil record, and how these species are related to each other. As a result, there are differing interpretations of how to place the various hominin species into a phylogeny. There is debate over how many and which particular morphological traits should be used, and discussion over whether a particular trait represents intraspecies variation or is indicative of species differentiation. These questions are part of the splitters versus lumpers debate, as discussed in Chapter 10.

In this introductory book, we will present and discuss one interpretation of the evolutionary relationships between the various hominin species (Figure 11.9). This phylogeny reflects the discussion in this and

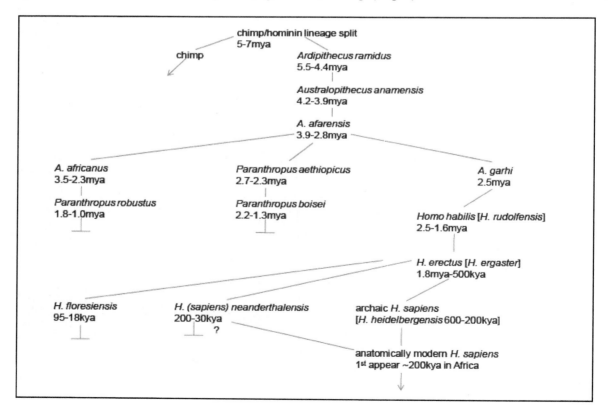

Figure 11.9: Hominin evolution, phylogeny.

the previous two chapters concerning which hominin fossil sets represent distinct species and which do not. For example, the phylogeny subsumes *Australopithecus bahrelghazali* and *Kenyanthropus platyops* into *Australopithecus afarensis*.

The phylogeny begins with the branching from a common ancestor between 7 mya and 5 mya into two lineages, one leading to modern chimpanzees and bonobos, and one leading to modern humans. Early hominin species include *Ardipithecus ramidus*, *Australopithecus anamensis*, and *Australopithecus afarensis*. After 3.5 mya, three lineages branch from *Australopithecus afarensis*. A southern African branch includes *Australopithecus africanus* evolving into *Paranthropus robustus*, which became extinct. An eastern African branch includes *Paranthropus aethiopicus* evolving into *Paranthropus boisei*, which also became extinct. A second eastern African branch includes *Australopithecus garhi*, the ancestor of later *Homo* species. The early *Homo* species include *Homo habilis* and *Homo rudolfensis*, one of whom was ancestral to later *Homo* species, including *Homo ergaster*, *Homo erectus*, *Homo heidelbergensis*, and anatomically modern *Homo sapiens*. Both *Homo neanderthalensis* and *Homo floresiensis* descended from *Homo erectus*. The debate over what happened to the Neanderthals is indicated by the question mark.

EVIDENCE FOR CULTURE

The earliest archaeological physical evidence for human culture dates to 2.6 mya in the form of ancient intentionally modified stone tools found at the site of Gona, Ethiopia, in east Africa (Semaw et al. 2003). The presence of culture among the hominins prior to 2.6 mya can be inferred, since chimpanzees in the wild manufacture and use tools.

These early stone tools are relatively simple, where one stone has been used to chip (flake) three to five small pieces from a second stone in order to create a rough cutting edge, a process known as direct percussion (Figure 11.10). Both the modified stone (referred to as a core or chopper tool) and the flake removed (referred to as a flake tool) were utilized. Tools of this type occur during the earlier part of the Lower Paleolithic time period, continue until 1.4 mya, and are named the Oldowan tool industry after Olduvai Gorge in Tanzania, where Louis and Mary Leakey first recovered them in the 1930s. Oldowan tools have been found at sites in north, east and south Africa. By approximately 1.6 mya, Oldowan tools found at some sites become a little more refined with more flakes removed, forming a rough point. These tools are referred to as the Developed Oldowan. The majority view is that Oldowan tools were made and used by early *Homo* and *Homo ergaster*, since the first appearance of Oldowan tools and early *Homo* are contemporaneous, and that they are frequently found in association with early *Homo* and *Homo ergaster*, and only rarely with australopithecines. Although it was originally thought that the production of the core tools was the primary purpose, subsequent analysis indicates that the flakes

Figure 11.10: Oldowan chopper tool, 1.8 mya (Olduvai Gorge, Tanzania).

Figure 11.11: Acheulean handaxe, 1.2 mya (Olduvai Gorge, Tanzania).

were mostly used (Toth 1985). Microscopic analysis of use-wear polish found on flakes indicates they were used for cutting and scraping meat from bones and for cutting plants (Schick and Toth 1993).

The later part of the Lower Paleolithic is characterized by the Acheulean tool industry, spanning from 1.4 mya to 200,000 years ago. Acheulean stone tools are more complex than those of the Oldowan, with an increasing variety of tool types, including hand axes, scrapers, and points (Figure 11.11). More flakes have been removed in order to achieve more regular and symmetrical shapes. Innovations that first appear with the Acheulean industry include the production of bifacial tools, where flakes have been removed from both sides of the pebble so that often none of the original surface remains, and retouching where small flakes have been removed from the cutting edge in order to refine and sharpen the cutting edge. The Acheulean industry is found in Africa, Europe, and western Asia, and is associated with *Homo erectus* and archaic *Homo sapiens*.

During the latter part of the Lower Paleolithic, associated with *Homo erectus*, there is increasing evidence for the active hunting of larger game. Prey bones found at many sites during this time show evidence of stone tool cut marks, with the absence of large carnivore tooth marks indicating hunting rather than scavenging. At the sites of Torralba and Ambrona in Spain (dated to 400,000 years ago), elephant bones were found in association with Acheulean tools. And at Olorgesailie in Kenya (700,000 years ago), hundreds of hand axes were found in association with the bones of several animal species.

Also during this period, *Homo erectus* began to colonize temperate regions of the Old World, where adaptation to cold winter temperatures was necessary. Adaptations for keeping warm included the controlled use of fire and the utilization of animal hides as rudimentary clothing. At the site of Zhoukoudian in northern China, dating to 670,000 years ago, in addition to *Homo erectus* fossils, thin seams of charcoal and many charred bones are interpreted as the remains of ancient hearths. Earlier evidence for the control of fire is less conclusive. For example, 1.5 mya, patches of baked earth found at Koobi Fora in Kenya suggest the remains of campfires. Alternatively, these may be the result of naturally occurring fires. In addition to warmth, fire may also have been used for light, to scare away predators, as part of hunting, and for cooking. Since animals are afraid of fire, wooden torches may have been used to drive animals over cliffs. Cooking food, particularly meat, makes it more easily digested and increases the utilization of nutrients.

Toward the end of the Lower Paleolithic after approximately 400,000 years ago, there is disputed evidence for the construction of shelters that comes from several sites. For example, at Terra Amata in southern France, dated to 250,000 years ago, the remains of a hut are suggested by artifact scatters (including what have been interpreted

Figure 11.12: Hut reconstruction (Terra Amata, France).

as hearths) surrounded by a series of postholes arranged in an oval (Figure 11.12). At Bilzingsleben in Thuringia, Germany, dated to 400,000 years ago, three concentrations of artifacts and animal bones found with large stones and bones have been interpreted as the remains of structures (Mania et al. 1994).

After 200,000 years ago, the production of stone tools became more complex with the innovation of a standardized technique for the production of flakes, which were further modified into particular tool types. This marks the beginning of the Middle Paleolithic in Europe, Asia, and North Africa and the Middle Stone Age (MSA) in sub-Saharan Africa. This stage continues until 40,000 years ago, at which time more advanced tool technologies appear. In Europe, the Middle Paleolithic is associated with Neanderthals and is characterized by the Mousterian tool industry. This industry is characterized by the appearance of hafting (the production of a composite tool by, for example, attaching a long handle to a stone point to make a spear). A point was attached to a handle using natural glues (for example, tree resin) and sinews for binding. Cores were prepared in a specific way for flake production. One common method was the Levallois technique, where initially, flakes were removed from the perimeter of the core, and then flakes were removed circumferentially from each of the two major surfaces of the core. Finally, from one of those

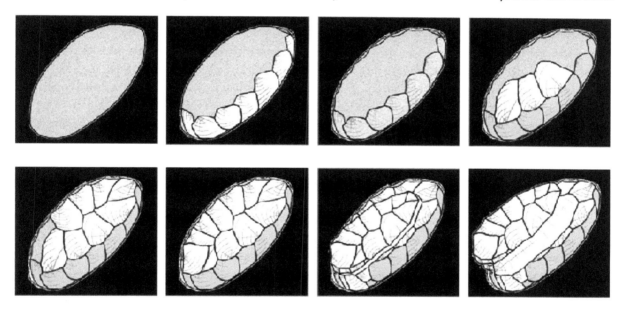

Figure 11.13: Levallois technique.

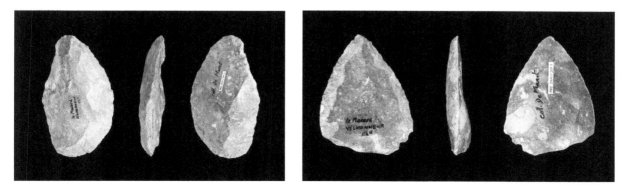

Figure 11.14: Mousterian tools, (left) scraper, Le Placard Cave, France, and (right) retouched Levallois point, Le Placard Cave, France.

surfaces, a large flake was removed (the Levallois flake), which was then further retouched into a particular tool type (Figure 11.13). Although the Mousterian tool industry includes core tools such as the hand axe), it is characterized by a predominance of flake tools, including points and scrapers (Figure 11.14).

Until recently, the Middle Paleolithic and the Middle Stone Age were viewed as technologically equivalent, with both Neanderthals in Europe and early anatomically modern *Homo sapiens* in Africa using the same tool kit. However, this view has been recently questioned. Traditionally, the production of blades (discussed in greater detail in Chapter 12) has been considered a defining characteristic of later Upper Paleolithic technologies. McBrearty and Brooks (2000) suggest that evidence of blade production during the Middle Stone Age found at some African sites (for instance, Howieson's Poort in South Africa, dated to 80,000 years ago) has been given too little attention, and that this represents a deeper time history for modern human technological behavior.

Neanderthals tended to live in areas where there were numerous caves and rock shelters, several of which have been identified as containing living spaces. The earliest evidence for intentional burial of the dead comes from the Middle Paleolithic. Burials of many Neanderthals have been found in caves. As a result, Neanderthal skeletal remains are the best represented of any premodern human species. These burials include articulated skeletons often placed in specific positions (in the fetal position, for example), and often include what are interpreted as grave goods. Grave goods include any object placed with a body in a burial pit, and may possibly reflect some sort of rudimentary spirituality or funerary ritual; in other words, evidence of symbolic thought. Objects found with Neanderthal burials include tools, animal bones, and plant remains. One example comes from Shanidar Cave in Iraq, where a Neanderthal individual was buried with pine boughs and flowers (Trinkaus 1983). The contention that Neanderthals intentionally included grave goods has been questioned by some (for instance, Sommer 1999), who suggest that plant remains may have naturally blown into the burial. Objects such as red ocher (a natural pigment) and items of personal adornment (beads) have been occasionally found in association with Neanderthals, suggesting that human expression through art has its roots in the Middle Paleolithic (D'Errico 2003).

Evidence from burials at Shanidar Cave and other sites is highly suggestive of Neanderthals caring for disadvantaged individuals. For example, one Shanidar burial is that of an older male who sustained severe injuries many years prior to his death, including injuries to the left tibia, right humerus, and right side of the head (Trinkaus 1983). The degree of healing of the bones indicates that this individual survived for many years after incurring these injuries. He would not have been able to provide for himself, and would have survived only with the care of other members of his group.

Question: Were Neanderthals capable of language? The evidence discussed above indicates that Neanderthals had some capability for symbolic behavior, which raises the question of whether they were capable of symbolic language that was comparable to that of modern humans. By reconstructing the vocal anatomy of Neanderthals, Lieberman and Crelin (1971) conclude that Neanderthals were limited as compared with modern humans in their ability to vocalize some vowel sounds, thus limiting their language capabilities. However, the discovery of an intact Neanderthal hyoid (a bone located in the neck that is associated with sound production) that is nearly identical in size and shape to that of a modern human hyoid suggests that the capability to vocalize sounds was similar for both (Arensberg et al. 1990). The debate continues.

CRITICAL REASONING QUESTIONS

- What feature distinguishes the genus *Homo* from the australopithecines?
- Why do the majority of researchers separate the early *Homo* fossil set into two species?
- How was the diet of early *Homo* different from that of the australopithecines?
- How did early *Homo* obtain meat? Briefly describe the evidence that tells us this.
- What was the geographic range of Neanderthals? How did Neanderthals physically evolve to the environment in which they lived?
- What are two innovations that distinguish the Acheulean from the Oldowan industries? What advantages did these innovations provide?
- Briefly define hafting. In which tool industry does it first appear?
- Which tool industry is associated with the Levallois technique? What was the Levallois technique used for?

REFERENCES AND SUGGESTED READINGS

Arensberg, B., L. A. Schepartz, A. M. Tillier, et al. (1990). A reappraisal of the anatomical basis for speech in Middle Paleolithic hominids. *American Journal of Physical Anthropology* 83:137–146.

Brown, P., T. Sutikna, M. J. Morwood, and R. P. Soejono (2004). A small-bodied hominin from the Late Pleistocene of Flores, Indonesia. *Nature* 431:1055–1061.

D'Errico, F. (2003). The invisible frontier: A multiple species model for the origin of behavioural modernity. *Evolutionary Anthropology* 12:188–202.

Finlayson, Clive, Francisco Giles Pacheco, Joaquín Rodríguez-Vidal, Darren A. Fa, et al. (2006). Late survival of Neanderthals at the southernmost extreme of Europe. *Nature* 443:850–853.

Isaac, G. L. (1978). The food-sharing behaviour of proto-human hominids. *Scientific American* 238:90–108.

Joris, O., and M. Street (2008). At the end of the 14C timescale—The Middle to Upper Palaeolithic record of Western Eurasia. *Journal of Human Evolution* 55:782–802.

Krings, M., A. Stone, R. W. Schmitz, et al. (1997). Neandertal DNA sequences and the origin of modern humans. *Cell* 90(1):19–30.

Leakey, L. S. B., P. V. Tobias, and J. R. Napier (1964). A new species of genus *Homo* from Olduvai Gorge. *Nature* 202:7–9.

Lewin, Roger (2005). *Human evolution: An illustrated introduction*. Malden, MA: Blackwell Publishing Ltd.

Lieberman, P., and E. S. Crelin (1971). On the speech of Neanderthal. *Linguistic Inquiry* 2:203–222.

Mania, D., U. Mania, and E. Vlček (1994). Latest finds of skull remains of *Homo erectus* from Bilzingsleben (Thuringia). *Naturwissenschaften* 81:123–127.

McBrearty, S., and S. B. Brooks (2000). The revolution that wasn't: A new interpretation of the evolution of modern human behavior. *Journal of Human Evolution* 39:453–563.

Potts, R. (1988). *Early hominid activities at Olduvai*. Chicago: Aldine.

Schick, K. D., and N. Toth (1993). *Making silent stones speak: Human evolution and the dawn of technology*. New York: Morrow.

Semaw, Sileshi, Michael J. Rogers, Jay Quade, et al. (2003). 2.6-million-year-old stone tools and associated bones from OGS-6 and OGS-7, Gona, Afar, Ethiopia. *Journal of Human Evolution* 45(2):169–177.

Serre, David, André Langaney, Mario Chech, et al. (2004). No evidence of Neandertal mtDNA contribution to early modern humans. *PLoS Biology* 2:313–317.

Shipman, P. (1986). Scavenging or hunting in early hominids. *American Anthropologist* 88:27–43.

Sommer, J. D. (1999). The Shanidar IV "flower burial": A re-evaluation of Neanderthal burial ritual. *Cambridge Archaeological Journal* 9:127–129.

Toth, N. (1985). The Oldowan reassessed: A close look at early stone tools. *Journal of Archaeological Science* 2:101–120.

Trinkaus, E. (1983). *The Shanidar Neanderthals*. New York: Academic Press.

Ungar, P. S., F. E. Grine, M. F. Teaford, and S. El Zaatari (2006). Dental microwear and diets of African early *Homo*. *Journal of Human Evolution* 50:78–95.

Walker, A., and R. E. Leakey, eds. (1993). *The Nariokotome Homo* erectus *skeleton*. Cambridge, MA: Harvard University Press.

Anatomically Modern Humans

By Roman Gastrell Harrison

T he earliest anatomically modern inhabitants of Europe are commonly referred to as Cro-Magnons, named after remains found at the site of the Cro-Magnon rock shelter in southwestern France in 1868. At the time of the discovery, it was not known how ancient these remains were, but subsequently were dated to 28,000 years ago. Since 1868, many more ancient anatomically modern *Homo sapiens* fossils have been found, not only in Europe, but also in other parts of the world. This chapter will discuss the fossil evidence for early anatomically modern humans, the source of early modern humans, and associated cultural evidence, including tool industries and art.

EARLY ANATOMICALLY MODERN *HOMO SAPIENS*

When compared with other hominin species, anatomically modern *Homo sapiens* have a more gracile postcranial skeleton, have an average brain size of approximately 1300–1400 cc, a more rounded cranium, reduced subnasal prognathism, and a protruding chin.

Intelligence is poorly correlated with raw brain size, but has a good correlation with the proportion of brain to body size. Neanderthals' brains were larger than those of anatomically modern *Homo sapiens*, averaging 1520 cc, and their bodies were more heavily built. Modern humans have larger brains in proportion to body size. This, in combination with cultural evidence (discussed below), indicates that early modern humans had an increased level of intelligence relative to Neanderthals, particularly in terms of symbolic thought.

During the 19th and early 20th centuries, the majority of the evidence—both fossil and cultural—for early anatomically modern *Homo sapiens* was recovered from European sites. This led to the conclusion that modern humans originated in Europe. However, more recently, many other early modern human sites have been found outside of Europe. Currently, the oldest dating anatomically modern *Homo sapiens* fossils come from Africa. For example, Omo-Kibish in Ethiopia dates to 195,000 years ago, Herto in Ethiopia dates to 160,000 years ago, and Klasies River Mouth in South Africa dates to 120,000 years ago. Only later do anatomically modern *Homo sapiens* fossils appear outside of Africa, dating as early as approximately 120,000–110,000 years ago in the Middle East, 50,000–40,000 years ago in east Asia, and 40,000–35,000 years ago in Europe. Colonization of the Americas occurred somewhat later, where the earliest archaeological evidence for human occupation dates to as early as 20,000 years ago.

SOURCE OF MODERN HUMANS

There has been vigorous debate surrounding the origin of anatomically modern *Homo sapiens*. Broadly, this debate involves two models (Figure 12.1). The Multiregional Continuity model suggests that anatomically modern *Homo sapiens* evolved from earlier archaic humans in several different parts of the Old World at about the same time. In this model, at about the same time, early modern Europeans would have evolved from European Neanderthals; early modern Asians would have evolved from Asian archaic *Homo sapiens*;

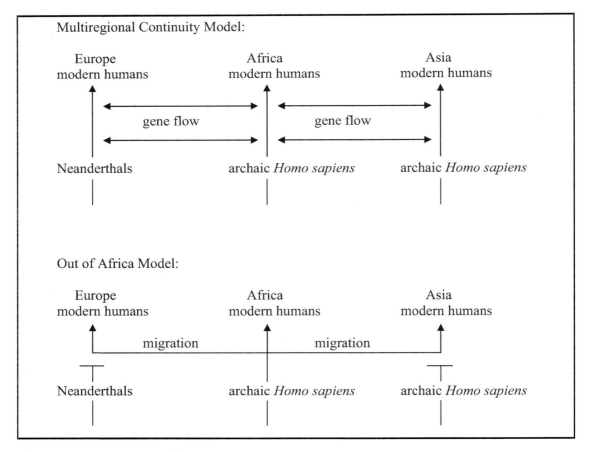

Figure 12.1: Source of modern humans—models.

and early modern Africans would have evolved from African archaic *Homo sapiens*. Gene flow would have been extensive between these geographical regions. In contrast, the Out of Africa model suggests that anatomically modern *Homo sapiens* evolved in one single location, Africa, and then later migrated to other parts of the world and outcompeted the archaic humans they encountered, resulting in the archaic humans becoming extinct. This model suggests there was little or no interbreeding between the in-migrating modern humans and the preexisting archaic humans. Fossil, genetic, and archaeological evidence has been cited in relation to this debate.

Before the advent of our ability to analyze the similarity of DNA, debate focused on the fossil evidence. Only recently has the antiquity of the earliest African modern human sites been recognized, either because of their recent discovery or because of recent reanalysis of their dating. As mentioned above, the earliest anatomically modern *Homo sapiens* fossils are found in Africa, dating as early as approximately 200,000 years ago, and only later are found in regions outside of Africa. An increasing majority of researchers maintain that this timing fits best with the Out of Africa model. Both anatomically modern *Homo sapiens* and Neanderthals were occupants of Europe for a period of time between approximately 40,000 and 30,000 years ago. Neanderthals and anatomically modern *Homo sapiens* do not appear to form an ancestor-descendant relationship, as would be expected in the Multiregional Continuity model. Some researchers suggest that the skeleton of a four-year-old child from Lagar Velho in Portugal (found in 1998), dating to 24.5 thousand years ago, possesses a mosaic of Neanderthal and anatomically modern traits and is evidence of interbreeding between the two groups, thereby supporting the Multiregional Continuity model (Duarte et al. 1999), while others maintain that this fossil is that of a stocky—but fully modern—human. In addition, some researchers interpret the fossil evidence from east Asia as representing continuity between archaic and modern human populations (Brown 2001).

In the late 1980s, the significance of using information derived from DNA in relation to the question of modern human origins became apparent. These early studies used mitochondrial DNA (mtDNA) (Cann et al. 1987). Subsequent studies have analyzed nuclear microsatellite DNA (short strands of DNA) and DNA from the Y chromosome. By comparing the similarities and differences of the DNA of individuals from modern human populations across the world, a phylogeny of those populations can be constructed. Since

the rate of genetic mutation is roughly constant, the date when a particular set of physical traits (and associated genes) first appears in a population and the antiquity of that population can be determined. Populations with a more ancient origin will show a larger degree of genetic variation because there has been a greater amount of time for that population to accumulate mutations, whereas populations with a more recent origin will show less genetic variation. Most of these studies indicate that anatomically modern *Homo sapiens* appeared relatively recently, approximately 200,000 years ago, and that their place of origin was sub-Saharan Africa (Relethford 2008).

In the traditional view, modern human behavior first appears about 40,000 years ago at the beginning of the Upper Paleolithic. In this

Figure 12.2: Blade, Upper Paleolithic, La Placard Cave, France.

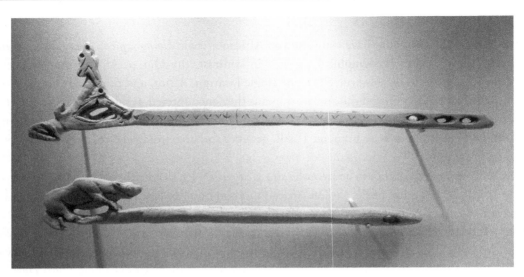

Figure 12.3: Atlatls, (upper) La Madeleine Rockshelter, France, (lower) Le Mas d'Azil, France.

view, the appearance of modern behavior was a sudden event marked by an increase in symbolic behavior, a "creative revolution" (Pfeiffer 1985). It has been suggested this was precipitated by a genetic mutation that occurred approximately 40,000 years ago (Klein 1995). More recently, it has been recognized that some features characteristic of the Upper Paleolithic can be seen in Middle Stone Age sites in Africa, indicating a more gradual transition to fully modern behavior. Examples of this evidence include bone points found at the site of Katanda in the Democratic Republic of the Congo dating to 90,000 years ago (Yellen et al. 1995); the production of blades in the Howieson's Poort industry in South Africa dating to 80,000 years ago (McBrearty and Brooks 2000); beads made from shells with drilled holes found at Blombos Cave in South Africa dating to 75,000 years ago (Henshilwood et al. 2004); and evidence of fishing at Klasies River Mouth in South Africa dating to between 120,000 years ago and 70,000 years ago (Klein 1979). The archaeological evidence is more equivocal than the fossil and genetic evidence, and can be used to support both the Out of Africa and Multiregional Continuity models.

Taken together, the fossil, genetic, and archaeological evidence provides greater support for the Out of Africa model than for the Multiregional Continuity model. As a result, there is currently a sizable consensus that modern humans originated in a single region—Africa—some 200,000 years ago, and later migrated to other parts of the world.

Question: Did modern humans and Neanderthals come in contact with each other? The evidence from Europe indicates that there was a time when both Neanderthals and modern humans were present. There is debate over the length of this period. The earliest unambiguous evidence (including both fossil and cultural evidence) of anatomically modern *Homo sapiens* in Europe dates to between 37,000–40,000 years ago. However, as discussed in Chapter 11, while some researchers suggest the evidence points to a Neanderthal presence in Europe as late as 28,000 years ago, others maintain that Neanderthals had disappeared by 35,000 years ago. Therefore, the period of European overlap between Neanderthals and modern humans may have been as little as 2000 years and as much as 12,000 years.

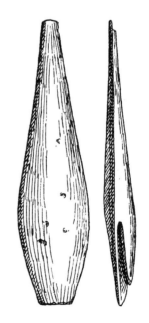

Figure 12.4: Aurignacian bone point.

In the Middle East, cave sites in Israel show evidence of both Neanderthals and modern humans. Evidence of Neanderthals is found at Tabun cave (dated to as early as 120,000 years ago) and Kebara and Amud caves (60,000–50,000 years ago), while evidence of anatomically modern humans is found at Qafzeh and Skhul caves (110,000–90,000 years ago) (Bar-Yosef 1993; Hublin 2000). These caves are located within a few kilometers of each other. It appears that Neanderthals first occupied this area, followed by modern humans, and then later once again by Neanderthals, suggesting possible contact between the two. The temporal relationship of these sites indicates that Neanderthals and modern humans did not form an ancestor-descendant relationship, as suggested by the Multiregional Continuity model.

In southern Europe, both Neanderthal and modern human sites occur in relatively close proximity in both time and space, suggesting that they were at the least aware of each other. What is debated is the nature of this potential contact. As discussed in Chapter 11, studies comparing Neanderthal and modern human DNA show that the analyzed Neanderthal sequences fall outside the range of modern humans, intimating little or no interbreeding between the two groups. In contrast, some researchers maintain that the fossil remains found at Lagar Velho, Portugal, are evidence of interbreeding. This debate surrounding the amount of interbreeding—if any—between Neanderthals and modern humans remains unresolved.

EVIDENCE FOR CULTURE

After 40,000 years ago, the evidence for modern human behavior increases significantly. Tool industries of the Upper Paleolithic are characterized by an increased use of bone and antler and the production of stone blades. Blades are flakes that are at least twice as long as they are wide, with parallel sides. Although there is debate over whether evidence of blade technology is present during the Middle Stone Age in Africa, the traditional viewpoint is that the appearance of blade technology is associated with the beginning of the Upper Paleolithic.

Blades were made by first preparing a core by forming a striking platform, a flat surface on the upper part of the core. Long thin flakes (blades) were then removed from the core, using a hammer and punch or through pressure flaking. This method is a more efficient use of stone, since several blades may be removed from a single core, whereas fewer flakes per core were produced using earlier methods such as the Levallois technique. Fine-grained stone such as obsidian or chert was preferred for blade production. Blade

Figure 12.5: Gravettian burin (Brassempouy, France).

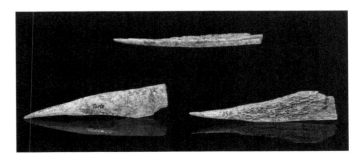

Figure 12.6: Bone awl (Tarte, France).

technology allowed stone tools to be thinner, longer, and narrower, producing a more pointed tool, making them more effective.

Blades may have been used without further modification or may have been further retouched to produce specific tool types, including scrapers, burins, knife blades, and spear points (Figure 12.2). Points made from blades were thinner than earlier flake points, resulting in lighter-weight spears that could be thrown further. During the Upper Paleolithic, lighter-weight spears using points carved from bone and antler were also produced. When hunting, these lighter-weight throwing spears may have given anatomically modern *Homo sapiens* an advantage over the heavier thrusting spears used by Neanderthals.

By approximately 25,000 years ago, the invention of the spear thrower (atlatl) further increased hunting efficiency. An atlatl is a wood or bone stick with a prong at one end and a hand grip at the other end used to launch a spear (Figure 12.3). The atlatl functions as a lever, and increases the propulsive power and the distance that a spear can be thrown, providing an advantage during hunting. Often, stone weights were attached to the shaft of the atlatl in order to increase the throwing power. The subsequent invention of the bow and arrow further increased hunting efficiency. The earliest direct evidence for the use of the bow and arrow appears late in the Upper Paleolithic. For example, at the Stellmoor site in Germany, dated to 10.5 thousand years ago, over 100 wooden arrows were found (Bokelman 1991). However, earlier indirect evidence in the form of small tanged points that have been interpreted as being arrowheads is found in Solutrean sites (Davidson 1974).

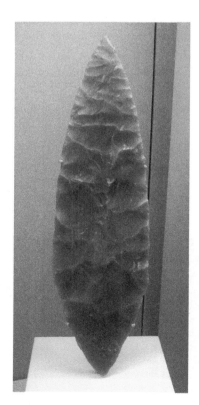

Figure 12.7: Solutrean leaf-shaped point (Volgu, Rigny-sur-Arroux, Saone-et-Loire, France).

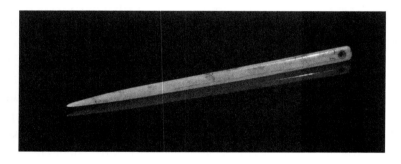

Figure 12.8: Magdalenian bone needle (Gourdan, France).

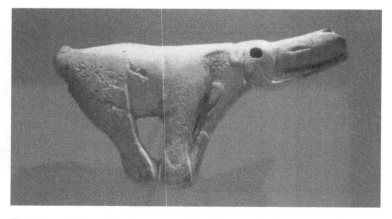

Figure 12.9: Magdalenian mammoth atlatl (Montastruc, France).

The Upper Paleolithic of Europe is commonly divided into five major cultures that are defined by their tool industries. Four of these industries are associated with anatomically modern *Homo sapiens*, and the fifth is associated with Neanderthals. The earliest of the Upper Paleolithic industries associated with anatomically modern *Homo sapiens* is the Aurignacian, dating to between 38,000 and 30,000 years ago. It is characterized by relatively large blades and with the introduction of bone points (Figure 12.4). Overlapping in time with the Aurignacian is the Châtelperronian tool industry, 36,000 to 32,000 years ago. The Châtelperronian is associated with Neanderthals and is characterized by large blades, indicating that Neanderthals were capable of producing Upper Paleolithic blade technology. There is discussion over whether Neanderthals independently invented blade technology or whether they acquired it from anatomically modern *Homo sapiens* (Hublin et al. 1996).

Blades became smaller with increasingly parallel sides in the Gravettian tool industry, associated with anatomically modern *Homo sapiens* and dating to between 30,000 and 23,000 years ago (Figure 12.5). This industry also marks the appearance of awls carved out of bone, a tool used for piercing (Figure 12.6). The Solutrean industry, dating to between 24,000 and 18,000 years ago, is characterized by distinctive leaf-shaped points (Figure 12.7). The Solutrean also provides evidence for tailored clothing in the form of bone needles with small carved holes for the eye (Stordeur-Yedid 1979) (Figure 12.8). Hides would have been cut into specific shapes and sewn together, using sinews for thread. Toward the end of the Upper Paleolithic, tools were increasingly manufactured from bone and antler. In the Magdalenian tool industry, 18,000 to 12,000 years ago, many of these tools incorporate artistically carved or engraved shapes (Figure 12.9). For example, bone atlatls may have an artistically carved protrusion on the shaft that functionally serves as the atlatl weight.

Subsistence strategies during the Upper Paleolithic included the gathering of a variety of wild plants and the hunting of terrestrial animals, including deer, ibex, bison, mammoth, and reindeer. Finely carved bone fish hooks first appear in middle Upper Paleolithic sites, and barbed harpoons from later Upper Paleolithic sites suggest that people were including fish and sea mammals in their diets (Figure 12.10). Stable isotope analysis of human bone from Gravettian burials (dating to 27,000 years ago) from central and eastern Europe indicate that 50 percent of the diet consisted of riverine resources (Richards et al. 2001). Remains interpreted as fish traps have been found in western Europe dating to 14,000 years ago. Although it has

Figure 12.10: Bone harpoon head (Mas d'Azil, France).

Figure 12.11: Mammoth bone dwelling—reconstruction based on one found at Mezhirich, Ukraine.

Figure 12.12: Bone flute (Geissenklösterle, Germany).

been suggested that people at this time were exploiting salmon runs (Jochim 1983), few fish bones have been found in associated sites (Mellars 1985). Faunal remains of waterfowl found at several later Upper Paleolithic sites provide evidence for the hunting of birds (Richards et al. 2001).

Evidence for the construction of shelters increases during the Upper Paleolithic. For example, in more northerly regions with few trees closer to the ice sheets, shelters were constructed using the bones of large animals, with the supports covered with hides. At Mezhirich in Ukraine, dated to 35,000 years ago, the remains of a mammoth bone and hide hut were discovered (Soffer 1985) (Figure 12.11). Mammoth tusks were used for the main supports, with vertebrae forming the walls. In more southerly areas where trees were more abundant, wooden poles were used for the supports of huts, which were covered with hides or sod. At Dolni Vestonice in the Czech Republic, dated to 27,000 years ago, people wintered in several wood-and-hide huts (Soffer et al. 1998).

Burial of the dead became more elaborate during the Upper Paleolithic, often including a greater abundance and variety of grave goods. Some burials include two or three individuals. For instance, at Sunghir in western Russia, dated to 24,000 years ago, two individuals, one male and one female and both of whom died in their teen years, were buried with grave goods that included spears, engraved items, ivory beads, and other jewelry (Formicola and Buzhilova 2004).

It is unclear when art first began to be produced. During the Middle Paleolithic, bones with linear engraving have been found associated with Neanderthals. There is disagreement over whether this evidence constitutes art. It is not until after 40,000 years ago that undisputed examples of art appear. Beginning in the early part and continuing throughout the Upper Paleolithic, evidence of art becomes ever more abundant. Items of personal adornment—including beads, pendants, and perforated animal teeth and shells—are frequently found associated with Upper Paleolithic burials. Evidence for the production of music is provided by the presence of artifacts interpreted as musical instruments; for example, a flute made from bone (Figure 12.12). Carved figurines of the human female form, often referred to as "Venus" figurines, appear during the Gravettian, approximately 25,000 years ago. One of the more famous examples is the Venus of Willendorf from Austria (Figure 12.13). These figurines typically have exaggerated breasts or buttocks and have highly stylized features

Figure 12.13: Venus of Willendorf, Austria.

of the head. Nose, eyes, and mouth are not depicted naturalistically or are absent. The hair is typically portrayed in a nonnatural design. A variety of suggestions explaining the function of these figurines has

Figure 12.14: Cave painting detail (Lascaux, France).

been made (McDermott 1996). A common theme in explanations is that they relate to fertility, either that of human females specifically or in a more general sense, and may have been used in rituals. The hunter/gatherers of the Upper Paleolithic were dependent on the fertility of the natural environment in which they lived, including the abundance of wild animals to hunt and plants to gather. Other suggestions include female status signifiers, that they were self-portraits, or that they were pornography for males. It may be that they served more than one function and that their function varied between groups.

Upper Paleolithic cave art is best known from European sites, including Altamira in Spain (dating to 17,000 years ago), Grotte de Chauvet (30,000 years ago), and Lascaux (15,000 years) in France (Figure 12.14). Paintings are often located in less accessible chambers of caves, not associated with living spaces. Artificial light would have been required to produce and to view these paintings. Most often depicted are large herbivorous mammals, including ibex, mammoth, deer, aurochs, and horses. These are represented in a naturalistic manner. These were animals frequently hunted by Upper Paleolithic people, as evidenced by bones found in associated sites. Rarely are carnivores depicted. Humans only appear infrequently and are highly schematic. Some are fantastic, combining human and animal forms. Hand prints were produced by placing the hand on the cave wall and blowing or brushing paint around the hand. These may have functioned as some sort of signature. Interpretations of these paintings include that they were used as a ritual to ensure a good hunt; that they reflected society's social structure; or that they were produced by shamans depicting their visions while in a trance (Lewin 2005).

CRITICAL REASONING QUESTIONS

- On which continent are the earliest anatomically modern *Homo sapiens* fossils found? How old are they? How old are the earliest anatomically modern *Homo sapiens* fossils in other parts of the world?
- What does DNA evidence tell us about the source of anatomically modern *Homo sapiens*? What does DNA evidence tell us about the disappearance of the Neanderthals?
- What innovation distinguishes Upper Paleolithic tool industries from earlier industries? What were the advantages of this innovation?

- What is an atlatl? How did this invention increase hunting efficiency?
- What evidence indicates that fish and sea mammals were included in Upper Paleolithic diets?
- What is the significance of the Mezhirich site?
- When did art first begin to be produced?
- What is the subject matter of cave paintings? What was the purpose of these paintings?

REFERENCES AND SUGGESTED READINGS

Bar-Yosef, O. (1993). The role of western Asia in modern human origins. In *The Origins of Modern Humans and the Impact of Chronometric Dating*, M. J. Aitkin, C. B. Stringer, and P. A. Mellars, eds., pp. 132–147. Princeton, NJ: Princeton University Press.

Bokelmann, K. (1991). Some new thoughts on old data on humans and reindeer in the Ahrensburgian tunnel valley in Schleswig-Holstein, Germany. *CBA Research Report* 77:72–81.

Brown, P. (2001). Chinese Middle Pleistocene hominids and modern human origins in east Asia. In L. Barham and K. Robson-Brown, eds., *Human Roots: Africa and Asia in the Middle Pleistocene*, pp. 135–147. Bristol, UK: Western Academic and Specialist Press.

Cann, R. L., M. Stoneking, and A. Wilson (1987). Mitochondrial DNA and human evolution. *Nature* 325:31–36.

Davidson, I. (1974). Radiocarbon dates for the Spanish Solutrean. *Antiquity* 48:63–65.

Duarte, Cidália, João Maurício, Paul B. Pettitt, et al. (1999). The early Upper Paleolithic human skeleton from the Abrigo do Lagar Velho (Portugal) and modern human emergence in Iberia. *Proceedings of the National Academy of Sciences* 96(13):7604–7609.

Formicola, V., and A. P. Buzhilova (2004). Double child burial from Sunghir (Russia): Pathology and inferences for Upper Paleolithic funerary practices. *American Journal of Physical Anthropology* 124:189–198.

Henshilwood, C., F. d'Errico, M. Vanhaeren, et al. (2004). Middle Stone Age shell beads from South Africa. *Science* 304(5669):404.

Hublin, J.-J. (2000). Modern-non modern human interactions: A Mediterranean perspective. In O. Bar-Yosef, and D. Pilbeam, eds., *The Geography of Neanderthals and Modern Humans in Europe and the Greater Mediterranean*, pp. 157–182. Cambridge, MA: *Peabody Museum Bulletin* 8, Harvard.

Hublin, Jean-Jacques, Fred Spoor, Marc Braun, et al. (1996). A late Neanderthal associated with Upper Paleolithic artefacts. *Nature* 381(6579):224–226.

Jochim, Michael (1983). Paleolithic cave art in ecological perspective. In G. N. Bailey, ed., *Hunter-Gatherer Economy in Prehistory*, pp. 212–219. Cambridge, MA: Cambridge University Press.

Klein, Richard G. (1979). Stone Age exploitation of animals in southern Africa. *American Scientist* 67:23–32.

——— 1995 Anatomy, behavior, and modern human origins. *Journal of World Prehistory* 9:167–198.

Lewin, Roger (2005). *Human evolution: An illustrated introduction*. Malden, MA: Blackwell Publishing Ltd.

McBrearty, S., and S. B. Brooks (2000). The revolution that wasn't: A new interpretation of the evolution of modern human behavior. *Journal of Human Evolution* 39:453–563.

McDermott, L. (1996). Self-representation in Upper Paleolithic female figurines. *Current Anthropology* 372:227–275.

Mellars, Paul (1985). The ecological basis of social complexity in the Upper Palaeolithic of southwestern France. In T. Douglas Price and James Brown, eds., *Prehistoric Hunter-Gatherers: The Emergence of Cultural Complexity*, pp. 271–297. Orlando, FL: Academic Press.

Pfeiffer, John (1985). The creative explosion: An inquiry into the origins of art and religion. Ithaca, NY: Cornell University Press.

Relethford, J. H. (2008).Genetic evidence and the modern human origins debate. *Heredity* 100:555–563.

Richards, M. P., P. B. Pettitt, M. C. Stiner, and E. Trinkaus (2001). Stable isotope evidence for increasing dietary breadth in the European mid-Upper Paleolithic. *Proceedings of the National Academy of Sciences* 9811:6528–6532.

Soffer, Olga (1985). *The Upper Palaeolithic of the central Russian Plains*. New York: Academic Press.

Soffer, Olga, James M. Adovasio, David C. Hyland, et al. (1998). Perishable technologies and the genesis of the eastern Gravettian. *Anthropologie* 36(1):43–68.

Stordeur-Yedid, D. (1979). Les aiguilles a chas au Paleolithique. *Gallia Prehistoire Supplement* 13.

Yellen, J. E., A. S. Brooks, E. Cornelissen, et al. (1995). A Middle Stone Age worked bone industry from Katanda, Upper Semliki Valley, Zaire. *Science* 268:553–556.

13

Human Variation

By Roman Gastrell Harrison

Although there is variation between individuals, all modern humans are similar enough to each other that we are all members of the same species. All modern humans are a little bit different in terms of physical features. Even identical twins, with identical DNA, are not completely physically identical. This is due to differences in the life history of each twin. For example, if one twin contracts a childhood disease, that twin's growth will be inhibited compared to the twin who does not contract the disease, resulting in slightly different adult heights.

Some of us are a little taller, some a little shorter. Some people are a little slimmer, some a little heavier. Some of us have brown eyes, some have blue eyes. Some have a darker skin color, some lighter. Different groups of humans have variable frequencies of these and other physical traits. In the past, it was believed that certain specific physical traits could be used to classify an individual into a particular group or "race." We now know that this is not possible. This chapter will discuss the variation in frequency of selected physical traits between human populations, evolutionary reasons for that variation, and whether the concept of race is valid from a biological point of view.

WHAT IS A CLINE?

The frequency of occurrence of many physical traits is not the same in all human populations. For example, populations living closer to the equator have higher frequencies of darker skin color, whereas those living closer to the poles have higher frequencies of lighter skin color. These differences in frequency have become less pronounced over the past century or two due to the increased movement of people from one part of the world to another.

Through natural selection, individuals who possess traits that are favorable to the environment in which they live have an increased chance of surviving, reproducing, and passing on those favorable traits. Over time, the frequency of favorable traits will increase in that population, and the frequency of unfavorable traits will decrease. Because the environment determines which traits are favorable and which are not, the selective pressure affecting different human populations living in different environments will not be the same. For example, darker skin color provides an evolutionary advantage in environments where the sun is more intense, and therefore has been selected for in populations living closer to the equator.

For the majority of traits with varying frequencies in different populations, the difference in frequency between adjacent populations is not large. For contiguous populations, there is a gradual change in the frequency of a trait forming a gradient through space, referred to as a cline. Clinal variation can be plotted on a map, depicting how the frequency of a particular trait varies through space. Skin color is an example of a trait that forms a cline. For example, in Egypt, the frequency of darker skin colors increases from north to south along the Nile Valley.

GEOGRAPHICAL VARIATION IN FREQUENCY OF TRAITS BETWEEN POPULATIONS

Among humans, the phenotypic expression of many traits may have more than one form. Traits that may be expressed in more than one way are called polymorphisms. The genetic loci controlling polymorphic traits have two or more alleles. Skin and eye color are examples of polymorphic traits. Polymorphisms have varying frequencies in different populations.

Skin color is a polygenic trait, with continuous variation from extremely light to extremely dark. The color of skin is determined by three substances: hemoglobin, carotene, and melanin. Of these, the degree of darkness is most influenced by the amount of melanin. Melanin is produced by cells in the skin called melanocytes. All humans have about the same number of melanocytes per unit area of skin, but vary in the amount of melanin produced by each melanocyte. Individuals with darker skin produce more melanin than lighter-skinned individuals.

Geographical variation of skin color is continuous and forms a clinal distribution. As a generalization, darker skin color has a higher frequency in populations toward the equator, and lighter skin color is more frequent in populations toward the poles (Figure 13.1). In the Old World, skin color varies from almost white at higher latitudes (for instance, in Scandinavia) to almost black in some regions near the equator (east Africa and southern India, for example). In the New World, there also exists a cline of darker-to-lighter skin color from the equator toward the poles. However, the degree of difference from the equator to the poles is not as great as is found in the Old World. Archaeological evidence indicates that humans first entered the New World by crossing the Bering Land Bridge into Alaska approximately 20,000 years ago, and

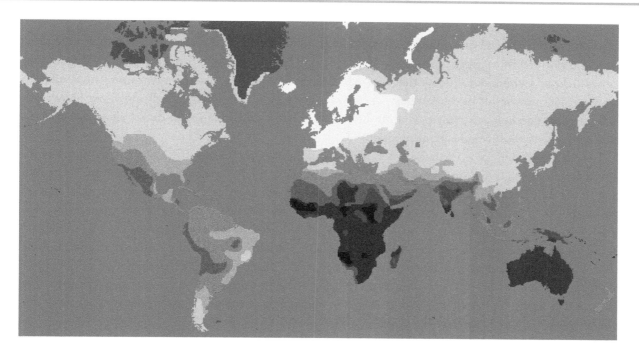

Figure 13.1: Variation in skin color. Darker map areas indicate darker skin colors.

then over time migrating southward and eastward, populating all of the New World. Human occupation of the New World has not been long enough for the evolution of the extremes of skin color found in Old World populations. For example, the skin color of modern Inuit peoples, whose ancestors first occupied the eastern Arctic of Canada and Greenland approximately 5,000 years ago, is darker than that of Old World populations living at the same latitude.

Question: Why did populations toward the equator evolve darker skin color? The evolution of skin color is related to the intensity of ultraviolet radiation. Toward the equator, the sun is directly overhead more frequently; the intensity of UV radiation reaching the Earth's surface is greater than toward the poles. Melanin absorbs UV radiation and acts as a natural sun block. Prolonged exposure to UV radiation can cause damage to the skin, and may result in skin cancer. It has been suggested that darker skin color evolved in populations living toward the equator as a way to reduce the chance of getting skin cancer. However, skin cancer develops over a long period of time and usually does not kill people until later in life, after they have reproduced. Since skin cancer does not affect reproductive potential in most individuals, it is not an adequate evolutionary explanation. An alternate explanation for the evolution of darker skin color in equatorial populations is related to folate levels. Exposure to intense UV radiation reduces folate levels, particularly in lighter-skinned individuals. Insufficient folate levels in men may affect spermatogenesis and in pregnant women may cause brain and spinal cord defects in the embryo, both affecting reproductive potential. Darker skin was selected for in regions with more intense UV radiation to prevent folate break-down (Jablonski and Chaplin 2000).

Question: Why did populations toward the poles evolve lighter skin color? The general consensus among researchers maintains that the evolution of lighter skin color toward the poles is related to the synthesis of vitamin D, commonly referred to as the vitamin D hypothesis (Loomis 1967). Most human diets do not provide sufficient vitamin D, with the exception of diets containing a high proportion of certain fish and oils (for example, the traditional Inuit diet). However, adequate vitamin D can be synthesized from other dietary nutrients through a chemical reaction that requires UV radiation in order for it to occur. Toward the poles, the sun is at a lower angle, reducing the intensity of UV radiation reaching the surface of the

Earth, increasing the risk of insufficient vitamin D synthesis. Additionally, colder temperatures necessitate increased clothing for warmth, resulting in less of the skin being exposed to sunlight. Vitamin D deficiency causes rickets, a childhood disease that weakens and deforms bones, making them more susceptible to breakage; this may result in death, affecting reproductive potential in afflicted individuals. At higher latitudes, lighter skin color maximizes vitamin D synthesis, while individuals with darker skin color have an increased risk of producing insufficient vitamin D.

In addition to skin color, eye color is also related to the pigment melanin. Eye color is determined by the wavelength of the light reflected from the iris of the eye. The density of melanin granules and their distribution in the different layers of the iris varies between individuals, and determines the wavelength of light in the visible light spectrum that is reflected from the eye. As the density of melanin in the iris increases, eye color becomes darker, from blue through green to brown. As with skin color, increased density of melanin in the iris provides increased protection from UV radiation. Melanin density and distribution and resulting eye color are controlled by several genes, some of which also play a role in the determination of skin color. Since some genes control for both skin and eye color, there is a degree of correlation between these two features. For example, individuals with darker skin color more frequently have brown eyes, whereas blue eyes are more frequently associated with lighter skin color.

Question: Why do some dark-skinned people have blue eyes? The correlation between the degree of darkness of eye and skin color is a generalization. Other contrasting combinations occur in many individuals; for example, dark skin color combined with blue eyes. These occur as a result of the transfer of traits through gene flow between populations. Individuals with light skin color may have dark-colored eyes, and those with dark skin color may have light-colored eyes.

The shape of the eye varies between individuals. Some aspects of eye shape have variable frequencies of occurrence between populations. The epicanthic fold—an extra flap of skin on the upper eyelid—is one example. The epicanthic fold occurs in high frequencies among east Asian populations, moderate frequencies in some Arctic Native American populations, and low frequencies in other populations. It is not currently understood why high frequencies of the epicanthic fold occur in east Asian populations. One suggestion is that while the epicanthic fold serves no direct biological function, it is a secondary feature that results when a low nasal bridge is combined with a fatty eyelid, two traits which may be associated with adaptation to colder climates (Brues 1977).

Hair color is a polygenic trait and for most colors is determined by the amount of melanin in hair strands, ranging from blond through brown to black. Red hair occurs when there are increased levels of a second pigment, keratin. Since melanin is the predominant pigment involved with both hair and skin color, there is a general correlation between the two. In the Old World, darker hair color predominates in populations closer to the equator, while lighter colors have increased frequencies in populations closer to the poles, in particular those of Europe. North-south regional variation in hair color frequency can also be observed. For instance, in Italy, blond hair occurs in higher frequency in more northerly parts of the country. Darker hair colors have very high frequencies in all New World populations, including those from the Arctic. The absence of lighter hair colors in northern New World populations is the result of their recent (approximately 5,000 years ago) migration to this region not providing enough time for the evolution of lighter colors, and the darker-haired northeast Asian source populations from which they originated.

Hair color in some individuals may become darker with age. Hair color, for example, may darken during adolescence in many Europeans whose hair was blond in early childhood. With increasing age, melanin production decreases, leading to gray and white colors. The age at which graying begins is extremely variable between individuals and is not correlated with skin color.

Although light hair color has a high degree of correlation with light skin color, some populations do not follow this pattern. For instance, in some Aboriginal populations of Australia, blond hair has a relatively high rate of occurrence, contrasting with a darker skin color. In these groups, many individuals have blond hair in childhood that darkens in adolescence, while some individuals retain blond hair all their lives. While blond hair in some Australian Aboriginals may be the result of admixture with Australians of European descent, this is not the case with all blond Aborigines. Evidence obtained from meticulously compiled genealogical records, combined with the absence of other non-Aboriginal traits in these individuals, indicate a population-specific genetic origin for the blond trait in these groups, and not admixture (Birdsell 1981).

Hair among humans ranges from straight to wavy/curly to woolly/spiral. Hair form is a polygenic trait; the specific form is determined by the shape of the hair strands in cross section. Straight hair is round in cross section, while wavy/curly hair is oval, and woolly/spiral hair is flat. As a generalization, higher frequencies of straight hair occur in east Asian and Native American populations, higher frequencies of wavy and curly hair occur in European, Middle Eastern, south Asian, and Polynesian populations, and higher frequencies of woolly and spiral hair occur in sub-Saharan African, Melanesian, and Australian Aboriginal populations. Although the adaptive significance of hair form is unclear, woolly hair may have evolved in equatorial regions as insulation against intense heat by increasing the air space between the scalp and outer edge of the hair; straight or wavy hair may have evolved in colder environments in order to keep the ears, neck, and shoulders warm.

The ABO blood group is a trait that has variable frequencies of types between populations. ABO blood type is a simple genetic trait with three alleles, where A and B are codominant, and O is recessive. Genotypes AA and AO are associated with blood type A, BB and BO with blood type B, AB with blood type AB, and OO with blood type O. Antibodies are molecules that react with foreign substances in the blood (antigens), causing clumping of the red blood cells. There are two kinds of antigens (A and B antigens) and two kinds of antibodies (anti-A and anti-B antibodies). The different blood types possess different combinations of antigens and antibodies (Figure 13.2), causing some blood type combinations to be incompatible. For this reason, not all donor-recipient blood type combinations are compatible. For example, a person with type A blood cannot receive type B blood because that person's anti-B antibodies will react with the B antigens in the donated type B blood. ABO blood type and associated allele frequencies vary between populations, with the frequency of the O allele ranging between 0.46 and 1.00, the A allele ranging between 0.00 and 0.50, and the B allele ranging between 0.00 and 0.34 (Roychoudhury and Nei 1988).

blood type	genotype	antigens	antibodies
A	AA, AO	A	anti-B
B	BB, BO	B	anti-A
AB	AB	A, B	none
O	OO	none	anti-A, anti-B

Figure 13.2: ABO blood groups, genotypes, antigens, antibodies.

Question: Why do ABO blood type and allele frequencies vary between populations? High or low allele frequencies may have evolved for a variety of reasons within a particular population. For example, low frequencies of blood type A in populations on the Indian subcontinent may be related to the historical prevalence of smallpox into the 20th century in that part of the world. The smallpox virus is chemically similar to the type A antigen. Blood type A individuals do not possess anti-A antibodies, and therefore have depressed resistance to smallpox and are more likely to die of the disease, resulting in lower frequencies of blood type A individuals (Vogel 1975). Very high frequencies of particular blood types found in some populations may be explained by the founder effect. For instance, the frequency of blood type O approaches 1.00 in indigenous populations of South America, indicating that the small group of original colonizers of the continent possessed a very high frequency of the O allele (Cavelli-Sforza 1997). Similarly, frequencies greater than 0.9 among northern Australian Aboriginals likely also were the result of the founder effect.

Evidence from biological anthropology, in combination with archaeological and linguistic information, provides strong support for northeast Asia as being the source region from which the earliest inhabitants of the Americas originated. Both Native American and northeast Asian populations have high frequencies of a suite of dental traits called sinodonty. Sinodont features include shovel-shaped incisors, single-root first premolars of the upper jaw, and triple-root first molars of the lower jaw. The high frequency of sinodont traits in both populations indicates that the source region of early American populations was northeast Asia (Turner 1984). Genetic information has provided evidence for the timing of migration into the Americas. Studies of mtDNA (inherited through the female line) and DNA from the Y chromosome (inherited through the male line) from Native American and northeast Asian populations implies an initial migration into the Americas between 20,000 and 15,000 years ago, with up to four subsequent migrations (Schurr 2004). This time range correlates with the earliest archaeological evidence for human occupation of the Americas, which the majority of researchers put at approximately 15,000 years ago.

THE QUESTION OF RACE

The term race is commonly understood to mean the classification of humans into categories which are defined by the presence or absence of certain traits. Most people associate specific traits with a particular race, and conclude that someone belongs to one race or another if they possess the traits of that race. Race is identified by the presence of specific—usually physical—traits. For example, an individual who has dark skin, brown eyes, a broad nose, and woolly hair would be categorized as a member of the African, or Negroid, race. This idea of race implies that there exists a set of unique traits that all members of a race possess, and that no nonmembers possess. This is what is referred to as the folk concept of race. In this conception, different intellectual and moral qualities are ascribed to the different races. Although most people in the past (and a minority of people today) believed that intellectual and moral qualities correlate with race, no reputable scientific study has ever shown this to be the case.

Question: Is the folk concept of race valid? Ever since their first appearance, humans have moved from one area to another, coming into contact and interbreeding with other humans. Throughout human history, gene flow has facilitated the transfer of genes and physical traits between populations. For this reason, there are always some individuals in a race who will possess traits that are not characteristic of that race, and lack traits that are characteristic of that race. In other words, there are no unique traits that can be used to definitively classify people into races, contrary to the common folk concept of race.

The terminology we commonly use to name the races does not entirely make sense. For example, "black" people are not black; they come in a variety of shades of brown. "White" people are not white; they come in an assortment of shades of beige. Sometimes, those shades of beige are darker than those shades of brown. This illustrates that the range of variation *within* populations is greater than the range of variation *between* populations, and that there is overlap in the ranges of variation of populations.

Biological anthropologists recognize these problems with the folk concept of race, and therefore no longer attempt to formulate rigid categories defined by the presence or absence of specific unique traits. However, in the past, the belief of the existence of unique traits led to numerous attempts at formulating classifications of humans into races. The various classifications vary in the number of traits used for classification and in the number of categories, ranging between 3 and 37 races. For example, the ancient Egyptians during the New Kingdom three thousand years ago based their classification on skin color: they referred to people who lived to the south as "black" people; those to the east, "yellow" people; those to the north, "white" people; and themselves as "red" people. Skin color is one of the most frequently used physical features in racial classification, although often in combination with other features. In 1946, for instance, Earnest Hooton used skin color, eye color, hair color, and hair form to classify humans into three main races, each of which contained several subraces.

We now recognize that no trait is unique to a particular population, but that many traits differ in frequency between populations. A trait may occur in extremely high frequency in a population, but there will always be some individuals who do not possess that trait. Biological anthropologists seek to understand the evolutionary reasons that explain why a particular trait is adaptive, and thus why that trait has a high frequency in a particular population; in other words, they seek to understand the adaptive significance of phenotypic and genotypic variation between populations.

In the past it was believed that identifiable human biological races exist, and that cultural qualities correlate with the various races. During the late 1800s, a concept named social Darwinism proposed that natural selection not only operated on human biology, but also human culture, and was used to explain the existence of inequality between individuals and between groups. Those individuals in a society who have more wealth and power are more "fit" and hence superior, while those who are poor with little power are less fit and inferior. Victorious nations (races) were more fit than conquered nations (races) as a result of natural selection. The problem with the idea of social Darwinism is that it applies a biological theory to social phenomena. The rules of natural selection are biological. The rules that govern biology are not the same as those that govern culture.

The social Darwinists believed that there was a biological basis for the inequality of individuals and races, and that evolution acted to gradually decrease the number of poorer "unfit" individuals and increase the number of fit individuals. This belief led to the idea of eugenics, proposed by Francis Galton in 1883, which proposed that society could be improved by encouraging mating among successful, fitter individuals and limiting mating among unsuccessful, less fit individuals. The idea that fitness was correlated with race led to the enactment of miscegenation laws regulating intermarriage between the races in many jurisdictions, including Nazi Germany and apartheid South Africa. In the southern United States, the enforcement of miscegenation laws ceased during the 1960s with the civil rights movement, although in some states these laws were not repealed until quite recently, for example in Alabama in 2001.

Although anthropologists and others now recognize that the concept of race has no basis in biology, many members of the general public consider race as something real. A minority of these people also maintain that some races are inferior to others, that not all races have the same level of intelligence and moral character, and that these differences are genetic. Studies that purport to show differences in intelligence between the races are problematic in terms of their methodology, assumptions, or interpretation of the data. An example is the book *The Bell Curve* (Herrnstein and Murray 1994), which uses data from other selected studies to conclude that intelligence is mostly inherited, that success is highly correlated with intelligence, that IQ accurately reflects intelligence, and that the lower socioeconomic status of African Americans compared with European Americans was due to their lower intelligence, as reflected in their IQ scores. Critics of Herrnstein and Murray point out that the degree of heritability of intelligence is highly disputed, that the racial groups are not genetically distinct, and that IQ test scores are influenced by culture (Molnar 1996). Herrnstein and Murray ignore the influence of environment. Even if a correlation did exist between race and intelligence, correlation does not prove causation.

In another example, J. Philippe Rushton (1995) argues that race is a valid biological concept, and that the three main races (Mongoloid, Caucasoid, and Negroid) differ in several behavioral traits, including parenting techniques, sexual practices, and social deviance. Rushton also maintains that these traits have a genetic basis that originated with the initial migration of humans from Africa 100,000 years ago. Rushton bases his analysis on data from selected modern nations. If his conclusions are correct, then all modern populations of a particular race should possess the same set of traits. Subsequent analysis using a more comprehensive data set concludes that of Rushton's 26 racially distinctive behaviors, the majority showed no correlation with race, and five had an opposite correlation to his prediction (Peregrine et al. 2003).

The flaws in these and other similar studies suggest that there may be an element of bias or racism on the part of the authors, which influences the research and associated conclusions. For instance, Rushton has been subject to criticism from the scientific community over his association with the Pioneer Fund, which he headed from 2002 until 2012. The Pioneer Fund was established in 1937 "to advance the scientific study of heredity and human differences"; critics of the fund cite its support of research on race and intelligence and its connections with racist individuals and white supremacist groups.

These views are in the minority. Currently, the majority view recognizes that intelligence cannot be easily quantified, that it is influenced by both environment and genetic inheritance, and that there is no valid evidence showing a correlation between intelligence and race.

CRITICAL REASONING QUESTIONS

- What is a cline?
- Why is there a higher frequency of darker skin in populations toward the equator, and a higher frequency of lighter skin in populations toward the poles?
- Why do northern New World populations have darker skin than Old World populations living at the same latitude?
- Briefly describe the folk concept of race.
- Why is the folk concept of race invalid?
- What is social Darwinism? Why is social Darwinism invalid?
- Briefly define eugenics. What are miscegenation laws?
- What were Herrnstein and Murray's conclusions in *The Bell Curve*? What problems are there with the validity of these conclusions?

REFERENCES AND SUGGESTED READINGS

Birdsell, J. B. (1981). *Human evolution: An introduction to the new physical anthropology.* Boston: Houghton Mifflin.

Brues, A. M. (1977). *People and races.* New York: Macmillan.

Cavelli-Sforza, L. L. (1997). Genes, peoples, and languages. *Proceedings of the National Academy of Sciences* 94:7710–7724.

Herrnstein, R. J., and C. Murray (1994). *The bell curve: Intelligence and class structure in American life.* New York: Free Press.

Jablonski, N. G., and G. Chaplin (2000). The evolution of human skin coloration. *Journal of Human Evolution* 39:57–106.

Loomis, W. F. (1967). Skin-pigment regulation of vitamin D biosynthesis in man. *Science* 157:501–506.

Molnar, S. (1996). Book review: *The Bell Curve: Intelligence and Class Structure in American Life.* R. J. Herrnstein & C. Murray. New York: Free Press. *Current Anthropology* 37:S165–S168.

Peregrine, Peter N., Carol R. Ember, and Melvin Ember (2003). Cross-cultural evaluation of predicted associations between race and behavior. *Evolution and Human Behavior* 24:357–364.

Roychoudhury, A. K., and M. Nei (1988). *Human polymorphic genes: World distribution.* Oxford, UK: Oxford University Press.

Rushton, J. Philippe (1995). *Race, evolution, and behavior.* New Brunswick, NJ: Transaction Publishers.

Schurr, T. (2004). Molecular genetic diversity in Siberians and Native Americans suggests an early colonization of the New World. In David Madsen, ed., *Entering America: Northeast Asia and Beringia Before the Last Glacial Maximum,* pp. 187–238. Salt Lake City: University of Utah Press.

Turner, Christy (1984). Advances in the dental search for Native American origins. *Acta anthropogenetica* 8(1–2):23–78.

Vogel, F. (1975). ABO blood groups, the HL-A system and diseases. In F. M. Salzano, ed., *The Role of Natural Selection in Human Evolution,* pp. 247–269. Amsterdam: North-Holland Publishing Co.

14

Population History And Genetics

Thank Your Ancestors

By Gillian Crane-Kramer

When we consider important factors of the environment, disease-producing organisms represent one of the most important selective pressures in evolutionary history. The path of all plant and animal life on Earth has been profoundly influenced by encounters with infectious diseases in particular. Given their ability to wreak havoc, what is stunning is that most disease-causing entities are too small to be seen by the naked eye. This means that they were not even discovered by humans until well into the Renaissance, and viruses were only viewed for the first time in the 20th century, thanks to the invention of the electron microscope. Just to give you an idea of how significant a threat disease-causing microorganisms are, the agent of botulism food poisoning is far too small to be seen by the naked eye. Yet, a 12-ounce glass of the toxin it produces would kill every human being (all six billion of us!) living on the face of the Earth (Sherman 2006)! With power like that, humans would do best to pay attention. Unfortunately, today in the developed world, we tend to see disease (especially infectious disease) as having only a minor impact on our lives. We are cared for by physicians from the moment we are born; we are vaccinated as children; well nourished; and when illness rears its ugly head, we are treated with effective drugs and antibiotics. Thus, our perception of how devastating a social impact disease can have is lost to us. We have been lulled into a false sense of security by this reliance upon effective and sophisticated modern medical technology. This is a very dangerous position to be in, as disease-producing organisms are themselves constantly evolving, and new forms are constantly emerging to threaten living creatures indefinitely. The study of disease in humans is particularly tricky because we cannot only

Figure 14.1: Medieval man, sick in bed (Wellcome Trust Images).

Figure 14.2: Witch silhouettes (Wellcome Trust Images).

concentrate on biological causes. We have to take into account the profound influence that human culture (and thus behavior) has on the pattern of disease in any given population. Human behavior and technological innovations have always played a major role in the production of disease. It is typically human activities—including commercial travel and trade, warfare, social adaptations, technological improvements, and dietary modifications—that precipitate the rise and fall of diseases (Sherman 2006).

The word disease implies a state of imbalance or abnormality within the body. It is defined as: "a condition of the living animal or plant body or of one of its parts that impairs normal functioning" (Merriam-Webster 1998: 332). Therefore, disease in an organism results from infection or genetic defect. It is important to remember that humans had no concept of the actual causes of disease until the 19th century. Today, the modern medical establishment perceives the physical signs of disease as a biological process with a specific biological cause. However, before the establishment of the modern medical concept of germ theory, humans explained the cause of disease in a variety of ways. In ancient Greece and Rome, numerous scholars (from Hippocrates to Galen) developed rationalistic explanations of how disease developed and how epidemics spread throughout the population. The fourth-century BC Greek physician Hippocrates was the father of modern medicine. He was not aware of specific disease-causing organisms, but interpreted disease as an imbalance within the body and between the body and the natural world. Health can be restored by reestablishing balance in the body through a myriad of techniques (massage, reiki, acupuncture, cupping, etc.). Hippocrates is known as the father of humoral theory, the idea that the body is composed of four humors (black bile, yellow bile, blood, and phlegm), and different diseases result from too much or too little of these essential humors. This notion dominated medicine for over a millennium and severely impeded the development of germ theory.

Another explanation for disease that is still seen today in many traditional societies is witchcraft or sorcery. Accusations of witchcraft offer a commentary on social relationships within and between groups. In order for health to be restored, the conflict must be resolved. This can involve many members of a social group, not just the individual who is ill. Therefore, physical illness is a sign of social unrest on some level. In the past, astrological information (not just what we read with our coffee in the morning) was important in the treatment of illness. The exact time of one's birth (the minute, the day, month, and year) was thought to determine general personality traits and general health. In addition, disease was often believed to result from dangerous astrological conjunctions. For example, many contemporary sources explain the cause of the devastating outbreaks of bubonic plague in the 14th century as resulting from an unfortunate celestial conjunction of the planets. These unfortunate events were often representative of divine wrath. Disease resulted directly from religious or moral transgressions, and the only way to restore one's health was to appease the angry gods. This could be accomplished by way of various rituals, prayers and incantations, ceremonial baths, donations of considerable

Figure 14.3: Greek Evil Eye charms.

size to the Church, and sacrifices. Linked to this idea of divine wrath is the biblical notion that the sins of the fathers can be visited upon their descendants in terms of disease (presumably inherited). However, this idea predates biblical writings in a number of cultures, as King Tutankhamen paid for the transgressions of his ancestors by dying young, around the age of 18 years, likely as a result of tuberculosis (his lungs were severely affected by the disease). It was an ancient concept of disease as divine retribution.

Disease has also been explained as resulting from the evil eye. A number of amulets, prayers, and incantations were devised to protect oneself from the dangers of the evil eye. As in witchcraft accusations, belief in the evil eye is indicative of social unrest or conflict. One of the most common explanations for disease in the past was the notion of poisoned air, or miasma. Miasma is a poisonous atmosphere once thought to rise from rotting matter or swamps, believed to cause widespread disease. This notion of contaminated air extends well back to classical times; a great example is the ancient Roman term *malaria* (*mal-*, *bad* and *aria-*, air) to describe the devastating disease that came from the Pontine marshes around Rome to prey on Roman citizens. In addition to the idea

Figure 14.4: The Evil Eye, by John Phillip (Stirling Smith Museum and Art Gallery).

Figure 14.5: Miasma.

of miasma were a number of ideas about bad seeds, or contagia. Such things could be passed from one person to another via water, soil, air, or through fomites such as clothing, utensils, bedding, or other belongings of the sick.

We now know that disease results from infection by disease-causing organisms, dietary deficiencies, or genetic factors. Every environment is associated with specific pathogens, and thus individual human populations have had to adjust to unique pathogen circumstances for millennia. With the development of the field of population genetics in conjunction with modern medicine, we are now able to investigate in minute detail the genetic response to disease stressors. As a result, scientists discovered that human populations around the world have developed unique genetic responses to disease threats in their environments. If these genetic solutions actually increase the likelihood of survival and reproduction, then they should increase in the population over time. We all carry inside us the genetic history of our ancestors, whether successes or failures. This chapter will focus on an examination of how our genes make us either susceptible—or resistant—to disease organisms.

DO YOUR GENES GOVERN DISEASE SUSCEPTIBILITY?

It appears that there are differences in the distribution of genetic disease throughout the world. Sometimes, populations appear to have reduced risk of developing a disease, but just as commonly, our genetic heritage can make us more vulnerable to certain conditions. Many genetic disorders are found in increased frequency in certain populations. A good example of this is the increased rates of **hypertension** observed in African Americans. Sodium is necessary for normal cell functioning, but prior to the development of agriculture, it was a minor component of the human diet. In addition, some areas of the world are associated with higher reserves of natural salt deposits than others, a factor that would become significant for African Americans after transportation to the New World during the period of slavery. Salt is typically used by humans to flavor foods and for food processing, preservation, and storage. The increased consumption of salt in the agricultural

Figure 14.6: African American male.

(and particularly modern) diet has been linked to increased rates of hypertension (high blood pressure), and African Americans appear to be significantly more at risk than other groups in the United States (Winick 1980). This clear difference in the prevalence of hypertension in African Americans requires explanation. Something about their ancestral journey has made them more at risk for developing hypertension; the trick is to figure out what.

There are many examples where founder effect has greatly increased the presence of genetic disease in particular populations. This is illustrated by the high rate of the BRCA1 gene mutation that places women at risk for developing **breast cancer** in eastern European

Figure 14.7: Ashkenazi Orthodox Jews.

Jews (Ashkenazim). The BRCA1 gene is found at a rate 20 times higher in female Ashkenazim than in the rest of the world. While over 300 mutations in the gene have been identified globally, Ashkenazim express only two of those mutations, indicating a genetic bottleneck resulting from founder's effect (Abel 2001, Risch et al. 2003, Motulsky 1995, Goodman 1979). This is also seen with the genetic disease **porphyria** variegata in Dutch South Africans. It is a genetic disease with a wide range of phenotypic expressions from little to no symptoms to severe expressions of delirium, abdominal pain, and dark red/black urine. Unbeknownst to him, one of the original Dutch settlers to South Africa carried the gene for porphyria. As a result, today, South Africans of Dutch descent (Afrikaaners) have a higher rate of porphyria than any other population in the world (Marks 2011).

DO YOUR GENES CONFER GENETIC RESISTANCE TO DISEASE?

Recent discoveries of higher frequencies of genes that are typically defined as deleterious in certain populations suggest that these genes may confer resistance to other conditions in those that are carriers. What we have here is called a balanced polymorphism; in these cases, natural selection appears to be favoring those individuals who are heterozygous (or carriers having only one copy of the negative allele). As they only have one copy rather than two, they do not express the disease state. However, the mating of two carriers always has a 25 percent chance of producing an affected child with two copies of the negative mutation. It appears that when lethal disease threats are present, this is a risk worth taking.

Cystic fibrosis is a genetic disease that affects epithelial tissue and is principally a disease of the lungs and pancreas. It is found in its highest frequency among Caucasian people of northern and western European ancestry (Ratjen and Döring 2003). Symptoms include excessive production of thick mucus in the lungs, coughing fits, and breathing difficulty. Cystic fibrosis affects the salt/water balance in our bodies. People with

Health Problems with Cystic Fibrosis

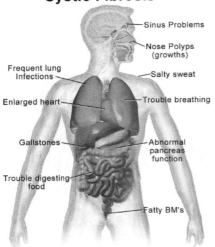

- Sinus Problems
- Nose Polyps (growths)
- Salty sweat
- Trouble breathing
- Abnormal pancreas function
- Fatty BM's
- Frequent lung Infections
- Enlarged heart
- Gallstones
- Trouble digesting food

Figure 14.8: Symptoms of cystic fibrosis.

the disease (rather than being a carrier and having only one copy of the dangerous recessive allele) have such an abnormal imbalance that it causes thick mucus to build up in the lungs. This mucus in turn provides the perfect environment for disease-causing bacteria to flourish, and places individuals at tremendous risk for pulmonary infections like pneumonia. Prior to the 20th century, people born with cystic fibrosis did not reach sexual maturity. Even today, the disease is associated with a significant reduction in life expectancy. It is estimated that in the Unites States, 1 in 27 people of European ancestry are heterozygous (have one copy) for the trait. Several hundred mutations have been identified for the gene. Interestingly, roughly 90 percent of Danish carriers of cystic fibrosis carry one specific mutation known as ΔF508. This gene is found in 75 percent of Dutch carriers, 70 percent of French carriers, and 50 percent of Spanish carriers (Marks 2011, Wailoo and Pemberton 2006). This implies that both genetic drift and possibly selection are involved. The two magic questions that instantly arise are: When can we identify this gene in the European population? and Why would northwestern Europeans have the highest frequency of this negative mutation in the world?

The most prevalent mutation causing the disease appears to be much older than anyone had imagined. Recent research suggests that the mutation arose in Europe by chance in the middle of the Stone Age, when humans were still living in mobile, small bands of hunter/gatherers. It spread with these nomadic populations throughout the north and west of the continent. The estimate for the mutation is based upon a study that collected genetic samples from 15 different European groups in order to reconstruct the evolutionary history of the CF mutation. The researchers concluded that the mutation is at least 52,000 years old, as much as 10 to 20 times the age considered previously (Morral et al. 1994). Furthermore, scholars assert that the F508 appeared in a population that was genetically distinct from any present European population. It then moved throughout Europe in chronologically distinct expansions, which explains the different frequencies of the F508 mutation in Europe today.

Figure 14.9: Medieval Town (Karl Eduard Biermann c. 1830).

The second million-dollar-question is, Why is it in the largest frequency there today? This is a tricky question, and is likely to be developed over time. However, it is probable that the frequency is elevated in this region because it offers some form of selective advantage when one is a carrier. Morral et al. (1994) suggest that the gene may provide some form of genetic resistance against the serious diarrheal infections like cholera, which lead to rapid dehydration and death and have been some of the greatest killers of humanity. Some scholars propose that historically, in European urban centers where diarrheal diseases like cholera were a constant threat to survival, those individuals who were carriers of one copy of the CF gene may have had a selective advantage for survival. The gene may assist in the retention of salt and water, and this could be a crucial protection against the excessive loss of fluids associated with gastrointestinal illnesses. The disease cystic fibrosis affects the cells' transportation of chloride ions, and interestingly, so does the bacterial toxin that causes cholera. It is very likely that this mutation did not confer any significant selective advantage until European populations began to live in large, permanent settlements. Diseases that cause serious inflammation of the intestines, particularly those that are waterborne, have been some of the greatest scourges of humanity. These do not historically become a significant problem until the adoption of agriculture and the rise of large centers. Perhaps in those crowded and unhygienic conditions, those people who were carriers of the CF gene had a selective advantage, and were thus more likely to survive

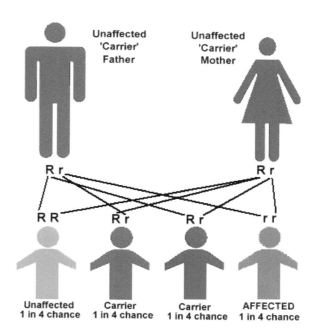

Figure 14.10: Inheritance of Tay-Sachs disease.

and reproduce. This is a very interesting suggestion, but the disease threat is likely to be something other than cholera, which appears to have emerged in India.

Another example of genetic susceptibility is found in the distribution of Tay-Sachs disease. **Tay-Sachs** is a rare condition that affects roughly only 1 in every 500,000 births worldwide. However, among the Ashkenazim (eastern European Jews), it is found at much higher frequencies—roughly 1 in every 2,500 births (Molnar 1998). Tay-Sachs disease is a fatal metabolic disease caused by an autosomal recessive gene. It causes an excessive accumulation of ganglio-sides in the brain's nerve cells, and this causes premature death of the cells. It is a devastating condition, with the most common form, infant Tay-Sachs, commencing at roughly six months of age and leading to death in the majority of cases before the age of four years. Why are the Ashkenazim the population that maintains the highest frequencies of a lethal allele? Could one copy again confer some form of selective advantage? Some suggest that heterozygous individuals may have a greater resistance against tuberculosis. Known as the White Death, tuberculosis moved like a scourge through urban environments. Pulmonary tuberculosis has been around for thousands of years, and continues to be one of the greatest threats to human health today. At some point,

Figure 14.11: Jewish family, Brooklyn, New York.

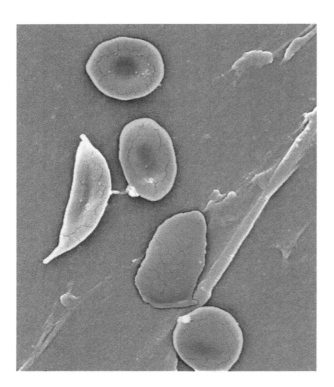

Figure 14.12: Sickled and normal red blood cells.

a mutation causing the disease appeared in the Ashkenazim. Throughout the 19th and 20th centuries (and earlier in many regions), this population was repeatedly persecuted and forced to live in crowded, stressful, unhygienic conditions. Tuberculosis thrives in these conditions, where the immune status is low and children and young adults are particularly vulnerable. Tuberculosis has always been particularly feared, as it is one of the few diseases that often carries off the young, healthy segment of the society. This has rippling demographic consequences as significant members of your reproductive pool are reduced. During World War II, tuberculosis was a large killer in Jewish settlements in eastern Europe. An interesting observation was made: seemingly normal and healthy family members of a Tay-Sachs child were often resistant to tuberculosis. If the Tay-Sachs gene did confer some resistance to tuberculosis, then one would expect that, in an environment where tuberculosis is a serious threat to survival, the Tay-Sachs gene should increase in frequency over time (Marks 1995). This happens in part because people who do not have it are more likely to contract and die from tuberculosis; thus, the people who survive to reproduce are the people with the gene. In addition, because the Ashkenazim married within their own community with little gene flow with other groups, the frequency would continue to increase. This is a very interesting idea, yet we must wait to understand how the Tay-Sachs gene actually functions to increase resistance before the debate is over. It is also possible that genetic drift plays a significant role in the frequency of the gene in Ashkenazim, as their populations have tended to live in small, rather isolated communities (Risch et al. 2003).

Without question, the most famous example of a balanced polymorphism in humans is the distribution of **sickle cell trait** around the world. In this case, the serious selective pressure is the disease malaria—one of the most deadly and wily of all of humanity's microscopic foes. For most of our history, as a lineage, we have lived in the tropics—in hot, wet conditions. While these environments have many tremendous advantages, one of the major downsides is the intense pathogen load.

Figure 14.13: *Anopheles stephensi* mosquito.

Temperate regions that experience periods of cold weather have a far lower pathogen load, as the cold acts as a filter for the majority of pathogens that are heat adapted.

Sickle cell anemia is caused by a negative point mutation on a gene located on Chromosome 11 (which leads to an error: the replacement of the amino acid valine for glutamic acid in the subsequent protein). The result of this condition is that the actual structure of the red blood cells is altered, and their ability to transport oxygen effectively is severely impaired. Debilitating symptoms of the disease include anemia, impairment of circulation, joint swelling and pain, enlargement of the spleen, and

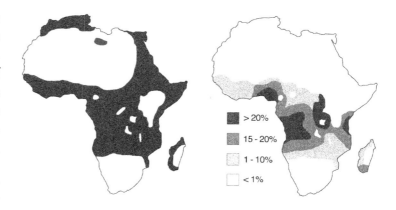

Figure 14.14: Distribution of sickle cell trait and malaria (original work by Anthony Allison).

frequent infections. For the majority of human history, people with the disease did not typically survive to contribute their genes to the next generation. For the frequency of sickle cell to have reached its present levels—as high as 40 percent in some African populations—the selective environmental pressure must have been very significant (Stanford et al. 2013). Some suggest that throughout human history, malaria may have killed more people than any other infectious disease. According to the World Health Organization, there were about 219 million cases of malaria in 2010 (with an uncertainty range of 154 million to 289 million) and an estimated 660,000 deaths (with an uncertainty range of 490,000 to 836,000). Most deaths occur among children living in Africa, where a child dies every minute from malaria. It is estimated that over a million children under the age of six years die every year from the disease. The disease not only places tremendous stress upon the medical system, but it also has rippling effects on other political, economic, and social realms of society.

Malaria is caused by a protozoa belonging to the family *Plasmodium*. There are over a hundred different species in this genus, and four of them are known to cause malaria. The life cycle of the *Plasmodium* requires a stage in both a human and mosquito host, and the disease is transmitted to humans via the bite of an infected female Anopheles mosquito. The most lethal form of the disease is caused by *Plasmodium falciparum*, and this form causes roughly 95 percent of all malarial deaths. The connection between sickle cell trait and malaria was established by the British geneticist Anthony Allison through work conducted in east Africa in 1953. His initial study focused upon whether or not individuals who were heterozygous for the trait demonstrated an elevated protection against the severe *Plasmodium falciparum* infections. This required Allison to examine children between four months and four years of age, a time when the risk of illness and death from the disease is at its greatest. The study was done in Ugandan villages where antimalarial drugs were not

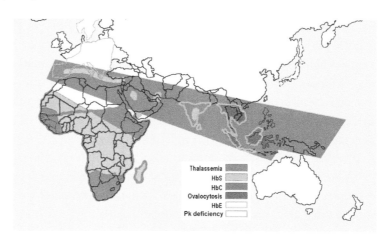

Figure 14.15: Distribution of red blood cell abnormalities.

used. Allison found that children in this age group carrying one copy of the sickle cell gene had significantly lower malaria parasite counts than children with normal hemoglobin. In addition, he observed that in areas affected by malaria, especially along Kenya's coast (southeast) and near Lake Victoria (southwest), a remarkably high number of people (20–30 percent) carried the gene for sickle cell anemia. In the highlands (west) of Kenya, where there was no malaria, Allison noted that less than one percent of the population carried the sickle cell gene. Allison correctly concluded that individuals with one copy of the sickle cell gene were resistant to malaria, and that in malarial areas, natural selection is acting upon that gene. Thus, carriers of the gene are much more likely to survive and reproduce than are noncarriers. As the gene had a significant impact upon survival, it increased over time in the populations where malaria was a constant and long-term threat. Recently, another interesting study looking at the frequency of the trait in a cohort of 1022 Kenyan children living near Lake Victoria supported Allison's earlier results (Aidoo et al. 2002). If high frequencies of sickle cell trait are maintained in malarial areas, why do we still find the allele in one out of every 12 African Americans? This is a legacy of their descent from West African populations, where one in three people are carriers of the gene today (Kwiatkowski 2005, Marks 2011). However, the presence of this gene is slowly declining in African American populations, as it no longer confers an advantage to survival (as malaria is no longer a health threat here).

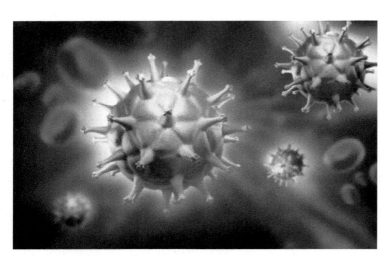

Figure 14.16: HIV virus and blood cell.

Interestingly, scientists have discovered other alleles affecting blood physiology that also appear to confer protection against malaria. This includes alleles for the thalassemias, which are conditions where there is also abnormal hemoglobin structure. Thalassemia has a high frequency in some Mediterranean populations, including Greeks and southern Italians. The name is derived from the Greek word for sea (*thalassa*), presumably the Mediterranean Sea, and blood (*heme*) (Ingram and Stretton 1959). Glucose-6 phosphate dehydrogenase deficiency is a condition where important metabolic pathways are affected. It is present in all human cells, but is a particularly important enzyme to red blood cells. This mutation is sex linked, and is commonly found in Mediterranean, African, and other populations. G6PD deficiency is the most common enzyme deficiency in humans; it is estimated to affect roughly 400 million people (Beutler 2008). While there are several mutations at this locus, two alleles attain frequencies of 20 percent or greater in African and Mediterranean populations: these are termed the A- and Med mutations (Tishkoff and Verelli 2004). It has been observed that malarial parasites are significantly more often observed in normal red cells than in enzyme-deficient cells (Luzzatto 1979). An evolutionary genetic analysis of malarial selection on G6PD deficiency genes has been published by Tishkoff and Verelli. Studies of the distribution of this mutation demonstrate that it is only common in many countries that are, or have had, a history of malaria.

A final fascinating example of a balanced polymorphism in humans is the **delta 32 mutation** and resistance to bubonic plague and the HIV virus. In humans, the CCR5 gene that encodes the CCR5 protein is located on the short (p) arm at position 21 on Chromosome 3. Inheritance of the delta 32 mutation results in the genetic deletion of a portion of the CCR5 gene. A few individuals carry a mutation known as CCR5-Δ32 in the CCR5 gene, protecting them against these strains of HIV. CCR5-Δ32 is a deletion mutation of a gene that influences how T cells function (Buseyne et al. 1998). At least one copy of CCR5-Δ32 is found in about 4–16 percent of people of European descent. Up to 20 percent of ethnic western Europeans carry this mutation, which is rare or absent in other ethnic groups (Zimmerman et al. 1997, Stephens et al. 1998, Majumder and Dey 2001). This suggests that the CCR5-Δ32 mutation was strongly selected for at some time during European history.

Many strains of the HIV virus—as well as the bacteria *Yersinia pestis*, which causes bubonic plague—initially use CCR5 to enter and infect host cells. The virus HIV normally enters a cell via its CCR5 receptors, especially in the initial stage of a person becoming infected. But in people with receptors impeded by the CCR5-Δ32 mutation, the HIV virus is blocked from entry into the cell, providing immunity to AIDS for homozygous carriers and significantly slowing the progress of the disease in heterozygous carriers.

Some researchers propose that the mutation would have been favored by natural selection when plague epidemics repeatedly swept through Europe during the Middle Ages (Duncan et al. 2005). However, recent experiments in mice suggest that *Yersinia pestis*, the cause of plague, can infect mammalian cells by other means, and recent research questions whether or not this is the correct selective disease pathogen (Faure and Royer-Carenzi 2008). Some scientists maintain that smallpox, which is caused by the variola virus, was the selection agent that historically caused CCR5-Δ32 carriers to survive in Europe (Galvani et al. 2003, Elvin et al. 2004, Mecsas et al. 2004). Some argue that in Europe, the mutation would have awarded significant protection against the tremendous killer smallpox, especially in the principal port and trade cities and in isolated islands and archipelagos like Iceland and the Azores (Freitas et al. 2006). There is also research suggesting that CCR5-Δ32 impedes the development of cerebral malaria from *Plasmodium* infection, and that it may also play a role in slowing the progression of multiple sclerosis (Belnoue et al. 2003, Barcellos et al. 2000, Kantor et al. 2003).

Clearly, we all carry inside us a record of our ancestors' long-standing relationships to the pathogens in their environments. Sometimes, nature randomly provides a chance mutation in a population that may not provide a significant survival benefit at the time. However, some of these mutations do allow for differential resistance to some of the world's greatest infectious killers. These genes increase over time, as it was the individuals who had these genes who survived to reproduce and pass them on to

Figure 14.17: Bubonic plague pit mass grave in Martigues, France 1720–21.

their offspring. It is an exciting time, as science is only at the beginning of identifying and understanding these amazing genetic responses to disease stress. No doubt we can expect to discover many more in the future. The implications for medicine in terms of future prevention and treatment of illness is profound with these genetic discoveries.

DO YOUR GENES MAKE YOU MORE SUSCEPTIBLE TO DISEASE?

The first portion of this chapter concerns itself with a discussion of genetic resistance in diverse populations throughout the world. It is marvelous to think that our ancestors have handed down to us—over countless generations—this arsenal of genetic weapons that can greatly increase our likelihood of survival. (Maybe you appreciate the people in those old black-and-white photos at home a little bit more!) Nevertheless, for every beneficial gift, there also usually is a downside. The downside to genetic heritage is that sometimes your genes also can make you more vulnerable to developing certain conditions. This means you will always have to be concerned about certain health-related issues, but knowledge is power. If you know that a particular condition is commonly displayed in your family or ethnic group, you can make medical and lifestyle choices that reduce your risk. We are all in this together, as no human population escapes their own unique genetic risks.

This impact of genetic heritage and lifestyle choices is well demonstrated by Native American populations and their increased risk for **diabetes mellitus type 2**. Adult-onset diabetes appears to be triggered by a high caloric intake, although there is no question that a genetic component is also involved. Native Americans present the highest levels of adult-onset diabetes in America today. This is because their traditional diets have been replaced by high quantities of processed and manufactured foods. Native Americans appear to be significantly more susceptible to developing type 2 diabetes than Caucasians. Diabetes occurs when the body either is not able to produce enough insulin to break down sugar from food, or when the body's cells fail to recognize the insulin it does produce. Why do we see such elevated rates of adult-onset diabetes in Native American populations? Is it something cultural, genetic, or a combination of both? The traditional Native American diet was full of wild meats, a large fiber plant component, and very little sugar. The only sugar available came from naturally sweet, seasonal foods like berries and other fruits and honey. There is no question that the Native American diet was greatly transformed in the 19th and 20th centuries as the traditional diets were abandoned in favor of the "American" diet,

Figure 14.18: Diane Douglas-Willard, Haida Indian.

Figure 14.19: A Kali'na hunter and female gatherer (from *Na'na Kali'na: Une histoire des Kali'na en Guyane*).

especially processed foods. This transformation can be seen as major changes observed in the modern glycemic index of Native individuals. The glycemic index is measured on a scale of 1 to 100, and is a measure of how fast a food's energy is absorbed into the bloodstream. Foods at the lower end of the scale represent those that are absorbed more slowly, and thus have the least effect on blood sugar. Traditional Native groups would have eaten a diet with foods well below a glycemic index of 50, but this has been replaced with foods that have a very high glycemic index (like breads, fried and processed foods, refined sugar) (Reinhard et al. 2012). If Americans of European descent are eating these new foods as well, why do we see these elevated rates only in Native Americans? Perhaps there is some genetic difference?

The idea of the **thrifty gene** was proposed by the geneticist James V. Neel in the early 1960s (Neel 1962, 1982, 2009). He was particularly

Figure 14.20: Stop Diabetes sign.

interested in diabetes, and felt that there was clearly a genetic component to the disease (later, this idea was also extended to address the great increase in obesity). Thrifty genes are genes that enable individuals to efficiently collect and process food to deposit fat during periods of food abundance. This allows people to survive on reserves during the lean times of year (feast or famine). Neel argues that in hunter-gatherer groups (especially women of reproductive age), the thrifty genotype would have been advantageous because it would allow them to increase their fat levels more quickly during times of abundance. The assumption is that larger (i.e., fatter) individuals who had the thrifty genes would be more likely to survive during times of food scarcity. Those individuals who were better able to survive the cyclical patterns of feast and famine were at a significant advantage for survival. Yet, in the first world today, there is a constant abundance of food—there is no famine to prepare for anymore. This genotype is still preparing us for starvation around every possible turn, but the lean times never take place. The result of this disconnect between the modern diet and the ancient environment to which we are adapted is the development of large-scale chronic obesity and related health problems like diabetes and heart disease. For a long time, scholars suggested that the thrifty gene or genes that were acquired through this long-standing adaptation to a cycle of feast and famine is what makes Native American populations significantly more at risk for developing chronic diseases like diabetes. It appears that the diet of ancient hunter-gatherers was associated with a much higher level of plant fiber than the modern diet, and our intestinal system is designed to ideally process this high level of fiber. In a very short period, Native Americans, who traditionally subsisted on a reasonably low-calorie and high-fiber diet for millennia, have adopted a diet with a very high glycemic index (Stöger 2008ab).

The thrifty gene hypothesis has received tremendous attention, with both supporters and critics. Other explanations have been presented to explain the present increase and distribution of diabetes. It appears that globally, diabetes is substantially more prevalent in northern populations. Moalem et al. (2005) suggest that recent animal research demonstrates that developing elevated levels of glucose, glycerol, and other sugar derivatives may in fact be a physiological means of cold adaptation. In elevated concentrations, these substances depress the freezing point of body fluids and prevent the formation of ice crystals in cells. They describe

Figure 14.21: Eating sushi.

Figure 14.22: Asian woman eating salad.

this effect as a form of "super-cooling," and it provides a type of "cryoprotectant," or antifreeze, for important tissues and vital organs. The ability to develop elevated levels of glycerol, glucose, and other sugar derivatives may have been selected as an adaptive measure in very cold climates. The authors suggest that northern Europeans would have had a selective advantage with this "cryoprotective" adaptation, which offered them considerable protection during periods like the Younger Dryas around 14,000 years ago, when the climate became dramatically colder. There is nothing mutually exclusive about these two suggestions; it is possible that both issues come into play. This would really stack the cards against Native American populations, who live in more northerly temperate zones, in terms of chronic conditions such as obesity and diabetes.

Another interesting relationship between a population and disease is the high rate of **stomach cancer** in Japanese (and some other Asian) populations. There is no question that the expression of this disease is multifactorial. However, many studies indicate there is a link between severe gastritis, stomach cancer, and diet. Diet has long been suggested as a causative factor in the development of certain forms of gastric cancer, with both salt and nitrate intake involved (Neugat et al. 1996, Gonzalez et al. 1985). In this case, dietary behavior may play an important role in the development of some forms of cancer.

Studies also imply that antioxidants such as vitamins A, C, and E may be protective (Ekstrom et al. 2000). It appears that a diet composed principally of fresh fruit and vegetables reduces the risk of developing stomach cancer, perhaps because they contain high levels of antioxidant vitamins. In particular, vitamin C–rich foods, in concert with other fresh foods, may help to prevent damage to the stomach lining, which can lead to cancer. Vitamin A is shown to protect against stomach cancer; it is also suggested that vitamin B6 may offer some protection (http://www.cancerresearchuk.org/cancer-help/type/stomach-cancer/about/stomach-cancer-risks-and-causes). This may explain why vegetarians appear to have a lower risk of stomach cancer than meat eaters. The EPIC study shows an increased risk of stomach cancer for people who eat a lot of red meat. But we need more studies to confirm this (http://epic.iarc.fr/ (Epic Project International Agency for Research on Cancer, WHO).

The typical Western diet has less salt than the Japanese diet, and animal models indicate that a high-salt diet causes acute gastritis (Fox et al. 1999). The incidence rates around the world vary, with the highest frequency of stomach cancer for males occurring in the Republic of Korea, followed by Mongolia and

Japan. About 73 percent of stomach cancer cases occur in less developed countries. The highest incidence of stomach cancer is in eastern Asia, central and eastern Europe, and South America, with the lowest incidence in western, northern and southern Africa (http://www.wcrf.org/cancer_statistics/data_specific_cancers/stomach_cancer_statistics.php (World Cancer Research Fund International).This may be explained to some extent by differences in diet, as a diet high in very salty foods increases the risk of stomach cancer. Stomach cancer levels are very high in Japan, where very salty pickled foods are popular. This suggestion is supported by the observation that a diet high in certain preserved foods may also increase your risk. Several studies and a large, ongoing research study called EPIC have found a small increase in the risk of stomach cancer in people who eat a lot of preserved meat and pickled foods (think of what is in most of our sandwiches every day). Preserved meat includes bacon, sausages, lunchmeats, and ham. Thus, in populations around the world like in Korea and Japan, where there is a high level of salted and pickled components in the diet, they express increased rates of

Figure 14.23: Breast Cancer ribbon.

gastritis and stomach cancer. This is supported by studies that compare rates of gastritis between United Kingdom and Japanese patients, and found it to be more common and severe in Japanese patients (Naylor et al. 2006). The authors conclude that this is in part due to the enriched amount of salt in the Japanese versus the British diets (surprising, given all those lovely British bangers and meat dishes).

Why do Western women between the ages of 35 and 70 demonstrate significantly higher rates of **breast cancer** than women in the developing world or in Eastern industrial nations? One in six American women will be affected by the disease. The difference is even more marked if we compare North American and hunter-gatherer women. There is roughly a hundredfold difference between rates of breast cancer in the

two. When compared to other groups, West Africans have one-twelfth the rates and Japanese women one-fourth the rates based upon differences in reproductive behavior (Boaz 2002).The distribution of breast cancer seems to be related to high-fat, -calorie, or -protein diets and high levels of estrogen (either produced within the body or taken artificially in medication). The risk is reduced for women who bear and nurse a number of children and higher for those who have no children or who bear their first child at a later age (Eaton et al. 1994, Eaton and Eaton 1999). Interestingly, recent studies show an elevated risk for breast cancer in Catholic nuns, as they neither bear or breast-feed children and often take hormone replacement at menopause. (For ages,

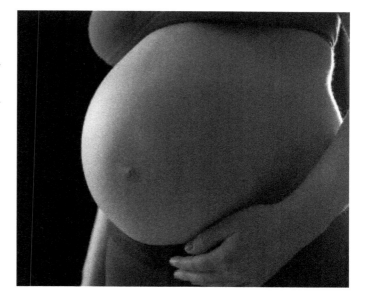

Figure 14.24: Pregnant woman's stomach.

breast cancer was known as nuns' disease). This relationship was later supported by large-scale studies that showed that a woman's chances of developing breast, uterine, or ovarian cancer are strongly related to the number of menstrual cycles she experiences (hence the exposure to elevated levels of estrogen). Estrogen wears many hats in the body, but most importantly here, it is a considerably potent stimulator of cell division in a woman's breasts, ovaries, and uterus (Lieberman 2013).

The evolutionary biologist Daniel Lieberman addresses this relationship from an evolutionary perspective in humans. With

Figure 14.25: Woman eating hamburger.

each menstrual cycle, a woman is exposed to elevated levels of estrogen, progesterone, and other related hormones. When one does not have a child, in every cycle, there is this increased surge of hormones that leads uterine cells to multiply and breast cells to divide. This means that at every cycle, as your reproductive cells replicate, there is an increased chance of a negative cancerous mutation occurring and those new mutant cells increasing. By having children at a young age and having multiple children, a woman reduces the number of menstrual cycles significantly over her lifetime. Thus, she reduces her overall exposure to elevated levels of reproductive hormones.

Lieberman argues that for millions of years, natural selection favored females who devoted whatever extra energy they had toward reproduction. We must remember that for probably 99 percent of our history as a species, we have lived in band-level societies associated with small population size and a mobile lifestyle. Hunter-gatherer women typically begin to menstruate by the age of 16, and then spend a significant portion of their adult lives either pregnant or breast-feeding, both of which are extremely calorically demanding (Cohen and Crane-Kramer 1997). It is estimated that hunter/gatherer women experience a total of only about 150 menstrual cycles. This is in contrast to Western and Eastern industrialized women, who generally begin menstruating between 12 and 13 years old and have only a few children due to access to affordable birth control. Western women typically experience between 350 to 400 menstrual cycles. The increased levels of body fat in Western industrial women has led to the commencement of menstruation roughly two years earlier than normal. This means two extra years of exposure to elevated estrogen levels (Boaz 2002). With this greatly increased number of menstrual cycles and the increased rush of hormones that accompany them, it should not surprise us that there has been a significant increase in reproductive cancers as birth control techniques became readily

Figure 14.26: Yanomamo woman and child.

available. As lactation often suppresses the ovulation cycle, hunter-gatherer women often extend the age of breast-feeding well beyond the third year of life. Western women rarely breast-feed for even 12 months, which means they resume their menstrual cycles much earlier than their hunter-gatherer counterparts. Natural selection never designed the female human body to deal with an abundance of energy or elevated hormones. Some suggest that Western women could reduce their breast cancer risk by nearly 60 percent if they returned to preindustrial levels of fertility

Figure 14.27: African American family.

and breast-feeding. With each successful pregnancy, the risk of breast cancer decreases by 7 percent; for every year the woman breast-feeds, there is a further decline of 4.3 percent. It is estimated that Western women could reduce their risk of breast cancer every year by 5 percent if they breast-fed their children for an extra six months (http://epic.iarc.fr/ (Epic Project International Agency for Research on Cancer, WHO).

A second significant risk factor for modern Western women is the relationship between fat and hormone levels. Hunter-gatherer women do not get fat. Okay, maybe in rare cases there is a fat hunter-gatherer woman who lives traditionally, but that is an anomaly. These women live very active and physically demanding lives. Hunter-gatherer women generally do maintain fat levels that are conducive for pregnancy and lactation. However, they are generally associated with lean body types and low overall fat levels. Human females are particularly well adapted to storing extra energy in fat cells. Obese women can have 40 percent higher estrogen levels than women who are not overweight. As a result, rates of reproductive tissue cancers among women are strongly correlated with obesity after menopause (Scapira et al. 1990, Stoll 1996). In a study conducted by the World Health Organization between 1973 and 1991, there was a 9 percent increase in obese women in the United States (from 16 percent to 25 percent of females). The present estimate of the level of obesity in black American women is 49 percent (WHO 1998). In one study of more than 85,000 American women who were postmenopausal, those who were obese had twice the risk of developing breast cancer than those who were not overweight. Women who are overweight—and thus have considerable deposits of adipose tissue (fat)—are at the highest risk for developing breast cancer after menopause (Boaz 2002). The message is loud and clear in terms of the link between the Western industrial lifestyle and breast cancer. These women are at high risk because of factors such as early menarche, late pregnancy, reduced numbers of pregnancy, reduced lactation, the use of hormonal birth control, and hormone replacement at menopause. Add this to a high-fat, high-protein diet in this affluent society, and you have a recipe for disaster. This is a classic example of how human biology and behavior interact to influence health and illness.

The last case we will examine in terms of genetic susceptibility is the relationship between African Americans and hypertension. **Hypertension** is commonly known as high blood pressure. It is a major risk factor for heart attack and stroke. Hypertension is typically associated with a thickening of the arteries that transport blood and the deposition of plaques that can lead eventually to arteriosclerosis, or hardening of the arteries. Both the brain and the kidneys can also be harmed by hypertension, as these are the organs associated with the highest amount of blood flow (Boaz 2002). From an evolutionary perspective, it appears that hypertension is essentially absent in hunter-gatherer populations (Wilson and Grim 1993). This is likely because the diets of hunter-gatherer groups are low in saturated fats and carbohydrates and high in fiber, vitamins, and minerals that are essential for normal functioning. It has been suggested that hypertension is linked to a high sodium (salt) diet.

Let us see if this is relevant to earlier preagricultural groups. If we examine a traditional people like the Yanomamö Indians of Brazil, whose diet relies principally upon low-sodium bananas, they excrete a very small amount of salt daily (only around 10 milligrams), which is only about a thousandth of the daily salt excretion of Americans (Diamond 2006). This suggestion is also supported by the work of biomedical scholar Staffan Lindeberg, which he conducted with the Kitava people of the Trobriand Islands in the South Pacific. Lindeberg (1994) took blood pressure readings from rural people of all ages, and

Figure 14.28: African slave child (Zanzibar).

found that the Kitava people have very low levels of hypertension. This is particularly fascinating, in light of the fact that their cholesterol readings were off the charts! How can this be? The diet of the Kitava offers us some tantalizing clues. Although the islanders consume a lipid-dense diet based on coconuts, they have low rates of obesity due to living a physically active lifestyle. Their diet is also very low in salt. Lindeberg argues that this suggests that high cholesterol may exacerbate high blood pressure, but it is not directly the cause. A diet high in salt can directly lead to increased frequencies of hypertension. Some indicate that the traditional salt intake of hunter-gatherer groups—both today and by extension, in the past—was approximately one gram per day. By comparison, the average American consumes between 9–12 grams a day (Boaz 2002). In order to avoid hypertension, recommended doses of no more than four grams per day are recommended (De Wardener 1996). As African Americans have adopted the standard Western diet that is very high in sodium, the rates of hypertension have escalated in this population.

When we look at the demographic distribution of the disease in the United States today, African Americans clearly demonstrate the highest rates of hypertension and heart disease per capita. When compared to American whites of the same sex and age, African Americans typically have higher blood pressure, twice the risk of developing hypertension, and are ten times as likely to die from it. Hypertension is a serious risk factor for heart and kidney disease, and American blacks have a risk for kidney disease that is 18 times greater than that of whites. Although African Americans constitute roughly ten percent of the population, they represent two-thirds of the people who suffer from hypertensive kidney disease in the United States (Diamond 2006).

Why are African Americans at highest risk for hypertension in the United States? It is suggested that this high risk of hypertension in this group is related to the fact that they have developed a highly efficient storage system for sodium (salt). This resulted from limited access to salt in West Africa and during the period of slavery. Thomas Wilson (1986) argues that a large portion of the African continent is associated

Figure 14.29: Two San Bushmen making a fire.

with hot and arid conditions. As a result, Africans developed a genetic adaptation that allows for greater kidney resorption of salt. He argues that hypertensive heart disease explains the high levels of dropsy (fluid accumulation) documented historically among slave populations of the West Indies. The root of this high degree of hypertension was a diet focused heavily on salted meats and fish, as well as the common use of added salt as a condiment.

Another possible way to explain the elevated salt-storing ability of African Americans (which is typically higher than ancestral Africans) is that it results from the very high mortality from salt depletion that occurred during sea transportation to the Americas as slaves. Those who had genes that allowed for greater salt retention were more likely to survive and reproduce. One cannot help but think that it also contributed to the survival of the male slaves, who would have been sweating and losing tremendous quantities of water and salts while working in the fields. While African Americans today do not gain any selective advantage from the higher ability to retain salt and water, it is still handed down to them as a relic of their ancestral past.

It is clear from the above examples (and they are by no means exhaustive) that over countless generations, human populations respond to changing conditions in their environment. Sometimes, a chance genetic mutation actually confers protection against major infectious pathogens, as in the case of sickle cell trait and the $\Delta 32$ mutation, for example. We would expect that these genes would increase in frequency over time, as it is those who have the gene who survive to reproduce. While our genetic heritage clearly protects us from harm in some instances, it also can predispose us to be more vulnerable to certain conditions. A reminder that we have strayed quite far from the normal Paleolithic hunter-gatherer diet is never more apparent than when we look at the increased rates of diabetes in Native Americans and the high rate of hypertension in African Americans. In this fast-paced modern world, we forget that despite our great achievements, we are still trapped in the bodies of mobile hunter-gatherers. The fact that we often live and eat in ways that are completely contrary to this original state explains why we have seen a veritable epidemic of the noncontagious diseases of civilization emerge in the last few centuries.

CRITICAL REASONING QUESTIONS

- Write down the ethnic background of members of your immediate and extended family. Given what you know about your own genetic legacy, what conditions might you be more vulnerable to? Do you also have a likelihood of greater resistance to certain conditions?
- Humans and other primates are some of the only mammals that have lost the ability to produce their own vitamin C. Why do you think that this occurred, and what effects might this have on our health?
- What risk factors place Catholic nuns right at the head of the line for developing breast cancer in the Western world?
- How did humans perceive the cause of disease prior to the development of germ theory? How did this affect our ability to understand and combat disease pathogens?
- There is truth to the statement "You are what you eat." What examples can you think of that show how diet can dramatically affect the expression of disease?
- Why are traditional peoples less likely to develop hypertension? How can people in the developed world decrease their risk?

REFERENCES AND SUGGESTED READINGS

Abel, E. L. (2001). *Jewish genetic disorders: A layman's guide*. Jefferson, NC: McFarland.

Aidoo M., D. J. Terlouw, M. S. Kolczak, et al. (2002). "Protective effects of the sickle cell gene against malaria morbidity and mortality." *Lancet* 359 (9314):1311–1312.

Allison, A. C. (1954). "Protection afforded by sickle-cell trait against subtertian malarial infection." *British Medical Journal* 1 (4857):290–294.

Allison, A. C., and D. F. Clyde (1961). "Malaria in African children with deficient erythrocyte glucose-6-phosphate dehydrogenase." *British Medical Journal* 1 (5236):1346–1349.

Barcellos, L. F., A. M. Schito, J. B. Rimmler, et al. (2000). "CC-chemokine receptor 5 polymorphism and age of onset in familial multiple sclerosis." *Immunogenetics* 51(4–5):281–288.

Baschetti, R. (December 1998). "Diabetes epidemic in newly westernized populations: Is it due to thrifty genes or to genetically unknown foods?" *Journal of the Royal Society of Medicine* 91 (12):622–625.

Belnoue, E., M. Kayibanda, J.-C. Deschemin, et al. (2003). "CCR5 deficiency decreases susceptibility to experimental cerebral malaria." *Blood* 101(11):4253–4259.

Beutler, E. (2008). "Glucose-6-phosphate dehydrogenase deficiency: A historical perspective." *Blood* 111 (1): 16–24.

Boaz, N. T. (2002). *Evolving health: The origins of illness and how the modern world is making us sick*. New York: John Wiley and Sons, Inc.

Buseyne, F., G. Janvier, J. P. Teglas, et al. (October 1998). "Impact of heterozygosity for the chemokine receptor CCR5 32-bp-deleted allele on plasma virus load and CD4 T lymphocytes in perinatally human immunodeficiency virus-infected children at 8 years of age." *Journal of Infectious Disease* 178 (4):1019–1023.

Cohen, M. N., and G. M. M. Crane-Kramer, eds. (2007). *Ancient health: Skeletal indicators of agricultural and economic intensification.* Gainesville: University Press of Florida.

De Wardener, T. W. (1986). "Sodium and hypertension." *Arch. Mal. Coeur Vaiss.* 89: Spec. No. 4.

Diamond, J. (2006). "The saltshaker's curse: Physiological adaptations that helped American blacks survive slavery may now be predisposing their descendants to hypertension," pp. 32–36. Annual Editions *Physical Anthropology* 06/07. Dubuque, IA: McGraw-Hill.

Duncan, C. J., et al. (March 2005). "Reappraisal of the historical selective pressures for the CCR5-delta32 mutation." *Journal of Medical Genetics* 42(3):205–208.

Eaton, S. B., et al. (1994). "Women's reproductive cancers in evolutionary context." *Quarterly Review of Biology* 69:353–367.

Eaton, S. B., and S. B. Eaton III (1999). "Breast cancer in evolutionary perspective." In W. R. Trevathan, E. O. Smith, and J. J. McKenna, eds., *Evolutionary Medicine*, pp. 429–442. New York: Oxford University Press.

Elvin, S. J., E. D. Williamson, J. C. Scott, et al. (July 2004). "Ambiguous role of CCR5 in *Y. pestis* infection." *Nature* 430(6998):417.

Ekstrom, A. M., M. Serafini, O. Nyren, et al. (July 2000). "Dietary anti-oxidant intake and the risk of cardia cancer and non-cardia cancer of the intestinal and diffuse type: A population-based case-control study in Sweden." *International Journal of Cancer* 87(1):133–140. http://epic.iarc.fr/ (Epic Project International Agency for Research on Cancer. WHO).

Faure, E., and M. Royer-Carenzi (December 2008). "Is the European spatial distribution of the HIV-1-resistant CCR5-Delta32 allele formed by a breakdown of the pathocenosis due to the historical Roman expansion?" *Infect. Genet. Evol.* 8 (6):864–874.

Fox, J. G., C. A. Dangler, N. S. Taylor, et al. (October 1999). "High salt intake induces gastric epithelial hyperplasia and parietal cell loss, and enhances *Helicobacter pylori* colonisation in C57BL/6 mice." *Cancer Research* 59(19):4823–4828.

Freitas, T., A. Brehm, and A. T. Fernandes (December 2006). "Frequency of the CCR5-delta32 mutation in the Atlantic island populations of Madeira, the Azores, Cabo Verde, and São Tomé e Príncipe." *Human Biology* 78 (6):697–703.

Galvani, A. P., and M. Slatkin (December 2003). "Evaluating plague and smallpox as historical selective pressures for the CCR5-delta-32 HIV-resistance allele." *Proceedings of the National Academy of Sciences of the USA* 100(25):15276–15279.

Gonzalez, C. A., E. Riboli, J. Badosa, et al. (1985). "Nutritional factors and gastric cancer in Spain." *American Journal of Epidemiology* 139(5):466–473.

Goodman, R. M. (1979). *Genetic disorders among the Jewish people.* Baltimore: Johns Hopkins University Press.

Hales, C. N., and D. J. Barker (November 2001). "The thrifty phenotype hypothesis." *British Medical Bulletin* 60 (1):5–20.

Harrison, G. A., J. S. Weiner, J. M. Tanner, and N. A. Barnicot (1977). *Human biology: An introduction to human evolution, variation, growth, and ecology*, 2nd ed. Oxford, UK: Oxford University Press.

Ingram, V. M., and A. O. Stretton (1959). Genetic basis of the thalassaemia diseases. *Nature* 184 (4703):1903–1909.

Liu, R., W. A. Paxton, S. Choe, et al. (August 1996). "Homozygous defect in HIV-1 coreceptor accounts for resistance of some multiply-exposed individuals to HIV-1 infection." *Cell* 86(3):367–377.

Kantor, R., et al. (2003). "A mutated CCR5 gene may have favorable prognostic implications in MS." *Neurology* 61(2):238–240.

Kaplan, N. L., P. O. Lewis, and B. S. Weir (1994). "Age of the ΔF508 cystic fibrosis mutation." *Nature Genetics* 8:216.

Karlen, A. (1995). *Man and microbes.* New York: Putnam.

Kawamura, T., et al. (2003). "R5 HIV productively infects Langerhans cells, and infection levels are regulated by compound CCR5 polymorphisms." *Proceedings of the National Academy of Sciences of the USA* 100(14):8401–8406.

Koeslag, J. H., and S. R. Schach (1984). "Tay-Sachs disease and the role of reproductive compensation in the maintenance of ethnic variations in the incidence of autosomal recessive disease." *Annals of Human Genetics* 48 (3):275–281.

Kwiatkowski, D. P. (2005). "How malaria has affected the human genome and what human genetics can teach us about malaria." *American Journal of Human Genetics* 77:171–192.

Lieberman, D. E. (2013). *The story of the human body: Evolution, health and disease.* New York: Pantheon (Random House).

Lindeberg, S., et al. (1994). "Cardiovascular risk factors in a Melanesian population apparently free from stroke and ischaemic heart disease—the Kitava study." *Journal of Internal Medicine* 236:331–334.

Luzzatto, L. (1979). "Genetics of red cells and susceptibility to malaria." *Blood* 54 (5):961–976.

Majumder, P. P., and B. Dey (October 2001). "Absence of the HIV-1 protective del-ccr5 allele in most ethnic populations of India." *European Journal of Human Genetics* 9(10):794–796.

Marks, J. (1995). *Human biodiversity: Genes, races, and history.* New York: Aldine de Gruyter.

———(2011). *The alternative introduction to biological anthropology.* New York: Oxford University Press.

McNeill, W. H. (1976). *Plagues and peoples.* New York: Doubleday.

Mecsas, J., et al. (July 2004). "CCR5 mutation and plague protection." *Nature* 427(6998):606.

Mish, F. C., ed. in chief (1998). Merriam Webster's Collegiate Dictionary, 10th ed. Springfield, MA: Merriam-Webster Inc.

Moalem, S., Storey, K., Percy, M., et al. (2005). "The sweet thing about Type 1 diabetes: A cryoprotective evolutionary adaptation." *Medical Hypotheses* 65 (1):8–16.

Moe, P. G., and T. A. Benke (2005). *Neurologic and muscular disorders: Current pediatric diagnosis and treatment,* 17th ed. New York: McGraw-Hill.

Molnar, S. (1998). *Human variation: Races, types and ethnic groups,* 4th ed. New Jersey: Prentice Hall.

Morral, N., J. Bertranpetit, X. Estivill, et al. (1994). "The origin of the major cystic fibrosis mutation (ΔF508) in European populations." *Nature Genetics* 7:169–175.

Motulsky, A. G. (February 1995). "Jewish diseases and origins." *Nature Genetics* 9 (2):99–101.

Naylor, G. M., T. Gotoda, M. Dixon, et al. (November 2006). "Why does Japan have a high incidence of gastric cancer? Comparison of gastritis between UK and Japanese patients." *Gut* 55(11):1545–1552.

Neel, J. V. (1962). "Diabetes mellitus: A 'thrifty' genotype rendered detrimental by 'progress?'" *American Journal of Human Genetics* 14 (4):353–362.

———(1982). "The thrifty genotype revisited." In *The Genetics of Diabetes Mellitus.* J. Kobberling and R. Tattersall, eds., p. 293 New York: Academic Press.

———(2009). "The 'thrifty genotype' in 1998." *Nutrition Reviews* 57 (5):2.

Neugat, A. I., H. Hayek, and G. Howe (June 1996). "Epidemiology of gastric cancer." *Seminars in Oncology* 23(3):281–291.

O'Brien, J. S. (1983). "The gangliosidoses." In J. B. Stanbury, et al., *The Metabolic Basis of Inherited Disease,* pp. 945–969. New York: McGraw Hill.

Ratjen, F., and G. Döring (2003). "Cystic fibrosis." *Lancet* 361:681–689.

Reinhard K. J., K. L. Johnson, S. LeRoy-Toren, et al. (2012). "Understanding the pathoecological relationship between ancient diet and modern diabetes through coprolite analysis." *Current Anthropology* 53(4):506.

Risch, N., H. Tang, H. Katzenstein, and J. Ekstein (2003). "Geographic distribution of disease mutations in the Ashkenazi Jewish population supports genetic drift over selection." *American Journal of Human Genetics* 72 (4):812–822.

Schapira D. V., et al. (1990). "Abdominal obesity and breast cancer risk." *Annals of Internal Medicine* 1990; 112(3):182–186.

Sherman, I. W. (2006). *The power of plagues*. Washington, DC: ASM Press.

Stephens, J. C., et al. (June 1998). "Dating the origin of the CCR5-del32 AIDS-resistance allele by the coalescence of haplotypes." *American Journal of Human Genetics* 62(6):1507–1515.

Stöger, R. (2008a). "The thrifty epigenotype: An acquired and heritable predisposition for obesity and diabetes?" *BioEssays* 30(2):156–166.

——— (2008b). "Epigenetics and obesity." *Pharmacogenomics* 9(12):1851–1860.

Stoll, B. A. (1996). "Obesity and breast cancer." *International Journal of Obesity and Related Metabolic Disorders: Journal of the International Association for the Study of Obesity* 20(5):389–392.

Tishkoff, S. A., and B. J. Verelli (2004). "G6PD deficiency and malarial resistance in humans: Insights from evolutionary genetic analysis." In K. Dronamraju, ed. *Evolutionary Aspects of Infectious Disease*. Cambridge, UK: Cambridge University Press.

Wailoo, K., and S. Pemberton (2006). *The troubled dream of genetic medicine: Ethnicity and innovation in Tay-Sachs, cystic fibrosis, and sickle-cell disease*. Baltimore: Johns Hopkins University Press.

Wald, P. (2006). "Blood and stories: How genomics is rewriting race, medicine, and human history." *Patterns of Prejudice* 40:303–331.

Winick, M. (1980). *Nutrition in health and disease*. New York: John Wiley. http://www.who.int/mediacentre/factsheets/fs094/en/ (World Health Organization). http://www.wcrf.org/cancer_statistics/data_specific_cancers/stomach_cancer_statistics.php (World Cancer Research Fund International). http://www.cancerresearchuk.org/cancer-help/type/stomach-cancer/about/stomach-cancer-risks-and-causes

World Health Organization (1998). About obesity. International obesity task force. Available at www.iaso.org/

Wilson, T. W. (1986). "Africa, Afro-Americans, and hypertension: An hypothesis." *Social Sciences History* 10:489–500.

Wilson, T. W., and C. E. Grim (1993). "Hypertension." In K. F. Kiple, ed., *The Cambridge World History of Human Disease*, pp. 789–794. Cambridge, UK: Cambridge University Press.

Zagury, D., et al. (1998). "C-C chemokines, pivotal in protection against HIV type 1 infection." *Proceedings of the National Academy of Sciences of the USA* 95(7):3857–3861.

Zimmerman, P. A., et al. (1997). "Inherited resistance to HIV-1 conferred by an inactivating mutation in CC chemokine receptor 5: Studies in populations with contrasting clinical phenotypes, defined racial background, and quantified risk." *Molecular Medicine* 3(1):23–36.

15

Modern Human Adaptation And Acclimatization

By Gillian Crane-Kramer

The human species is the most geographically diverse species on Earth. We live in exceedingly hot deserts; we live in the frigid tundra, and every imaginable scenario in between. There is no question that cultural behavior has been our great companion, and it allows us to adjust through artificial means to environments we are not biologically adapted to under normal circumstances. Lest we become too cocky, we also relied heavily on the help of other animal species in order to adapt to new environmental circumstances (think dogs, llamas, or camels, for example). For thousands of years, human populations have been responding to the unique local climatic and environmental circumstances in which they find themselves. As a result, we see biological differences emerging that can be explained through the process of **adaptation** and **acclimatization**. As discussed in Chapter 13, there is no biological basis for dividing humans into different races. There is more genetic variation within supposed racial categories than between them, and these divisions are really a result of the fact that our brain is designed to think typologically. The human brain has to process a dizzying amount of information every day, and the way that we make things manageable and intelligible is by organizing things according to classes of objects. Thus, we have the tendency to overlook observable variation, and concentrate instead on wider, often visible categories. Today, biological anthropologists recognize that humans are all members of the same polytypic species, meaning that we are composed of local populations that differ from each other in the frequency of one or more genes. If we have now established that all humans—regardless of where they live—are the same species, then how can we explain the significant differences that we observe between different groups?

Figure 15.1: Human variation.

Figure 15.2: Solar radiation and skin color.

As scientists, we have an obligation to explain these differences in a meaningful way, and as this is a book about evolution, we are obligated to explain them in evolutionary terms.

The way an organism responds to the stresses in its environment is through this process that we call adaptation. In terms of human variation, when we speak about adaptation, we are talking about changes that occur at the level of the genes. They occur in populations, and take multiple generations to occur. Sickle cell trait is a great example of a genetic adaptation. However, individual organisms are also capable of responding to their environment. This is through a process called acclimatization, which is a physiological change that occurs in individuals. It takes typically from a few weeks to a few months to occur, and it is not generally a permanent alteration. Breathing more rapidly and deeply in high altitude environments is a good example of acclimatization. Individuals develop this at higher elevations, but breathing rates will return to normal when the individual returns to sea level.

In Chapter 12, we explained the distribution of human skin color as a response to differing global levels of solar radiation. Those people who have lived for many generations in the tropics, where solar radiation is high, have dark skin. This is because dark skin is better able to protect against the harmful effects of solar radiation. The evolution of light skin color probably only occurred in the last 100,000 years as humans settled permanently in northern temperate zones. Light skin appears to be more efficient at producing vitamin D, and is more cold resistant. Given the global distribution of human skin colors, it is not difficult to see from an evolutionary standpoint why there are very elevated levels of skin cancer in white Australians. Here, we have an evolutionary anomaly. Due to colonialism (and criminal transportation), you have in Australia what never should have been: light-skinned people in the tropics! This is probably no different from when my fellow graduate student Caesar from Ghana told me that only crazy people would chose to live in Canada during the winter (there are days when I agree with him). The amazing movement of people that has taken place in the last few centuries has offered human populations new environmental challenges to overcome. Fortunately, the human species has a great deal of biological plasticity, and we can observe a wide range of different responses that have developed over millennia around the world.

HEAT, HUMIDITY AND COLD: MY KINGDOM FOR MILD TEMPERATURES!

When we compare ourselves to polar bears or arctic foxes, it is abundantly obvious that humans are not really well adapted to the cold. There is a logical explanation for this, in that for the vast majority of our evolutionary history, our family has lived in the tropics. A constant core temperature of roughly 98.6 degrees is necessary for normal body and brain functioning. Humans can handle some fluctuation around this temperature norm, but extended periods of increased body temperature above 104–107 degrees rapidly leads to organ failure and death. The ape-human split likely occurred at some point around six million years ago. Our ancestors lived exclusively in hot, humid climates until very recently in our history, and our close ape cousins all still live in tropical zones. The challenge for people living in hot climates is how to effectively dissipate heat. In fact, the human body can adjust more easily to heat load than cold. When we examine modern humans, we would expect to discover biological solutions to dealing with heat stress (Mitchell et al. 1976, Wyndham et al. 1976).

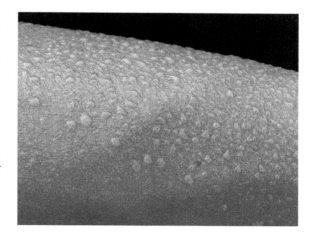

Figure 15.3: Polar bear and cub.

The amount of heat stress that a population experiences is dependent upon location. Those who live in the tropical areas of the world live with the constant threat of heat stroke, whereas people who live in temperate climes have a seasonal risk. In hot, arid weather, the humidity levels are low, and sweat evaporates readily. Because of this, we typically feel much more comfortable in dry desertlike conditions than we do at the same temperature in humid, hot, tropical rainforests. The higher the desert temperatures, the greater the cooling effect we get from evaporation. As is the case with many environmental stressors, young children and the elderly are most at risk for developing heat stroke. When we examine the effects of heat stress on the human body, we must take into account two forms of heat production—internal and external. Internal heat is produced by the body's own metabolic processes, particularly during periods of movement like walking, running, or physical labor. External heat stress is generated by the environment in which the organism lives. When the body senses an elevation in body temperature, the immediate physiological response is a vasodilation of the blood vessels. Vasodilation involves the expansion of blood vessels near the body's surface; as the blood vessel diameter increases, blood pressure decreases, and the body is capable of moving more blood (and thus heat) away from the body's core to the body's surface. The red face of a person (like my redheaded son's) on a hot day or after a tough hockey practice is a visible sign of vasodilation.

Perhaps the most important biological response developed by humans in response to heat stress is **sweating**. Sweat is produced by the eccrine glands (located throughout the body), and is principally composed of water. As one sweats, a thin layer of water is evaporated from the surface of the skin, which makes us feel cool. Essentially, when we sweat, we are transferring our heat to the surrounding air, and this reduces our temperature. The water that we sweat through our pores is at a

Figure 15.4: Perspiration.

higher temperature than the water our body retains, and this assists us in radiating heat to the air. Finally, our kidneys are able to concentrate our urine, meaning that we lose less water when we urinate, but still expel all the harmful waste from our bodies. Humans are capable of sweating a remarkable volume of fluid. The fact that we can sweat such a large volume of water indicates that this process must be very important in terms of

Figure 15.6: Yali man, Papua New Guinea.

Figure 15.5: People of South Asia and Oceania.

our functional adaptation to heat. We are a tropical species, and it makes sense that over countless generations, humans have devised a very efficient system for contending with heat stress. It is estimated that the evaporation of one liter of sweat releases 560 kcal of heat from the body, and people are capable of sweating up to four liters an hour (Beall and Steegmann 2000). At maximum sweating capacity, the body can lose its entire sodium pool in just three hours, which can be fatal. Amazingly, many populations around the world like the Bantu people of Africa or the Australian Aborigines have been making accommodations to intense heat for millennia, able to maintain thermal homeostasis with a lower body fluid loss (Frisancho 1993).

If sweating is such a great solution to heat stress, then why are we the only primates to have developed this strategy? One will notice that primates (except for humans) have a significant covering of body hair. The ability to sweat is less effective in areas of the body associated with hair cover. This fact suggests that sweating evolved as a thermoregulatory adaptation that developed at the same time as the loss of body hair. The loss of body hair in humans is unique among the primates, so it appears that the association between this and sweating is an adaptation unique to our species. Human populations such as native Equatorial Africans or tropical Southeast Asians who have lived in hot climates for long periods of time have the same number of sweat glands as other populations. This seems odd at first glance, that Equatorial Africans and the Inuit people of the Arctic should have the same number of sweat glands. However, we have only inhabited cold temperate areas very recently in our history, not enough time to alter the number of sweat glands, for one. Plus, northern peoples also live physically demanding lives and sweat to release heat (think of how hot you feel when you shovel snow in winter). So, it appears that because we need to release heat regardless of the hot or cold climate that now surrounds us, we still have the same number of sweat glands. Interesting new research on the subject is emerging all the time. For example, Wei Cheng et al. (2012)

Figure 15.7: Fulani woman, Africa.

state that some human nerve cells have proteins on their surfaces that allow them to differentiate between several different temperatures in the slightly warm to hot range. This response may play an important part in the way we respond to hot temperatures physiologically.

A further issue for populations living in hot climates is the level of humidity. Evaporation occurs less efficiently in humid conditions, and this makes it more difficult to release heat in hot, humid conditions than in hot, dry climates. Some scholars suggest that nose shape can be related to levels of humidity. The shape of the nose is recorded in terms of the "nasal index," which is the width of the nose divided by the height multiplied by 100. Common values for the nasal index range from roughly 64 percent to 104 percent (Molnar 1998, Molnar and Molnar 2000). In cold climates with low humidity, the nose is narrow. In warm climates, where the relative humidity is high, the nose is wide. This would represent a genetic adaptation, as Australian Aborigines living in the hot humid parts of the continent typically have to deal with 70–80 percent relative humidity. In groups living in the Arctic—where the absolute humidity in the air is low—narrow noses are the norm. Narrow noses are also typically found in populations that live in desert environments, which are also characterized by low levels of moisture in the air. Thus, populations in arid climates have narrow noses, and those in humid climates have wide noses (Franciscus and Long 1991). Researchers indicate that narrow noses may be better humidifiers of air than wider noses are. In addition, the greater internal surface area of high, narrow noses allows greater moisturizing of the air in dry regions. This general relationship is a good example of a genetic adaptation to low humidity conditions.

For the majority of their history, humans and their ancestors have not had to contend with the stressors of a cold environment. Permanent settlement in temperate zones has only occurred in roughly the last 100,000 years. Thus, humans are typically better adapted to dealing with heat stress than they are cold stress. When we look around the world today, the populations that are at significant risk for cold stress are

Figure 15.8: Depiction of Aborigines at King George's Sound, Western Australia (colored lithograph).

Figure 15.9: Inuit women eating Maktaaq delicacy (bowhead whale blubber).

those that experience cold periods in temperate climates: people at the Earth's magnetic poles (i.e., Arctic groups) and those living at high altitudes above 10,000 feet. The danger in cold climates is the risk that tissue temperature will drop to the point of hypothermia (low body temperature), which results from exposure to very cold air or immersion in very cold water, and leads to rapid tissue death. Hypothermia begins to occur when the core body temperature drops to 94°F (34.4°C). There is an escalation in body cooling below 85°F (29.4°C), as our temperature regulating system (in the hypothalamus) typically fails at this juncture. Death from hypothermia can occur very quickly, as in the Titanic disaster of 1912. The vast majority of the ship's crew and passengers did not actually die with the sinking of the ship, but died from hypothermia from being left to float for roughly two hours in frigid Atlantic temperatures hovering around 28°F before help arrived.

Many populations around the world have had to adjust to extremely cold temperatures. They have done this in a variety of ways, most of which appear to be acclimatization. A common physiological reaction to cold is **shivering**. The body begins to shiver when it senses a core temperature decline of two to three degrees C. The increase in muscle use does help us to feel warmer, but this is a temporary solution because it is very costly in caloric terms. The body's first response to cold conditions involves vasoconstriction of the blood vessels. This involves the reduction (narrowing) in diameter of blood vessels beneath the skin (the exact opposite of what happens when exposed to heat) and a subsequent reduction in peripheral blood flow. This narrowing of the blood vessels reduces blood flow and heat loss from the internal core of the body to the skin surface. When we look at populations around the world, one way humans have adapted to cold conditions is through a **redistribution of heat to the extremities**. This is accomplished through a cycle of vasodilation and vasoconstriction of the blood vessels. When one is exposed to cold conditions, there is first an intense vasoconstriction response, followed after about five minutes by a period of vasodilation, and this continues cyclically to prevent the tissue temperature from dropping to dangerous frostbite levels. This cycling is known as the **Lewis hunting phenomenon**. This reaction was first described by Sir Thomas Lewis in 1930 about Inuit hunters. He observed that vasoconstriction alternates with periods of vasodilatation, so that the extremities receive a sudden and occasional burst of warmth, enough to restore normal functioning (Dana et al. 1969). We see this solution in East Coast Maritime fishermen, who spend all day with their hands in the frigid Atlantic waters, and yet are able to avoid frostbite. After prolonged exposure to cold water immersion baths, Inuit individuals maintain higher hand temperature readings than do European and African Americans (Meehan 1955).

A further way to buffer the cold is to increase **overall metabolic rate**. To measure heat production, scholars take a specific kind of measurement called a BMR (basal metabolic rate). The BMR is the rate at which an organism's body, while at rest, expends energy only to maintain basic bodily functions. It is measured by the amount of heat emitted per kilogram of body weight. For people such as the Inuit/Aleut of the Canadian and American north and the native Indians of Tierra del Fuego of southern South America, who live in very demanding subarctic regions, they increase their metabolic rates by consuming large levels of high-calorie fatty foods. The Inuit people's high BMR is achieved by consuming a high-fat diet, often of raw meat. It is high in animal fat and protein (about nine calories per gram) and low in carbohydrates (about three calories per gram). This significantly increases the basal metabolic rate, which in turn results in the production of extra body heat. Populations that have been living in harsh, cold conditions for countless generations have also developed a myriad of cultural practices to help them positively adjust to a very difficult environmental situation. They wear very heavy and well-designed clothing with strategically placed venting;

Figure 15.10: Maritime fishermen, Newfoundland, Canada.

they design their houses to maximize heat retention; they sleep huddled together to conserve body heat; and they remain physically active when outdoors. A final response to cold stress is called insulation acclimatization, where individuals have cooler skin surface temperatures, but maintain core body temperatures.

This adjustment has evolved in warm environments where the temperatures do not approach freezing, and frostbite is not a concern. This adaptation is seen in Australian Aborigines and in the Ju/'hoansi of southwestern Africa, both of whom often sleep naked at night in temperatures only slightly above freezing (Ward 1960, Wyndham and Morrison 1958, Wyndham 1964). In these populations, individuals develop thick fat deposits around the vital organs of the chest and abdomen to ensure that vital functions do not become impaired. As the skin temperatures cool, heat loss is reduced, and the core body temperature remains within the normal range. It is believed that this adaptation must have developed in warm climates, where temperatures do not ultimately drop low enough for frostbite to occur. Several studies have generated results suggesting that Australian Aborigines resist cold stress by elevating the core temperature through vasoconstriction and by tolerating mild-to-moderate hypothermia without

Figure 15.11: Aleut woman, Attu.

compensating metabolically (Scholander, Hammel, et al. 1958, Hammel et al. 1959). This response would not be adaptive for the Aborigines or the Ju/'hoansi if they lived in environments where the temperature regularly dropped below 0 degrees with the threat of frostbite present. As their body fat is concentrated in the torso to protect vital organs, the appendages (fingers, toes, ears, and nose) would be at particular risk for tissue damage and death. This physiological adaptation is highly beneficial in circumstances where temperature rarely dips below freezing, and where traditional peoples do not have abundant high-calorie fatty foods. It is believed that this adaptation must have developed in warm climates, where temperatures do not ultimately drop low enough for frostbite to occur.

A very interesting potential adaptation to extreme cold conditions is the development of the classic Mongoloid (Asian) face. These adaptations include a reduction of the brow ridges and frontal sinuses,

Figure 15.12: Asian woman smiling.

widening and flattening of the orbital and malar (cheekbone) regions to permit more fat padding, non-projecting nose and ears, short limbs, the epicanthic fold of the eyes, and lower surface-to-mass ratio. Some suggest that the evolution of Mongoloid (Asian) features and the identification of the Lewis hunting reaction in these groups is an adaptation to the cold of the Mammoth steppe (Takeru and Sathmåry 1996). From an evolutionary perspective, for countless generations, the ancestors of modern Asian peoples had to adapt to cold, wind-swept environments. The shorter limb length in Mongoloid populations results from Allen's ecological rule, which states that the greater the distance from the equator, the shorter the length of the appendages (Takasaki et al. 2003). This is a cold adaptation designed to reduce the overall surface area and retain heat.

Some also suggest that the narrow and high nose characteristic of Inuit, Caucasian, and Neanderthals is an adaptation to an arid, cold environment, as it contributes to warming and moisturizing the air and the retention of heat and moisture from expired air (Hernández et al. 1997). This notion that the Mongoloid face may have developed as a cold adaptation is supported by a study that examined the survival of rats in the cold (Steegmann and Platner 1968, So 1980). Those rats who had narrow nasal passages, broader faces, shorter tails, and reduced leg length (and thus shorter appendages) had a higher survival rate in the cold. The authors then correlated these observations with features of Mongoloid people like the Inuit and Aleut, who live in Arctic or subarctic environments. They imply that Mongoloid groups who are cold adapted have developed similar features to those observed in other warm-blooded animals; all in accordance with Allen's rule. This includes fairly broad and long heads, narrow nasal passages, large jaws, fairly large bodies, and short limbs. There are always exceptions to every rule, but one must take into account that evolution is a very slow process that takes countless generations to effect noticeable change. The cephalic index of many indigenous Americans seems to indicate an exception to Allen's rule (Beals 1972). Native people of the tropical Americas appear to have cold-adapted, high cephalic indexes. Beals notes that as these people have only recently moved into hot climates, they still demonstrate the high cephalic index of their cold-adapted Mongoloid ancestors.

BODY SIZE AND SHAPE: LONG AND LEAN OR SMALL AND CURVACEOUS

When we examine the geographic distribution of humans around the world, there appears to be a general correlation between latitude and body size/shape. The relationship between body size and shape and climate is best described by two biogeographic rules: Bergmann's and Allen's rules. In warm-blooded organisms (mammals and birds), there are changes in body mass as one moves either north or south, away from the equator. **Bergmann's rule** focuses upon body size. The 19th-century English zoologist Carl Bergmann was interested in the relationship between body mass, surface area, and the production of heat in warm-blooded animals. He states that in warm-blooded organisms, heat-adapted organisms will have smaller bodies than will cold-adapted ones. He notes that populations who live in colder areas tend to have short, compact bodies (think of the Inuit of the Arctic). This body shape has less surface area relative to mass than more linear bodies. Thus, this shorter, compact body form conserves heat. In contrast, populations who live in warm areas tend to have long, linear bodies that absorb less heat. Relative to body volume (mass), small bodies

Figure 15.13: Henry Foy with Kenyan people (Wellcome Images).

have greater surface area allowing them to dissipate heat more effectively. Large bodies have less surface area in order to conserve heat. Therefore, it appears that increased body mass is a benefit for organisms that are adapted to the cold. In the vast majority of cases, the average body weight of populations in hot regions is significantly lower (in all continents) than that in temperate and cooler climates. Hence, organisms adapted to warm climates tend to be smaller and have narrower, more linear bodies. In addition, as temperature of the environment increases, there also tends to be an increase in the relative size of protruding organs such as the ears (and tails).

The other general rule is **Allen's rule**. This rule is concerned with the length of the appendages. It states that warm-blooded organisms that live in hot climates will have long limbs, which maximizes the surface area for heat dissipation. People who live in hot areas have longer arms and legs, which allows for a greater skin surface for sweating and cooling. Human populations living in cold areas tend to have short arms and legs, which reduces the surface area from which to lose heat. Charbonneau-Roberts et al. (2005) show that the ratio of sitting height to total height reduces as mean annual temperature increases. Thus, the lower limbs tend to be longer in hotter climates and shorter in colder climates. This observation of increasing length of limbs in hotter climates is also seen in the upper limbs, since the ratio of arm span to height becomes greater in hot climates. The dimensions of the trunk of the body also become reduced in hotter climates, which results in a more linear trunk shape. These rules also appear to apply to other animal species. Paterson (1996) found that Japanese macaques who were moved to a northern location increased in overall size over time, adhering to both Bergmann's and Allen's rules.

Figure 15.14: Maasai boy.

We can clearly see evidence of these biogeographical principles when we look at some of the world's populations. If we compare Inuit or Mongolian populations to the Maasai of Africa or the Australian Aborigines, it is clear that these groups have adapted over countless generations to very different environmental conditions. The correlations between average temperature and body size and shape account for about 50–60 percent of the total interpopulation variance, which indicates that other factors influence this variation in body shapes (like nutrition). An indication that body size and shape involve a complex interaction between both environmental and genetic factors is suggested by the fact that when children are raised in a climate that is different from their ancestors, they tend to grow in patterns that are similar to the indigenous children (Roberts 1968, 1978, Malina 1975).

Apparently, general cranial size and shape also adhere to these climatic rules. Beals (1972) compared cephalic index (measure of head size) and climate around the globe, and concludes that people in colder climates have wider skulls than people in hot climates. This was especially marked between tropical groups and cold-adapted groups that experience periods of frost. He argues that the shape of the upper portion of the skull is related to heat retention or loss. Rounded skulls (with a high cephalic index) retain heat better, and thus are seen in cold-adapted populations. By extension, then, narrow skulls lose heat more rapidly, and thus would be beneficial in hot climates.

The data on the subcutaneous fat levels of different populations is not clear. In humans, the best form of natural insulation is subcutaneous fat; and in general, the greater the fat layer, the lower the total heat loss (Frisancho 1993). In one interesting study, men were exposed to cold water at 15°C for 30 minutes. The results demonstrate that the greater the skin-fold thickness (and thus the fat layer), the smaller the drop in rectal temperature (Keatinge 1979). The fact that the intensity and frequency of shivering are higher in thin people—and that they also have increased heat production during cold immersion—results from these lower levels of fat insulation (LeBlanc 1975, Buskirk et al. 1963). In the United States, African Americans clearly have a smaller mean and range of skin fold thickness than American whites; this suggests that Inuit groups have a thicker fat covering than Africans do. There are always exceptions to every rule. The Lapps of northern Scandinavia are thin. However, there is a general correlation between latitude and body shape that may extend back over a million years ago. Consequently, populations living in hot climates tend to have small, narrow bodies with long limbs (like the Maasai of Kenya), and groups living in cold climates tend to have large, wide bodies with short limbs, like the Inuit peoples. The long-standing association between climate and body size suggests that this is a genetic adaptation.

MY, THE AIR IS THIN UP HERE: HIGH-ALTITUDE STRESS

One of the most stressful environments in which to live on Earth is a high-altitude environment. Today, there are millions of people who live in high-altitude conditions at altitudes between 3500 and 4000 meters (roughly 11,000 to 13,000 feet). Multiple stressors converge at high altitude to place tremendous stress on the human body. In high-altitude environments, the most pressing stress results from the reduced availability of oxygen that occurs with reductions in barometric pressure. This means that at high altitudes, living creatures are always at risk for developing **hypoxia** (oxygen deprivation). However, high-altitude populations also have to contend with the added pressures presented by high solar radiation, cold temperatures, high wind, low humidity in the air, and reduced access to important nutritional components. For example, in most high-

Figure 15.15: Nepalese sherpa and pack.

altitude regions, winter temperatures are very low. In Tibet at 5000 meters, for instance, temperatures regularly are as low as −33°C; even in the summer, the temperatures rise to only 13°C. Humans respond to this cold stress at high altitudes by cultural means like wearing warm clothing and building well-designed shelters to maximize heat retention.

Oxygen constitutes about 21 percent of the atmosphere by volume; hence, the pressure of oxygen is roughly one-fifth of the total barometric pressure. The lower air pressure means that hemoglobin molecules in red blood cells take in fewer oxygen molecules with each breath—about one-third less at 4000 meters than at sea level (Beall 2001, Harrison et al. 1988, Frisancho 1993.). Although plants also do not thrive in low-oxygen environments, there is cultivated land in Tibet at altitudes of 2700–4500 meters. In the Andes, there are permanent settlements at 5200 meters, and daily work visits (for mining) occur at levels of roughly 5800 meters. The areas above 4000 meters are predominantly pastoral land with some agriculture, with the reverse seen at lower altitudes. Hypoxia results in mountain sickness. Oxygen deprivation results in symptoms like headache, nausea and loss of appetite, loss of ability to concentrate, tunnel vision, disorientation, and breathlessness occurring at about 8,000 feet during rest, and about 6500 feet during physical activity. Both acclimatizations and adaptations have been identified in response to high-altitude stress. When one moves from a lower altitude to a high-altitude setting, the immediate response to lack of oxygen (anoxia) is an increase in the volume of air breathed in per minute. People simply begin to breathe more rapidly and deeply. This elevated respiration rate has only a limited effect in improving the oxygen supply. As high-altitude environments are associated with low barometric pressure, when breathing in the air, less oxygen ultimately reaches the lungs. The body accommodates itself to this reduction in available oxygen by increasing its production of red blood cells to increase the transportation of oxygen. This elevated red blood cell production continues for several months, but there are limits to the efficacy of this response for most individuals. These changes are temporary acclimatization and will disappear when one returns to a lower altitude.

Genetic adaptations have also been identified in populations that have lived at high altitudes for countless generations. In these groups, scholars have identified respiratory, cardiovascular, and circulatory adjustments to life at high altitudes. In the Andes, some populations produce 30 percent more red blood cells than populations at sea level. In some groups, the right ventricle of the heart is larger, which assists the heart in pumping more blood to the lungs. In turn, this allows a more rapid transportation

Figure 15.16: Inca woman and child, Peru.

Figure 15.17: Indigenous women of Peru.

of oxygen to vital tissues. The chamber on the right side of the heart receives venous (deoxygenated) blood from the right atrium, and forces it into the pulmonary artery to be shipped to the lungs to be reoxygenated. In populations with a long history of living in high-altitude environments, the pulmonary arterial pressure is higher than in populations at sea level because of this enlargement of the right ventricle (called right ventricular hypertrophy). Therefore, these native groups have higher cardiac outputs than populations at sea level. When we examine people who have a long history at high altitudes like native Ethiopians and peoples of the Andes and Himalayas, we notice they have larger chest cavities than do populations at low altitudes, reflecting the high-altitude populations' inherited increases in lung volume. In Peruvian populations at high altitude, lung volume and chest dimensions were greater in all age categories (Frisancho and Baker 1970, Beall et al. 2002, Beall et al. 2010). Research comparing Tibetans who were born and raised at altitudes above 3600 meters with Han Chinese who were born at sea level and acclimatized to higher altitudes in adulthood proves very insightful. It concludes that the native Tibetans have larger lung volumes than the Han (Moore et al. 1991, Droma et al. 1991). In high-altitude native groups of the Andes, scholars also report that when allowances are made for differences in overall body size, these groups have larger lung volume and residual volumes than native groups at sea level (Frisancho et al. 1973, Hurtado et al. 1956). Clearly, there are multiple ways that humans have adjusted to high altitude, and both the size of the lungs and chest dimensions are influenced by genetic and developmental factors that interact differently in different groups (Greksa 1990, 1996). It has also been noted that humans who are born and raised in high-altitude conditions are generally shorter at most ages than low-altitude groups; this results from delayed maturation (Frisancho and Baker 1970). Widespread growth retardation results from the increased energy required to live in cold environments with little oxygen and poor nutrition. In high-altitude situations where adequate nutrition is available, growth is slower in children, but the total growth period is prolonged; hence, overall size is not decreased. While native Peruvian groups tend to demonstrate smaller stature and a delayed maturation, this reduced stature is not characteristic of all high-altitude populations. This leads scholars to

Figure 15.18: Tibetan child.

question whether or not smaller stature actually does result from hypoxia and cold stress. Leonard et al. (1990) observe that nutrition plays a major role in the development of shorter stature in Peruvians. They argue that this shorter stature in Peru is related to low socioeconomic status and inadequate access to proper nutrition. In other high-altitude groups like Ethiopians, there does not appear to be a reduction in adult stature. This is because the period of growth is slower, but longer in these groups, so that they attain the same height

Figure 15.19: Tibetan nomads.

as populations at lower altitudes (Frisancho and Baker 1970).

In the Andes, women give birth to lower-birth-weight babies. However, the placenta that nourishes the baby is larger. This ensures that the fetus receives adequate supplies of oxygen in utero. Cynthia Beall and colleagues (2000, 2001, 2010) found that Tibetan women with genes for high oxygen saturation in their hemoglobin—which enhances the body's access to oxygen—have more surviving children. It appears

Figure 15.20 Himalayas mountains.

that variants of the gene EPAS1 (related to red blood cell production) appears to have undergone strong selection pressure in Tibetans (Beall et al. 2010). Thus, hypoxia at high altitudes can act as an agent for natural selection.

GOT MILK? MAYBE NOT!

Everywhere we look in North America, we see signs encouraging us to drink milk. Milk prices are regulated by the government, since it is considered a necessary food staple. As a result, it is not surprising that we think everyone in the world also consumes milk as adults. In this we would be seriously incorrect. Nutritional behavior has long been an important element in human evolution. The most widely known adaptation to dietary factors is known as lactose persistence or **lactose tolerance**, which involves the ability to process milk products into adulthood. This ability is a genetically determined trait. Up until roughly the age of four years, all human children can produce **lactase**, the enzyme that breaks down the **lactose** (milk sugar) in dairy products. This ability to digest milk makes sense in light of the importance of breast milk in early life. All newborn mammals—including human infants—have the ability to digest milk. This is due to the fact that they produce lactase in the cells covering the walls of the small intestine. The ability to digest any kind of milk after age four

Figure 15.21: Man drinking a glass of milk.

depends upon the activation of a single dominant gene on the somatic (body) chromosome 2 (Swallow 2003). Lactose is a disaccharide (meaning that it is a sugar composed of two smaller sugars: monosaccharides). This enzyme allows us to split the milk sugar lactose into one molecule each of glucose and galactose (Hollox et al. 2001). In the majority of the world's populations, this ability to produce lactase is turned off after infancy, which leads to lactose intolerance. The genes that are responsible are called **regulatory genes**, and they turn other genes on or off at appropriate times during growth and development. If too much milk is ingested after the age of five, the undigested lactose ferments in the large intestine, leading to gas, bloating, diarrhea, colic, and severe gastrointestinal upset (Beall and Steegmann 2000).

In all human populations, infants and young children can digest milk. This makes sense in evolutionary terms, as baby formula and cereals were nonexistent. For the vast majority of human history, the only food available for infants and toddlers was breast milk, which is extremely nutritious and rich in vital vitamins and essential minerals. The increase of the gene that confers lactase persistence offers a good example of a more rapid form of natural selection. The domestication of milk-producing animals (cattle, sheep, goats, yak, etc.) only occurred less than 12,000 years ago.

Figure 15.22: Mother breast feeding.

The mutation that caused the ability to digest milk must have occurred after this time, when dairy farming first began. New research suggests that the mutation likely occurred independently more than once, but the subsequent results were the same in each population. For example, European and Kenyan populations have different mutations for lactose persistence, but they share the same level of tolerance. Research conducted by Sarah Tishkoff et al. (2007) suggest that the **LCT gene** is a mutation that arose independently in east Africa and northern Europe. The study examined 470 individuals from 43 different

Figure 15.23: Nguni cattle, Mkhaya Game Reserve.

African ethnic groups from Sudan, Kenya, and Tanzania, and these showed that the genetic variants of the LCT gene are different from those seen in European groups. They estimate that the mutation and the strong natural selection for it occurred within the last 7,000 years. This is supported by the work of other scholars, who suggest that selection for the LCT gene occurred around 7500 years ago in the dairy farming and agricultural communities of central Europe (Itan et al. 2009). The gene then moved with these migrating dairy farming groups, and this appears to correlate well with archaeological evidence from the European Neolithic Linearbandkeramik (LBK) culture (Concolly et al. 2008, Itan et al. 2009).

Scholars are still not clear today about whether or not lactose tolerance is an inherited trait in all circumstances. Several family studies have been conducted in places like Israel and Nigeria. They suggest that tolerance may be inherited by a single dominant condition, although it is not known how the gene functions. However, the situation is not entirely straightforward, as there is evidence that adults who have little or no lactase can slowly learn to tolerate quite high intakes of lactose without negative effects.

Figure 15.24: Tutsi cattle herd.

Figure 15.25: Tuareg woman, Mali.

Since this adaptation is not accompanied by a rise of their lactase levels, it is presumably due to a change in the intestinal flora (Scrimshaw and Murray 1988).

Among the majority of the world's populations—especially in native groups across Asia, Africa, Australia, southern Europe, and both North and South America—

Figure 15.26: Thai child from Hill Tribes.

most adult individuals are intolerant of milk. Thus, this form of food is not a normal part of the adult diet. Why do such differences occur in lactose tolerance among human populations? Throughout the Stone Age (prior to 10,000 years ago), milk was generally not available after weaning in hunter/gatherer groups. Thus, the distribution of lactose-tolerant populations indicates the role of cultural practices on this trait. Globally, we see the highest proportion of lactose persistence in three geographic regions: northern Europe (particularly around the Baltic and North seas), eastern Africa (Sudan, the Sahara, Kenya, Tanzania, and in the Uganda-Rwanda area of the interior), and the arid regions of the Middle East. This includes groups like the Tuareg of the Sahara, the Fulani of the West African Sahel, and the Beja and Kabbabish of Sudan, as well as the Tutsi population of Uganda-Rwanda (Patterson 2000). Another locus of lactose tolerance is in northern India (Babu et al. 2009).

It appears that in Chinese, Japanese, Thai, and Inuit populations, 80 percent or more of these groups are lactose intolerant, whereas in certain African and western European groups, the figure is between 5 percent and 25 percent. European groups, who are generally lactose tolerant, are partially descended from groups of the Middle East. Lactose intolerance in African Americans is between 70 to 77% percent (Allen and Cheer 1996, Lerner and Libby 1976, Molnar 1998). Roughly 77 percent of European Americans and only 14 percent of African Americans have the LCT gene; most human populations around the globe reach the African American frequency. It is estimated that 30 to 50 million Americans are lactose intolerant, including 75 percent of Native Americans and African Americans, and 90 percent of Asian Americans (Allen and Cheer 1996, Lerner and Libby 1976, Molnar 1998). The Fertile Crescent of the Middle East is where domestication first occurred, and populations in this region have been relying on milk products as an important component in their diets for millennia. Therefore, these early dairy farming groups raised cows,

Figure 15.27: Yoruba drummers, Kwara State, Nigeria.

sheep, goats etc., and likely consumed considerable quantities of milk. Strong selection pressures would act in this cultural environment to shift the gene frequencies in the direction of more lactose tolerance. The **cultural historical hypothesis** states that for those populations where dairy farming emerged early (over 9000 years ago, potentially in the Middle East), there has been strong selection for individuals who are lactose tolerant (Simoons 1978, 2001, McCracken 1971). Milk is a very nutritionally rich food (naturally; it is designed for babies!). It is very rich in fats, carbohydrates, and proteins, as well as calcium and phosphorus. In environments where rich food may not always be available, those individuals who could digest milk had a selective advantage for survival and reproduction. Modern European descendants of these populations have apparently retained this ancient ability. The gene spread rather quickly from one dairy farming group to another. It took almost 400 generations for this mutation to get to 90 percent tolerance, where it is today in northern Europe. Even fairly modest selective advantages that increase fitness by five to ten percent could account for the high frequencies of lactose tolerance found in northern Europe over a period of roughly 6000 years (Feldman and Cavalli-Sforza 1989, Aoki 1986).

Groups such as the Fulani, Tutsi, and Maasai, who have been pastoralists (animal herders) for thousands of years, have much lower rates of lactose intolerance then non-pastoralists. The Fulani are nomadic cattle herders, and milk is an extremely important component of the diet in all age categories. They have the lowest level of lactose intolerance in Africa at roughly 22 percent. African populations such as the Ibo, Ganda, Yoruba, or !Kung-San Bushmen—hunting/gathering people or agricultural groups who did not practice dairy farming—are as much as 99 percent lactose intolerant (Lerner and Libby 1976, Molnar 1998). Traditional hunter/gatherer populations did not have access to milk products after weaning. This explains the very high percentage of lactose intolerance in these groups. It appears that the geographic distribution of lactose tolerance is related to a history of cultural dependence upon milk products (Holden and Mace 1997, Leonard 2000).

There are some populations that culturally rely on dairy farming that are not characterized by high lactose levels: Mediterranean populations (Greek, Italian, etc.) and central and southern Asians, for instance. These groups do not typically consume their milk in raw form. Instead, these populations have traditionally consumed their milk produce as cheese and other derivatives (yogurt,

Figure 15.28: Greek feta cheese.

Figure 15.29: Greek yogurt.

sour cream, cottage cheese), in which the lactose has been metabolized through bacterial action to lactic acid. This partially fermented milk is much more easily digested than raw milk. In adult populations, the

Figure 15.30: Cattle herder.

elderly in particular may have benefited from the consumption of milk products, as they are rich in calcium and vitamin D, which helps to maintain strong, healthy bones and reduces the risk of osteoporosis (Boaz 2002).

DAIRY PRODUCTS, RICKETS, AND DIABETES: WHAT'S THE CONNECTION?

Very interesting research is emerging that suggests there may be a connection between lactose tolerance, dairy farming, and latitude. Calcium is absolutely essential for normal bone growth and maintenance, and vitamin D is very important for the proper absorption of calcium. Today, we have multivitamins and food like milk and cereal that are fortified with this vitamin. However, for most of human history (and in many parts of the world today), the only source of vitamin D was sunlight. Exposure to ultraviolet radiation stimulates our bodies to synthesize vitamin D. We know from our discussion about the evolution of human skin color in Chapter 13 that the degree of solar radiation varies tremendously across the globe. It is most intense around the equator, becoming less intense the farther away from the equator one moves.

Consequently, some argue that as populations moved out of the tropics and into the temperate zones that are associated with far lower levels of solar radiation, they would have always been at risk for developing rickets, the vitamin D deficiency. Rickets results from inadequate levels of vitamin D, which in turn leads to

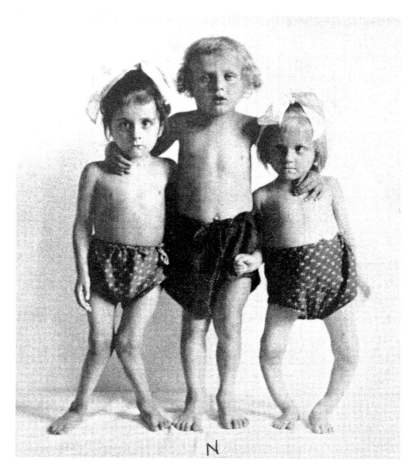

Figure 15.31: Children with vitamin D deficiency, rickets.

improper absorption of calcium, affecting both normal bone growth and maintenance. In these temperate zones, lactose tolerance would provide a selective advantage for survival because lactose increases calcium absorption (Allen and Cheer 1996, Beall and Steegmann 2000). Interestingly, there is some correlation between lactose intolerance and latitude, but it is not a perfect picture. The Fulani prove a good exception to this rule, as they live in the tropics, characterized by a constant year-round exposure to intense solar radiation, and thus have no need to worry about adequate vitamin D production. It is very possible that this trait developed for different reasons in different groups—for some, it may have been related to the necessity for a highly nutritious food, while others may have required it for proper calcium absorption in nontropical zones (Relethford 2005).

The scholars Allen and Cheer (1996) suggest that lactose tolerance may be related in an evolutionary sense to the development of non–insulin dependent diabetes mellitus (adult diabetes, rather than juvenile onset). Diabetes results from an inability to properly metabolize the simple sugar glucose. Allen and Cheer argue that as human populations began to rely on dairy products as a significant component of their diets, there was a significant rise in the amount of lactose in the diet (remember, lactose is broken down into the simpler sugars glucose and galactose). Consequently, it can be argued that diabetes is the price that dairy farming people have to pay for the increased lactose in their diets, and demonstrates beautifully how human behavior can quickly affect our biology.

When we look around at our human groups in diverse parts of the planet, it is clear we have taken our own individual evolutionary paths in response to very specific environmental and climatic conditions. We have developed biological means of responding to significant environmental pressures, in terms of heat stress, cold stress, high-altitude stress, and dietary stress. Some of these adjustments are temporary acclimatizations that develop over a short period of time and typically disappear when the individual is removed from the environment. Other adjustments have a genetic basis, and these represent long-term adaptations in populations to environmental stressors over countless generations.

CRITICAL REASONING QUESTIONS

- What is the difference between acclimatization and genetic adaptation? Distinguish between the two in terms of adjustments to high-altitude and hot environments.
- When you go out in cold or hot temperatures, what physiological responses do you notice? How do these changes assist you in maintaining homeostasis (equilibrium)?
- List what features define the Asian face. What environmental factors might have influenced the development of these characteristics?
- The Maasai people of east Africa are tall and slender, while Inuit groups of the Arctic are shorter and heavier. What biogeographical rules explain this observation? Can you see this in other animal species?
- People who live at high altitudes have to endure a wide range of environmental stresses. What are these selective pressures, and how have different high-altitude groups responded to them?
- Lactose tolerance is one of the few genetic adaptations that have been linked to nutritional behavior. Explain the distribution of this trait around the world.
- If most of the human population cannot digest milk as adults, why does the first world send milk as a primary source of food aid? Does this make any sense?
- Lactose tolerance may protect us from rickets, but it makes us more vulnerable to diabetes. Why?

REFERENCES AND SUGGESTED READINGS

Allen, J. S., and S. M. Cheer (1996). "The non-thrifty genotype." *Current Anthropology* 37:831–842.

Aoki, K. (1986). "A stochastic model of gene-culture coevolution suggested by the 'cultural-historical hypothesis' for the evolution of adult lactose absorption in humans." *Proceedings of the National Academy of Sciences* 83:2929–2933.

Babu, J., S. Kumar, P. Babu, et al. (2009). "Frequency of lactose malabsorption among healthy southern and northern Indian populations by genetic analysis and lactose hydrogen breath and tolerance tests." *American Journal of Clinical Nutrition* 91 (1):140–146.

Beall, C. M., and A. T. Steegmann (2000). "Human adaptation to climate: Temperature, ultraviolet radiation, and altitude." In S. Stinson, B. Bogin, R. Huss-Ashmore, and D. O'Rourke, eds., *Human Biology: An Evolutionary and Biocultural Perspective*, pp. 163–224. New York: Wiley-Liss.

Beall, C. M. (2001). "Adaptations to altitude: A current assessment." *Annual Review of Anthropology* 30:423–456.

Beall, C. M., G. L. Cavalleri, L. Deng, et al. (2010). "Natural selection of EPAS1 (HIF2a) associated with low hemoglobin concentration in Tibetan highlanders." *Proceedings of the National Academy of Sciences.* 107:11459–11464.

Beall, C. M., M. J. Decker, G. M. Brittenham, et al. (2002). "An Ethiopian pattern of human adaptation to high-altitude hypoxia." *Proceedings of the National Academy of Sciences.* 99:17215–17218.

Beals, K. L. (1972). "Head form and climatic stress." *American Journal of Physical Anthropology* 37:85–92.

Bloom, G. S. P. (2005). "Dairying barriers affect the distribution of lactose malabsorption." *Evolution and Human Behavior* 26:301.

Boaz, N. (2002). *Evolving health: The origins of illness and how the modern world is making us sick.* New York: John Wiley and Sons.

Buskirk, E. R., R. H. Thompson, and G. D. Whedon (1963). "Metabolic response to cold air in men and women in relation to total body fat content." *Journal of Applied Physiology* 18:603–612.

Charbonneau-Roberts, G., H. Saudny-Unterberger, H. V. Kuhnlein, and G. M. Egeland (2005). "Body mass index may overestimate the prevalence of overweight and obesity among the Inuit." *International Journal of Circumpolar Health* 64(2):163–169.

Cheng, W., F. Yang, S. Liu, et al. (2012). "Heteromeric heat-sensitive TRP channels exhibit distinct temperature and chemical response." *Journal of Biological Chemistry* 287(10):7279–7288.

Concolly, J., S. Colledge, and S. Shennan (2008). "Founder effect, drift, and adaptive change in domestic crop use in early Neolithic Europe." *Journal of Archaeological Sciences* 35(10):2797–2804.

Copley, M. S., R. Berstan, S. N. Dudd, et al. (2003). "Direct chemical evidence for widespread dairying in prehistoric Britain." *Proceedings of the National Academy of Sciences USA* 100:1524–1529.

Copley, M.S., R. Berstan, A. J. Mukherjee, et al. (2005). "Dairying in antiquity. III. Evidence from absorbed lipid residues dating to the British Neolithic." *Journal of Archaeological Science* 32:523–546.

Craig, O. E., C. P. Heron, L. H. Willis, et al. (2005). "Did the first farmers of central and eastern Europe produce dairy foods?" *Antiquity* 79:882–894.

Dana Jr., A. S., I. H. Rex Jr., and M. H. Samitz (1969). "The hunting reaction." *Archives of Dermatology* 99(4):441–450.

Droma, T. S., R. G. McCullough, et al. (1991). "Increased vital and lung capacities in Tibetan compared to Han residents of Lhasa (3,658 m)." *American Journal of Physical Anthropology* 86:341–351.

Feldman, M. W., and L. L. Cavalli-Sforza (1989). "On the theory of evolution under genetic and cultural transmission with application to the lactose absorption problem." In M. W. Feldman, ed., *Mathematical Evolutionary Theory,* pp. 145–173. Princeton, NJ: Princeton University Press.

Franciscus, R. G., and J. C. Long (1991). "Variation in human nasal height and breadth." *American Journal of Physical Anthropology* 85:419–427.

Frisancho, A. R. (1993). *Human adaptation and accommodation.* Ann Arbor: University of Michigan Press.

Frisancho, A. R., and P. T. Baker (1970). "Altitude and growth: A study of the patterns of physical growth of a high altitude Peruvian Quechua population." *American Journal of Physical Anthropology* 32:279–292.

Frisancho, A. R., T. Velasquez, and J. Sanchez (1973). "Influences of developmental adaptation on lung function at high altitude." *Human Biology* 45:583–594.

Greksa, L. P. (1990). "Developmental responses to high-altitude hypoxia in Bolivian children of European ancestry: A test of the developmental adaptation hypothesis." *American Journal of Human Biology* 2:603–612.

——— (1996). "Evidence for a genetic basis to the enhanced total lung capacity of Andean highlanders." *Human Biology* 68:119–129.

Hammel, H. T., R. W. Elsner, D. H. Le Messurier, et al. (1959). "Thermal and metabolic responses of the Australian aborigine exposed to moderate cold in summer." *Journal of Applied Physiology* 14:605–615.

Hammel, H. T., J. S. Hildes, D. C. Jackson, and H. T. Anderson (1962). "Thermal and metabolic responses of the Kalahari Bushmen to moderate cold exposure at night." *Technical Report 62–44.* Fort Wainwright, AL: Arctic Aeromedical Laboratory.

Harrison, G. A., J. S. Weiner, J. M. Tanner, and N. A. Barnicot (1977). *Human biology: An introduction to human evolution, variation, growth, and ecology*, 2nd ed. Oxford, UK: Oxford University Press.

Hernández, M., C. L. Fox, and C. Garcia-Moro (1997). "Fueguian cranial morphology: The adaptation to a cold, harsh environment." *American Journal of Physical Anthropology* 103:103–117.

Holden, C., and R. Mace (1997). "Phylogenetic analysis of the evolution of lactose digestion in adults." *Human Biology* 69:605–628.

Hollox, E. J., M. Poulter, M. Zvarik, et al. (2001). "Lactase haplotype diversity in the Old World." *American Journal of Human Genetics* 68:160–172.

Hurtado, A., T. Velasquez, et al. (1956). "Mechanisms of natural acclimatization: Studies on the native residents of Morococha, Peru, at an altitude of 14,000 feet." *Report 56–1*. Randolph Field, TX: Air Force School of Aviation Medicine.

Ingram, C. J., M. F. Elamin, C. A. Mulcare, et al. (2007). "A novel polymorphism associated with lactose tolerance in Africa: Multiple causes for lactase persistence?" *Human Genetics* 120:779–788.

Itan, Y., A. Powell, M. A. Beaumont, et al. (2009). The origins of lactase persistence in Europe. *PLoS Comput Biol* 5(8):e1000491. doi:10.1371/journal.pcbi.1000491

Keatinge, W. R. (1969). *Survival in cold water: The physiology and treatment of immersion hypothermia and of drowning.* Oxford, UK: Blackwell Scientific Publications.

LeBlanc, J. (1975). *Man in the cold.* Springfield, IL: Charles C. Thomas.

Leonard, W. H., T. L. Leatherman, J. W. Carey, and R. B. Thomas (1990). "Contributions of nutrition versus hypoxia to growth in rural Andean populations." *American Journal of Human Biology* 2:613–626.

Leonard, W. R. (2000). "Human nutritional evolution." In S. Stinson, B. Bogin, R. Huss-Ashmore, and D. O'Rourke, eds., *Human Biology: An Evolutionary and Biocultural Perspective*, p. 295–343. New York: John Wiley and Sons.

Lerner, I. M., and W. J. Libby (1976). *Heredity, evolution, and society.* San Francisco: W. H. Freeman.

Malina, R. M. (1975). *Growth and development: The first twenty years in man.* Minneapolis: Burgess.

McCracken, R. D. (1971). "Lactase deficiency: An example of dietary evolution." *Current Anthropology* 12:479–517.

Meehan, J. P. (1955). "Individual and racial variations in vascular response to cold stimulus." *Military Medicine* 116:330–334.

Mitchell, D., L. C. Senay, C. H. Wyndham, et al. (1976). "Acclimatization in a hot, humid environment: Energy exchange, body temperature, and sweating." *Journal of Applied Physiology* 40:768–778.

Molnar, S. (1998). *Human variation: Races, types and ethnic groups*, 4th ed. Englewood Cliffs, NJ: Prentice Hall.

Molnar, S., and I. M. Molnar (2000). *Environmental change and human survival: Some dimensions of human ecology.* Upper Saddle River, NJ: Prentice Hall.

Moore, L. G., J. G. Zhuang, R. G. McCullough, et al. (1991). "Increased lung volumes in Tibetan high altitude residents." *American Journal of Physical Anthropology* 12 (abstract):134.

Paterson, J. D. (1996). "Coming to America: Acclimation in macaque body structures and Bergmann's rule." *International Journal of Primatology* 17:585–611.

Patterson, K. D. (2000). "Lactose tolerance." In K. F. Kiple, ed., *The Cambridge World History of Food.* Cambridge, UK: Cambridge University Press.

Relethford, J. H. (2005). *The human species: An introduction to biological anthropology*, 6th ed. New York: McGraw-Hill.

Roberts, D. F. (1968). "Genetic effects of population size reduction." *Nature* 220:1084–1088.

——— (1978). *Climate and human variability*, 2nd ed. Menlo Park, CA: Benjamin Cummings.

Scholander, P. F., H. T. Hammel, J. S. Hart, et al. (1958). "Cold adaptation in Australian Aborigines." *Journal of Applied Physiology* 13:211–218.

Scrimshaw, N. S., and E. B. Murray (October 1988). "The acceptability of milk and milk products in populations with a high prevalence of lactose intolerance." *American Journal of Clinical Nutrition* 48(4):1079–1159.

Simoons, F. J. (1978). "The geographic hypothesis and lactose malabsorption. A weighing of the evidence." *American Journal of Digestive Disorders* 23:963–980.

——— (2001). "Persistence of lactase activity among northern Europeans: A weighing of the evidence for the calcium absorption hypothesis." *Ecology of Food and Nutrition* 40:397–469.

So, J. K. (1980). "Human biological adaptation to Arctic and subarctic zones." *Annual Review of Anthropology* 9:63–82.

Steegmann, A. T., and W. S. Platner (1968). "Experimental cold modification of cranio-facial morphology." *American Journal of Physical Anthropology* 28:17–30.

Swallow, D. M. (2003). "Genetics of lactase persistence and lactose intolerance." *Annual Review of Genetics* 37:197–219.

Takasaki, Y., S. F. Loy, and H. W. Juergens (2003). "Ethnic differences in the relationship between bioelectrical impedance and body size." *Journal of Physiological Anthropology and Applied Human Science* 22:233–235.

Takeru, A., and E. J. E. Sathmåry (1996). *Prehistoric Mongoloid dispersals*. New York: Oxford University Press.

Tishkoff, S. A., F. A. Reed, A. Ranciaro, et al. (2007). "Convergent adaptation of human lactase persistence in Africans and Europeans." *Nature Genetics* 39(1):31–40.

Ward, J. S., G. A. C. Bredell, and H. G. Wenzel (1960). "Responses of Bushmen and Europeans on exposure to winter night temperatures in the Kalahari." *Journal of Applied Physiology* 15:667–670.

Wyndham, C. H., and J. F. Morrison (1958). "Adjustment to cold of Bushmen in the Kalahari Desert." *Journal of Applied Physiology* 13:219–225.

Wyndham, C. H. (1964). "Southern African ethnic adaptation to temperature and exercise." In P. T. Baker and J. S. Weiner, eds. *The Biology of Human Adaptability*. Oxford, UK: Clarendon Press.

Wyndham, C. H., G. G. Rogers, L. C. Senay, and D. Mitchell (1976). "Acclimatization in a hot, humid environment; cardiovascular adjustments." *Journal of Applied Physiology* 40:779–785.

16

It Seemed Like A Good Idea At The Time

Evolution and Human Behavior

By Gillian Crane-Kramer

One thing that makes humans a particularly difficult subject of study is the complicated interaction between our biology and our culture. In terms of human health and illness, human disease does not just result from a complex set of biological factors. One must also take into account both the natural and social environments, and the influence these have on the course of a disease-causing microorganism. In this chapter, we will discuss how our behavior affects our health in terms of diet, as well as other factors such as economic strategy, ritual behavior, and more. We often don't think about how our behavior influences our health. We think of it in a passing way in that we wash our hands after being in the bathroom, or we cover our faces when we sneeze. However, we don't often ponder how important aspects of our daily lives—like the architectural style of your house, or taking Communion at church, or planting wheat for food—can dramatically influence our biological well-being. Our lives are busy, so most people do not stop to think how things like human diet, activity levels, population density, and degree of mobility have changed throughout the course of our evolutionary history as a species.

It is crucial for us to remember that disease-producing organisms (nasty critters like bacteria, viruses, and fungi) are themselves evolving in response to our protective measures. This is why we are now seeing mosquitoes that are resistant to some antimalarial drugs and antibiotic-resistant strains of old foes like tuberculosis and staphylococcus emerging. It is like an endless dance—sometimes, as during the ancient pandemics of bubonic plague or the modern scourge of HIV, it appears that the pathogens govern the steps. However,

223

Figure 16.1: Washing hands, Senegal, Africa.

Figure 16.2: Bacteria cells.

humans have also devised an arsenal of weapons against these enemies—sterilization, pasteurization, antibiotics, and well-trained physicians on the front lines—that allow us to take the lead on occasion. We must not allow ourselves to become complacent when it comes to our health, whether this relates to proper diet or infectious pathogens. Whether we like it or not, our behavior does profoundly affect our health, both for individuals and on a group basis. For the vast majority of our history as a family, humans have lived in small, mobile bands of hunter/gatherers. We did not have cities or farms or domesticated plants or animals (okay, maybe dogs). We moved around with the seasons or when resources became depleted in an area. The diet was well balanced for the most part, and small band groups tended to be extremely knowledgeable about the local flora and fauna. In other words, we were pretty well adapted to this way of life, and managed to subsist on a relatively diverse set of dietary components. For millions of years, our family has lived like this. But as far as the longer history of our lineage (over roughly the last five million years), human diet and society have changed in an inconceivable way over the last 10,000 years. When we made the change from a mobile hunter/gatherer lifestyle to a sedentary agricultural one, it forever changed our relationship to wild species, to our natural environments, and to ourselves. Therefore, humans as a biological species have had to contend with an overwhelming amount of change in a very short period of time. Not surprisingly, we have risen to the challenge of these new stresses, sometimes with more success than others. There is no shame in making mistakes. The shame comes in not learning from them.

SORRY, DARLIN': YOU ARE WHAT YOU EAT

When we look at the diets of other primates, we can see that the human diet has undergone some changes in the last five million years or so. All other primates (with the exception of common chimpanzees and bonobos) have exclusively vegetarian diets (maybe with the occasional bug thrown in for good measure). The vast majority of primates, then, are either principally folivorous (leaf-eating) or frugivorous (fruit-eating). While humans, particularly hunter-gatherer groups, have a considerable plant component in their diet, humans are clearly unique in adding the meat component. Humans are omnivores (I do apologize to the vegetarians), and we do require both animal and plant food sources for nutritional health. Like all creatures, humans require a proper balance of nutritional elements for optimal health. This proper nutrition is necessary for body growth and maintenance, particularly from birth through adolescence, when we grow rapidly. Vitamins are classified as either water-soluble or fat-soluble. In humans, there are 13 different vitamins: nine are water-soluble (vitamin C and eight B vitamins), and four are fat-soluble (A, D, E, and K). Water-soluble vitamins are not stored in the body, and any excess is excreted from the body in urine, to the degree that urinary output is a strong predictor of vitamin consumption (Fukuwatari and Shibata 2008, Lieberman and Bruning 1990). Different vitamins and minerals fulfill different roles in maintaining nutritional health. For example, vitamin C is essential for normal collagen production (collagen is the most common protein in your body and a very important constituent of all connective tissue like bone, muscles, and blood vessels). It helps you maintain and repair bone and other important tissues, and it assists in the healing of wounds and the formation of scar tissue. Humans and other primates have lost their ability to create their own vitamin C, likely because we lived in environments where we were exposed to a continuous source of vitamin C–rich foods like fruit and vegetables (Leonard 2000). To maintain healthy nutrition, it is not only the specific foods that are important (and hence specific vitamins and minerals), but also the combination of foods. Some nutrients are required to properly absorb others, and some elements inhibit the absorption of others. For example, elevated doses of vitamin A can inhibit the absorption of vitamin K. However, vitamin C increases the absorption of iron and chromium. Some vitamins are involved in the transportation of other vitamins into the body.

Figure 16.3: Baby gorilla.

Copper is necessary for the proper absorption of iron. Vitamin D increases the absorption of both calcium and magnesium, and inhibits excretion of calcium through the urine. Without vitamin D, calcium is not well absorbed in the body. Fat-soluble vitamins A, D, E, and K require fats to be absorbed (Lieberman and Bruning 1990). Intestinal disorders such as celiac disease or Crohn's disease decrease the absorption of all nutrients, including the fat-soluble vitamins.

The energy that we take in as food is measured in calories and includes carbohydrates, fats, and proteins. Proteins in particular are very important for certain metabolic activities. The components of proteins are amino acids, and we require 20 amino acids for normal biological functioning. Adults require eight different amino acids that can only be obtained through food;

Figure 16.4: Healthy vegetables.

children require nine (Relethford 2005). The best source of protein for humans is acquired from animal products like meat, eggs, milk, and fish. While plants provide proteins as well, they lack certain amino acids, and thus must be consumed in combination to provide balanced nutrition.

We cannot be absolutely sure when humans (or their ancestors) became hunter-gatherers, but we have a good idea that it was over two million years ago. Humans lived in this manner until around 12,000 years ago, when we begin to see the emergence of early agriculture in some regions of the world. We know that the modern distribution of hunter/gatherers is a pale reflection of their distribution in the past. Prior to the Neolithic period associated with agriculture, all of the world's populations lived as hunter/gatherers, yet their diets varied quite dramatically. Naturally, hunter/gatherer groups like the Aleut of the arid, cold Arctic have a diet composed of very different foods than the Aborigines of the hot, dry Australian desert. Populations that live in resource-rich environments tend to move less frequently than those in regions with fewer resources.

Figure 16.5: Kitchen still life, Jacopo da Empoli, 16th century.

Movement then occurs when either food or water resources become depleted. While hunting provides an important protein component to the diet, the majority (70–80 percent) of the diet comes from gathering, and includes things like tubers, nuts, seeds, and other plants. Among the !Kung San of the Kalahari Desert in southern Africa, two-thirds of their daily caloric intake comes from plant foods and nuts (Lee 1968). This is also true for the Aboriginals of central Australia, where the principle portion of their diet is plant based, particularly involving nuts and seeds (Molnar and Molnar 2000). The specific plant-to-animal food ratio in the Paleolithic diet is the cause of considerable debate. The average diet among modern hunter-gatherer societies is estimated to consist of 64–68 percent of animal calories and 32–36 percent of plant calories (Cordain et al. 2002), with animal calories further divided between fished and hunted animals in varying proportions (typically with hunted animal food comprising 26–35 percent of the overall diet). There is significant variation in the meat component between hunter/gatherer groups themselves. The animal-derived calorie percentage ranges from 25 percent in the Gwi people of southern Africa, to

Figure 16.6: San Bushmen, Botswana.

as high as 99 percent in the Alaskan Nunamiut. The animal-derived percentage value is elevated in polar hunter-gatherer societies, who have no choice but to eat animal food because of the inaccessibility of plant foods. In general, hunter/gatherer populations consume a diet that has a meat component of at least 20 percent, except in certain groups like the Inuit or Nunamiut, where the meat component of the diet is elevated due to a limited plant resource availability (Relethford 2005).

THE MESOLITHIC AND THE BROAD-SPECTRUM REVOLUTION: NOT IN KANSAS ANYMORE, DOROTHY

The Mesolithic period is this rather poorly defined period approximately 12,000 years ago that occurs at the end of the Pleistocene Epoch. This is a period of dramatic environmental change around the world, with a recession of the glaciers, a rise in sea level, and a warmer, milder climate. With all this major environmental change come tremendous changes in the distribution of plants and animals, notably a major reduction in mega fauna around the world. Apparently, increasing strain was being placed upon the traditional hunter-gatherer lifestyle due to these dramatic climatic changes, perhaps in conjunction with an increase in population size as well. When your resource base reduces, you can combat this in a number of different

Figure 16.7: Perito Moreno Glacier, Los Glaciares National Park, Argentina.

ways. First, you can simply forage and hunt farther away from home, but naturally constraints are placed by distance. Secondly, you can incorporate new regions into your territory that have been formerly neglected. Third, you can add new dietary elements to the diet, which include things like small animals, seafood, and new plant species. Lastly, you can grow your own food. This last solution seems to have been the dominant one for the last 8,000 years, at least. With this shift to an agricultural diet called the **Neolithic Revolution**, humans dramatically changed the types of food in their diet. It seems that in most cases, we settled for quantity over quality with this shift, and many modern diseases of civilization stem from this critical economic choice. In Chapter 15, we talked about the idea of a thrifty gene in hunter-gatherer groups. This gene allowed humans to retain fat more efficiently during periods of abundance so that they could survive during the lean times or in periods of famine. The typical hunter-gatherer diet is high in protein and low in carbohydrates and sugars. The level of physical activity is high; the level of obesity is low. This low-fat, low-sugar diet—in conjunction with a high physical activity level—means that hunter-gatherers are associated with far lower levels of conditions like heart disease and stroke, diabetes, and many forms of cancer. Boyd Eaton and Konner (1985, 1999) have reconstructed what

Figure 16.8: Native American woman gathering seeds, Coast Pomo.

they believe to be the average Paleolithic (hunter-gatherer) diet from a number of modern and archaeological sources. They argue that this hunter-gatherer diet is fundamentally different from the modern agricultural one, in both quality and composition. The hunter-gatherer diet is high in essential micronutrients, fiber, protein and potassium, and low in sodium (salt) and fat. They argue that although the carbohydrate and caloric intake between modern agriculturalists and hunter-gatherers is roughly equivalent, hunter-gatherers have a much more active lifestyle, requiring a higher calorie load. In addition, hunter-gatherers acquire their carbohydrates mostly through vegetables and fruits, whereas today, we get them from processed cereals and refined sugars. We have simply not had enough time in evolutionary terms to adjust to this new nutritional environment; as a result, we are seeing a dramatic rise in nutritionally related illnesses. We see this discordance today in the high rates of diabetes in traditional hunter-gatherer peoples. In groups like the Pima-Papago Indians of the American Southwest, the diabetes rates are as high as 50 percent of the population, and elevated rates have been observed in many other Pacific Islander, Asian, and African American groups who have recently adopted the Western diet (Neel 1962, 1982, 2009, Knowler et al. 1980).

Due to their small group size and nomadic lifestyle, hunter-gatherers have traditionally been far less at risk for infectious pathogens (especially the crowd diseases like cholera, smallpox, and tuberculosis). This is in large part the result of small population size, which cannot sustain many of the dangerous infectious pathogens. However, hunter-gatherers are more at risk for developing parasitic infections and chronic infections. Zoonoses are diseases that are transmitted from animals to humans (or vice versa), and hunter-gatherers typically come into contact with these through insect bites, exposed wounds, butchering, or consumption of an infected animal. These can include conditions like malaria, yellow fever, anthrax, salmonella, or rabies. Humans can also be exposed to numerous lethal anaerobic bacteria—including germs that cause botulism, tetanus, or gangrene—through contact with the intestinal contents of infected animals during butchering (Sherman 2006). The consumption of raw or undercooked game is a potentially dangerous practice. One potential threat is the trichina worms that cause trichinosis. These parasites are

Figure 16.9: Naro Bushmen, Botswana, Africa.

Figure 16.10: Hadza archery, Lake Eyasi, Tanzania.

found in animals that consume other animals (carnivores and omnivores). Today, we associate the disease particularly with pork that is not properly cooked, but the infection has been observed in many different mammal species.

This disease could ravage people in historically modern times as well. The Danish ship *Unicorn* set sail in 1619 to find the fabled Northwest Passage, the water route across North America between the Atlantic and Pacific oceans. Sixty-one of the 64 crewmen suffered terrible deaths in Canada's frozen Hudson Bay in 1620. Canadian historian Delbert Young learned from the memoirs of the captain of the *Unicorn* that the men became ill after consuming raw polar bear meat. In 1897, infected bear meat also caused the deaths of Swedish explorers who had tried to reach the North Pole by balloon. Many years later, their frozen supplies were discovered and found to contain *Trichinella* parasites (Young 1969).

Figure 16.11: Camp fire, Chippewa Village, Itasca State Park Minnesota, 1926.

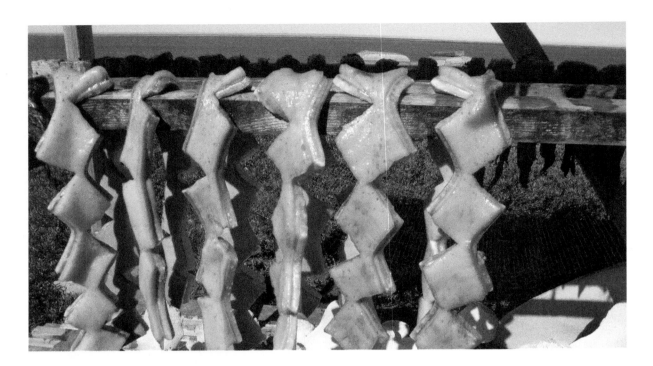

Figure 16.12: Beluga blubber drying at Point Lay, Alaska.

The other primary group of infections that affected hunter-gatherer groups includes infections of a chronic nature. Transmission from person to person occurs from contaminated objects or food, skin-to-skin contact, the oral-fecal route, or through droplet infection (sneezing or coughing). A classic example of a chronic infection is yaws, caused by a spirochete from the genus *Treponema*. This illness is associated with nonindustrialized populations, and typically manifests itself as a disease of childhood. It is transmitted through skin-to-skin contact and the sharing of contaminated objects. A number of conditions, often referred to as heirloom diseases, have probably been passed down to us from our earlier primate ancestors. These conditions have plagued human populations throughout our evolutionary history. This includes various classes of bacteria such as staphylococcus, streptococcus, pneumococcus, herpes, and salmonella, as well as a number of amoebic infections, viruses, and intestinal protozoa.

Figure 16.13: Kenyan woman eating.

Hunter-gatherer populations typically demonstrate higher levels of dental attrition (wear) than agricultural groups. Wild foods tend to have a tougher composition, and are typically consumed raw or slightly cooked. They are also associated with a greater amount of grit and soil. Thus, the teeth are exposed to significant wear, and often are simply worn down prior to old age, making the processing of course vegetable matter extremely difficult. The benefit of a tougher diet associated with hunters and gatherers is that they have substantially lower rates of dental caries compared to agriculturalists. The coarse nature of their typical diet precludes the adherence of food residues on the teeth, and this significantly reduces the ability of cavity-producing bacteria to attack the surfaces of the teeth (Cohen and Crane-Kramer 2007, Cohen and Armelagos 1984).

One way of overcoming the problem of lower-quality foods for infants is to significantly extend the period of breast-feeding. Breast milk is a wonderful source of nutrition, and hunter/gatherer women often breast-feed their children into the fifth year of life. This has the added benefit of repressing the ovulation cycle in women, assuring that the mother's system will be able to recover from the nutritional drains of pregnancy before conception occurs again. We see a very different pattern in resource consumption and management between hunter-gatherer and agricultural groups. For the most part, the transition to agriculture is not one that benefited us nutritionally, but it allowed us to sustain dense, large urban populations. We end up relying on what is termed "**third-quality foods**" (grains and tubers) that are often deficient in essential dietary components.

Figure 16.14: Hadzabe woman and child, Tanzania.

THE RISE OF AGRICULTURE AND DIET: NOT A PRETTY PICTURE

With the emergence of agriculture, we see dramatic shifts in human health and illness. It is a trade-off, really. Agriculture made it possible to sustain large populations and provide adequate caloric energy, but this occurred at the cost of individual and group health. Agricultural strategies are associated with a reduction in the amount of animal protein consumed. This in part results from the fact that there is a heavier reliance on produced vegetable staples, and the absence of wild game in relation to sedentary communities. A decline in food quality results from a reliance on third-quality foods, the very foods that eventually became crucial staples in agricultural societies.

Today, the majority of our food intake comes from cereal staple crops. The types of plants and animals that were selected for domestication were characterized by some important features. People selected plants that produced high yields, stored well, and tasted pleasant (no one wanted to domesticate stinkweed). Domesticated animals are typically herbivores or omnivores, and are herd/pack animals with a natural social hierarchy. They are able to reproduce in captivity and grow fairly quickly, and they taste good (hence why no one tried to domesticate the grizzly bear). With the advent of agriculture at the dawn of the Neolithic period, we see a shift, where quantity begins to outshine quality. Agriculture

Figure 16.15: Thai farmers reaping the rice with sickles.

produces large yields that are able to sustain large, permanently settled populations. However, the overall quality of the grasses that constitute the majority of the modern diet (wheat, barley, rice, millet, etc.)

Figure 16.16: Sami reindeer herder, Sweden.

is generally pretty nutrient deficient. It is likely that early subsistence agriculturalists continued to collect wild plant and animal resources to supplement their diets, and thus still had a fairly diverse range of different species in their diets.

Animal foods are the best source of complete protein (protein with the best balance of amino acids) for human health. Animal resources are also the best source of vitamins like A, B12, and D. Minerals like iron and zinc are more readily available in meat sources, as well as necessary fat. As agriculture intensifies, wild animals are hunted to extinction or simply move out of the area, and farmers emphasize the growth of dense grasses over other vegetable staples. As agriculture intensifies, the meat component of the diet decreases, as does the variety of the diet. The elevated contribution of carbohydrates from grains to the human diet following the adoption of agriculture has effectively diluted the protein content of the human diet (Mann 2007). In modern hunter-gatherer diets, dietary protein is characteristically elevated (19–35 percent of energy) at the

Figure 16.17: Healthy foods (National Cancer Institute, 1986).

Figure 16.18: Sample of grains, Glenbow Museum, Calgary, Canada.

expense of carbohydrates (22–40 percent of energy) (Cordain et al. 2000, 2002). On the other hand, even though modern hunter/gatherers gain as much energy from animal products as westernized groups, the meat of wild animals is much leaner than their domestic counterparts, and thus there is far less fat. The modern Western diet is high in fats, sugars, and carbohydrates—a complete opposite of the hunter/gatherer diet. Our diet is defined by a high level of fat (roughly 40 percent energy) and this is 40–50 percent saturated fat, obtained mostly from animal and dairy products or contained within manufactured foods (Frisancho 2012).

Figure 16.19: Sweet potatoes—tubers.

HUMAN BEHAVIOR AND DIETARY DISEASE: TOO MUCH OR TOO LITTLE OF A GOOD THING?

Figure 16.20: Esta Mamae carries pana in a basket outside a traditional food storage hut.

As noted above, in order to maintain health, there must be a balance in the nutrients that are consumed (there were no multivitamins in the past). Each individual nutrient must be ingested in specific quantities, and must also be in a form that can be absorbed by the body's digestive system. An imbalance in consumed nutrients leads either to too much or too little of a dietary component, typically with negative consequences. Many of the most devastating nutritional diseases result from deficiencies in one or more essential nutrients. These deficiencies can result either from the consumption of foods deficient in some nutrients or by the processing of food, which can remove important nutritional components.

One of the most common scourges related to farmers is **iron-deficiency anemia**, which results from inadequate absorption of iron. This can result from several different factors, including lack of access to or availability of iron-rich foods; food choices and the combination of foods in the diet; food preparation techniques; pregnancy and lactation; and the presence of parasites. The human body can only absorb iron in specific forms and food combinations (Cohen and Crane-Kramer 2007). If iron levels become too reduced in the diet, this can lead to the development of iron-deficiency anemia. The important cereal grain staples all contain a class of chemicals called phytates; these often impede the absorption of important dietary nutrients like iron, calcium, and zinc. This is also the case with many staple tubers like sweet potatoes, cassava, and yams (Winick 1980, Jelliffe and Jelliffe 1982, El-Najjar 1977). The heavy reliance on these cereal and tuber species makes populations vulnerable to conditions such as anemia and pellagra. It has been seen in Old World sites like the late Roman period cemetery at Poundbury in England. Out of over 1400 burials retrieved from the site, as many as 28 percent of the skulls displayed evidence of anemia in their upper eye sockets (cribra orbitalia) (Molleson 1989). Maize in particular is a poor source of certain amino acids such as lysine and the vitamin niacin, and is low in iron content. Particularly in the New World, populations that relied on maize as their principal cultigen were at an elevated risk of developing iron-deficiency anemia. With the advent of agriculture, increased rates of iron-deficiency anemia have commonly been observed on the skull (as porotic hyperostosis and cribra orbitalia) by scholars who work in areas associated with a heavy reliance on these particular crops.

A widespread condition in the past, **pellagra** was often called the Red Plague. The first description of the disease comes from Spain in 1735, where it was called *mal de la rosa* because the disease appeared as a red rash that covered the hands and feet and formed a butterfly pattern across the neck. The word pellagra comes from the Italian *pelle-* (skin) and *-agra* (rough) (Sherman 2006). This patterned reddening of the skin is a classic sign of the disease, which also includes a staggering gait, loss of balance, diarrhea, and nonsensical ramblings. In severe cases, people could become insane or die from the disease; the clinical symptoms of pellagra were described as the 4 D's: dermatitis, diarrhea, dementia, and death.

In the early 1900s, this nutritional deficiency was commonplace in the American South. Ground corn is very low in niacin, as well as the amino acid tryptophan, which the body uses to process niacin. The Southern diet—particularly of the poor—was principally composed of cornmeal. The disease would appear as a spring fever that appeared just before mid-February, gradually become worse through May and June, and then decline. In the American South, the fatality rate from pellagra could be as high as 40 percent; in 1916, it was the second highest cause of death in South Carolina. From 1730 to 1930, pellagra apparently caused roughly 500,000 deaths worldwide. Interestingly, greatly elevated levels of the disease were recorded in federal troops imprisoned in Andersonville, Georgia, during the Civil War (Roe

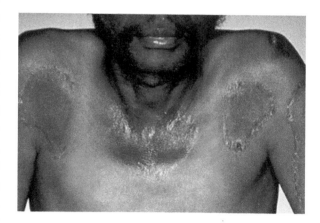

Figure 16.21: Patient suffering from pellagra, caused by vitamin B (niacin) deficiency.

1973, Wood 1979). Between 1900 and 1947, there were around 3 million cases in the United States, with about 100,000 deaths (Sherman 2006, Barnes 2005). The condition was essentially eradicated in the West by 1950. Pellagra is a disease of corn: corn mush, hominy grits, and corn bread all lack adequate levels of niacin (a water-soluble B vitamin). It is a disease of poverty, and is associated with a heavy reliance upon corn in the diet. The connection between a niacin deficiency and pellagra was discovered by Dr. Joseph Goldberger in the 1920s. He suggested that the disease could be prevented by adding fresh meat, eggs, milk, and vegetables to the diet. Interestingly, the reason that Mexican and other Central and South American groups did not suffer from pellagra when it was endemic in the American South was their practice of soaking the cornmeal in hot limewater before making tortillas. This processing releases the bound niacin and therefore prevents pellagra. The Southern tradition of the prolonged boiling of corn meal in water means that only approximately 20 percent of the niacin is released. Thus, the alkaline nature of the limewater, in addition to boiling above 80°C, allows all of the niacin to be released and ingested (Sherman 2006).

Rice—the major staple of Asia—is a poor source of protein, and this low protein quality further inhibits the activity of Vitamin A in the body. A heavy reliance on rice can lead to condition called **beriberi**. This disease results from

Figure 16.22: Mexican woman making maize tortillas.

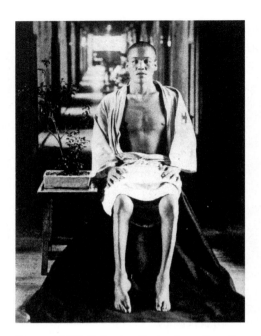

Figure 16.23: Patient suffering from the vitamin B1 (thiamine) deficiency beriberi.

a deficiency in vitamin B1 (thiamine), a water-soluble vitamin that is essential for glucose metabolism and for the proper conversion of carbohydrates into energy. Thiamine also plays an important role in muscle, nerve, and heart function. Dietary sources of thiamine are whole, fortified, or enriched grains, pork chops, and soy milk. Beriberi occurs when the brown husk of the rice is removed and polished rice becomes part of a person's diet. Chinese documentary evidence concerning the use of polished white rice as a staple crop extends back as far as the third century BC, from where it spread to other portions of Asia (Wood 1979). Beriberi is associated with symptoms such as a progressive loss of strength, swelling of the ankles and thighs, tremendous pain in the joints of the legs, loss of the ability to speak, heart failure, emaciation, and death from asphyxia and convulsions (Pfeiffer 1975, Scrimshaw 1975). Natural rice is quite nutritious; however this disease is related to the processing of rice to produce milled, polished white rice. The cooking of rice without polishing allows all of the vitamin B complex to remain intact. Parboiled rice loses the majority of the B vitamins, but retains niacin, thiamine, and riboflavin from the B complex. Polished rice loses all of the B vitamins, except for small traces of folic acid (Kirschmann 1975, McElroy and Townsend 1989). In 1870, steel rollers were invented for milling rice, and tons of rice could be milled using steam power. The milling process removed the outside covering—the

Figure 16.24: Asian woman eating white rice.

pericarp, or husk—leaving the white polished rice behind. This polished white rice is stored for much longer; thus, the usable yield from each harvest increases, owing to less spoilage. Larger numbers of people could be fed, and the cost of the rice was reduced as well. Consequently, this form of processed rice became the staple for the military and many institutions like hospitals, orphanages, and prisons. These populations in particular were at significant risk for developing the disease. Beriberi was the main cause of death among prisoners of war interned by the Japanese in World War II (Barnes 2005).

The storage of food resources is associated with a trade-off situation. Although it allows for a more reliable food source, the storage of many fruit and vegetable products leads to a substantial loss in vitamin content, particularly vitamin C and other water-soluble vitamins (vitamin B). Stored food is also vulnerable to infestation by rodents and insects. As populations rely more on stored food products, they reduce their exposure to products associated with different water and soil sources. This reduction in exposure to different soil and water supplies means that people often do not have access to vital dietary components such as iodine and fluorine. This can lead to the development of conditions such as **goiter**, which is associated with deficient levels of iodine. Iodine is stored by the thyroid gland at the base of the neck; it is used to form thyroxine, a hormone that controls metabolic processes (Barnes 2005). Prior to the modern era, people obtained the necessary levels of iodine through consuming salt or drinking water. For coastal populations, both kelp and seafood are good sources of iodine. The majority of the world's mountainous areas and regions in all continents—like the Pyrenees and the Alps in Europe, the Atlas Mountains of North Africa, Papua New Guinea in the Pacific, the Andes of South America, the North American Pacific Northwest, and the Himalayas, to name a few (Barr 1951, Aufderheide and Rodriguez-Martin 1998)—are associated with poor sources of iodine. Populations in these regions have traditionally traded with other groups for salt or seafood. Symptoms of iodine deficiency include the retention of salt and water, muscle weakness and fatigue, menstrual disturbances, and lowered resistance to infection (DeGroot 1975, Sodeman 1956). There are many descriptions in the past of encounters with populations suffering from goiter. In the 13th century, Marco Polo describes widespread goiter in central Asians,

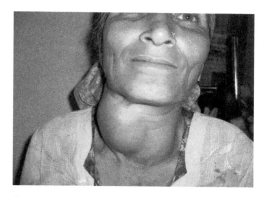

Figure 16.25: Indian woman with a large goiter due to iodine deficiency.

and Roman historians describe it as present in people of the Alps. It has also been identified in an 18th-century male from Sicily and a Nazca woman from southern Peru dating to 100 BC (Guggenheim 1981, Aufderheide and Rodriguez-Martin 1998).

While pellagra, iron-deficiency anemia, and beriberi are all diseases that result from deficiencies of essential dietary elements, there are also conditions that result from overabundance. They include such conditions as gout, obesity, diabetes, celiac disease, and Crohn's disease. **Gout** results from a disturbance of uric acid metabolism, occurring predominantly in males. It is characterized by painful inflammation of the joints, especially of the feet and hands, and arthritic attacks that can become chronic and result in deformity. The gout epidemic in 18th-century England was in part saturnine gout, which results from lead deposition in the kidneys, impairing the ability of these organs to excrete uric acid due to the importation of fortified Iberian wines (Sherman 2006). To make matters worse, the Georgian diet was full of rich, fatty foods, particularly meats. Purines are components of nucleic acids, and they are metabolized mainly to uric acid. Many rich foods contain a lot of purines, but all meats—especially

organ meats—are particularly enriched in purines. This combination of high quantities of alcohol and purine-rich foods was literally a recipe for disaster. Not surprisingly, this was considered an affliction of the affluent. We can imagine that gout has been essentially nonexistent as a condition for most of human history. Hunter-gatherers do not consume the dietary components that lead to this affliction, nor did agriculturalists for most of their history. This is a modern ailment: a direct result of the fact that we have this discordance between our

Figure 16.26: An Obese Gouty Man Drinking Punch with Two Companions (Wellcome Trust Images, colored etching by J. Gillray 1799).

Figure 16.27: Gluten is the common name for the proteins in certain grains.

hunter-gatherer biological selves and our modern dietary behavior.

Celiac disease, also known as gluten intolerance, is a genetic disorder that affects at least 1 in 133 Americans. It is estimated that perhaps one percent of the American population has celiac disease (Rewers 2005). Celiac disease (CD) is a lifelong inherited autoimmune condition that can occur in children and adults. When people with CD eat foods that contain gluten, it creates an immune-mediated toxic reaction. It is an autoimmune digestive disease that damages the villi of the small intestine and interferes with absorption of nutrients from food. Even small amounts of gluten in foods can induce symptoms in those affected. Gluten is the common name for the proteins in certain grains. These proteins are found in all forms of wheat (including durum, semolina, spelt, kamut, einkorn, and faro) and related grains like rye, barley, and triticale (Di Sabatino and Corazza 2009). The disease mostly affects people of European (especially northern European) descent, but recent studies show that it also affects Hispanic, Black, and Asian populations as well. Symptoms of celiac disease can range from the classic features such as diarrhea, dermatitis, irritability, weight loss, and malnutrition, to latent symptoms such as isolated nutrient deficiencies with no gastrointestinal symptoms (Wiley and Allen 2009). It is estimated that 83 percent of Americans who have celiac disease are undiagnosed or misdiagnosed with other conditions. Evidently, between 5–22 percent of celiac patients have an immediate family member (first-degree relative) who also

Figure 16.28: Ancient Egyptian farmer from the Burial Chamber of Sennudem.

has celiac. Celiac disease can lead to a number of other disorders including infertility, reduced bone density, neurological disorders, some cancers, and other autoimmune diseases.

Humans first started to cultivate grains in the Neolithic period (beginning about 9500 BCE) in the Fertile Crescent in western Asia, and it is likely that celiac disease did not occur before this time. When we look at diets around the world, we expect to find evidence of celiac only in groups who consume wheat, oats, barley, rye, or buckwheat. Thus, it probably did not occur in groups that relied principally on corn (like in the Americas), rice (east and south Asia) and other cultigens like taro, manioc, and millet (Wiley and Allen 2005). Some suggest that celiac disease happened most frequently in groups who have had little historic exposure to wheat or other gluten-containing cultigens (Simoons 1981). We would then expect that groups in the Middle East—where domestication first occurred (and whose populations have been consuming wheat for the longest period of time)—should have the lowest rates of celiac disease. However, this does not appear to be the case, as Middle Eastern groups appear to demonstrate the same levels of celiac disease as northern Europeans, in an area where domestication occurred much later in time (Rostami et al. 2004). Interestingly, as wheat (traditionally a staple of the West) is becoming a commonly consumed staple in south Asia, particularly among the middle and upper classes, celiac disease is now widely recognized in this region today, where historically the rates have been very low (Accomando and Cataldo 2004, Lindenbaum 1987).

The earliest skeletal case of celiac disease comes from the Roman port colony of Cosa, southwest of Tuscany in Italy during the first century AD. At this site, the skeleton of an 18-to-20-year-old young female showing clinical signs of malnutrition (short stature, osteoporosis, linear enamel hypoplasia, and cribra orbitalia) was discovered. These indirect signs of anemia were interpreted as indicative of celiac disease. In order to confirm the diagnosis of celiac disease, Gasbarrini et al. (2012) extracted DNA from parts of the skeleton, and studied **HLA polymorphisms** known to be involved in susceptibility to celiac disease. The young female displays the HLA DQ 2.5 haplotype, which is associated with the highest risk of celiac disease. The traditional Roman diet was rich in wheat products, and therefore gluten. The authors suggest that the death of this young female resulted from severe malnutrition, rooted in celiac disease. The possibility of poor availability of food was excluded, as there are multiple indicators that she came from a wealthy family. This includes the jewelry found with her and the overall quality of the tomb (Gasbarrini et al. 2010). A final tale involves the increased rates of intestinal and digestive disorders that accompany the agricultural diet. Many conditions involving the intestinal and digestive tracts have been linked to low levels of fiber in the modern diet. We have already discussed the fact that the modern "civilized" diet is associated with far lower levels of dietary fiber than the traditional hunter-gatherer diet. As a result, for potentially millions of years, our intestinal and digestive systems have

Figure 16.29: Portrait of a Roman Woman (Anselm Feuerbach,1862/66).

been accustomed to processing large quantities of wild vegetable matter daily. A lack of adequate dietary fiber is linked to constipation; this in turn is related to increased frequencies of conditions such as hiatal hernia, diverticulitis, varicose veins, and hemorrhoids (Trowell and Burkitt 1981, Cohen 1989). The loss of dietary fiber also seems to lead to a reduced number of bowel movements, which means that stools spend a longer time in the intestinal tract. This leads the intestinal wall to have an increased period of exposure to microbes associated with decay. Some suggest that elevated exposure to these microbes or their by-products

Figure 16.30: Fried chicken and soda—high fat, high sugar Western modern diet.

is related to increased frequencies of appendicitis and cancers of the colon, rectum, and small intestine (Trowell and Burkitt 1981, Story and Kritchevsky 1980, Hughes and Jones 1985, Basu et al. 1973, Cohen 1989). In addition, low dietary fiber has also been linked to the development of gallstones (Story and Kritchevsky 1980, Basu et al. 1973).

Clearly (and these are only a few of a much wider number of cases that could be discussed), dietary behavior has a tremendous impact upon health. The shift from hunting and gathering to intensive agriculture led to a fairly generally accepted downward spiral in terms of overall nutritional quality. There is no question that the quantity of food increased dramatically, as did our ability to store food for a later date. However, pellagra, celiac disease, and beriberi are not conditions that plagued our hunter-gatherer ancestors. Gout, like obesity and diabetes, is really a disease of affluence. The increased fats, carbohydrate, and sugar levels of the modern Western diet predisposes us to develop these conditions, which we know are essentially absent or very geographically restricted in the historic and archaeological past.

CHANGING OUR WORLD: HUMAN BEHAVIOR AND OUR DISEASE EXPERIENCE

When we go over to watch the football game with our friend who has the sniffles or take a sip of water from the cup of our coughing friend, the fact that we have just been complicit in our exposure to disease does not enter our minds. Every day, we humans engage in behaviors that either protect us or place us at increased risk for disease. Sometimes we engage in behaviors that substantially reduce our risk of disease: when we get vaccinated, quit smoking, or raise our houses on stilts above the fly zone of malaria-carrying mosquitoes. Humans are smart (usually), and over time, we tend to learn effective countermeasures to some disease stressors. However, we must remember that humans are the most widely dispersed species geographically on Earth. This means we have had to adapt to a remarkable number of diverse ecosystems over very long periods of time. These adjustments and accommodations are a work in progress, but what has already been achieved occurs in both the biological and cultural realms. In this section, we will look at how human culture (particularly agriculture and population movement) has dramatically altered the relationship we have to the pathogens in our environment. This is where biology and culture collide!

In Chapter 14, we discussed the serious threat that malaria represents to survival in much of the tropical and subtropical world when we mentioned the development of sickle cell trait. **Malaria** is a very ancient disease, and it has likely plagued human (and ancestral) populations for millions of years. We know from many documentary sources that malaria was a serious problem in the ancient world, with descriptions of the disease from China, India, and Mediterranean Europe in particular. The disease ravaged populations in the United States (both George Washington and Abraham Lincoln suffered from malaria) well into the 20th century; parts of Europe battled the disease until after World War II. An indication of how prolific and deadly the disease could be is reflected in the ancient Chinese myth describing the three demons that bring disease. One of the demons carries a hammer that causes a pounding, painful headache; another demon carries a bucket of ice water to chill the victim; and the third carries a stove to cause fever (Learmonth 1988, Wiley and Allen 2009).

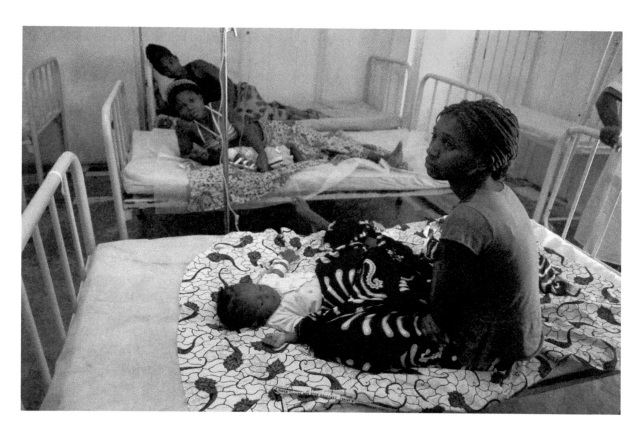

Figure 16.31: Woman sits while her sick children are treated for malaria at the municipal hospital of M'banza, Congo, Zaire province.

It is estimated that roughly between 350 and 500 million people globally suffer from malaria today, and around 1 million people (mostly children under the age of five years) die from the disease every year. It is the fourth leading cause of death in children under the age of five years (Centers for Disease Control 2008). The burden of disease is overwhelmingly carried by sub-Saharan Africans, as 60 percent of all malarial cases and roughly 80 percent of malarial deaths take place in this region (Centers for Disease Control 2008). There are four separate species of *Plasmodium* that transmit malaria; the less severe forms (*P. ovale, P. vivax,* and *P. malariae*) have a longer evolutionary history with humans and our hominid and primate ancestors. The acute severe form of the disease is caused by *Plasmodium falciparum*—probably a more recent variant—and accounts for roughly 95 percent of all malarial deaths. The disease is transmitted in sub-Saharan Africa by two species of the genus *Anopheles*. Some scholars argue that prior to horticulture and more intensive cultivation in Africa, when people were mobile hunter-gatherers, the rates of malaria were relatively low. *Anopheles* mosquitoes feed off of other African mammals, and the infection of humans was relatively rare and accidental. Livingstone (1958) presents an explanation for changes observed over time in the sickle cell gene. He argues that many thousands of years ago,

Figure 16.32: *Anopheles gambiae* mosquito.

the African continent was not a good environment for malaria, since it was mostly covered by dense forests; the mosquitoes that transmit the disease prefer sunny conditions and stagnant water. Dense forest prevents much sunlight from reaching the ground, and little water also accumulates on the ground in this type of

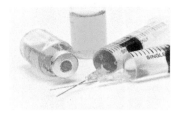

Figure 16.33: Vaccine with hypodermic syringe and needle.

ecosystem. Far fewer mosquitoes around, far fewer infections from things like malaria and yellow fever.

This situation changed dramatically, though, with the advent of agriculture and the movement of iron-using, Bantu-speaking peoples in sub-Saharan Africa around 2000 years ago. Vast areas of forest were cleared for agriculture (often employing the slash-and burn technique), and this greatly improved the breeding possibilities for *Anopheles* mosquitoes. The permanent settlement of people in these cleared areas was an ideal situation for malaria to thrive: mosquitoes now have a sunny location associated with small pools of stagnant water, and they have a permanent reservoir of blood meals available. Over time, we became the mammal meal of choice for these mosquito species, with a subsequent dramatic rise in malarial infection. It is not surprising that any mutation that could confer protection against this deadly disease would increase over time in this cultural and natural environment. This illustrates very well the reason for the high frequency of the sickle cell trait in these malarial areas today, as well as demonstrating how human behavior can have profound consequences in terms of disease.

A similar situation can be seen today with one of the most deadly of all African diseases: **African sleeping sickness**. It is seen in the area of Africa known as the tsetse zone, which extends in Africa roughly from 20 degrees north and 20 degrees south,

Figure 16.34: Slash-and-burn agriculture, Madagascar.

an area of over 10 million square miles and larger than the continental United States. The threat of this disease is so severe that it makes farming of ungulates extremely difficult and unprofitable. Just to give a real understanding of how significant a reduction we are talking about, in terms of animal protein, the productivity in the tsetse zone is only 1/70th of that seen in Europe on the equivalent portion of land. The annual loss in terms of dairy products, meat, manure, hides, and animal work hours is roughly $5 billion, and 30 percent of the 150 million cattle in the region are at risk of infection (Sherman 2006). While preventives are available, the cost is absolutely prohibitive for most small-scale African farmers. African sleeping sickness is caused by protozoa of the genus *Trypanosoma*, which are transmitted to humans by the bite of the tsetse fly (genus *Glossina*). The tsetse flies are infected via infected human beings or from animals (ungulates, typically) infected with the human parasites. Other parasite species and subspecies of the *Trypanosoma* genus are pathogenic to animals and cause animal trypanosomiasis in wild and domestic animal species. The disease in cattle is called nagana, a Zulu word meaning "to be depressed." Animals can host the human parasites; thus domestic and wild animals are an important parasite reservoir (WHO 2013).

Sleeping sickness occurs in 36 sub-Saharan Africa countries, and the highest-risk groups are those people who live in rural areas and depend upon hunting, agriculture, fishing, or animal husbandry. *Trypanosoma brucei gambiense* (*T.b.g.*) accounts for more than 98 percent of reported cases of sleeping sickness (WHO

2013). In the first stage, the trypanosomes reproduce in tissue below skin, blood, and lymph. This stage involves bouts of headaches, fever, joint pains, and itching. In the second stage, the parasites cross the blood-brain barrier to infect the central nervous system. This is known as the neurological phase, and involves changes in behavior, sensory disturbances, confusion, and poor coordination. A disturbance of the sleep cycle is an important feature of the second stage of the disease. Without treatment, sleeping sickness is fatal (WHO 2013). We can imagine that hunter-gatherers were probably not really at risk for this

Figure 16.35: Tsetse fly.

condition. It is typically restricted to wild ungulates (hoofed animals who typically have a mild disease experience), and the hunter-gatherers did not have domesticated animals and were mobile. The problem arose when animal husbandry began.

The tsetse zone was one of the very last areas to be permanently inhabited in Africa because of the tremendous disease burden. Many African cultures like the Dinka, Nuer, and the Maasai have large herds of cattle, the principle source of wealth and status. Movement into the tsetse zone had the potential to be disastrous for pastoral groups. We have observed a dramatic rise in African sleeping sickness since the late 19th century; this is a direct result of European colonialism in the region. When Europeans settled in this region of Africa, they brought with them herds of European cattle. Prior to this time, a kind of stand-off developed between humans, domesticated and wild ungulates, and tsetse flies.

With the European cattle came the introduction of a formerly unknown lethal disease into Africa, known as rinderpest. The introduction of rinderpest led to enormous mortality in both wild and domesticated ungulates. This not only had tremendous economic and social consequences, but it also had devastating health consequences. Now, the tsetse fly fed upon another large mammal in the environment—the human—resulting in dramatic increases in human infection (McNeil 1976, Huygelen 1997, Sherman 2006). As the number of grazing animals sharply declined, the savanna grasses grew ever taller, offering new breeding

Figure 16.36: Ploughing with cattle in southwestern Ethiopia, Tsetse Zone.

opportunities for the tsetse flies. The high mortality of domesticated cattle herds led to a dramatic reduction in the animal protein component of the African pastoral diet, leading to increases in conditions like kwashiorkor (protein-energy malnutrition) and reduced resistance to other infections (Sherman 2006, Nash 1969, Lyons 1991, 1992).

The creation of dams has also had devastating consequences in many regions of the world today. No more is this more apparent than in the case of the fluke-worm infection schistosomiasis. The disease **schistosomiasis** results from infection by fluke worms (trematodes), but these flukes differ from other species, in that there are two distinct sexes and they inhabit the blood vessels of the host. Widespread and chronic infection with schistosomiasis is one of the leading health problems in the tropical world today. After malaria, schistosomiasis is the second most socio-economically devastating parasitic disease. Today, roughly 200 to 300 million people in over 70 countries in Africa, Asia, and South America harbor the parasite. Globally, it will kill about 800,000 people annually (Kheir et al. 1990, Mott 1987, Sherman 2006, McNeil 1976). The schistosomes weaken and kill their host by causing a number of unpleasant symptoms such as bladder damage, epilepsy, cirrhosis of the liver, kidney failure, lesions of the lungs, and even cancer. Schistosomiasis is often referred to as bloody-bladder disease because the early sign of the disease, often occurring at puberty, is urine filled with red blood.

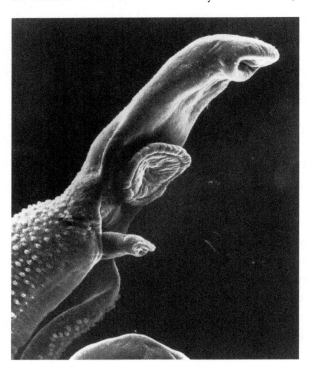

Figure 16.37: Schistosome fluke worm.

Transmission of the disease typically occurs when an individual (usually a child) is swimming or bathing in water contaminated by schistosomes. The fluke worm must complete part of its life cycle in freshwater snails that thrive in warm shallow waters associated with human habitations (wells, irrigation channels, etc.). The schistosome is often commonly transmitted to farmers who wade through shallow water that is infected with the parasite's larvae. This is often the case in areas where wet rice agriculture is traditionally practiced. Records of a disease resembling schistosomiasis extend as far back as ancient Mesopotamia (Sumerian, Assyrian, and Babylonian records). Food production begins in the Middle East circa 8000 BC. The natural flooding of the Nile River provided an ideal environment for the domestication of plants and animals, and large communities soon developed in this region. The earliest civilizations of the Fertile Crescent (Assyrian, Babylonian, Sumerian, and Egyptian) were based upon agriculture, and agriculture requires irrigation. With its shallow ditches, irrigation farming, particularly in tropical regions, created the perfect environment for the freshwater snails that harbor the schistosomes. In Egypt, infection may have originally been a seasonal event that came with the annual flooding of the Nile. However, once the ancient Egyptians established extensive irrigation channels, the disease became a constant year-round problem (Sherman 2006). Today, the construction of dams for hydroelectric power has greatly increased the rates of schistosomiasis. Two of the most disastrous examples came with the building of the Aswan High Dam (completed in 1971) in Egypt and the Volta River Dam in Ghana. In both cases, enormous lakes of standing water were formed with miles of shoreline, and these became the perfect breeding grounds for the freshwater snails that are vectors of the disease. With the Aswan Dam, the annual flooding of the river with its periodic outbreaks of schistosomiasis has now been replaced by an environment that is supplied with a

Figure 16.38: Ancient city of Babylon.

constant supply of irrigation water due to the control of the water levels in Lake Nasser. Now the disease can exist all year round rather than seasonally, and greater numbers of infected snails are now found in the Nile Delta and upstream (Wilkens 1987, Grove 1980). Prior to the construction of the Aswan Dam, the prevalence of schistosomiasis in the Nile Delta was 60 percent, but in the 500-mile portion of the river between Aswan and Cairo (where only annual flooding occurred), the prevalence was only 5 percent. Within four years of the dam's construction, the average prevalence rate between Aswan and Cairo had multiplied by seven (35 percent) (Sherman 2006). In recent years, as a result of the erection of large dam systems, the infection rate has risen to 90 percent or more in areas where the disease traditionally was unknown. In order to eradicate the disease, the chain of transmission must be broken. Besides the administration of effective drug therapy, in order to eradicate the disease, one can target the vectors of schistosomiasis with molluscicides (snails are mollusks) and drainage programs. Further contributing factors to the widespread distribution of schistosomiasis is the rapid deforestation occurring in tropical regions today, the human use of local water as latrines due to inadequate water treatment systems, and the establishment of artificial management systems (Barnes 2005).

Figure 16.39: Aswan Dam, Egypt.

Figure 16.40: Sailor at the Port of Copenhagen (Albert Edelfelt, 1890, Port of Copenhagen).

Long-distance travel has also contributed to increased rates of nutritional and infectious disease. After famine, scurvy is responsible for more suffering than any other nutritional disease in history. It is first described in the 15th century, and it is not merely a coincidence that the disease is described at a time when long sea voyages from Europe became common. **Scurvy** results from a lack of the water-soluble vitamin C. Most animals can produce their own vitamin C, but humans, other primates, fruit-eating bats, and guinea pigs have lost this ability over time. Fresh fruits and vegetables are the best sources of vitamin C,

Figure 16.41: Lemon and lime.

which is essential for normal health. Vitamin C is vital to the production of the protein collagen, a major constituent of connective tissues like tendons and ligaments and the walls of blood vessels. Scurvy is characterized by symptoms such as swollen appendages, exhaustion, swelling and ulceration of the gums, and hemorrhages into the skin and from the mucous membranes. These symptoms make sense in light of the fact that the capillary walls require vitamin C for collagen to retain their permeability and strength. A vitamin C deficiency, scurvy was a common problem for sailors. It results from the monotonous diet of salted meats and the lack of fresh vegetables, fruits, and other sources of vitamin C in the diet. The English were the first to discover the cause of scurvy in the 18th century. After this time, long sea voyages were supplied with large quantities of lemons and limes. The rates of scurvy dropped significantly (Harvie 2002, Carpenter 1988, Sherman 2006).

Ritual behavior is also a major source of disease transmission. For those who practice Christianity, a visit to church on Sundays is often accompanied by participation in Communion. The act of **Communion** is a shared event in the Christian faith. As such, congregations all partake of the wine and bread communally. The sharing of the wine glass during Communion can lead to the transmission of a number of pathogens such as the common cold and influenza. This risk can be avoided by providing the wine in individual glasses. In Yemen, the communal use of ritual ceremonial

Figure 16.42: Holy Communion (Hungarian Codex, 17th century).

baths during certain religious events greatly increases the rates of schistosomiasis exposure. **Kuru** is a prion disease of humans that is related to Creutzfeldt-Jakob disease (CJD). The term kuru derives from the Fore word *kuria/guria* (to shake), a reference to the body tremors that are a classic symptom of the

disease. The Fore also call it the laughing sickness because it is characterized by pathological bursts of laughter. Kuru is a lethal neurological disease that takes between 5 to 20 years to express symptoms (Collinge et al. 2006). Once symptoms begin, death occurs within 12 months. This condition was endemic among the Fore tribe of Papua New Guinea and was confined to that tribe and those nearby populations with whom they practiced intermarriage (Gibbs and Gajdusek 1970). Gajdusek concludes that kuru was transmitted by the ritualistic consumption of the brains of deceased relatives, which was practiced by the Fore. He then proves this hypothesis by successfully transmitting the disease to primates and demonstrating that it had an unusually long incubation period of several years (Gajdusek et al. 1967, Gibbs et al. 1980). Symptoms of the disease include truncal ataxia (uncoordinated movements), preceded by headaches, shaking of the limbs, and joint pain. Some highland peoples of Papua New Guinea practiced ritual cannibalism. Relatives of the deceased consumed their bodies in order to

Figure 16.43: Fore tribesmen, Papua New Guinea.

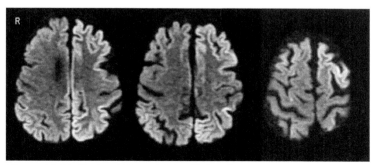

Figure 16.44: Brain of Fore child suffering from kuru.

return their life force to the community. The disease had a very interesting frequency among the Fore, being eight to nine times more prevalent in women and children than in men at its height. This is because the men of the village took the premier pieces and the women and children would eat the rest of the body, including the brain, where the prion was concentrated. There is also the strong possibility that it was passed on to the women and children because it was their responsibility to clean the relative's body after death. Transmission could result from entry of the prion through cuts and sores on the hands. Kuru was already declining among the Fore by the mid-1960s, although cases continued to appear for several more decades. The last sufferer died in 2005. However, the average incubation period of the disease is 14 years, and cases were reported with latencies as long as 40 years or more for those who were most genetically resilient (McElroy and Townsend 2009).

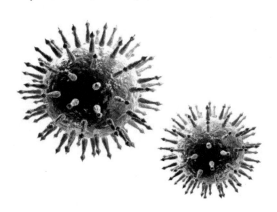

Figure 16.45: Influenza virus.

A final example involves the dreaded influenza virus. **Influenza**—commonly called the flu—is a viral infection that attacks the upper respiratory tract, including the nose, throat, and the major airways leading into the lungs. It is spread through talking, sneezing, and coughing; infection results from droplet inhalation. Generally, the illness caused by influenza is completed within ten days, with an incubation period between one to three days. Typically, influenza infections are not life threatening, with a mortality rate of less than one percent in vulnerable individuals. Symptoms encompass fever, painful frontal headache, backache, sore muscles, exhaustion, reduction in appetite, stuffy, runny nose, and sore throat with dry cough. It is common for dizziness, sweating, sore eyes, and light sensitivity to occur as well. Globally, influenza today is an important infectious disease, with roughly 20 percent of children and 5 percent of all adults developing symptoms. The death rate can be as high as five percent (McNeil 1976, Sherman 2006). Influenza is a "crowd" disease, requiring a large, dense population in order to be maintained over time. Such large, permanent settlements do not appear until the intensification of agriculture. Farmers are associated with far lower levels of mobility than hunter-gatherers. This is a good thing and a bad thing. The good thing is that it finally allows populations to develop levels of immunity to local pathogens. Hunters and gatherers are always moving between a diverse range of different microenvironments that are often associated with different pathogens. This population simply rarely stays in any location long enough to develop any long-term immunity.

Ticks also tend to move away from the disrupted land that surrounds agricultural communities, which would lead to reductions in conditions like Lyme disease, Rocky Mountain spotted fever, and scrub typhus, to name a few. The negative is that you cannot be a farmer, and simply wander off and leave your crops and animal herds unattended. Permanent structures are a must, and they are attractive to vermin and insect species (who are attracted to stored foods, garbage, and human and animal waste) who are often vectors for pathogens. For example, the aedine mosquitoes that carry both dengue (breakbone) fever and yellow fever have a preference for permanent habitations; they are usually associated with standing water, either inside or outside the structures. The building of permanent structures also is associated with poor air circulation, and this greatly increases the risk of airborne diseases such as influenza and the common cold. These viruses do not easily survive outside, and they are easily transmitted in warm, poorly ventilated buildings. In northern climates, the rates of respiratory infections like the common cold and influenza dramatically rise during

Figure 16.46: Rooftops of a Dogon village near the Bandiagara Escarpment, Mali.

the winter. There is little air ventilation because windows are closed for several months. In addition, people tend to spend much more time inside and in closer contact in the winter, which promotes transmission from person to person.

The increased frequency of respiratory ailments in the winter in temperate climes may also be related to a seasonal decline in the amount of ultraviolet radiation. This reduction may reduce the likelihood of the virus being damaged or killed by direct radiation damage or indirect effects (ozone concentration). It is also suggested that colder and drier conditions may lead to dehydration of the mucous membranes, and this inhibits the body from effectively defending against respiratory infection. The virus may also remain longer on exposed surfaces (doorknobs, telephones, etc.) in colder temperatures. (Shaman and Kohn 2009, Lowen et al. 2007, Sherman 2006).

Every day, people engage in countless behaviors that can either directly or indirectly affect their health in a complex number of ways. We are a product of the culture in which we grow up. Dietary choices and preparation techniques are learned within a specific cultural framework. The economic transition from a hunter-gatherer economic strategy to an agricultural strategy resulted in profound changes in the quality and quantity of food. There is a complex and dynamic interrelationship between the environment, human biology, and human behavior. Often, we engage in behaviors with little thought as to their ultimate impact

Figure 16.47: Winter Landscape with Snowfall near Antwerp (Lucas van Valckenborch, 1575).

Figure 16.48: Port Sulphur, Louisiana after Hurricane Katrina.

upon our individual or group health. We do this at our own peril, and we must continue to question and reevaluate our choices in terms of our role in the allocation of essential resources. The way we manage this relationship with the natural world will determine how long we remain a successful species in evolutionary terms. As much as we like to think that human ingenuity, progress, and technology can buffer us from the natural world, this is a very dangerous bubble within which to exist. Events like tsunamis, hurricanes, disease epidemics, and famine remind us that we cannot control everything.

CRITICAL REASONING QUESTIONS

- What are some of the defining features of the hunter-gatherer lifestyle? How does this influence their relationship to disease-causing organisms?
- How did the transition to agriculture change the quality and quantity of foods?
- Name two diseases that result from affluence. How about two diseases associated with poverty?
- Name three ways in which human behavior can influence levels of health in a population.
- How did the practice of slash-and-burn agriculture in Africa greatly increase people's risk of exposure to malaria?
- How can ritual behavior affect your health?
- Write a list of some the behaviors you engaged in for the last 24 hours. Did you get enough sleep? What did you eat? Did you shower? Drive? and so on. How do these behaviors affect your risk of illness?

REFERENCES AND SUGGESTED READINGS

Accomando, S., and F. Cataldo (2004). "The global village of celiac disease."'. *Digestive and Liver Disease* 36(7):492–498.

Aiello L. C., and P. Wheeler (1995). "The expensive-tissue hypothesis." *Current Anthropology* 36(2):199–221.

Aufderheide, A. C., and C. Rodriguez-Martin (1998). *The Cambridge encyclopedia of human paleopathology*. Cambridge, UK: Cambridge University Press.

Azevedo, M. J. (1978). *Disease in African history: An introductory survey and case studies*. Durham, NC: Duke University Press.

Barnes, E. (2005). *Diseases and human evolution*. Albuquerque: University of New Mexico Press.

Basu, T. K., et al. (1977). Interrelationships of nutrition and cancer. *EFN* 2:193–199.

Boaz, N. T., and A. J. Almquist (2002). *Biological anthropology: A synthetic approach to human evolution*, 2nd ed. Upper Saddle River, NJ: Prentice Hall.

Carpenter, K. (1988). *The history of scurvy and vitamin C*. Cambridge, UK: Cambridge University Press.

Centers for Disease Control and Prevention (2008). "Malaria facts: Malaria worldwide." http//www.cdc.gov/malaria /facts.htm#WorldMalaria

Cohen, M. N. (1989). *Health and the rise of civilization*. New Haven, CT: Yale University Press.

Cohen, M. N., and G. J. Armelagos, eds. (1984). *Paleopathology at the origins of agriculture*. Orlando, FL: Academic Press.

Cohen, M. N. and G. M. M. Crane-Kramer (2007). *Ancient health: Skeletal indicators of agricultural and economic intensification*. Gainesville: University of Florida Press.

Colagiuri, S., and J. Brand-Miller (March 2002). "The 'carnivore connection': Evolutionary aspects of insulin resistance." *European Journal of Clinical Nutrition* 56 (1):S30–S35.

Collinge, J., J. Whitfield, E. McKintosh, et al. (June 2006). "Kuru in the 21st century: An acquired human prion disease with very long incubation periods." *Lancet* 367 (9528):2068–2074.

Collins, D. (1973). *Background to archaeology: Britain in its European setting*, rev. ed. Cambridge, UK: Cambridge University Press.

Cordain L., J. B. Miller, S. B. Eaton, et al. (March 2000). "Plant-animal subsistence ratios and macronutrient energy estimations in worldwide hunter-gatherer diets." *American Journal of Clinical Nutrition* 71 (3):682–692.

Cordain, L., J. B. Miller, S. B. Eaton, and N. Mann (December 2000). "Macronutrient estimations in hunter-gatherer diets." *American Journal of Clinical Nutrition* 72 (6):1589–1592.

Cordain, L., S. B. Eaton, J. B. Miller, et al. (March 2002). "The paradoxical nature of hunter-gatherer diets: Meat based, yet non-atherogenic." *European Journal of Clinical Nutrition* 56 (Suppl 1):S42–S52.

Cordain, L., S. B. Eaton, A. Sebastian, et al. (2005). "Origins and evolution of the Western diet: Health implications for the 21st century." *American Journal of Clinical Nutrition* 81 (2):341–354.

DeGroot, L. J. (1975). "Endemic goiter." In P. B. Beeson and W. McDermott, eds., *Textbook of Medicine*, 14th ed., pp. 1727–1728. Philadelphia: W. B. Saunders.

Di Sabatino, A., and G. R. Corazza (April 2009). "Coeliac disease." *Lancet* 37 (9673):1480–1493.

Eaton, S. B. (2003). "An evolutionary perspective on human physical activity: Implications for health." *Comparative Biochemistry and Physiology. Part A, Molecular and Integrative Physiology* 136 (1):153–159.

El-Najjar, M. Y. (1977). "Maize, malarias and the anemias in the pre-Columbian New World." *Yearbook of Physical Anthropology* 28:329–337.

Elton, S. (2008). "Environments, adaptations and evolutionary medicine: Should we be eating a 'stone age' diet?" In P. O'Higgins and S. Elton, eds., *Medicine and Evolution: Current Applications, Future Prospects*. London: Taylor and Francis.

Frisancho, A. R. (2012). *Human adaptation and accommodation. Enlarged and revised edition of human adaptation.* Ann Arbor: University of Michigan Press.

Fukuwatari, T., and K. Shibata (2008). "Urinary water-soluble vitamins and their metabolite contents as nutritional markers for evaluating vitamin intakes in young Japanese women." *Journal of. Nutr. Sci. Vitaminol.* 54 (3):223–229.

Gasbarrini, G., L. Miele, G. R. Corazza, and A. Gasbarrini (August 2010). "When was celiac disease born? The Italian case from the archeologic site of Cosa." *Journal of Clinical Gastroenterology* 44(7):502–503.

Gajdusek, D. C., C. J. Gibbs Jr., and M. Alpers (1967). "Transmission and passage of experimental 'kuru' to chimpanzees." *Science* 155 (3759):212–214.

Gibbs, C. J. Jr., and D. C. Gajdusek (1970). "Kuru: Pathogenesis and characterization of virus." *American Journal of Tropical Medicine and Hygiene* 19 (1):138–145.

Gibbs C. J., H. L. Amyx, A. Bacote, et al. (August 1980). "Oral transmission of kuru, Creutzfeldt-Jakob disease, and scrapie to nonhuman primates." *Journal of Infectious Diseases* 142 (2):205–208.

Gremillion, K. J. (2011). *Ancestral appetites: Food in prehistory.* Cambridge, UK: Cambridge University Press.

Grove, D. I. (1980). "Schistosomes, snails and man." In N. F. Stanley and R. A. Joske, eds., *Changing Disease Patterns and Human Behavior*, pp. 187–204. New York: Academic Press.

Guggenheim, K. Y. (1981). *Nutrition and nutritional diseases.* Lexington, MA: Collamore Press, D. C. Heath.

Harvie, D. (2002). *Limeys: The story of one man's war against ignorance, the establishment and the deadly scurvy.* Phoenix Mill, UK: Sutton.

Hibbert, C. (1982). *Africa explored: Europeans in the Dark Continent 1769–1889.* London: Allan Lane.

Hughes, R. E., and E. Jones (1985). Intake of dietary fiber and age of menarche. *AHB* 12:325–332.

Huygelen, C. (1997). "The immunization of cattle against rinderpest in eighteenth-century Europe." *Medical History* 41 (2):182–196.

Jelliffe, E. F., and D. B. Jelliffe, eds. (1982). *Adverse effects of food.* New York: Plenum.

Jones, M. (2007). *Feast: Why humans share food.* Oxford, UK: Oxford University Press.

Kheir, M. M., I. A. Eltoum, A. M. Saad, et al. (February 1999). "Mortality due to schistosomiasis mansoni: A field study in Sudan." *America Journal of Tropical Medicine and Hygiene* 60 (2):307–310.

Kirschmann, J. D. (1975). *Nutritional almanac.* New York: McGraw-Hill.

Knowler, W. C., D. J. Pettitt, P. J. Savage, and P. H. Bennett (1980). "Diabetes incidence in Pima Indians: Contributions of obesity and parental diabetes." *American Journal of Epidemiology* 113(2):144–156.

Kopp, W. (May 2006). "The atherogenic potential of dietary carbohydrate." *Preventive Medicine* 42 (5):336–342.

Learmonth, A. (1988). *Disease ecology: An introduction.* New York: Basil Blackwell.

Lee, R. B. (1968). "What hunters do for a living, or how to make out on scarce resources." In R. B. Lee and I. Devore, eds., *Man the hunter*, pp. 30–48. Chicago: Aldine.

Leonard, W. R. (2000). "Human nutritional evolution." In S. Stinson, B. Bogin, R. Huss-Ashmore, and D. O'Rourke, eds., *Human Biology: An Evolutionary and Biocultural Perspective*, pp. 295–343. New York: John Wiley and Sons.

Leonard, W. R. (December 2002). "Food for thought: Dietary change was a driving force in human evolution." *Scientific American* 287 (6):106–115.

Lieberman, S., and N. Bruning (1990). *The real vitamin and mineral book.* New York: Avery Group.

Lindenbaum, S. (1979). *Kuru sorcery: Disease and danger in the New Guinea highlands.* Palo Alto, CA: Mayfield.

——— (1987). "Loaves and fishes in Bangladesh." In M. Harris and E. B. Ross, eds., *Food and Evolution*, pp. 427–443. Philadelphia: Temple University Press.

——— (June 2005). "Palaeolithic diet ('stone age' diet)." *Scandinavian Journal of Food & Nutrition* 49 (2):75–77.

Livingstone, F. B. (1958). "Anthropological implications of sickle cell gene distribution in West Africa." *American Anthropologist* 60:533–562.

Lowen, A. C., S. Mubareka, J. Steel, and P. Palese (October 2007). "Influenza virus transmission is dependent on relative humidity and temperature." *PLoS Pathogens* 3 (10):e151.

Lyons, M. (1991). African sleeping sickness: An historical review. *International Journal of STD and AIDS* 2 (Supplement 1):20–25.

——— (1992). *The colonial disease: A social history of sleeping sickness in northern Zaire, 1900–1940*. Cambridge, UK: Cambridge University Press.

Mann, N. (September 2007). "Meat in the human diet: An anthropological perspective." *Nutrition & Dietetics* 64 (4):S102–S107.

Marlowe, F. W. (2005). "Hunter-gatherers and human evolution." *Evolutionary Anthropology* 14 (2):15294.

McElroy, A., and P. K. Townsend (2009). *Medical anthropology in ecological perspective*, 2nd ed. Boulder, CO: Westview Press.

McNeill, W. (1976). *Plagues and peoples*. New York: Anchor Press/Doubleday.

Milton, K. (2002). "Hunter-gatherer diets: Wild foods signal relief from diseases of affluence." In P. S. Ungar and M. F. Teaford, *Human Diet: Its Origins and Evolution*, pp. 111–22. Westport, CT: Bergin and Garvey.

Molleson, T. (1989). "Social implications of the mortality patterns of juveniles from Poundbury Camp, Romano-British cemetery." *Anthropologische*r *Anzeiger* 47:27–38.

Molnar, S., and I. M. Molnar (2000). *Environmental change and human survival: Some dimensions of human ecology.* Upper Saddle River, NJ: Prentice Hall.

Mott, K. E. (1987). "Schistosomiasis control." In D. Rollinson, and A. J. G. Simpson, eds., *The Biology of Schistosomes: From Genes to Latrines*, pp. 429–450. London: Academic Press.

Nash, T. A. M. (1969). *Africa's bane: The tsetse fly*. London: Collins.

Neel, J. V. (1962). "Diabetes mellitus: A 'thrifty' genotype rendered detrimental by 'progress?'" *American Journal of Human Genetics* 14 (4):353–362.

——— (1982). "The thrifty genotype revisited." In J. Kobberling and R. Tattersall, eds., *The Genetics of Diabetes Mellitus*, pp. 933. New York: Academic Press.

——— (2009). "The 'thrifty genotype' in 1998." *Nutrition Reviews* 57 (5):2.

O'Keefe, J. H., and L. Cordain (January 2004). "Cardiovascular disease resulting from a diet and lifestyle at odds with our Paleolithic genome: How to become a 21st-century hunter-gatherer." *Mayo Clinic Proceedings* 79 (1):101–108.

Pfeiffer, C. C. (1975). *Mental and elemental nutrients*. New Canaan, CT: Keats Publishing.

Relethford, J. H. (2005). *The human species: An introduction to biological anthropology*, 6th ed. New York: McGraw-Hill.

Rewers, M. (April 2005). "Epidemiology of celiac disease: What are the prevalence, incidence, and progression of celiac disease?" *Gastroenterology* 128 (4 Suppl 1):S47–S51.

Richards, M. P. (December 2002). "A brief review of the archaeological evidence for Palaeolithic and Neolithic subsistence." *European Journal of Clinical Nutrition* 56 (12):1270–1278.

Roe, D. A. (1973). *A plague of corn: The social history of pellagra*. Ithaca, NY: Cornell University Press.

Rostami, K., R. Malekzadeh, et al. (2004). "Coeliac disease in Middle Eastern countries: A challenge for the evolutionary history of this complex disorder?" *Digestive and Liver Disease* 36(10):694–697.

Scrimshaw, N. S. (1975). "Deficiencies of individual nutrients: Vitamin diseases." In P. B. Beeson and W. McDermott, eds., *Textbook of Medicine*, 14th ed., pp. 1368–1375. Philadelphia: W. B. Saunders.

Shaman J., and M. Kohn (March 2009). "Absolute humidity modulates influenza survival, transmission, and seasonality." *Proceedings of the National Academy of Sciences USA* 106 (9):3243–3248.

Sherman, I. W. (2006). *The power of plagues*. Washington, DC: ASM Press.

Simoons, F. J. (1981). "Celiac disease as a geographic problem." In D. N. Walcher and N. Kretchmer, eds., *Food, Nutrition and Evolution: Food as an Environmental Factor in the Genesis of Human Variability*, pp. 179–199. New York: Masson.

Sodeman, W. A. (1956). "Nutritional factors: Protein and fat metabolism." In W. A. Sodeman, ed., *Pathologic Physiology: Mechanisms of Disease*, pp. 25–55. Philadelphia: W. B. Saunders.

Story, J. A., and D. Kritchevsky (1980). "Nutrients with special functions: Dietary fiber." In R. B. Alfin-Slater and D. Kritchevsky, eds., *Human Nutrition*. New York: Plenum.

Trowell, H. C., and D. P. Burkitt, eds. (1981). *Western diseases: Their emergence and prevention*. London: Edward Arnold.

Voegtlin, W. L. (1975). *The stone age diet: Based on in-depth studies of human ecology and the diet of man*. New York: Vantage Press.

Wiley, A. S., and J. S. Allen (2009). *Medical anthropology: A biocultural approach*. New York: Oxford University Press.

Wilkins, H. A. (1987). "The epidemiology of schistosome infections in man." In D. Rollinson, and A. J. G. Simpson, eds., *The Biology of Schistosomes: From Genes to Latrines*, pp. 279–397. London: Academic Press.

Winick, M. (1980). *Nutrition in health and disease*. New York: John Wiley.

Wood, C. S. (1979). *Human sickness and health: A biocultural view*. Palo Alto, CA: Mayfield Publishing.

World Health Organization (June 2013). African sleeping sickness. http://www.who.int/mediacentre/factsheets/fs259/en/

Young, D. A. (1969). *Last voyage of the unicorn*. Toronto: Clarke, Irwin.

17

Where Do We Go From Here?

By Gillian Crane-Kramer

The form of social organization in which we have lived for most our history as a family is the band. Hunter-gatherers typically live in small, mobile groups without any permanent structures or domesticated species. These nomadic human groups—who move around their territory according to the seasons or resource depletion—leave a very small signature on the natural landscape. Hunter-gatherers do not clear land for planting; they do not build irrigation channels; and they do not live in large, crowded settlements. They also do not typically drive other species to extinction by overconsumption or habitat destruction. They do not pollute the oceans, damage the ozone layer, or engage in rapid deforestation. You get the picture now, I think. When we lived as these small mobile populations, we lived as part of the natural ecosystem, rather than separate from it. In a funny kind of way, incipient (early) agriculturalists probably had the best set-up of all. They still lived in small communities, and they still obtained some of their food from wild plants and animals, as well as domesticates.

With the intensification of agriculture came a dramatic population increase in a very short period of time. Until the development of agriculture around 10,000 years ago, it is estimated that the world population stabilized at about three million people, living a hunting-gathering lifestyle that is associated with a low population density. The total world population probably never exceeded 15 million inhabitants before the invention of agriculture (Teller 2009). As agriculture intensified and the supply of food increased, population continued to increase. There has been an accelerated and continuous increase in world population growth from the end of the Great Famine and the Black Death in the

257

Figure 17.1: Hadzabe men starting fire, Tanzania.

Figure 17.2: Hadzabe hut, Tanzania.

mid-14th century, when the population was around 370 million people (Birabin 1980). We are now at over six billion people, with numbers that increasingly place a strain upon our natural resources. There is no organism in the history of Earth that has so profoundly altered the natural world. These dramatic alterations of the landscape lead to the emergence of new and complex challenges—not only for us, but for all the other creatures on Earth who have to survive what we do. (Sorry, I know that sounds a little preachy, but we really should be the guardians of this planet, rather than the alternative.) We could write several books on how the modern world is influencing the course of evolution, but we will have to let a few examples suffice.

One of the serious issues that concerns the overall health and well-being of the world's biodiversity is the enormous **deforestation** that is occurring at a very alarming rate. Roughly 30 percent of the world's land masses are covered by forests. What is tremendously disturbing is that parcels as large as Panama are lost each year. At this rate, the world's rain forests could completely disappear in a hundred years at the current rate of deforestation (National Geographic 2013). Deforestation occurs for a number of reasons. Profit from lumbering is a major incentive, but the biggest factor involved in the clearing of the world's forests is agriculture. Cleared land is required for planting, grazing of animals, and the erection of ever larger human habitations. The lumber industry, which is responsible for supplying the world's wood and paper products, is responsible for a huge level of deforestation annually. Deforestation due to lumbering has led to serious outbreaks of yellow fever, both in West Africa and Central and South America and dengue fever in the New World. Both yellow and dengue fevers are arboviruses that are carried by mosquitoes, ticks, sand flies, and midges (Lederberg et al. 1992). We humans appear to be accidental victims who become infected when we intrude upon the habitat of the normal hosts of the vectors (birds and mammals). Both of these illnesses can present with a range of symptoms that are related to the form of virus transmitted and the immune status of the host. Milder forms of the disease can express influenza-like symptoms, with or without joint pain (although dengue fever isn't called breakbone fever for nothing). More severe expressions of disease include the development of encephalitis and hemorrhagic symptoms (Benenson 1995). **Yellow fever** is transmitted through the bite of a female Aedes mosquito (typically *Ae. africanus* and *Ae. simpsoni* in Africa and *Ae. aegypti* in the New World). This virus has probably coexisted with West African tropical monkey species for millennia; infection typically does not result in a serious disease experience in these primates. However, woodcutters in both Africa and Central/South America move into these tropical zones and fell trees that bring both the monkey hosts and the infected mosquitoes to the ground. The mosquitoes are happy to feed on the closest convenient primate hosts—in this case, the woodcut-

Figure 17.3: The city of Toronto, Canada, at night.

ters (Barnes 2005). These men carry the infection back to their villages, where local mosquitoes become infected. The increased clearing of tropical forest for agriculture also has brought humans into closer contact with primate hosts. The mosquito species can adjust to reproducing in stagnant water associated with human habitations, instead of laying their eggs high up in the rain forest canopy.

Thus, humans, monkeys, and mosquitoes are brought into ever closer contact, with outbreaks of yellow fever resulting (Cooper and MacCallum 1984). In this way, yellow fever (and dengue fever as well in the tropical Americas and Southeast Asia) is transferred from high up in the rain forest canopy to human settlements; even today, this disease has become a common childhood illness in West Africa (Burnet and White

Figure 17.4: Deforestation south of Sante Fé, Panamá.

Figure 17.5: Deer in the grass.

1972). In addition to the removal of trees, the building of access roads in remote forested environments leads to increasing damage. When we think of deforestation, we typically think of the removal of trees, but just as important is the loss of essential grasslands around the world. Grassland/savanna environments are very important because grass species fulfill a number of functions. Many grass species fix nitrogen and moisture in the topsoil; they physically prevent erosion; and they are essential food resources for a wide range of different ruminant species.

The increased incidence of Lyme disease is another good example of how disrupting our environment changes our risk of disease. Since 1980, **Lyme disease** has become the most common insect-borne disease in North America. This is directly related to alterations in land use patterns over the last two centuries (Lederberg et al. 1992). Throughout the last two centuries, enormous swathes of previously forested land have been cleared for agriculture. This massive deforestation dramatically changed the life cycle of the vector tick that carries the condition because there was a dramatic reduction in their host animal habitat (particularly for the deer), and Lyme disease then became a rare disease (Barnes 2005). As farmland became available in the American Midwest, many farmers abandoned their eastern farms and moved. This al-

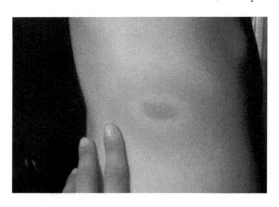

Figure 17.6: Bull's eye rash of Lyme disease.

lowed a regeneration of the eastern woodlands, and by the mid-20th century, offered an ideal dense regrowth forest environment for white-footed mice and white-tailed deer, the natural hosts of these ticks. As humans and these animal vectors were brought into ever closer proximity, the rates of Lyme disease have increased tremendously. Many European countries are also experiencing increasing rates of Lyme disease due to massive reforestation programs implemented after World War II (Lederberg et al. 1992).

Deforestation has a negative impact on the environment in a number of ways. Perhaps the most serious and worrisome impact is the loss of habitat for millions of species; it is estimated that as much as 70 percent of the planet's land animals and plants live in forests. It is interesting (and terrifying, actually) to think that if roughly 70 percent of the Earth's terrestrial biodiversity is found in forests, then 70 percent of the world's land pathogens are also there. The fact that we are rapidly moving into these areas without any concern as to the hidden terrors we might unleash is really quite extraordinary, certainly not thinking ahead. In addition, we must accept that with this wide-scale deforestation comes the potential extinction of a countless number of species, and consequently a dramatic reduction in global biodiversity. Deforestation also drives climate change. Forest soils are moist because of the vegetation's extensive root systems, but without the protection accorded by sun-blocking trees, they quickly dry out. Trees also help sustain the water cycle by returning

Figure 17.7: Timber from a Malaysian forest at sawmill for export.

water vapor back into the atmosphere. Without trees to fill these functions, many former forest lands can quickly become barren deserts (National Geographic 2013). Additionally, deforestation also results in more extreme fluctuations in temperature as the trees block the sun's rays during the day and hold in heat at night. Finally, trees also play a critical role in absorbing the greenhouse gases that lead to global warming. Fewer forests means that larger amounts of greenhouse gases will enter our atmosphere. In turn, this will increase the speed and severity of global warming (National Geographic 2013).

Global warming also poses a serious threat to a wide number of plant and animal species. Based upon the analysis of ancient paleoclimate, it appears that the surface temperatures in the mid- to late-20th century are warmer than in the last 600 years—in many regions, thousands of years (Nicholls et al. 1996). Of great concern is how rapidly the temperature is increasing. From the period between 1906 and 2005, the global average temperature increased by 0.74 degrees C, and by 2100, the average global temperature is estimated to rise between 1.8 degrees and 4 degrees C (Solomon et al. 2007). There is no question that

Figure 17.8: Global warming—cloud cover over Elephant Island, Southern Ocean.

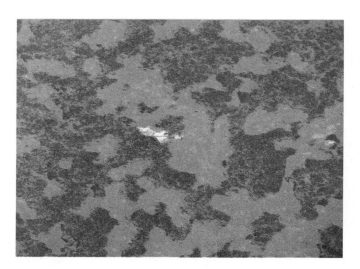

Figure 17.9: Bloom of cyanobacteria (blue-green algae).

global warming has occurred, and although part of this process may result from cyclical global changes in weather, scientists are also aware that it is primarily caused by increasing concentrations of greenhouse gases produced by human activities such as the burning of fossil fuels and processes like deforestation. The planet's warming has led to dramatic changes in our weather patterns, thus allowing both tropical and subtropical diseases to expand their territories. As the disease vectors increase their range, we must be aware that formerly absent conditions may become established in new regions. Malaria once extended in North America from the Deep South right up to Montreal, and it may again. Conditions like the SARS virus, the H5N1 influenza virus, Rift Valley fever, and West Nile virus all flourish in warm conditions; it is likely that we will experience a fairly rapid increase in their range globally (Nakazawa 2008). It is also possible that global warming will allow the vectors that carry diseases like dengue fever to survive as far North as New York City (Armelagos 2010).

Global warming presents a myriad of challenges to living creatures. Ocean surface temperatures have also increased substantially over the last 100 years (especially the last 35 years). In the period between 1995 and 2004, scientists recorded the highest average sea surface temperatures ever (Trenberth 2005). This sea surface warming greatly increases the potential for flooding and coastal erosion in low-lying regions. In addition to this warming, this climate change is also associated with the acidification of the oceans, which is the result of higher carbon dioxide levels. Although we do not yet fully understand the full effects of ocean acidification, scientists believe that it might particularly threaten marine shell-forming organisms like coral and their dependent species (Solomon et al. 2007).

There is also great concern that these elevated sea temperatures may threaten many fish populations; for example, the recent slowing of the North Atlantic Gulf Stream might reduce the levels of plankton, a major source of food for fish larvae (Pauly and Alder 2005). A decline in larval fish populations will further impede the recovery of already overexploited species, and this will in turn negatively affect coastal and island populations, where fish is the principal source of dietary protein. Globally, fish represents approximately 16 percent of consumed animal protein. In some areas, it can be higher—as high as 26 percent in some regions of Asia, for example (Frumkin 2010). These reductions in fish also profoundly affect a wide range of bird and mammal species that rely on fish as

Figure 17.10: Blue starfish (*Linckia laevigata*) resting on hard acropora coral, Lighthouse, Ribbon Reefs, Great Barrier Reef, Australia.

major parts of their diets. This increase in temperature and sea level cannot help but have significant effects upon the marine ecosystem at all levels.

In addition, with these rises in temperature, we have witnessed an increase in hurricane and severe weather events (heat waves, floods, wildfires), a considerable decline in the polar ice caps, increases in sea level, increases in dangerous algae blooms, drought ,and desertification, to name a few. Thomas et al. (2004) estimate that between 15 and 37 percent of 1103 endemic or near-endemic known plant and animal species will be committed to extinction

Figure 17.11: Digging for drinking water in a dry riverbed, Turkana, northern Kenya.

by 2050, although it is difficult to assess the actual risk of extinction (Thuiller et al. 2004, Araújo et al. 2005). In terms of the impact upon agriculture, many suggest that drought will greatly exacerbate global malnutrition, which is already at a level of 800 million undernourished people (WHO 2002). Additionally, roughly 1.7 billion people today (roughly one-third of all people on Earth) live in water-stressed regions; this number is estimated to rise to 5 billion people by the year 2025 (Frumkin 2010). The glaciers of the Tibetan plateau are expected to be completely melted by the year 2035; they supply water to over 1 billion people in the dry season (Parry et al. 2007). This reduction in water supplies will lead to increases in diarrheal disease and conditions such as Trachoma (one of the leading causes of blindness in the world), scabies, conjunctivitis, and many more conditions associated with poor hygiene and sanitation and a lack of adequate clean-water supplies (Patz 2001, Patz and Kovats 2002). No pun intended—this is but the tip of the iceberg.

BAD AIR AND FAST TRAVEL: AIR POLLUTION AND THE VIRAL SUPERHIGHWAY

Air pollution is one of the most significant contributors to human illness, including conditions like asthma, COPD, cardiovascular disease, and premature death. This is not a new problem, but it certainly is not one that affected most mobile hunter-gatherers. One must take into account that air pollution emissions have many natural (biogenic) and human (anthropogenic) sources. The danger of air pollution was recognized as early as the fourth century BC, when Hippocrates, the father of medicine, observed that people's general health could be affected by the air they breathe, and that the quality of the air was different in different regions (Bell and Samet 2010). The air pollution was so high (and the air quality so poor) in London in the 13th century that a commission was established to investigate and solve the problem (Brimblecombe 1986). In the past, pollution was principally generated by kilns, furnaces, and hearths. The level of contaminants in the air would have been very dependent on the population. With the rise of industrialization and the use of fossil-fuel–based vehicles, we have greatly increased the level of contaminants released into the air.

The vitamin D deficiency rickets is the first real disease from air pollution—it moved like a scourge through industrial Europe, especially devastating to children. **Rickets** is the result of a deficiency in exposure to solar ultraviolet radiation, which is necessary for the normal growth and maintenance of bone. Bones with inadequate calcium do not mineralize properly, causing soft bones, best illustrated by the bowing of the lower limbs that is a classic sign of rickets. It became epidemic in England after 1650, when soft coal became the principal fuel source. The disease became endemic in northern Europe after this time due to the high levels of coal dust contaminants in the air, plus the fact that the majority of the poor lived in narrow, sunless alleys in urban slums and factory towns (Sherman 2006). The children of the poor were especially vulnerable, as they were often put to work in factories and workhouses for most of the daylight hours, and spent little time outside exposed to sunlight. During the colder times of year, when the solar radiation levels are already significantly reduced in temperate zones, the risk would have become even more elevated. The connection between exposure to sunlight and rickets was made in the late 19th century, when it was noted in Britain and Germany that the disease was seasonal. In 1884, it was observed that children who were born in the fall and died in the spring had rickets, and children who were born in the spring and died in the fall did not (Sherman 2006).

Over the last five centuries in particular, long-distance transportation has become a commonplace occurrence. Consequently, the damaging effects of air pollution can now develop far from their source (Bell and Samet 2010). Air pollutants can be either gases or particles; pollutants that are aerosols are composed of small liquid or solid particles suspended in air. Therefore, air pollution is actually a mixture of a number of distinct pollutants (kind of like a toxic cloud) that contains things like sulfur dioxide, carbon monoxide, and tropospheric ozone (Bell and Samet 2010, Holgate et al. 1999). The ozone layer in our atmosphere protects living creatures by absorbing UVB rays, the most dangerous wavelength of ultraviolet radiation. The damage to the atmosphere's ozone layer means that more ultraviolet radiation is reaching the Earth's surface. As far as human health, this translates into increased rates of skin cancer, suppression of the immune system,

Figure 17.12: Air pollution—dense haze over eastern China (view looks eastward across the Yellow Sea toward Korea).

and damage to the eyes (McElroy and Townsend 2009).

One of the most dangerous by-products of vehicle exhaust fumes is dioxin. People who live in urban centers associated with large levels of exhaust contaminants in the air inhale high levels of dioxin compared to rural groups. Dioxin is a recognized immune suppressor, and is increasingly being linked to various forms of cancer and developmental disorders (Nakazawa 2008). We know that this increased rate of air pollution is having a very serious impact on our health. A large and important study was conducted in six major U.S. cities on the relationship between air pollution and mortality in both children and adults. People

Figure 17.13: Lines of traffic, Algarve, Portugal.

living in the city with the highest air pollution levels had a 26 percent higher mortality rate than those in cities with less pollution (Dockery et al. 1993). **Asthma** is the fastest growing health condition in urban regions around the world. During the period between 1979 and 1989, severe asthma attacks requiring hospitalization increased by 43 percent in the United States. During the period 1982 to 1992, deaths caused by asthma increased by 50 percent in the United States and Canada, Great Britain, New Zealand, and Sweden (Barnes 2006). It takes only relatively small levels of allergens to trigger a wave of asthma attacks, especially when ozone levels rise (Regush 1992). It has been estimated that as many as 60,000 new chemicals have been commercially released in the last 50 years alone. Chemical fumes that are released by household cleaners, paints, glues, and artificial carpet fibers are only a few examples of these new irritants. Furthermore, the increase in asthma and other respiratory infections is also related to the establishment of energy-saving closed indoor environments that recycle indoor air and greatly increase the concentration of indoor pollution. Particularly in temperate climates, people also spend a considerable part of the year indoors with little air circulation, which also contributes to increased seasonal cycles of disease in these regions (Barnes 2006).

The long-distance transportation that facilitates the movement of pollutants around the world is also a major factor in the transmission of disease over large distances. For most of human history, disease that emerged in a particular region remained isolated due to the limited long-distance contact between human groups. Now, we have the Viral Superhighway, in the sense that there is little to impede the global hitchhiking of a vast array of hitherto restricted pathogens (Armelagos 2010). Today, within a few days, you can fly from Hong Kong to Toronto and carry a new virus that sends the medical systems of other countries into overload (like in the outbreak of the SARS virus in the early 21st century). The **SARS virus** (severe acute respiratory syndrome) was first identified in Vietnam in 2003. It rapidly spread throughout Southeast Asia, particularly as a result of air travel. It arrived in North America via an infected Chinese businessman from Hong Kong, but fortunately, a prepared medical system was able to contain any potential outbreak. It is a serious condition, with mortality rates as high as 50 percent in those who are

Figure 17.14: Passenger at airport.

Figure 17.16: Brown tree snake (*Boiga irregularis*), Guam.

Figure 17.15: A vector averaging current meter encrusted with zebra mussels (*Dreissena polymorpha*).

at high risk (Liu 2003, Whitby and Whitby 2003, Barnes 2006).). It is not surprising that we now see diseases in North America like Lyme disease, West Nile virus, and SARS—none of which ever existed in this region of the world until the modern era.

Long-distance transportation is also a serious issue in terms of disease risk for plants and animals, as new and exotic animals are continuously imported (legally or illegally) around the world, and **invasive species** hitch rides on airplanes and ships (especially in ballast water). This is a huge threat to biodiversity, particularly in isolated ecosystems like islands. For example, Hawaii is aggressively fighting to prevent the invasion of the brown tree snake, which has caused tremendous economic and ecological problems in Guam. The snake has destroyed bird, lizard, and bat populations, as well as being responsible for increased numbers of snake bites and power outages from climbing electrical wires. It is estimated that this species alone could cost the state of Hawaii over $100 million.

The mongoose was introduced to Hawaii (also to Fiji and Jamaica) in the mid-19th century to control the large rat populations living in the sugarcane fields (Hoagland et al. 1989, Espeut 1882). Today, the mongoose population has grown so large that it is a very serious threat to ground nesting birds. Vector species of insects also hitch rides (like the mosquito species that carry yellow fever from Africa to the New World), and this process is escalating as global transportation explodes. Zebra mussels (the scourge of boat owners), originally indigenous to the lakes of southern Russia, have become a serious invasive species problem in Europe and North America. They were first identified in the Great Lakes region of Canada and the United States in the late 1980s. Apparently, they were accidentally introduced into the lakes in the ballast water of ocean-traveling vessels using the St. Lawrence Seaway. Zebra mussels are responsible for the near extinction of a number of mussel and clam species in the Great Lakes; they clog essential water intake pipes, lead to several cut feet and trips to the hospital every year, and may be the source of avian botulism (Mackie et al 1989). The regular transportation of humans and other plant and animal species either intentionally or unintentionally has profoundly altered the state of equilibrium in many ecosystems. Unfortunately, this is a force that once begun is extremely difficult to control.

ALLERGIES AND PSYCHOLOGICAL DISEASE: IS OUR MODERN WORLD HURTING US?

There is no question that there is a feedback system between the physical and mental systems of the body. Mental health affects physical health, and vice versa. What we often do not consider is that there is also a dynamic relationship between our biology and our immediate surroundings. Environmental pollutants, noise pollution, and stress have a profound effect upon our overall well-being—not just in terms of physical health, but also our mental health. When viewing populations around the world, it is clear that both asthma and allergies are most common by far in industrialized nations. In the last few decades, the rates of allergies and asthma have exploded, and it is estimated that today, roughly one-fifth of all Americans suffer from asthma or allergies, a rate double that of 20 years earlier (Wiley and Allen 2005). Although these conditions are essentially unknown among many

Figure 17.17: Child playing in the dirt, Ethiopia.

populations (especially those in Africa and Amazonia), when people from these regions move to industrialized countries, the rates of their children rise to those of industrial kids. Clearly, environment is a serious factor in the development of these conditions.

Allergies result from exposure to antigens or foreign proteins that are not disease causing (although the immune system interprets them as so). The most common allergies are to pet dander, dust mites, pollens, molds, and foods (particularly peanuts, milk, shellfish, and eggs). The classic immune response associated with allergies is an elevated level of the antibody IgE, which is a rare—but potent—antibody. Why are industrialized people suffering from such high levels of allergies and asthma? One very interesting suggestion is the **hygiene hypothesis**, which states that this rapid increase in allergic diseases (asthma, hay fever, etc.) may result from a lower incidence of infection in early childhood (Strachan 2000). Today, this idea has

Figure 17.18: House dust mites.

Figure 17.19: Allergies sign.

Figure 17.20: Man using asthma inhaler.

Figure 17.21: Man suffering from depression.

been extended beyond an explanation for allergic diseases, and may also be relevant to the development of conditions such as type 1 diabetes, multiple sclerosis, some forms of depression, and cancer (Stene and Nafstad 2001, Okada et al. 2010, Raison et al. 2010, Rook et al. 2013).

The rise in the developed world of acute lymphoblastic leukemia in young people has also been explained by the hygiene hypothesis (Smith et al. 1998, Okada et al. 2010). Some suggest that autism spectrum disorders demonstrate features of an immune disease (Ashwood and Wakefield 2006, Gupta et al. 1998, Zimmerman et al. 2005, Croonenberghs et al. 2002, Wiley and Allen 2005). Since allergies and many other chronic inflammatory diseases appear to have become serious health concerns only in roughly the last century, one cannot ignore the relationship between this trend and the establishment of public health protocols. During the latter part of the 19th century—particularly after the establishment of germ theory—there were radical improvements in water quality (both in drinking water and sewage treatment), sanitation, and food safety. The implementation of higher standards of hygiene led to a dramatic reduction in infectious disease (particularly in children), especially during the period 1900–1950, and the development of immunizations and antibiotics added to this arsenal greatly reduced the infectious disease experience in developed nations. The reduction in the practice of breast-feeding, particularly since the 1960s, has also contributed to the increased rates of allergies and asthma. Breast-feeding has been shown to be protective against a number of illnesses, including upper and lower respiratory ailments, ear infections, allergies, asthma, intestinal disorders, colds, and a number of other bacteria and viruses (La Leche League 2013).

Figure 17.22: Image of a pair of *Schistosoma mansoni* helminths. The smaller female lives in the gynecophoral canal of the male.

A fascinating extension of the hygiene hypothesis is the **helminth hypothesis**, which particularly emphasizes the huge reduction of helminth (worm) infections with the rise of allergies in the industrial world. The sole purpose of the IgE antibody appears to be to combat helminths, but in the absence of worm infections, it responds to other allergens that have similar antigen proteins to helminths (Wiley and Allen 2009). The idea is that many commonplace allergens are similar in their chemical signatures and molecular weight to helminthic antigens. When one looks at food allergies, they are typically related to the consumption of plant (peanut) or marine protein sources, not mammalian meats. This is likely because the mammalian protein signature is very similar to the human; thus those proteins are not recognized by our bodies as foreign (Wiley and Allen 2009). Research demonstrates a clear inverse relationship between helminth infection and the risk of developing allergies or asthma. It is suggested that this relationship may result from the fact that worm antigens appear to stimulate the body to produce anti-inflammatory cytokines that inhibit airway inflammation, characteristic of both allergies and asthma (van den Biggelaar et al. 2000, Wiley and Allen 2009). Populations with a long history of infection by helminths like hookworm, pinworm, and roundworm may have been affected by selection to have elevated IgE levels. When people move to industrial nations where there is little to no helminth threat, these individuals have an especially high risk of developing allergies or asthma.

Something as simple as the novel use of wool blankets in Papua New Guinea led to alarming increases in asthma (Dowse et al. 1985). Since worm infections were commonplace in industrial nations until well into the 20th century (and still are in most of the developing world), rates of these modern conditions were very low. Urban poverty is also a contributing factor to the development of allergies and asthma, as low-income housing is often associated with cockroach antigen (Barnes et al. 1999). This may explain

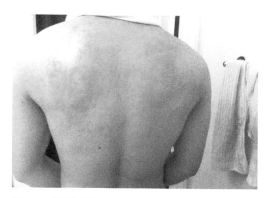

Figure 17.23: Hives on the back from an allergic reaction.

why African Americans tend to have higher rates of allergies than Americans of European origin (Le Souef et al. 2000). There is no question that increased rates of these conditions also occurred with the rise of permanent settlements. The modern industrial house is full of carpets, drapes, pillows, bedding, and pet beds—wonderful places for dust mites to reproduce in high numbers. Yet again, it appears that our behavior is at odds with our biology, and this time, it is a major source of chronic inflammatory disease.

A very interesting area of new research involves the possible development of psychological disorders with viral or bacterial infection. Some suggest that one of the principal causes of autism could be an autoimmune response to the streptococcus bacteria (similar to strains that cause strep throat). Infection with the streptococcus bacteria can lead to the infected individual producing antibodies that mistakenly attack the basal ganglia in the brain, in addition to the strep bacteria itself (Waltz 2002). Studies also indicate that infection with viral agents (like those that cause meningitis and encephalitis) can lead to the development of severe autistic-like symptoms, and greatly elevated rates have been observed in children who were infected with both German measles and mumps during the same period (Waltz 2002, Frith 1989).

It also appears that depression has a genetic component in many instances. **Depression** (not an easy term to define) is the most common form of mood disorder in the developed world. Modern brain imaging studies examining brain anatomy and function have identified several areas of the brain that differ between people who are depressed and not depressed (Drevets 2000, Beyer and Krishnan 2002). First-degree relatives of an individual with a depressive disorder are 1.5 to 3 times more likely to develop the condition than the general population (American Psychiatric Association 1994). Furthermore, recent molecular genetics studies have identified some genes that are believed to be linked to depression susceptibility (Craddock and Forty 2006).

Recent research implicates an infectious agent as a possible cause of schizophrenia. The disease toxoplasmosis is caused by a small protozoon called *Toxoplasma gondii*, which typically causes only mild infections in humans, birds, and other animals. The reservoir for the parasite is wild and domestic rodents, a favorite meal of cats, and the disease is transmitted to humans via contact with cat feces or infected dust particles in the air. In cat-owning humans, the infection rate is between 20 and 60 percent of people (Jones 1975); it is estimated that roughly 50 percent of the American population may be infected, without their knowledge in most cases (Yaeger 1985). This protozoon has recently emerged as a prime causative candidate for schizophrenia. Schizophrenia is a neuropsychiatric disorder with a global distribution that has a devastating impact upon affected individuals and their families. Schizophrenia also exerts an enormous cost on the wider social group in terms of resources allocated to medical care, lost productivity, and social problems such as homelessness (Yolken et al. 2009). There are many similarities between schizophrenia and **toxoplasmosis** in an epidemiological sense. First, many studies report that in comparison to

Figure 17.24: Woman holding her pet cat.

control groups, individuals with schizophrenia have a higher prevalence of antibodies to *T. gondii*. Second, in rare instances, individuals with adult toxoplasmosis may develop psychotic symptoms that are similar to those of schizophrenia. Third, antipsychotic drugs that are effective in treating schizophrenia also inhibit some parasites, including *T. gondii*. Finally, studies show that compared to controls, individuals with schizophrenia have had greater exposure to cats in childhood (Yolken et al. 2009, Brown et al. 2005, Torrey and Yolken 1995, Torrey et al. 2007, Tamer et al. 2008, Zhu et al. 2007, Mortensen et al. 2007).

And now, a final thought about a very scary foe: **antibiotic-resistant microorganisms**. As we change our environments and develop new technology, we fool ourselves into thinking we are immune to infectious disease in the industrial world. If we actually get sick, we trust that the sophisticated medical technology and new medications will cure us. It is nice to take a trip to La-La Land periodically, but it is not good to live there permanently. To add to the horror of these new enemies, we have created the monsters ourselves. Human behavior has a tremendous impact upon our overall health. We have to consider factors like what we eat and drink, what clothes we wear, what our occupation is, what preventative health measures do we practice, and what is the quality of the air and water we ingest. This interaction between biology and culture involves issues such as how we build our houses, and how successfully can we buffer ourselves from

Figure 17.25: Plowing the field.

the stresses of the environment in which we live. How does what we choose to place on our bodies help us to be better adapted to our natural environments? When we are transported to locales that are not our natural environments, (migration, immigration, slavery, criminal transportation), how can we make adjustments to protect ourselves?

The health crisis we are experiencing today has occurred as we humans change our behavior and alter the fabric of our environment. We cannot complain entirely, as it is also this same behavior that has vastly improved the quality and length of our lives in many respects. The 20th century brought with it cleaner water and food, better living conditions, vaccinations and antibiotics, the eradication of smallpox, and huge reductions in killers such as tuberculosis, syphilis, cholera, and polio. Agricultural abundance soared in the developed world, and then in developing nations. With this surplus of food comes a general increase in longevity and population size. The deaths of infants, small children, and young adults—routine events for so long—became unusual tragedies. Life

Figure 17.26: Family Reunion (Frédéric Bazille, 1868).

spans increased, and in some places even doubled (Sherman 2006, McNeil 1976). The recognition and identification of new emerging illnesses deliver a powerful message to humans: that we have not overcome the world of microorganisms. As we continue to alter our social and natural environments, we create our own monsters. Clearly, the mid-20th-century optimism created by the discovery of antibiotics was premature. Hantavirus was first identified in the Four Corners region of the American Southwest. SARS emerged in Southeast Asia, and rapidly spread around the world. New antibiotic strains of staphylococcus are developing in response to our abuse of prescribed medicine. Many human diseases came from other species. Tuberculosis probably came from cattle or wild birds, SARS from civets, and the HIV virus that causes AIDS from African primates.

More than any species in the history of Earth, we have altered the natural world in which we live. Too often, this has had devastating consequences for human health and life expectancy. We provide ecological niches for microbes by clearing land and plowing fields, domesticating animals, and building homes, cities, and factories. The evolution of human habitations into urban centers has created artificial environments with a new set of stresses to the human body and mind. The creation of cities also dramatically alters the natural ecosystem and the balance between organisms within that environment. Sophisticated modern medical technology

Figure 17.27: Family leaning backward.

Figure 17.28: Ships docked in Singapore.

has lulled us into a state of complacency when it comes to the threat of infectious disease. This is a most dangerous state, as infectious pathogens are evolving and emerging at all times—and will continue to threaten human populations in the future.

Our world is much more vulnerable to epidemic disease than it was in the past. We have seen the reemergence of old enemies in antibiotic-resistant form, enemies like tuberculosis, streptococcus, pneumococcus, and staphylococcus. Both Old and New World diseases can emerge on the scene quickly and move rapidly throughout the world because of the rapid global movement of peoples and goods. With the help of fast-moving ships, planes, and trains, diseases that were previously remote and geographically restricted are now found in our midst. Good examples include severe acute respiratory syndrome (SARS), West Nile virus, mad cow disease, and new strains of avian flu. Toxic shock syndrome resulted from the introduction of improved menstrual tampons that provided an ideal environment for the growth of a lethal microbe (in this case, the bacterium *Staphylococcus aureus*). Legionnaires' disease was the result of the growth and spread of another deadly pathogen (*Legionella*) through a hotel's air conditioning system.

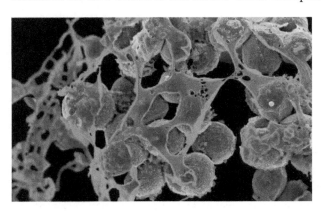

Figure 17.29: Scanning Electron Micrograph image of methicillin-resistant *Staphylococcus aureus*.

From the 20th century on, we have had great success in eliminating smallpox and dramatically reducing the presence of long-time killers such as polio, whooping cough, measles, mumps, and rubella. However, the improper administration and abuse of antibiotics and incomplete vaccination in populations has led to the recent resurgence of some old killers in scary new armor: antibiotic resistance. We have not conquered infectious disease; we have simply shifted the focus from some old pathogens to new ones. Pathogenic organisms are themselves evolving and responding to our innovations. Thus, new diseases will continue to emerge and present new challenges for all living creatures, whether plant or animal.

This world is an amazing, breathtaking place, with an incredible diversity of living species. It is this very diversity that keeps this planet healthy and strong. Whether we like it or not, we are part of the natural web of life, and as the dominant species on Earth (at least for now), we do have an obligation to examine how our actions affect the chain of life in different ecosystems. Loss of other living creatures does have a profound effect upon the quality of human life. Evolution is not a goal-directed enterprise. Sometimes, nature throws up new possibilities (mutations), and then tinkers with different combinations of these features. The direction in which a living organism evolves is dependent upon a complex range of different interrelated factors, but ultimately, the goal of any organism is to become as well adjusted as possible to their unique, individual, natural (and often social) environment. How successfully an individual accomplishes this goal is reflected in the number of offspring that it leaves behind, and thus the number of their genes that are passed on to future generations. How well a species rises to these challenges is the difference between survival and extinction.

We humans are a young species; we are shaped by the same forces as any other creature that has come (and many gone) from this planet. If we too wish to continue as a species, we must be diligent in assessing our actions and the wider impact that they have on the fabric of life on this planet. Until *Star Trek* becomes

Figure 17.30: Suspension bridge, Puerto Viejo de Sarapiqui, Costa Rica.

true and we can live in space and eradicate disease, we are stuck here. But what a marvelous, exciting place to be stuck, as long as we take the time to protect it, and by so doing protect ourselves. Thank you, Charles Darwin, for bringing this incredible idea to the attention of other people, and helping us to understand the stunning process by which life unfolds on this our beloved Earth.

CRITICAL REASONING QUESTIONS

- What behaviors have you engaged in over the last 24 hours that have had a negative impact upon the natural environment? How might you reduce your personal signature?

Figure 17.31: Human hands holding the world.

- How does the hunter-gatherer lifestyle protect one from diseases of civilization?
- How do deforestation and global warming negatively affect natural environments and the creatures that live within them?
- How has long-distance travel and trade greatly facilitated disease transmission and extinctions?
- What is it about the modern industrialized world that makes us so vulnerable to developing allergies and asthma? How can we reduce our risks?
- Are psychological diseases genetic, environmental, or both?

REFERENCES AND SUGGESTED READINGS

American Psychiatric Association (1994). *Diagnosis and statistical manual of mental disorders*, 4th ed. Washington, DC: American Psychiatric Association.

Armelagos, G. J. (2010). "The Viral Superhighway." In *Annual Editions of Physical Anthropology (2010/1011)*, pp. 184–188. New York: McGraw-Hill.

Araújo, M. B., R. J. Whittaker, et al. (2005). "Reducing uncertainty in projections of extinction risk from climate change." *Global Ecology & Biogeography* 14 (6):529–538(10).

Ashwood, P., and A. J. Wakefield (2006). "Immune activation of peripheral blood and mucosal CD3+ lymphocyte cytokine profiles in children with autism and gastrointestinal symptoms." *Journal of Neuroimmunology* 173 (1–2):126–134.

Barnes, E. (2005). *Diseases and human evolution*. Albuquerque: University of New Mexico Press.

Bell, M. L., and J. M. Samet (2010). "Air pollution." In H. Frumkin, ed., *Environmental Health: From Global to Local*. San Francisco: John Wiley and Sons.

Benenson, A. S. (1995). *Control of communicable diseases manual*, 16th ed. Washington, DC: American Public Health Association.

Beyer, J. L., and K. R. Krishnan (2002). "Volumetric brain imaging findings in mood disorders." *Bipolar Disorders* 4:89–104.

Biraben, J.-N. (1980). "An essay concerning mankind's evolution." *Population*, Selected Papers, vol. 4, pp. 1–13. Original paper in French: (b) Jean-Noël Biraben (1979). "Essai sur l'évolution du nombre des homes." *Population*, vol. 34 (no. 1), pp. 13–25.

Brimblecombe, P. (1986). *The big smoke: A history of air pollution in London since medieval times*. New York: Methuen.

Brown, A. S., C. A. Schaefer, C. P. Quesenberry, et al. (2005). "Maternal exposure to toxoplasmosis and risk of schizophrenia in adult offspring." *American Journal of Psychiatry* 162: 67–773.

Buer, Mabel C. (1926). *Health, wealth and population in the early days of the Industrial Revolution*, p. 30. London: George Routledge & Sons.

Burnet, M., and D. White (1972). *Natural history of infectious diseases*. Cambridge, UK: Cambridge University Press.

Caselli, G., J. Vallin, and G. Wunsch (2006). *Demography: Analysis and synthesis, four volume set: A treatise in population*. Burlington, MA: Academic Press.

Cohen, J. (1995). *How many people can the earth support?* New York: W. W. Norton & Co.

Cooper, J. I., and F. O. MacCallum (1984). *Viruses and the environment*. London: Chapman and Hall.

Craddock, N., and L. Forty (2006). "Genetics of affective (mood) disorders." *European Journal of Human Genetics* 14:660–668.

Croonenberghs, J., A. Wauters, K. Devreese, et al. (2002). "Increased serum albumin, γ globulin, immunoglobulin IgG, and IgG2 and IgG4 in autism." *Psychological Medicine* 32 (8):1457–1463.

Dockery, D. E., et al. (1993). "An association between air pollution and mortality in 6 U.S. cities." *New England Journal of Medicine* 329:1753–1759.

Dowse, G. K., K. J. Turner, G. A. Stewart, et al. (1985). "The association between dermatophagoides mites and the increasing prevalence of asthma in village communities within the Papua New Guinea highlands." *Journal of Allergy and Clinical Immunology* 75:75–83.

Drevets, W. (2000). "Neuroimaging studies of mood disorders." *Biological Psychiatry* 48:813–829.

Ehrlich, P., and A. Ehrlich (1990). *The population explosion*. New York: Simon & Schuster.

Espeut, W. B. (1882). "On the acclimatization of the Indian mongoose in Jamaica." *Proceedings of the Zoological Society of London* 1882:712–714.

Frith, U. (1989). *Autism: Explaining the enigma*. Victoria: Blackwell Publishing.

Frumkin, H., ed. (2010). *Environmental health: From global to local*, 2nd ed. San Francisco: John Wiley and Sons.

Gallant, R. (1990). *The peopling of the planet Earth*. New York: Macmillan.

Gupta, S., S. Aggarwal, B. Rashanravan, and T. Lee (1998). "Th1- and Th2-like cytokines in CD4+ and CD8+ T cells in autism." *Journal of Neuroimmunology* 85 (1):106–109.

Hilts, P. (2005). *Rx for survival: Why we must rise to the global health challenge*. New York: Penguin Press.

Hinze-Selch, D., W. Däubener, L. Eggert, et al. (2007). "A controlled prospective study of *Toxoplasma gondii* infection in individuals with schizophrenia: Before seroprevalence." *Schizophrenia Bulletin* 33:782–788.

Hoagland, D. B., G. R. Horst, and C. W. Kilpatrick (1989). "Biogeography and population biology of the mongoose in the West Indies." In C. A. Woods, ed., *Biogeography of the West Indies*, pp. 611–634. Gainesville, FL: Sand Hill Crane Press.

Holgate, S. T., J. M. Samet, H. S. Koren, and R. L. Maynard, eds. (1999). *Air pollution and health*. London: Academic Press: London.

Jones, T. C. (1975). "Toxoplasmosis." In P. B. Beeson and W. McDermott, eds., *Textbook of Medicine*, 14th ed., pp. 502–506. Philadelphia: W. B. Saunders.

La Leche League International. https://www.llli.org/faq/prevention.html

Lederberg, J., R. E. Shope, and S. Oaks Jr. (1992). *Emerging infections: Microbial threats to health in the United States*. Washington, DC: Institute of Medicine, National Academy Press.

Le Souef, P. N., J. Goldblatt, and N. R. Lynch (2000). "Evolutionary adaptation of inflammatory immune responses in human beings." *Lancet* 356:242–244.

Liu, J. (2003). "SARS, wildlife and human health." *Science* 302:53.

Mackie, G., W. Gibbons, B. Muncaster, and I. Gray. (1989). "The zebra mussel, *Dreissena polymorpha*: A synthesis of European experiences and a preview for North America." Canada: Ontario Ministry of Environment.

McElroy, A., and P. K. Townsend (2009). *Medical anthropology in ecological perspective*, 5th ed. Philadelphia: Westview Press.

McNeil, W. (1976). *Plagues and peoples*. New York: Anchor Press/Doubleday.

Mortensen, P. B., B. Nørgaard-Pedersen, B. L. Waltoft, et al. (2007). "*Toxoplasma gondii* as a risk factor for early-onset schizophrenia: Analysis of filter paper blood samples obtained at birth." *Biol Psychiatry* 61:688–693.

Nakazawa, D. J. (2008). *The autoimmune epidemic*. New York: Simon & Schuster.

National Geographic (2013). http://environment.nationalgeographic.com/environment/global-warming/deforestation-overview/

Nicholls, N., et al. (1996). "Observed climate variability and change." In J. Houghton, et al., eds., *Climate Change 1995: The Science of Climate Change*. Contribution of Working Group 1 to the Second Assessment Report of the Intergovernmental Panel on Climate Change. New York: Cambridge University Press.

Okada, H., C. Kuhn, H. Feillet, and J-F. Bach (2010). "The 'hygiene hypothesis' for autoimmune and allergic diseases: An update." *Clinical & Experimental Immunology* 160 (1):1–9.

Parry, M. L., et al. (2007). "Summary for policymakers." In *Climate Change 2007: Impacts, Adaptation, and Vulnerability*. Contribution of Working Group II to the Fourth Assessment Report of the Intergovernmental Panel on Climate Change. New York: Cambridge University Press.

Patz, J. A. (2001). "Public health risk assessment linked to climatic and ecological change." *Human and Ecological Risk Assessment* 7(5):1317–1327.

Patz, J. A., and R. S. Kovats (2002). "Hotspots in climate change and human health." *British Medical Journal* 325:1094–1098.

Pauly, D., and J. Alder (2005). "Marine fisheries systems." In R. Hassan, R. Scholes, and N. Ash, eds. *Ecosystems and Human Well-being: Current State and Trends*, vol. 1. Washington, DC: Island Press.

Raison, C. L., C. A. Lowry, and G. A. W. Rook (2010). "Inflammation, sanitation and consternation: Loss of contact with co-evolved, tolerogenic micro-organisms and the pathophysiology and treatment of major depression." *Archives of General Psychiatry* 67(12):1211–1224.

Regush, N. (May-June 1992). "Last gasp." *Equinox* 63:85–97.

Rook G. A. W., C. A. Lowry, and C. L. Raison (2013). "Microbial old friends, immunoregulation and stress resilience." *Evolution, Medicine and Public Health* 1:46–64.

Sherman, I. W. (2006). *The power of plagues*. Washington, DC: ASM Press.

Smith, M. A., R. Simon, H. D. Strickler, et al. (1998). "Evidence that childhood acute lymphoblastic leukemia is associated with an infectious agent linked to hygiene conditions." *Cancer Causes & Control* 9 (3):285–298.

Solomon, S., et al, eds. *Climate change 2007: The physical science basis*. Working Group 1 Contribution to the Fourth Assessment Report of the Intergovernmental Panel on Climate Change. New York: Cambridge University Press.

Stene L. C., and P. Nafstad (2001). "Relation between occurrence of type 1 diabetes and asthma." *Lancet* 2001 357:607.

Strachan, D. (2000). "Family size, infection and atopy: The first decade of the 'hygiene hypothesis.'" *Thorax* 55 (90001):S2–S10.

Tamer, G. S., D. Dundar, I. Yalug, et al. (2008). "The schizophrenia and *Toxoplasma gondii* connection: Infectious, immune or both?" *Adv Ther*. 25:703–709.

Teller, L. N., ed. (2009). *Urban world history: An economic and geographical perspective*. Quebec: Presses de l'Université du Québec.

Thomas, C. D., A. Cameron, R. E. Green, et al. (2004). "Extinction risk from climate change." *Nature* 427 (6970):145–148.

Thuiller, W., M. B. Araújo, R. G. Pearson, et al. (2004). "Biodiversity conservation: Uncertainty in predictions of extinction risk." *Nature* 430 (6995):1.

Torrey E. F., and R. H. Yolken. (1995). "Could schizophrenia be a viral zoonosis transmitted from house cats?" *Schizophrenia Bulletin* 21:167–171.

Torrey, E. F., J. J. Bartko, Z.-R. Lun, and R. H. Yolken (2007). "Antibodies to *Toxoplasma gondii* in patients with schizophrenia: A meta-analysis." *Schizophrenia Bulletin* 33:729–736.

Trenberth, K. (2005). "Uncertainty in hurricanes and global warming." *Science* 308:1753–1754.

van den Biggelaar, H. A., R. van Ree, L. C. Rodrigues, et al. (2000). "Decreased atopy in children infected with *Schistosoma haematobium*: A role for parasite-induced interleukin-10." *Lancet* 356:1723–1727.

Waltz, M. (2002). *Autistic spectrum disorders: Understanding the diagnosis and getting help*. Beijing: O'Reilly and Associates.

Whitby, N., and M. Whitby (2003). "SARS: A new infectious disease for a new century." *Australian Family Physician* 32(10):779–783.

World Health Organization. *World Health Report 2002: Reducing Risks, Promoting Healthy Life*. Geneva: World Health Organization.

Yaeger, R. G. (1985). "Coccidia, malarial parasites, *Babesia*, and pneumocystis." In P. C. Beaver and R. C. Jung, eds., *Animal Agents and Vectors of Human Disease*, pp. 50–77. Philadelphia: Lea and Febiger.

Yolken, R. H., F. B. Dickerson, and E. Fuller Torrey (November 2009). "Toxoplasma and schizophrenia." *Parasite Immunology* 31(11):706–715.

Zhu S., M.-F. Guo, Q.-C. Feng, et al. (2007). "Epidemiological evidences from China assume that psychiatric-related diseases may be associated with *Toxoplasma gondii* infection." *Neuro Endocrinol Lett* 28:115–120.

Zimmerman, A. W., H. Jyonouchi, A. M. Comi, et al. (2005). "Cerebrospinal fluid and serum markers of inflammation in autism." *Pediatric Neurology* 33 (3):195–201.

Appendix
Critical Reasoning Answers

Chapters 6–13

Chapter Six Answers:

1. Characteristics possessed exclusively by all primate species include flexible limbs, nails instead of claws, opposable thumbs, large brain size in proportion to body size, and flexible learned behavior. Primate limbs are flexible, particularly the arms. which can be rotated 360°. This flexibility facilitates effective movement in the arboreal environment. All primates have nails instead of claws at the ends of all of their digits, with the exception of the Strepsirhini species, which possess two claws, one on each index finger, used for grooming. All primates have opposable thumbs, and with the exception of humans, some degree of opposability of the big toe, which facilitates grasping.

2. The first true primate species appeared toward the end of the Paleocene epoch, 55 million years ago to 60 million years ago. These early primates are most similar to the modern prosimians: lemurs, lorises, and tarsiers.

3. Primates evolved as an adaptation to an arboreal environment, living in a forested environment and spending the majority of time up in the trees, where they took advantage of fruit as a major dietary resource.

4. The primates are classified into two suborders: The Strepsirhini include the lemurs and lorises, and the Haplorhini include the tarsiers, New World monkeys, Old World monkeys, apes. and humans.

5. Until recently, the term hominid was used to describe species in the human lineage. This was based on evolutionary systematics, which emphasize physical morphology in classification. Since humans look the least similar to orangutans, gorillas, common chimpanzees, and bonobos, the four of these species were classified into the family Pongidae, with only humans in the family Hominidae. Therefore, Hominidae (and hominid) were exclusively human terms. Currently, an increasing majority of researchers use cladistic systematics for classification, which only consider genetic distance data. Of the above five species, humans are not the least genetically similar; thus, humans are no longer the only species included in the family Hominidae, and hominid can no longer be used as an exclusive term for humans. In a cladistic classification, humans are the only species in the tribe Hominini; consequently, the word hominin is now used to describe the species in the human lineage.

6. The two species of chimpanzees are the most genetically similar species to humans, sharing a common ancestor five to seven million years ago. Studying modern chimpanzee behavior provides insight into the behavior of early hominin species.

Chapter Seven Answers:

1. Home range is the total area used by a primate social group for all daily and seasonal activities. It is not actively defended, and may overlap with the home ranges of other conspecific groups. The territory of a primate social group is an area that is exclusively used and actively defended against conspecific groups. It is a conscious construct in the animals' minds.

2. Resource defense territoriality may occur in a primate social group if certain resources—particularly food resources—are scarce and patchy or clumped in space, since it is to the group's benefit to maintain exclusive access to these scarce resources. Mate defense territoriality may occur if mating behavior includes a high degree of male competition for females. In this situation, restricting nongroup male access to the group's females reduces competition for the group's males.

3. Studies of path length (daily travel distance, including curves) and day range (straight-line distance from sleeping area to furthest point reached in a day) provide information on how efficiently the home range is used by a social group. These studies show that primates have conscious knowledge of their surroundings, including the locations of resources such as the water source and favored feeding locations. They travel from one location to another by the most efficient route, indicating that they possess a cognitive map: a conscious mental map of their surroundings.

4. Grooming behavior involves the cleaning of the fur of another animal. One purpose of grooming is hygiene, but more importantly, it serves to form and strengthen social bonds between individuals.

5. Dominance is the ability or power to influence another individual's behavior. Not all individuals in a social group have the same level of influence. Rank is an individual's relative dominance level within their social group.

6. At birth, an individual inherits the rank of the mother and keeps this rank until puberty. Individuals who leave their natal group at puberty and join another group lose their birth rank, and establish a new rank through interactions with members of their new group. Philopatric individuals who remain in their natal group for life retain their birth rank, but may be able to raise that rank through interactions with other individuals.

7. During field studies of macaques living on Koshima Island, Japan, researchers provided food on the beach in order to keep the animals in the same place for observation. Initially, sweet potatoes were provisioned. In time, initiated by one female and copied by other individuals, the group began to wash their potatoes in pools of water to wash off the sand before eating them. Later—again initiated by the same female—individuals began taking their potatoes to the ocean to wash them. Apparently, they preferred their potatoes with salt. Later still, the researchers changed the diet to rice, again leaving it on the beach, figuring that it would take some time for the macaques to separate the rice from the sand. However, this same female quickly learned that all she had to do was dump a handful of rice and sand into a pool of water so that the sand sank, the rice floated, and could then be easily skimmed off of the water's surface. This demonstrates flexible learned behavior.

8. The theory of mind is the ability to place oneself into the mind of another. It includes the ability to perceive another individual's state of mind, and the ability to distinguish between what you and others know, facilitating active teaching (as opposed to learning by copying).

Chapter Eight Answers:

1. Potassium-argon dating is a radiometric technique which measures the decay of K40 to Ar40. The half-life of K40 is 1.3 billion years, meaning that after this period, half of the original K40 in the sample

has decayed to Ar40. K-Ar dating is used to date volcanic rocks. The date of an archaeological layer can be bracketed by dating volcanic layers above and below.

2. The anthropoids include all monkey, ape, and human species. The hominoids include all ape and human species. The hominins include all human species. All three include humans.

3. The family Adapidae is similar to modern lemurs. The family Omomyidae is similar to modern tarsiers.

4. Much of our fossil evidence for early monkey species comes from the Fayum in Egypt. It dates to the Oligocene epoch and falls into two families, Propliopithecidae and Parapithecidae.

5. The apes, including those of the Miocene, do not have tails and have Y5 molar cusp pattern. In contrast, the monkeys have tails and X4 bilophodont molar cusp pattern.

6. During the middle Miocence, beginning approximately 16 million years ago, several ape species evolved and adapted to environments in Africa and Eurasia. This period is referred to as the Age of the Apes.

Chapter Nine Answers:

1. The distinguishing morphological feature of the hominins is habitual bipedal locomotion. Nonhuman primates usually move quadrupedally, although they may move bipedally for brief periods of time.

2. In fossil primates, specific skeletal features are used to identify mode of locomotion. In bipedal hominins, the foramen magnum is positioned more toward the base of the skull; the spine forms a gentle S-shape; the big toe is in line with the other toes; and the base of the foot forms a distinct arch, whereas in quadrupedal primates, the foramen magnum is more toward the back of the skull; the spine forms a gentle curve and is not S-shaped; the big toe diverges from the other toes; and the base of the foot is flatter, with no distinct arch.

3. The time of divergence of the chimpanzee and human lineages can be determined by comparing the degree of similarity of their DNA. Differences in the base sequence of chimpanzees and humans result from mutations accumulating over time, which occur at a constant known rate. This information is used to calculate the time that has elapsed since chimpanzees and humans shared a common ancestor. These studies bracket the time of divergence between 5 million and 7 million years ago.

4. During the period of the first appearance of the hominins at the end of the Miocene and beginning of the Pliocene epochs, the African environment was becoming cooler and drier. Tropical forests were shrinking and becoming more fragmented. Savanna grasslands were expanding, with an increase in mixed woodland/grassland areas. These changes were accompanied by increased seasonal variation.

5. The early hominin species migrated from the tropical forests of Africa, initially into mixed woodland/grassland forest fringe areas, and eventually colonized the expanding savanna grasslands. Hominin adaptation to these environments required a modification in diet. Fruit is a major component of the diet of apes, and is abundant in tropical forests where apes live. In fragmented forest fringe areas and on the savanna grasslands, less fruit is available, and is found in clumps of trees separated by grassland. The hominins adapted by supplementing what fruit they could find with other dietary items readily available on the savanna grasslands.

6. The environment that a hominin species lived in can be determined by examining plant and animal fossils that are found in the same stratigraphic layer and that are associated with the hominin fossil. For example, a savanna environment would be indicated by a predominance of grass plant species.

The remains of Sahelanthropus tchadensis *from Chad date to between 7.4 and 6.5 million years ago. The position of the foramen magnum is located between the base of the skull as is found in bipeds, and the rear of the skull as is found in quadrupeds. Its position is ambiguous in terms of mode of locomotion. While some researchers maintain that the location of the foramen magnum is close enough to the base of the skull to indicate bipedality, others suggest it is more toward the back of the skull, indicating quadrupedality. As a result, there is debate over whether* Sahelanthropus tchadensis *represents an early hominin, an early chimpanzee, the common ancestor of these two, or another ape species.*

Chapter Ten Answers:

1. In 1924, Raymond Dart discovered the first hominin fossil found in Africa at the site of Taung, South Africa, and named it *Australopithecus africanus.*

2. The fossil remains of Lucy were discovered in 1974 at the site of Hadar, Ethiopia. Lucy dates to 3.2 million years ago, and is a member of *Australopithecus afarensis.* Morphological features of the pelvis indicate that Lucy was female. In comparison with modern humans, Lucy was shorter, had a smaller cranial capacity, larger brow ridges, a greater degree of subnasal prognathism, and an increased proportional length of arms to legs.

3. In 1978, a series of footprints dated to 3.5 million years ago were uncovered in a volcanic ash layer at the site of Laetoli, Tanzania. Among these footprints were those left by hominins, as indicated by the presence of a distinct arch, the big toe in line with the other toes, and that they came in pairs, not fours. The significance of these footprints is that they provide conclusive evidence of bipedality by 3.5 million years ago, and that hominin foot morphology was essentially modern by this time.

4. Over the course of human evolution, the shape of the dental arcade changed from rectangular to U-shaped to parabolic. The diastema became smaller, and is correlated with a reduction in the size of the canine. The canine also became less pointed with reduced sexual dimorphism in a process named incisorization. The first premolar became less pointed and developed a second cusp in a process named molarization.

5. The gracile australopithecines are more lightly built in their cranial morphology in comparison to the robust australopithecines. Distinctive robust australopithecine cranial features include a sagittal crest, flared zygomatic arches, and a large mandible.

6. The robust australopithecines adapted to the savanna grasslands by concentrating their diet on readily available tough, crunchy plant foods. These foods required large temporalis muscles for mastication. The sagittal crest, flared zygomatic arches, and large mandible were muscle attachment sites for these large temporalis muscles.

Chapter Eleven Answers:

1. The genus *Homo* is distinguished from the australopithecines by significant enlargement of the brain. Whereas average cranial capacity of the australopithecine species ranges between 440 cc and 530 cc, that of early *Homo* ranges between 600 cc and 750 cc.

2. The majority of researchers consider the range of cranial capacity of early *Homo* to be too great to be that of a single species. The variation of early *Homo* cranial capacity falls into two overlapping groups, with the smaller group averaging 650 cc and the larger averaging 735 cc. A majority of researchers consider the difference in brain size between the two groups to be too great to represent males and females of a single species, and therefore separate the early *Homo* fossil set into two species: the smaller is *Homo habilis* and the larger is *Homo rudolfensis.*

3. The australopithecines adapted to the savanna grasslands by having a diet that was comprised of a high proportion of abundant tough, crunchy plant foods. In contrast, early *Homo* began incorporating meat into their diets, supplemented with what fruit they could find on the savanna grasslands.

4. Evidence indicates that early *Homo* obtained their meat primarily through scavenging. Prey bones associated with early *Homo* have cut marks made by both stone tools and the teeth of large carnivores. On many of these bones, the stone tool cut marks overlay the large carnivore tooth marks, indicating that early *Homo* accessed carnivore kill leftovers.

5. Fossil remains of Neanderthals have been found in Europe, the Middle East, and central Asia. The Neanderthals adapted to the cold Ice Age conditions of the late Pleistocene by evolving a shorter, stockier body shape. This body shape reduces skin surface area in proportion to overall body mass, reducing heat loss through the skin—an adaptation to a cold environment.

6. Two innovations that appear in the Acheulean industry are retouching and bifacial tools. Retouching involves removing small flakes from the cutting edge of a tool in order to refine and sharpen the cutting edge. Bifacial tools have had several flakes removed from the original pebble so that little or none of the original surface remains. This facilitates the production of more regularized shapes.

7. Hafting occurs when a handle is attached to produce a composite tool. For example, a long handle may be attached to a stone projectile point to produce a spear. Hafting first appears with the Mousterian tool industry.

8. The Levallois technique is associated with the Mousterian tool industry. It was used as a method for repeatedly producing flakes of standardized size and shape.

Chapter Twelve Answers:

1. The earliest anatomically modern *Homo sapiens* fossils are found in Africa and date to approximately 200,000 years ago. Anatomically modern *Homo sapiens* fossils appear later in other parts of the world: in the Middle East by approximately 120,000 years ago, east Asia by 50,000 years ago, Europe by 40,000 years ago, and later than 15,000 years ago in the Americas.

2. A majority of researchers agree that studies comparing the range of genetic variation in modern human populations (analyzing mtDNA and DNA from the Y chromosome) indicate that anatomically modern *Homo sapiens* originated in sub-Saharan Africa and first appeared approximately 200,000 years ago, supporting the out of Africa model. Studies comparing Neanderthal and modern human DNA show that Neanderthal sequences fall outside the range of variation found among modern human populations. This indicates that Neanderthals made little or no contribution to the modern human gene pool, and suggests that they became extinct.

3. Upper Paleolithic tool industries are distinguished by the presence of blade technology. Blades are flakes that are long and narrow, forming tools that are sharper and more pointed, thus making them more effective. The manufacture of blades facilitated the production of smaller, more delicate, and more precisely formed tools.

4. An atlatl is a tool that is used to launch a spear or dart. It may be manufactured from wood or bone, and has a prong at one end to anchor the base of the spear or dart and a hand grip at the other end. An atlatl acts as a lever and increases the propulsive power, increasing the distance and heft with which a spear or dart can be thrown.

5. Evidence that fish were included in Upper Paleolithic diets includes finely carved fish hooks and the remains of fish traps found in archaeological sites. Stable isotope studies indicate that the diet of some Upper Paleolithic populations consisted of 50 percent riverine resources. Barbed harpoon heads

carved from bone suggest that coastal Upper Paleolithic groups included larger fish and sea mammals in their diet.

6. Evidence for the construction of shelters was found at Mezhirich, Ukraine. The remains of a hut built using mammoth bones and hide were discovered here, dating to 35,000 years ago.

7. There is debate over when the production of art first occurred. One aspect of this debate involves the question of what constitutes art. Some researchers argue for the production of art in the Middle Paleolithic, citing as evidence bones with linear engraving associated with Neanderthals. Other researchers do not consider these to be art. Regardless of whether these Middle Paleolithic examples qualify as the first appearance of art, after 40,000 years ago, evidence for the production of art and the complexity of art forms increases.

8. The most frequent depictions represented in Upper Paleolithic cave art are those of large herbivorous animals that were frequently hunted; these figures were painted in a naturalistic manner. Carnivores appear less frequently. Occasionally, humans appear and are schematic in design. Some representations are fantastic, and combine human and animal forms. Handprints may signify a form of signature. Proposed explanations relating to the purpose of these cave paintings often include an aspect of ritual coordinated by a shaman acting as a medium with the spirit world, or may relate to a pictorial rendering of the structure of society.

Chapter Thirteen Answers:

1. A cline occurs when there is a gradual change in the frequency of a trait between contiguous populations through space. An example of a cline is the distribution of skin color in Egypt, where the frequency of darker skin color increases from north to south along the Nile Valley.

2. Melanin in the skin provides protection against harmful UV radiation from the sun. UV radiation breaks down folate in the body. Insufficient folate interferes with reproduction. Toward the equator, where UV radiation is more intense, darker skin is favorable because increased melanin blocks more UV radiation and reduces folate breakdown, increasing reproductive potential. Toward the poles, UV radiation is less intense. UV radiation is required for the synthesis of vitamin D by the human body. Insufficient vitamin D results in rickets, and may lead to death. At higher latitudes, lighter skin is favorable because reduced melanin blocks less UV radiation and maximizes vitamin D synthesis.

3. Northern regions of the New World were first occupied by humans far more recently (5,000 years ago) than northern regions of the Old World. As a result, compared with northern populations of the New World, populations living at the same latitude in the Old World have had a longer period of time to adapt to reduced UV intensity, resulting in the evolution of lighter skin in Old World northern populations.

4. The folk concept of race states that there are real categories, or races, of humans, and that an individual can be classified into one race or another according to whether that individual possesses certain physical traits. In other words, the races are defined by the presence of specific, distinctive, unique traits, with the implication that all members of a race will possess those distinctive traits. Often, intellectual and moral qualities are ascribed to the races.

5. The major problem with the folk concept of race is the idea that there exist distinctive traits that can be used to definitively classify an individual. Because gene flow has occurred between populations throughout human history, traits have been transferred between populations. For this reason, some members of a race will possess traits not distinctive of that race, and other members will lack some traits that are distinctive of that race. Put another way, there are no unique traits. There will always be

exceptions to the rule. A second problem with the folk concept of race is the correlation of intelligence and morals with the races. No reputable study has shown this to be the case.

6. Social Darwinism suggests that natural selection not only acts on human biology, but also human culture; it is used to explain and justify inequality between individuals and races. The problem with social Darwinism is that it incorrectly represents what natural selection explains. Natural selection is the explanation of how biological evolution works. It provides the "rules" that govern biological evolution. The social Darwinists apply these rules to human culture. However, the rules that govern human culture are not the same as the rules that govern human biology. For this reason, social Darwinism is invalid.

7. Eugenics is the idea that society can be improved by limiting the reproduction of less fit individuals and encouraging the reproduction of more fit individuals. Since fitness was thought to be correlated with race, many jurisdictions enacted miscegenation laws, which barred intermarriage between the races.

8. In *The Bell Curve*, Herrnstein and Murray conclude that intelligence is mostly inherited; that success is highly correlated with intelligence; that IQ accurately reflects intelligence; and that the lower socioeconomic status of African Americans compared with European Americans is due to genetically inherited lower IQ. These conclusions are problematic because, contrary to Herrnstein and Murray's premises, the degree of heritability of intelligence is not clearly understood, racial groups are not genetically distinct, and IQ scores are influenced by culture. For these reasons, the vast majority of researchers consider Herrnstein and Murray's conclusions invalid.

Credits

I would like to thank my graduate student, Mikayla Ploof for her creation of the PowerPoint slide to accompany the textbook.

1.1 Copyright © 2013 FreeDigitalPhotos.net/Naypong.

1.2 Copyright © 2010 FreeDigitalPhotos.net/Luigi Diamanti.

1.3 Copyright © 2014 FreeDigitalPhotos.net/Stuart Miles.

1.4 Creative Commons: Copyright © Hugo Heikenwaelder (CC BY-SA 2.5) at http://commons.wikimedia.org/wiki/File:Universum.jpg

1.5 Copyright © 2014 FreeDigitalPhotos.net/holohololand.

1.6 Creative Commons: Copyright © Wanida W. (CC BY-SA 3.0) at http://commons.wikimedia.org/wiki/Category:Yeti#mediaviewer/File:Abominable_snowman_yeti.JPG

1.7 Creative Commons: Copyright © Jsquish (CC BY-SA 3.0) at http://commons.wikimedia.org/wiki/Category:Scientists#mediaviewer/File:Scientists_montage.jpg

1.8 Copyright © Benoit Rochon (CC by 3.0) at http://commons.wikimedia.org/wiki/File:Colloque_scientifique_international_portant_sur_les_TIC_en_%C3%A9ducation_-_10.jpg.

1.9 Copyright in the Public Domain.

1.10 Copyright in the Public Domain.

2.1 Copyright in the Public Domain.

2.2 Copyright in the Public Domain.

2.3 Creative Commons: Copyright © Martin Kraft (CC BY-SA 3.0) at http://commons.wikimedia.org/wiki/%CE%9A%CE%BB%CE%B1%CF%8D%CE%B4%CE%B9%CE%BF%CF%82_%CE%A0%CF%84%CE%BF%CE%BB%CE%B5%CE%BC%CE%B1%E1%BF%96%CE%BF%CF%82#mediaviewer/File:Claudius_Ptolemaios_%28Nikolaikirche_Stralsund%29.jpg

2.4 Copyright in the Public Domain.

2.5 Copyright in the Public Domain.

2.6 Copyright in the Public Domain.

2.7 Copyright in the Public Domain.

2.8 Copyright in the Public Domain.

2.9 Copyright in the Public Domain.

2.10 Copyright in the Public Domain.

2.11 Copyright in the Public Domain.

2.12 Copyright © Fae (CC by 2.0) at http://commons.wikimedia.org/wiki/File:Georges_Louis_Leclerc,_Comte_de_Buffon._Lithograph._Wellcome_V0000889.jpg.

2.13 Creative Commons: Copyright © James.Leek at http://commons.wikimedia.org/
wiki/Robert_Hooke#mediaviewer/File:7_Hooke_%26_Pepys.JPG

2.14 Copyright in the Public Domain.

2.15 Copyright in the Public Domain.

2.16 Copyright in the Public Domain.

Fig. 2.17: Copyright © by Tangient LLC, (CC BY-SA 3.0) at https://hcevolution.wikispaces.com/4
%2C+How+do+environmental+changes+lead+to+evolution%3F+Jacob+and+Amber.

2.18 Copyright in the Public Domain.

2.19 Copyright in the Public Domain.

2.20 Copyright in the Public Domain.

2.21 Creative Commons: Copyright © Tomas Castelazo (CC BY-SA 3.0) at http://com-
mons.wikimedia.org/wiki/File:Grand_canyon_march_2013.jpg

3.1 Copyright in the Public Domain.

3.2 Copyright © 2013 FreeDigitalPhotos.net/cooldesign.

3.3 Copyright © 2011 FreeDigitalPhotos.net/dreamdesigns.

3.4 Copyright in the Public Domain.

3.5 Copyright © 2010 FreeDigitalPhotos.net/jscreationzs.

3.6 Copyright in the Public Domain.

3.7 Copyright in the Public Domain.

3.8 Copyright © 2010 FreeDigitalPhotos.net/dream designs.

3.9 Creative Commons: Copyright © PaleoBioJackie (CC BY-SA 3.0) at http://commons.
wikimedia.org/wiki/File:Mitochondrial_DNA_versus_Nuclear_DNA.gif

3.10 Copyright in the Public Domain.

3.11 Copyright in the Public Domain.

3.12 Creative Commons: Copyright © Dbachmann (CC BY-SA 2.0) at http://commons.wikimedia.org/wiki/
File:Australopithecus_africanus_adult_female_-_head_model_-_Smithsonian_Museum_of_Natural_History_-_2012-05-17.jpg

3.13 Creative Commons: Copyright © Photaro (CC BY-SA 3.0) at http://commons.wikimedia.
org/wiki/File:Skeleton_and_restoration_model_of_Neanderthal_La_Ferrassie_1.jpg

3.14 Copyright in the Public Domain.

3.15 Copyright in the Public Domain.

3.16 Copyright © 2014 FreeDigitalPhotos.net/cuteimage.

3.17 Copyright © Sailko (CC by 3.0) at http://commons.wikimedia.org/wiki/File:Mummie_di_cuzco_08.JPG.

3.18 Copyright in the Public Domain.

3.19 Copyright in the Public Domain.

4.1 Copyright © 2013 FreeDigitalPhotos.net/luigi diamanti.

4.2 Creative Commons: Copyright © Mart 1tin (CC BY-SA 3.0) at http://commons.
wikimedia.org/wiki/File:GEC_Anderson_paints_and_mat_brush.jpg

4.3 Copyright in the Public Domain.

4.4 Copyright in the Public Domain.

4.5 Copyright in the Public Domain.

4.6 Copyright © 2012 FreeDigitalPhotos.net/cbenjasuwan.

4.7 Copyright in the Public Domain.

4.8 Copyright in the Public Domain.

4.9 Copyright in the Public Domain.

4.10 Copyright © 2011 FreeDigitalPhotos.net/David Castillo Dominici.

4.11 Copyright © 2014 FreeDigitalPhotos.net/David Castillo Dominici.

4.12 Copyright © 2010 FreeDigitalPhotos.net/EA.

4.13 Copyright © Gadjoboy (CC by 2.0) at http://commons.wikimedia.org/wiki/File:Amish_On_the_way_to_school_by_Gadjoboy2.jpg.

4.14 Copyright in the Public Domain.

4.15 Creative Commons: Copyright © Gilles San Martin (CC BY-SA 3.0) at http://commons.wikimedia.org/wiki/File:Biston_betularia_20110529_102239_8073M.JPG

4.16 Copyright © 2013 FreeDigitalPhotos.net/nuttakit.

4.17 Copyright © 2011 FreeDigitalPhotos.net/puttsk.

4.18 Copyright © 2012 FreeDigitalPhotos.net/Ambro.

4.19 Copyright © 2011 FreeDigitalPhotos.net/Robert Nilson.

5.1 Copyright in the Public Domain.

5.2 Copyright in the Public Domain.

5.3 Creative Commons: Copyright © Flickr upload bot (CC BY-SA 2.0) at http://commons.wikimedia.org/wiki/File:Espanola_2010_09_29_0949.jpg

5.4 Copyright © 2011 FreeDigitalPhotos.net/David Castillo Dominici.

5.5 Copyright © 2013 FreeDigitalPhotos.net/David Castillo Dominici.

5.6 (Original to author)

5.7 Copyright © 2011 FreeDigitalPhotos.net/Maggie Smith.

5.8 Copyright © Inugami-bargho (CC by 2.0) at http://commons.wikimedia.org/wiki/File:Children_playing_with_a_dog.jpg.

5.9 Copyright in the Public Domain.

5.10 Copyright © 2011 FreeDigitalPhotos.net/lobster20.

5.11 Copyright © FlickrLickr (CC by 2.0) at http://commons.wikimedia.org/wiki/File:Noah%27s_hand.jpg.

5.12 Copyright © 2012 FreeDigitalPhotos.net/Victor Habbick.

5.13 Copyright © 2008 FreeDigitalPhotos.net/James Barker.

5.14 Copyright © 2012 FreeDigitalPhotos.net/luigi diamanti.

5.15 Copyright in the Public Domain.

5.16 Copyright in the Public Domain.

5.17 Copyright © ArthurWeasley (CC by 3.0) at http://commons.wikimedia.org/wiki/File:Pakicetus_BW.jpg.

5.18 Creative Commons: Copyright © de: Benutzer:Paddy (CC BY-SA 3.0) at http://commons.wikimedia.org/wiki/Category:Goose_bumps#mediaviewer/File:Gaensehaut.jpg

5.19 Copyright in the Public Domain.

5.20 Copyright © Fae (CC by 4.0) at http://commons.wikimedia.org/wiki/File:Development_of_human_embryo_at_five_stages._Wellcome_L0057765.jpg.

5.21 Copyright in the Public Domain.

5.22 Creative Commons: Copyright © David Monniaex (CC BY-SA 3.0) at http://commons.wikimedia.org/wiki/Dinosauria#mediaviewer/File:Palais_de_la_Decouverte_Tyrannosaurus_rex_p1050042.jpg

5.23 Copyright © Renata3 (CC by 2.0) at http://commons.wikimedia.org/wiki/Amber#mediaviewer/File:Spider_in_amber_%281%29.jpg.

5.24 Copyright © 2012 FreeDigitalPhotos.net/papaija2008.

5.25 Creative Commons: Copyright © Ghedoghedo (CC BY-SA 4.0) at http://commons.wikimedia.org/wiki/File:Kelaeno_scutellaris_Muensterella.JPG

5.26 Copyright in the Public Domain.

5.27 Copyright in the Public Domain.

5.28 Creative Commons: Copyright © Jillcurie (CC BY-SA 3.0) at http://commons.wikimedia.org/wiki/File:Relative_dating_of_fossils.png

5.29 Copyright in the Public Domain.

5.30 Copyright in the Public Domain.

5.31 Creative Commons: Copyright © Vesta (CC BY-SA 3.0) at http://commons.wikimedia.org/wiki/Archaeopteryx#mediaviewer/File:Archaeopteryx_lithographica_%28Eichst%C3%A4tter_Specimen%29.jpg

5.32 Creative Commons: Copyright © WolfmanSF (CC BY-SA 3.0) at http://commons.wikimedia.org/wiki/File:Horseevolution.png

5.33 Copyright © Magnus Manske (CC by 2.0) at http://commons.wikimedia.org/wiki/File:Gobiconodon_sp.jpg.

5.34 Copyright in the Public Domain.

5.35 Copyright in the Public Domain.

6.1 Copyright in the Public Domain.

6.2 (Original to author)

6.3 Copyright © Terpsichores (CC by 3.0) at http://commons.wikimedia.org/wiki/File:Propithecus_vertical_clinging_and_leaping.svg

6.4 Copyright © Alex Dunkel (CC by 3.0) at http://upload.wikimedia.org/wikipedia/commons/7/7c/Lemur_catta_004.jpg

6.5 Copyright © Joachim Huber (CC by 2.0) at http://upload.wikimedia.org/wikipedia/commons/2/2e/Galago.jpg

6.6 Copyright © mtoz (CC by 2.0) at http://upload.wikimedia.org/wikipedia/commons/7/7e/Bohol_Tarsier.jpg

6.7 Copyright © Miguelrangeljr (CC by 3.0) at http://upload.wikimedia.org/wikipedia/commons/8/88/A._paniscus_Zoo_SP.jpg

6.8 Copyright © D. Gordon E. Robertson (CC by 3.0) at http://upload.wikimedia.org/wikipedia/commons/2/20/Purus_Red_Howler_Monkey.jpg

6.9 Copyright © Flying Freddy (CC by 3.0) at http://upload.wikimedia.org/wikipedia/commons/6/6e/Macaque_ds.jpg

6.10 Copyright © A. Davey (CC by 2.0) at http://upload.wikimedia.org/wikipedia/commons/a/a0/Baboon_II_(5067551363).jpg

6.11 Copyright © derekkeats (CC by 2.0) at http://upload.wikimedia.org/wikipedia/commons/b/b5/Vervet_Monkey.jpg

6.12 Copyright © Mario Biondi (CC by 3.0) at http://upload.wikimedia.org/wikipedia/commons/1/10/Langur.jpg

6.13 Copyright in the Public Domain.

6.14 Copyright © risco 1492 (CC by 3.0) at http://upload.wikimedia.org/wikipedia/commons/0/08/Orang_Utan,_Semenggok_Forest_Reserve,_Sarawak,_Borneo,_Malaysia_crop.JPG

6.15 Copyright © Kabir Bakie (CC by 2.5) at http://upload.wikimedia.org/wikipedia/commons/3/3d/Gorilla_017.jpg

6.16 Copyright © Rennett Stowe (CC by 2.0) at http://upload.wikimedia.org/wikipedia/commons/b/ba/Chimpanzee_(3265647592).jpg

6.17 Copyright in the Public Domain.

6.18 Copyright © Rob Bixby (CC by 2.0) at http://commons.wikimedia.org/wiki/File:Bonobo_sexual_behavior_1.jpg.

7.1 Copyright in the Public Domain.

7.2 (Original to author)

7.3 Creative Commons: Copyright © Yosemite (CC BY-SA 3.0) at http://commons.wikimedia.org/wiki/File:Jigokudani_hotspring_in_Nagano_Japan_002.jpg

7.4 Creative Commons: Copyright © Mike Richey (CC BY-SA 2.5) at http://commons.wikimedia.org/wiki/File:BonoboFishing04.jpeg

8.1 (Original to author)

8.2 (Original to author)

8.3 Copyright © Ghedoghedo (CC by 3.0) at http://commons.wikimedia.org/wiki/File:Plesiadapis_cookei_skeleton.JPG.

8.4 Copyright © Reiserfs (CC by 3.0) at http://commons.wikimedia.org/wiki/File:Tetonus_homunculus_skull_big.jpg.

8.5 Copyright © Ghedoghedo (CC by 3.0) at http://commons.wikimedia.org/wiki/File:Notharctus_osborni.JPG.

8.6 Copyright © Ghedoghedo (CC by 3.0) at http://commons.wikimedia.org/wiki/File:Aegyptopithecus_zeuxis_paris.jpg.

8.7 Copyright © Ghedoghedo (CC by 3.0) at http://commons.wikimedia.org/wiki/File:Proconsul_africanus_4.JPG.

8.8 Copyright © Kippelboy (CC by 3.0) at http://commons.wikimedia.org/wiki/File:Almost_humans_exhibit_at_ICP_in_Sabadell_%2830%29.JPG.

8.9 Copyright © Durova (CC by 3.0) at http://commons.wikimedia.org/wiki/File:Gigantopithecusjaw.jpg.

9.1 Copyright in the Public Domain.

9.2 Creative Commons: Copyright © Didier Descouens (CC BY-SA 4.0) at http://upload.wikimedia. org/wikipedia/commons/f/fc/Sahelanthropus_tchadensis_-_TM_266-01-060-1.jpg

9.3 Creative Commons: Copyright © Lucius (CC BY-SA 3.0) at http://upload.wi-kimedia.org/wikipedia/commons/d/d1/Orrorin_tugenensis.jpg

9.4 Copyright © T. Michael Keesey (CC by 2.0) at http://upload.wikimedia.org/wikipedia/commons/e/e1/Ardi.jpg.

10.1 Creative Commons: Copyright © 120 (CC BY-SA 3.0) at http://upload.wi-kimedia.org/wikipedia/commons/3/31/Lucy_blackbg.jpg

10.2 Creative Commons: Copyright © Mpinedag (CC BY-SA 3.0) at http://upload. wikimedia.org/wikipedia/commons/5/51/LucySmithsonian.JPG

10.3 Creative Commons: Copyright © Momotarou2012 (CC BY-SA 3.0) at http://upload. wikimedia.org/wikipedia/commons/6/61/Laetoli_footprints_replica.jpg

10.4 Creative Commons: Copyright © Didier Descouens (CC BY-SA 3.0) at http://upload.wikimedia. org/wikipedia/commons/b/be/Australopithecus_africanus_-_Cast_of_taung_child.jpg

10.5 Creative Commons: Copyright © Pavel Svejnar (CC BY-SA 4.0) at http://upload.wikime-dia.org/wikipedia/commons/2/2c/Kenyanthropus_platyops,_skull_(model).JPG

10.6 Creative Commons: Copyright © Jose Braga:Didier Descouens (CC BY-SA 3.0) at http://upload. wikimedia.org/wikipedia/commons/a/a1/Original_of_Paranthropus_robustus_Face.jpg

10.7 Copyright in the Public Domain.

10.8 Creative Commons: Copyright © Guerin Nicolas (CC BY-SA 3.0) at http://upload.wikimedia. org/wikipedia/commons/2/28/Paranthropus_boisei_face_(University_of_Zurich).JPG

10.9 Creative Commons: Copyright © Guerin Nicolas (CC BY-SA 3.0) at http://upload.wikimedia.org/ wikipedia/commons/d/db/Paranthropus_aethiopicus_face_(University_of_Zurich).JPG

10.10 Creative Commons: Copyright © RegentsPark (CC BY-SA 3.0) at http://com-mons.wikimedia.org/w/index.php?title=File:Nutcracker_Man.jpg

11.1 (a) Copyright in the Public Domain and (b)Copyright in the Public Domain.

11.2 Human Origins Program, Smithsonian Institution, "SEM cut mark on a Fossilized Bone," http:// humanorigins.si.edu/human-characteristics/tools-food. Copyright © by Smithsonian Institution.

11.3 (left) Copyright © Claire Houck (CC by 2.0) at http://commons.wikimedia.org/wiki/File:Turkana_Boy.jpg. and (right) Copyright © Nachosan (CC by 3.0) at http://commons.wikimedia.org/wiki/ File:MEH_Homo_ergaster_29-04-2012_11-37-14_2592x3888.JPG.

11.4 Copyright © Luna04 (CC by 3.0) at http://commons.wikimedia.org/wiki/File:Homo_ergaster.jpg.

11.5 Copyright © Gerbil (CC by 3.0) at http://commons.wikimedia.org/wiki/File:Sangiran_17-02.JPG.

11.6 Copyright © We El (CC by 3.0) at http://commons.wikimedia.org/wiki/File:Spy_Skull.jpg.

11.7 Copyright © Uniesert (CC by 3.0) at http://commons.wikimedia.org/wiki/File:Neandertala_skulptajho,_1928.jpg.

11.8 Copyright © Ryan Somma (CC by 2.0) at http://commons.wikimedia.org/wiki/ Homo_floresiensis#mediaviewer/File:Homo_floresiensis.jpg.

11.9 (Original to author)

11.10 Copyright © BabelStone (CC by 3.0) at http://commons.wikimedia.org/wiki/ File:Olduvai_stone_chopping_tool_at_British_Museum.jpg.

11.11 Copyright © Johnbod (CC by 3.0) at http://commons.wikimedia.org/wiki/File:Olduvai_handaxeDSCF6959.jpg.

11.12 Copyright in the Public Domain.

11.13 Copyright © José-Manuel Benito Álvarez (CC by 2.5) at http://commons.wi-kimedia.org/wiki/File:Levallois_Preferencial-Animation.gif.

11.14 (left) Copyright © Didier Descouens (CC by 3.0) at http://commons.wikimedia.org/wiki/File:Racloir_Grotte_du_ Plaquard_MHNT_PRE2009.0.0205.6.jpg and (right) Copyright © Didier Descouens (CC by 3.0) at http://commons.wikimedia. org/wiki/File:Eclat_Levallois_retouch%C3%A9_-_Grotte_du_Placard_MHNT_PRE_2009.0.205.5_%283%29.jpg.

12.1 (Original to author)

14.18 Copyright in the Public Domain.

14.19 Copyright in the Public Domain.

14.20 Copyright © 2014 FreeDigitalPhotos.net/Stuart Miles.

14.21 Creative Commons: Copyright © CherryX (CC BY-SA 3.0) at http://commons.wikimedia.org/wiki/File:Eating_Sushi_on_a_wodden_floor.jpg

14.22 Copyright © 2011 FreeDigitalPhotos.net/artemisphoto.

14.23 Copyright © 2011 FreeDigitalPhotos.net/scottchan.

14.24 Copyright © 2014 FreeDigitalPhotos.net/Patrisyu.

14.25 Copyright © 2012 FreeDigitalPhotos.net/marin.

14.26 Creative Commons: Copyright © Cmacauley (CC BY-SA 3.0) at http://commons.wikimedia.org/wiki/Category:Yanomami#mediaviewer/File:Yanomami_Woman_%26_Child.jpg

14.27 Copyright in the Public Domain.

14.28 Copyright in the Public Domain.

14.29 Creative Commons: Copyright © Ian Sewell (CC BY-SA 2.5) at http://commons.wikimedia.org/wiki/Category:San_people#mediaviewer/File:BushmenSan.jpg

15.1 Copyright © 2012 FreeDigitalPhotos.net/stockimages.

15.2 Copyright © 2013 FreeDigitalPhotos.net/stockimages.

15.3 Copyright in the Public Domain.

15.4 Creative Commons: Copyright © Minghong (CC BY-SA 3.0) at http://commons.wikimedia.org/wiki/Category:Perspiration#mediaviewer/File:TranspirationPerspirationCommonsFL.jpg

15.5 Copyright © Christophe Cagé (CC by 2.0) at http://commons.wikimedia.org/wiki/Category:Aboriginal_Australians#mediaviewer/File:Populations_of_first_wave_of_migrations_in_southern_Asia_and_Oceania.jpg.

15.6 Copyright © Tubezlob (CC by 2.0) at http://commons.wikimedia.org/wiki/File:Yali_man_Baliem_Valley_Papua.jpg.

15.7 Creative Commons: Copyright © Rotatebot (CC BY-SA 2.0) at http://commons.wikimedia.org/wiki/File:FulaniWoman.jpg

15.8 Copyright in the Public Domain.

15.9 Creative Commons: Copyright © Ansgar Walk (CC BY-SA 2.5) at http://commons.wikimedia.org/wiki/Category:Inuit_people#mediaviewer/File:Maktaaq_2_2002-08-10.jpg

15.10 Copyright © Plismo (CC by 3.0) at http://commons.wikimedia.org/wiki/File:NflL_fishermen.jpg.

15.11 Creative Commons: Copyright © Malcolm Greany (CC BY-SA 2.0) at http://commons.wikimedia.org/wiki/File:Greany_Attu_Woman.jpg

15.12 Copyright © 2013 FreeDigitalPhotos.net/stockimages.

15.13 Copyright © Fae (CC by 4.0) at http://commons.wikimedia.org/wiki/File:Photograph_of_Henry_Foy_with_Kenyan_people._Wellcome_L0069011.jpg.

15.14 Creative Commons: Copyright © Flickr upload bot (CC BY-SA 2.0) at http://commons.wikimedia.org/wiki/Category:Maasai#mediaviewer/File:1993_167-19A_Masai_boy.jpg

15.15 Creative Commons: Copyright © Ranveig at http://commons.wikimedia.org/wiki/Category:Sherpa#mediaviewer/File:Nepalese_sherhpa_and_pack.jpg

15.16 Creative Commons: Copyright © File Upload Bot Magnus Manske (CC BY-SA 3.0) at http://commons.wikimedia.org/wiki/Category:People_of_Peru#mediaviewer/File:Incan.jpg

15.17 Copyright © David Stanley (CC by 2.0) at http://commons.wikimedia.org/wiki/Category:People_of_Peru#mediaviewer/File:Indigenous_Women_%287640964776%29.jpg.

15.18 Creative Commons: Copyright © Antoine Taveneaux (CC BY-SA 3.0) at http://commons.wikimedia.org/wiki/File:People_of_Tibet29.jpg

15.19 Creative Commons: Copyright © Davin7 (CC BY-SA 3.0) at http://commons.wikimedia.org/wiki/Category:People_of_Tibet#mediaviewer/File:MNga%C2%B4ris_%28Tibet%29_Nomaden_Dieter_Schuh.JPG

15.20 Copyright © CherryX (CC by 2.0) at http://commons.wikimedia.org/wiki/Category:Mountains_of_Tibet#mediaviewer/File:Mountains_in_Tibet.jpeg.

15.21 Copyright © 2011 FreeDigitalPhotos.net/Ambro.

15.22 Copyright © 2013 FreeDigitalPhotos.net/Jomphong.

15.23 Creative Commons: Copyright © Commonsuf (CC BY-SA 3.0) at http://commons.wikimedia.org/wiki/File:Nguni_cattle.jpg

15.24 Creative Commons: Copyright © Nic pocker (CC BY-SA 3.0) at http://commons.wikimedia.org/wiki/File:Tutsi_cows.jpg

15.25 Creative Commons: Copyright © Ras67 (CC BY-SA 2.0) at http://commons.wikimedia.org/wiki/Tuareg#mediaviewer/File:Tuareg_woman_from_Mali_January_2007.jpg

15.26 Copyright © File Upload Bot Magnus Manske (CC by 2.0) at http://commons.wikimedia.org/wiki/Category:Ethnic_groups_in_Thailand#mediaviewer/File:Thailand_Hill_Tribes_%282281687084%29.jpg.

15.27 Copyright © Martin H. (CC by 2.0) at http://commons.wikimedia.org/wiki/Category:Yoruba_people#mediaviewer/File:Kwarastatedrummers.jpg.

15.28 Copyright in the Public Domain.

15.29 Creative Commons: Copyright © ProjectManhattan (CC BY-SA 3.0) at http://commons.wikimedia.org/wiki/File:Fresh_greek_yoghurt.jpg

15.30 Creative Commons: Copyright © Ayaita (CC BY-SA 3.0) at http://commons.wikimedia.org/wiki/File:Ganado_La_Mochila.jpg

15.31 Copyright © Fae (CC by 4.0) at http://commons.wikimedia.org/wiki/Category:Rickets#mediaviewer/File:Rachitis,_stages_of_development_for_children_Wellcome_M0003399.jpg.

16.1 Creative Commons: Copyright © Piki-photow (CC BY-SA 4.0) at http://commons.wikimedia.org/wiki/File:AFRICA_BASIN_AND_PITCHER_FOR_WASHING_HANDS.jpg

16.2 Copyright © 2010 FreeDigitalPhotos.net/jscreationzs.

16.3 Copyright © 2011 FreeDigitalPhotos.net/M-Pics.

16.4 Copyright © 2013 FreeDigitalPhotos.net/BrianHolm.

16.5 Copyright in the Public Domain.

16.6 Copyright © Flickr upload bot (CC by 2.0) at http://commons.wikimedia.org/wiki/File:San_Bushmen_I.jpg.

16.7 Copyright in the Public Domain.

16.8 Creative Commons: Copyright © Christof01 (CC BY-SA 3.0) at http://commons.wikimedia.org/wiki/Glacier#mediaviewer/File:PeritoMoreno011.jpg

16.9 Creative Commons: Copyright © DVL2 (CC BY-SA 3.0) at http://commons.wikimedia.org/wiki/Category:San_people#mediaviewer/File:Botswana_051.jpg

16.10 Creative Commons: Copyright © Woodlouse (CC BY-SA 2.0) at http://commons.wikimedia.org/wiki/File:Hadzabe_Hunters.jpg

16.11 Copyright in the Public Domain.

16.12 Creative Commons: Copyright © jai MANSSON (CC BY-SA 2.0) at http://commons.wikimedia.org/wiki/Category:Inuit_food#mediaviewer/File:Beluga_blubber.jpg

16.13 Copyright © FlickrLickr (CC by 2.0) at http://commons.wikimedia.org/wiki/Category:People_eating#mediaviewer/File:Kenyan_woman_eating.jpg.

16.14 Creative Commons: Copyright © ldobi (CC BY-SA 3.0) at http://commons.wikimedia.org/wiki/File:Hadzabe4.jpg

16.15 Copyright © 2013 FreeDigitalPhotos.net/noppasinw.

16.16 Copyright © Mats Andersson (CC by 2.0) at http://commons.wikimedia.org/wiki/Category:Sami_people_with_reindeer#mediaviewer/File:Reindeer_herding.jpg.

16.17 Copyright in the Public Domain.

16.18 Copyright in the Public Domain.

16.19 Creative Commons: Copyright © Pdemchick (CC BY-SA 3.0) at http://commons.wikimedia.org/wiki/File:Sweet_potatoes,_Padangpanjang.jpg

16.20 Copyright © Russavia (CC by 2.0) at http://commons.wikimedia.org/wiki/File:Esta_Mamae_carries_pana_in_a_basket_on_her_head_outside_a_traditional_food_storage_hut._%2810694583373%29.jpg.

17.8 Creative Commons: Copyright © Geo Swan (CC BY-SA 2.0) at http://commons.wikimedia.org/wiki/Category:Global_warming#mediaviewer/File:Cloud_cover_on_Elephant_Island_by_Philip_Hall,_Austral_Summer_1993-1994_%28NOAA%29.jpg

17.9 Creative Commons: Copyright © Lamiot (CC BY-SA 3.0) at http://commons.wikimedia.org/wiki/Category:Algal_blooms#mediaviewer/File:Cyanobacteria_032.jpg

17.10 Creative Commons: Copyright © Vearthy (CC BY-SA 2.0) at http://commons.wikimedia.org/wiki/Category:Coral#mediaviewer/File:Blue_Starfish.jpg

17.11 Copyright © File Upload Bot Magnus Manske (CC by 2.0) at http://commons.wikimedia.org/wiki/Category:Drought#mediaviewer/File:Digging_for_drinking_water_in_a_dry_riverbed_%286220146368%29.jpg.

17.12 Copyright in the Public Domain.

17.13 Creative Commons: Copyright © OsvaldoGago (CC BY-SA 2.5) at http://commons.wikimedia.org/wiki/Traffic#mediaviewer/File:Auto_stoped_highway.JPG

17.14 Copyright © 2014 FreeDigitalPhotos.net/khunaspix.

17.15 Copyright in the Public Domain.

17.16 Copyright in the Public Domain.

17.17 Creative Commons: Copyright © russavia (CC BY-SA 2.0) at http://commons.wikimedia.org/wiki/File:Playing_in_the_Dirt,_Ethiopia_%288215960625%29.jpg

17.18 Creative Commons: Copyright © Gilles San Martin (CC BY-SA 2.0) at http://commons.wikimedia.org/wiki/File:House_dust_mites_%285247996458%29.jpg

17.19 Copyright © 2014 FreeDigitalPhotos.net/David Castillo Dominici.

17.20 Copyright © 2012 FreeDigitalPhotos.net/marin.

17.21 Creative Commons: Copyright © Sander van der Wel (CC BY-SA 2.0) at http://commons.wikimedia.org/wiki/Category:Depression#mediaviewer/File:Depressed_%284649749639%29.jpg

17.22 Copyright in the Public Domain.

17.23 Copyright in the Public Domain.

17.24 Copyright © juanedc (CC by 2.0) at http://commons.wikimedia.org/wiki/File:Mariya_y_Barik_%288229547232%29.jpg.

17.25 Creative Commons: Copyright © Pl 05 SIGIT (CC BY-SA 3.0) at http://commons.wikimedia.org/wiki/File:Plowing_the_field.JPG

17.26 Copyright in the Public Domain.

17.27 Copyright © 2013 FreeDigitalPhotos.net/stockimages.

17.28 Creative Commons: Copyright © William Cho (CC BY-SA 2.0) at http://commons.wikimedia.org/wiki/Category:Shipyards#mediaviewer/File:Blue_hour_@_West_Coast_Park_Singapore_%285486856602%29.jpg

17.29 Copyright in the Public Domain.

17.30 Copyright in the Public Domain.

17.31 Copyright © 2009 FreeDigitalPhotos.net/Danilo Rizzuti.